A Practical Guide to
Elementary Instruction

A Practical Guide to Elementary Instruction

From Plan to Delivery

Suzanne Borman
United States International University

Joel Levine
United States International University

Allyn and Bacon
Boston • London • Toronto • Sydney • Tokyo • Singapore

Series Editor: Frances Helland
Editorial Assistant: Kris Lamarre
Senior Marketing Manager: Kathy Hunter
Production Administrator: Annette Joseph
Production Coordinator: Holly Crawford
Editorial-Production Service: Lynda Griffiths, TKM Productions
Composition Buyer: Linda Cox
Photo Editor: Susan Duane
Manufacturing Buyer: Megan Cochran
Cover Administrator: Suzanne Harbison

Allyn & Bacon
A Viacom Company
160 Gould Street
Needham Heights, MA 02194
Internet: www.abacon.com
America Online: keyword: College Online

Library of Congress Cataloging-in-Publication Data

Borman, Suzanne.
    A practical guide to elementary instruction: from plan to
delivery / by Suzanne Borman & Joel Levine.
      p.   cm.
    Includes bibliographical references and index.
    ISBN 0-205-14188-9
    1. Elementary school teaching--Handbooks, manuals, etc.
    2. Classroom management--Handbooks, manuals, etc. I. Levine, Joel.
    II. Title.
    LB1555.B66 1996
    372.11'02--dc20   96-38717
                                                CIP

Printed in the United States of America

10 9 8 7 6 5 4 3 2 1   02 01 00 99 98 97

Figure Credit: p. 342: Excerpt from *Portfolio and Performance Assessment: Helping Students Evaluate Their Progress as Readers and Writers* by Roger Farr and Bruce Tone, copyright © 1994 by Harcourt Brace & Company, reprinted by permission of the publisher.

Photo Credits: p. 1: Stephen Marks; pp. 41, 233, 313: Will Faller; p. 145: Jim Pickerell.

To Kumarji of Mt. Cuchama
for Teaching by Example

Contents

SECTION III   *Strategic Classroom Planning*   *145*

SECTION IV   *Classroom Management*   *233*

Foreword

Whenever confronted with an issue of great importance and about which there are differences in opinion—such as What counts as teaching and how is teaching rightfully practiced?—we are wise to attend to the views and knowledge of those who have committed their lives to the question. This is so, even if ultimately the answer is our own.

The authors of *A Practical Guide to Elementary Instruction: From Plan to Delivery,* Suzanne Borman and Joel Levine, are exceptionally qualified to guide the work of novice and experienced teachers alike, for they have dedicated themselves to teaching and to the preparation of teachers. In this practical guide, they convey their range of scholarship and experience in helpful ways, inspiring and enlightening.

Teachers will find this a reader-friendly text, rich in strategies and examples for dealing with the many decisions to be made in classroom teaching. The book is unusual in its comprehensiveness. Instead of presenting a single procedure or method for given instructional problems, the text invites the reader to examine alternatives so that one's own purposes and situations can best be served. In addition, instead of either-or thinking, the authors assist the reader in recognizing when and for which purposes one approach is preferable to another.

Unlike many methods books that feature only the latest innovations in teaching, Borman and Levine combine the best of the old and the new, avoiding fashion for substance. Students of teaching will appreciate both the magnitude of topics and the organizing structure of the text, which simplifies their learning by showing how the different aspects of teaching are related to each other.

A Practical Guide to Elementary Instruction is a professional book that teachers will keep long after completion of a particular course. It is a valuable resource to which the teacher will turn when fresh perspectives and options are needed to resolve a classroom dilemma, when one wants a compendium of practical solutions to an instructional problem, and when it is necessary to renew enthusiasm about the work of a teacher.

John D. McNeil
Professor of Education Emeritus
University of California, Los Angeles

Preface

In writing this book, one overriding goal was always foremost: to provide a comprehensive set of ideas, procedures, and approaches that can be studied and continually referred to as the basis for running all aspects of a first-rate elementary classroom. *A Practical Guide to Elementary Instruction: From Plan to Delivery* is not simply a "how-to" workbook of practical solutions to selected classroom problems. Rather, it is a comprehensive look at all that faces you as you assume responsibility for a classroom. Its numerous strategies and examples require you to think deeply and creatively about how to adapt and apply these ideas to your style of teaching and classroom situation.

Much discussion today focuses on the teacher as a leader. Indeed, the teacher is a leader in every sense of the word. Leadership is not based on power or on the numbers of those being led; it can be best defined by the quality of care, support, nurturing, and guidance the leader brings to those he or she is leading. Certainly, in the world of education, the elementary teacher has the greatest opportunity to lead, and lead in a way that can make a real difference. An examination of what it takes to consistently and effectively provide such leadership will reveal that it comes down to making decisions. As a teacher, you will be required to make big and small decisions, complex and simple decisions, and long- and short-term decisions. This book is about helping you carefully do the thinking and planning and take the action necessary to make these decisions, which will deeply affect the lives of the children with whom you work.

Preparing for and assuming an elementary teaching position places great responsibility on your shoulders. Among the features of this book that will allow you to address these responsibilities and meet demands of this most rewarding task are the following:

- A detailed guide is presented on how to develop study skills in elementary-school children.
- A complete design, with examples, for creating a personalized classroom management system is given.

- The process of how to use five different planning models is discussed and classroom examples are given as guides.
- A discussion is provided on how to recognize and utilize the dynamics of diversity to expand classroom management skills.
- The *whys* and *hows* of cooperative learning are explained and 10 varied cooperative activity structures are given, with a systematic plan for using and adapting each one.
- One of the most clearly understandable examinations of learning styles in the field is provided and summarized through the Learning Styles Profile Continuum.
- A Resource Bank of Instructional Activities provides numerous activities, categorized for different learning and planning needs, with examples and instructions for their design and use.

Acknowledgments

We would like to extend our sincerest appreciation to all those who gave their time and effort in making this book a reality. This work could not have been completed without the support of our family of friends. Dr. Naomi Aschner's help was critical in making the text more readable. Ken Gerber, Suzanne Suprise, and Zachary Coffin were there when we needed their technical expertise to create the many graphic displays. Xiao Ming Guo provided valuable and generous computer assistance whenever needed. Phil Crowley always made sure our many packages containing various drafts were mailed in a timely and safe manner. Mark Jatczak made the time to copy materials with an amazingly short turnaround. Our university administrators provided the release time we needed to complete the work. At Allyn and Bacon, there are several who must be mentioned here. Frances Helland, our editor, was a driving force in getting the work into print. Thanks, too, to Nihad Farooq, Kris Lamarre, Annette Joseph, Holly Crawford, and Lynda Griffiths. Finally, we express our gratitude to our esteemed colleagues Douglas Brooks (Miami University), Margaret Kirwin (College of St. Rose), and Leone Snyder (Northwestern College), who so kindly and thoughtfully reviewed the manuscript and provided invaluable suggestions.

Section *I*

The Foundation

Few occupations are as complex and demanding as elementary school teaching. It is hard to think of anyone who has to make so many important decisions, day after day, that have a direct bearing on the growth and development of children. These decisions can be categorized into five major areas:

- Decisions concerning responsibilities in the context of a complex education system and social structure
- Decisions concerning what instructional strategies should be used to deliver instruction and promote learning
- Decisions concerning the design of the overall curriculum framework and daily lesson plans in each content area
- Decisions concerning how to create a positive, smoothly functioning classroom environment
- Decisions concerning what will determine student readiness for, progress toward, and achievement in learning

Within these five major decision areas, a myriad of related decisions need to be made. Sometimes a teacher will make these decisions spontaneously, sometimes after considerable reflective thought, and sometimes with the wise advice of others. Whatever the case may be, the decisions a teacher makes concerning his or her students are never made lightly—much is riding on those decisions.

This book has been designed and written with the goal of helping you make these decisions. Each section focuses on one of the five major decision areas and provides you with the background information, tools, creative ideas, and practical classroom examples to make these decisions in an effective and timely manner. The authors hope that this becomes the most "dog-eared" book you ever own, as you refer to various parts of it again and again to assist you in addressing your needs and problems.

Teaching is a complex endeavor that requires the integration of knowledge in various areas with the skills and understandings needed to utilize that knowledge in the classroom. Many variables influence the daily activities and exchanges that form the basis of a child's education, including research studies, state and district policies and curriculum, and local school culture and requirements, as well as community demographics. To demonstrate how the elementary classroom teacher can most effectively function in this environment is the goal of this book. This section provides insights into teaching and learning, which are at the heart of education.

C h a p t e r *1*

Teaching

The following topics will provide an orientation to essential aspects of teaching:

- What makes a good teacher
- Responsibilities of the teacher

What Makes a Good Teacher

When thinking about what makes a good teacher, three essential abilities come to mind: (1) the ability to manage student behavior and the classroom environment, (2) the ability to plan curriculum over the short and long term, and (3) the ability to carry out instruction through the use of various teaching strategies. Indeed, these two major aspects of classroom teaching are of paramount importance and, accordingly, are the focus of any program that prepares people to be teachers. It is, however, essential to understand that one's degree of success in developing skill in these three areas hinges on several key factors that are basic to one's own character and personality. Training alone does not make a good teacher! If that were not true, scholars would only need to design the ideal program and put through it everyone who wants to become a teacher. In reality, however, many people go through the same teacher-training program yet demonstrate very different levels of ability. Why is this so? Are there certain identifiable traits that predispose one to success on the path to becoming a good teacher? Yes, there definitely are personal characteristics that are highly correlated with success in teacher training and in transferring that training to the classroom.

Two of the most important among these characteristics are a genuine liking for children and an enthusiasm for life and learning. Other important characteristics include one's orientation to solving problems, being organized, communicating clearly and thoroughly, being flexible, and being creative.

3

Liking for Children

A liking for children and an enthusiasm for life and learning are inherent to one's being—a person has or does not have these characteristics. Teachers who have a genuine liking for children and are deeply concerned for their well-being will do whatever it takes to acquire the knowledge and skills needed to help their students. Ralph Tyler (1987), one of the twentieth century's leading educators, made an important statement on this subject in a featured presentation to the American Educational Research Association:

> *After a lifetime of working with teachers and those preparing to become teachers, I have found that the single most reliable predictor of success as a teacher is a sincere caring for children. To give you an example of what I mean, take the person who has an average GPA in college, but who cares deeply about children and has the desire to serve them as a teacher. My years of experience have shown that this individual will learn whatever she needs to learn, find whatever she needs to find—in short—overcome any academic deficiencies she may have so that she can deliver effective instruction for the benefit of her students.*

Enthusiasm for Life and Learning

Enthusiasm is a decidedly positive force in life. Individuals having an enthusiasm for life and learning are characterized by a keen interest in and awareness of people and events around them and often acquire an ever-increasing understanding of the world in which they live. An excellent example of how such enthusiasm can affect students' approaches to life and learning is demonstrated by the following instructional activity:

> One morning at an elementary school in lower Manhattan of New York City, Mrs. Gaffney was strongly advised by fellow teachers to take her kindergarten class out to the playground to avoid the noise and distraction that would be created by the custodian who was coming to repair the door to her classroom. Because of Mrs. Gaffney's interest in learning about a wide variety of things, she chose to remain in the classroom for a learning experience, assembling her children around the door as it was being repaired. As the custodian worked, the children eagerly asked him questions about what he was doing. From this, Mrs. Gaffney and the children found new words to add to their vocabulary list. This, then, became the basis for an art project where groups of children worked cooperatively to draw a picture of a door, labeling the parts they had learned about.

> The teacher sets the tone of the classroom; this atmosphere has a strong influence on the students, as does the teacher's enthusiasm. At the elementary school level, this influence is especially strong as "the personal interactions between teacher and pupils in the elementary school are greater in number and extent than at any other level" (Jarolimek & Foster, 1981, p. 42).

Problem-Solving Propensity

The classroom teacher has no dearth of problems to solve, whether they be interpersonal, instructional, resource related, behavioral, and so on. Effective teachers identify problems and take action to solve them; problems are not ignored. Let us look at two different examples to clarify this point.

Example 1

Mrs. Dunn, a first-grade teacher, followed a particular routine with her whole class at the start of the day; it included taking attendance, collecting lunch money, reviewing the calendar, and discussing the weather. After about a month of carrying out the routine in the same manner, Mrs. Dunn noticed her students were getting restless during this period. She concluded that they were getting bored with the routine. Although she wanted to continue the basic content of the introductory activities, Mrs. Dunn decided that she could find different ways of presenting the same material. When she began to vary the *format* of these activities, she once again had the full attention of her students.

Example 2

Mr. Martin, a third-grade teacher, was teaching a math unit on place value. Although he followed the suggested introductory activities in the math text, he noticed that when he questioned his students following the activities, quite a few did not understand the meaning of the values of the one's, ten's, and hundred's places. For example, when he asked them what the 9 represents in the number 493, the children were unable to respond that the 9 represents nine tens, or 90. They seemed to be having a hard time conceptualizing the idea that each position in a three-digit number represents a different value. Mr. Martin did not want to move on until all the students understood this important concept. He decided to reteach the same concept the next day, using manipulatives on a place-value chart. Each student was provided with a chart with three columns labeled appropriately *one's place*, *ten's place*, and *hundred's place*. To help the students understand what each place value means, he had them use single beans to represent individual units of one, ten beans glued to each popsicle stick to represent units of ten, and one hundred beans glued to a flat square to represent units of one hundred. Each student was given a set of these manipulatives to use while Mr. Martin demonstrated how to depict various numbers.

Mr. Martin grouped the students in such a way that each group contained at least one student who seemed to grasp the idea. He then called out numbers so the groups could practice placing the manipulatives on the place-value charts. He drew the students further into the activity by having them think of numbers to represent. Next, Mr. Martin reversed the process by demonstrating a number with the manipulatives and asking the students to write the number down. After ample practice using the manipulatives, Mr. Martin evaluated the students' understanding and was pleased to see that they were able to grasp the concept of place value.

Both of these examples show that the first thing the teachers did was identify that there was a problem. Mrs. Dunn noticed that her students were beginning to get a little restless during a particular period of the day, and Mr. Martin determined a lack of understanding by questioning his students. Many teachers fail to solve problems because they fail to *recognize* them. The authors have seen teachers deliver instruction according to their predetermined plan without regard to the students' responses to the instruction. Teachers must be alert to the clues that indicate how the instruction is being received by the students. Confused or vacant looks on the faces of the children is a large hint that it is time to stop and check for understanding.

The second thing that both Mr. Martin and Mrs. Dunn did was to consider possible solutions to the problems they had identified. For a new teacher, it is sometimes helpful to consult with an experienced teacher who has likely encountered the same problem and has tried different ways of solving it. Having decided on a solution, the next step is to try it out and, finally, to evaluate the results.

Inevitably, many kinds of unanticipated problems will arise in the classroom. Whether these problems are in the area of academics, behavior, scheduling, or resource support, the degree to which they will remain problems that interfere with the teacher's ability to teach will depend on what is called that teacher's *problem-solving propensity.* This refers to a *readiness to recognize a problem* as it occurs, the ability to *think of or search out possible solutions* to it, and a *tenacity to try out various alternatives* until the problem is solved.

Organized Approach

It is no exaggeration to say that being organized is absolutely critical to effective classroom teaching. Considering that the new teacher is faced with all the demands and responsibilities of the veteran teacher (minus the experience!), the ability to organize time, materials, and planning curriculum and instruction can well mean the difference between success and failure. It is difficult for someone who has never been an elementary school teacher to imagine the variety of noninstructional tasks that need to be dealt with in a single day. For example, an elementary school teacher will have to keep track of who has or has not turned in homework and class work; determine which students deserve which consequence or reward; assess who needs to go to a pull-out program and when; decide what calls to make or letters to send to parents; keep track of which students are scheduled for computer, learning center, or tutoring time and when; and set out the instructional aide's list of duties for the day. These tasks are only a few aspects of what a teacher needs to do on a daily basis at the elementary level. Add to this the major tasks of planning and carrying out instruction as well as implementing a classroom management system, and it becomes evident that the multiplicity of tasks can be accomplished only through an organized approach. In this way, the organized teacher creates a structured classroom environment in which students know what is expected of them academically and behaviorally. "The necessity to enforce control occurs infrequently among teachers who are good organizers and planners" (Jarolimek & Foster, 1981, p. 43).

Communication Skills

Communication, the imparting of information and ideas, is the basis of teaching. On a given day in the elementary school classroom, teachers continually are presenting and explaining content, giving directions, relating behavior expectations, and listening to students. In large part, the clarity and appropriateness (i.e., connecting with student levels of understanding) of these communications determine a teacher's degree of success. Frequently, student comprehension is dependent on the teacher's ability to clarify a concept, idea, or generalization. Good communication skills are essential in exchanges not only with students but also with parents, colleagues, and administrators. For example, in order to obtain a parent's meaningful involvement and cooperation in his or her child's learning, the teacher has to be able to communicate concerning the child's intellectual and social needs. In general, the ability to communicate is a key ingredient to productive and pleasant interactions with all members of the school community.

Adaptability

Teachers must adapt to changes and unexpected circumstances in the course of any teaching assignment. For example, consider the case of Mrs. Amalfitano:

> Mrs. Amalfitano is a first-year teacher with a combination K–1 bilingual class. Within the first five months, she has acquired a firm hold on the curriculum and delivery of instruction at two grade levels in two languages. During this time, she has had to deal with changing her instructional aide, absorbing three problem students, organizing an instructional fair day, and participating in a new parent-involvement program. Just when Mrs. Amalfitano was beginning to relax and feel comfortable in her routine, word came that she must accept another new student—one who is from a dysfunctional family and is emotionally disturbed. Fortunately, adjusting to new and changing circumstances has been Mrs. Amalfitano's mode of operation since she began teaching. In this way, what could have been a stressful situation is handled calmly with the necessary flexibility.

Creativity

Elementary school teachers spend every day for an entire school year with their students, instructing them in all subject areas. Those with an inclination for creativity continually find new and interesting ways to present lessons, involve students, use resources, arrange the room, and, in general, maintain a positive learning environment. The teachers whose classrooms are remembered most clearly and fondly are those who take the time to provide imaginative experiences for the students. Perhaps nothing is more indicative of a teacher's motivation to serve students and grow as a learner than the amount of effort made to design creative instructional activities. Such teacher motivation and creativity is directly linked to how well the students will become self-motivated learners.

Instruction and Management Skills

Classroom teaching is essentially instruction and management. All classroom learning experiences and social interactions emanate from and revolve around strategies the teacher employs in these two areas. The foundation of a teacher's knowledge of instruction and management strategies is laid in a teacher preparation program. This foundation needs to be built on throughout one's teaching career by staying in touch with the latest research and practices and by continually reflecting on the effects of strategies used. As knowledge continues to grow and society continues to change rapidly, strategies to promote student learning and manage the classroom environment must change accordingly.

> *The demographics of families and future students tell us that there is a need for a complex teaching repertoire—one with the variation necessary to meet the diversity of needs. Research indicates that if we are to be effective in teaching amidst such diversity, our repertoire must not include teaching strategies that make students passive learners (Mullis, Owen, & Phillips, 1990).*

Students of today and tomorrow require interactive teaching that promotes high levels of personal involvement. Figure 1–1 provides a summary of the characteristics of a good teacher.

The path to becoming a good teacher is an arduous one, requiring much effort—that is, a tremendous investment of one's time, energy, thoughts, and feelings. It would

FIGURE 1–1   Summary of What Makes a Good Teacher

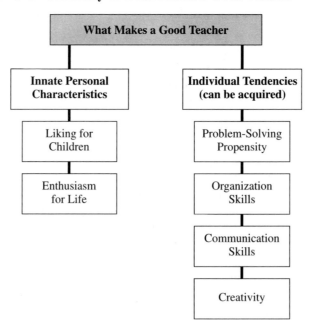

be very difficult to imagine making such effort without possessing, in some degree, the traits that have just been discussed. Individuals with these characteristics will make the most of the training and experiences they go through to become a teacher.

Responsibilities of the Teacher

Not only is teaching one of the most complex professions but it is also one where the highest level of responsibility is assumed. The teacher is in a pivotal position to influence significantly the lives of the students with whom he or she works over the course of his or her entire career. Just how significant this influence can be is readily seen when one considers that the main responsibility of the teacher is to provide for the intellectual, emotional, and physical growth of the students. To get a clear understanding of how to approach or even begin to assume and fulfill this overall responsibility, it is useful to look at the following six main areas of responsibility: (1) curriculum, (2) instruction, (3) classroom environment, (4) school community, (5) personal decorum, and (6) philosophy of education.

Curriculum

The curriculum is the subject matter content that is presented to students. The teacher's responsibility involves planning curriculum on both a long-term and short-term basis.

From a long-term perspective, it is necessary prior to the beginning of school to determine the overall structure for each subject for the year. This entails deciding what will be taught, to what depth, and in what sequence. To accomplish this long-term planning, the teacher has to review a variety of sources, including state curriculum frameworks, district curriculum guides, school guidelines, and relevant adopted textbooks. There is always scope for the teacher's creative input in the long-term planning process, which increases with experience. Procedures for orienting teachers to the curriculum vary greatly from school to school, from a high level of guidance and collaboration to no direction and support whatsoever. The wisest course, then, is to be prepared to assume full responsibility for the long-term phase of the curriculum-planning process, This means that the teacher must locate and procure the resources for long-term planning in a timely fashion, review them, and seek out additional help, as needed, to create an effective plan.

From a short-term perspective, the teacher's responsibility centers around three levels of planning: the unit, the weekly, and the daily lesson plan. All three levels are derived from and give life to the scope, depth, and sequence determined in the long-term plan. Short-term planning entails determining what is to be accomplished for any given segment of the overall curriculum. For example, stating the goals to be reached through the unit plan over a several-week period as the basis for designing a series of daily lesson plans is a part of the short-term planning process.

Curriculum planning is a crucial aspect of teaching. The long- and short-term plans are the blueprint for instruction. No matter how well versed a teacher is in various teaching techniques, his or her instruction will be ineffective unless that instruction is rooted in a sound curriculum plan. Further, poor or skimpy planning leaves the teacher without a point of reference for determining what does and does not work to promote student learning. It is impossible to reflect on and alter something that does not exist.

Instruction

Instruction is the implementation of the curriculum plan through various teaching strategies to create a series of student learning experiences. The success of instruction must ultimately be measured by the quality of student learning. Because student interest and involvement are the keys to their learning, it follows that the teacher's responsibility is to acquire and develop skill in a variety of teaching strategies (also referred to as teaching methods or techniques). Failure to do so dooms the students to one-dimensional instruction, which leaves them bored, uninvolved, and in a poor position to learn. An equally important reason for a teacher to acquire a repertoire of methodologies is so he or she is able to accommodate the various learning styles of the students in the class. With the growing recognition of the importance of learning styles in the students' abilities to acquire new skills and information, the facility of the teacher to use a variety of strategies and methodologies is essential.

Effective instruction depends not only on a good plan and skill in teaching strategies but also, in large part, on the spontaneous modification and/or enrichment of instruction according to the needs of the situation. Consider this example:

> The students in Mrs. Boyd's class had just returned from lunch and were seated for the usual 15-minute period when she reads literature to them. For the past two days, the students had been very attentive to the story. On this day, however, she noticed as she read that the students had blank expressions and seem bored. This was a signal to her that some adjustment was immediately necessary to save the activity. Realizing that this part of the story was a little more remote from the students' life experiences, she assigned several students to read aloud the parts of the characters in the story and directed them to interpret and project what their characters might be feeling and thinking. As a result, the students got involved in the story even more than usual and raised some very interesting questions about the story and their characters. The basis of Mrs. Boyd's success is her knowledge of many teaching methods that she can draw on and adapt at any moment as the situation demands.

In addition to the ability to use a variety of teaching strategies and the ability to implement any one of a variety of these strategies or methodologies on the spot, there are two more characteristics of good instruction that the teacher must acquire and continue to develop. One is the ability to engage in task analysis and the other is knowledge of subject matter.

The ability to engage in task analysis means that the teacher must be able to analyze a task and break it down into the smallest sequential steps possible. This is important because many children, especially younger ones, can only learn a task or skill by mastering, one at a time, each small step involved in performing the overall task. Many adults have difficulty in realizing the extent to which children need to learn things one small step at a time, and then in breaking the task down into small steps. This is precisely what must be done, however, to facilitate learning for many children.

Another necessity for good instruction is the knowledge of subject matter. This does not mean that the elementary school teacher must have expertise in all the subject areas he or she will be teaching. It does mean, though, that before teaching a topic or unit of instruction, it is the teacher's responsibility to thoroughly inform himself or herself about the topic. Only then can the teacher respond to students' questions and maintain the flow of instruction.

It is the responsibility of the teacher to provide the best possible instruction that he or she can. In order to do so, the following skills are necessary for the teacher to master: a variety of teaching strategies or methodologies, the ability to do task analysis, and the knowledge of subject matter.

Classroom Environment

Perhaps the most encompassing of all the teacher's responsibilities is to provide a classroom environment in which children are safe and can learn. The classroom environment consists of two main aspects: (1) the physical appearance and layout and (2) the nature of social interaction that occurs among the members of the classroom.

The first impression elementary school students have of a new classroom is its physical appearance and layout. This impression sends a crucial message to the students. It lets them know that they are in a caring, structured environment or in one where more or less anything goes. Just imagine the positive effect on students when they enter a classroom that can be described as follows: desks neatly and spaciously arranged, wall space attractively utilized, bulletin boards colorfully prepared to display student work, a generally clean and neat appearance, storage and supply areas well kept and clearly identified, and learning centers invitingly arranged and labeled (e.g., listening, library, and computer centers). It is the teacher's responsibility and a very wise investment of time and energy to have these physical aspects prepared before the start of school and to maintain them throughout the year.

The teacher sets the tone and expectations for social interaction in the classroom—that is, how all persons in the classroom are to deal and work with one another. To assume responsibility in this area, it is useful to do the following: Set limits on physical and verbal behaviors, foster respectful attitudes, provide for cooperative spirit and work, and create an atmosphere that encourages expression, participation, and risk taking. Although these social interactions are primarily developed through the normal course of day-to-day activities in the classroom, it is necessary periodically to teach these behaviors directly. This can be done through teacher-led discussions, weekly classroom meetings to air issues and feelings, and role-play activities that demonstrate desirable behaviors. Developing positive social behaviors can also be interwoven with instruction by coaching students to assume supportive and encouraging roles in cooperative learning groups and peer-tutoring sessions. The teacher can foster student expression, participation, and risk taking through his or her interest in and acceptance of students' logic, thought processes, and expressions of thoughts and feelings.

The environment in which one lives, breathes, and works for any length of time has a profound effect in shaping one's attitude toward remaining in and performing well in that environment. For elementary school students, who are at an impressionable and formative stage in their lives, the effects of the environment are magnified. Therefore, the teacher who creates a positive and supportive environment is more likely to have students who look forward to coming to school and who will be motivated to learn. On the other hand, a negative environment can severely damage a child's interest in school and learning for a long time to come.

School Community

The school community consists of the school itself and the surrounding community. To be successful as an elementary school teacher, one must assume several important responsibilities that go beyond those in the classroom. These include administrative and professional responsibilities.

As an institution, the elementary school functions and is sustained on a daily basis by carrying out numerous administrative tasks. Among these tasks, several fall under the responsibility of the teacher, including entering grades in a grade book; preparing and issuing report cards; maintaining cumulative record folders; conducting health and demographic surveys (i.e., handing out and collecting various forms); assuming yard, recess, lunch, and bus duty; and attending regular staff meetings. Looking over this list, one thing becomes apparent. All of these responsibilities are to be accomplished in a definite, timely manner. Woe to the teacher who fails to submit his or her grades on time. Not only will this make a less than favorable impression on the principal, parents, and students but it will also make the orderly functioning of the school more difficult. Similarly, the remaining administrative tasks have their part to play in the economy of a smoothly running elementary school. Serious repercussions are inevitable for the teacher who does not make allowance in his or her time and planning to execute these tasks efficiently. How long can a principal afford to keep a teacher on staff who does not do his or her part in the running of the school?

Of a different nature and equally important are the professional responsibilities of the teacher, which include staff relations, support of colleagues, knowledge of community events, awareness of legal issues, and involvement with the Parent/Teacher Association. In looking at this list of professional responsibilities, it is apparent that they require a different type of involvement than the administrative responsibilities. The administrative responsibilities are defined for the teacher and need to be accomplished at definite times, whereas the professional responsibilities are more ongoing and fluid in nature. Another and perhaps even more distinguishing characteristic of these professional responsibilities is the need for judgment to be exercised continually to fulfill what is expected in each of these areas.

The relationships that a teacher forms at a school site with support staff personnel, who can arguably be called the backbone of the school, are important. These individuals include custodians, school secretaries, attendance clerks, and food-service personnel. Consider this example:

Mr. Crawford had planned to meet with the school secretary during his preparation time to work out transportation arrangements for taking his second-grade class on a field trip to the zoo. As he entered the office, he recognized that Mrs. Jones, the school secretary, was in the midst of a particularly hectic morning. At this point, sound professional judgment would entail determining what is the greater need at the moment. Mr. Crawford realized that he still had a few days to make the transportation arrangements for this class and that there was no need to further burden the secretary.

Often, the elementary school teacher's day is, itself, hectic enough, so that gaining insights like Mr. Crawford displayed is not easy. Nonetheless, such exercise of judgment—whether it be remembering to put the classroom chairs up for the custodian, assisting the food-service personnel by properly organizing students in the lunchroom line, or generally just noticing how busy any of the support personnel are at a given moment—will go a long way toward contributing to the smooth functioning of the school.

Another professional responsibility in the area of interpersonal relations is providing support to colleagues. Teaching is a very demanding profession and all teachers experience days when frustration mounts to a seemingly unbearable level. In schools where teachers work together, sharing and planning, having close association, it is not uncommon for one teacher to invite another to bring his or her students in for a shared activity, thus freeing a stressed teacher from his or her students for a short time. Not only does this provide a break in which one can collect oneself but it also provides a psychological boost to know that a sympathetic colleague is aware of what one is going through. This support can make all the difference to a teacher who is having a bad day, and it creates a generally nurturing atmosphere in the whole school community. This kind of activity may not be listed in a job description, but it is an activity on the professional level that fosters a work environment that is beneficial to everyone. Therefore, teachers need to be aware of how their colleagues are doing and to offer support when appropriate.

An additional responsibility of teachers as professionals is to be aware of community events. Although it may not be possible for most teachers to be involved deeply in the local community, it is important for teachers to know of major events in the community so they can relate their instruction to the lives of their students. Teachers must exercise their own judgment as to the extent of their involvement in community events, but even minimal involvement helps them be in tune with the community.

Related to community involvement is involvement with the Parent/Teacher Association (PTA). Again, each individual teacher must evaluate personal needs and time issues and decide how much time he or she can give in this area; however, it is advisable to contribute as much as possible. Participation in the PTA strengthens the links between the school and the parent community—two major forces in the students' lives.

Regarding awareness of legal issues, it is important that teachers inform themselves of all responsibilities for which they are held legally accountable, such as never leaving a class unattended (i.e., students must be under the supervision of a certified adult) or reporting possible child abuse. Individual schools have procedures for these kinds of legal responsibilities, and all teachers should familiarize themselves with the individual school policy.

When teachers take their professional responsibilities seriously, their professionalism enhances the interactions and associations and enriches the lives of all those living and working in the school community.

Personal Decorum

A teacher's personal decorum refers to appearance and behavior, especially in terms of social interactions. Teachers are role models for their students. They are very important adults in the lives of their students, who watch them carefully and are influenced, often deeply, by them. Because of this, it is the teacher's responsibility to maintain a certain standard in appearance and social interactions. Of course, there is room for individual differences in dress style or manner of interacting with others, but a certain level of propriety must be maintained. For example, the teacher's appearance should be pleasant, clean, and neat, and the social behavior should reflect cultural norms in terms of manners and consideration of others.

The teacher's appearance is, in fact, a reflection of his or her respect for the children and the learning process. When the teacher takes the time and effort to appear attractive, it sends a message to the students that he or she considers the reason for which everyone is at school day after day an important endeavor that deserves to be taken seriously.

Through body language, mannerisms, tone of voice, and speech, people often reflect their inner states. For example, a person full of enthusiasm tends to project a positive, upbeat mood that is noticed and felt by others, whereas a very anxious person tends to have a nervous or unsettling presence. A person who stands before 32 students every day for six hours serving as a guide and role model has a great responsibility in terms of the kind of presence or mood he or she projects. After all, this mood or presence sends a message to the students that may inspire them to approach things in a positive, confident manner or to approach things fearfully and tentatively. Therefore, it is the teacher's responsibility to maintain a physically, mentally, and emotionally healthy state so that he or she projects an upbeat, positive outlook.

It is also important that the teacher, in his or her interactions with students and other members of the school community, maintain dignity and respect for the individual. Being respectful to students does not mean being weak willed or intimidated by them. It means that the teacher keeps a civilized level of behavior, even while dealing with the most difficult student. Firm limitations are enforced, but the teacher does so calmly and without temper or vindictiveness. Everyone has ups and downs in their personal lives, but a teacher has the responsibility to transcend this as much as possible when he or she is in the classroom, for the benefit of the children.

Philosophy of Education

Teachers, as professionals, are responsible for formulating and articulating beliefs about how children learn and how best to instruct them. Without a philosophy of education, many educators will be swayed by every fad that comes along without understanding why they are following those procedures. Teachers must take the time to study research, go to seminars, discuss issues with fellow teachers, and reflect on their own teaching experiences in order to formulate their own deeply held beliefs about teaching and learning. Of course, in this lifelong process, beliefs will change as one acquires more experience, studies new research, and so on. And this is as it should be. Teachers must continue to grow and change, just as they expect their students to do, and their beliefs will be modified in the process. Without carrying out the responsibility of the development and continued examination of a philosophy of education, an educator's level of teaching will remain one dimensional. In this area of responsibility, the teacher is beholden only to his or her own expectations, not to those of a site administrator or school community. That is the meaning of being a professional. The route to school improvement and a more effective education system is through the professionalism of teachers.

For a summary of the responsibilities of a teacher, see Figure 1–2.

FIGURE 1–2   Overview of Responsibilities of a Teacher

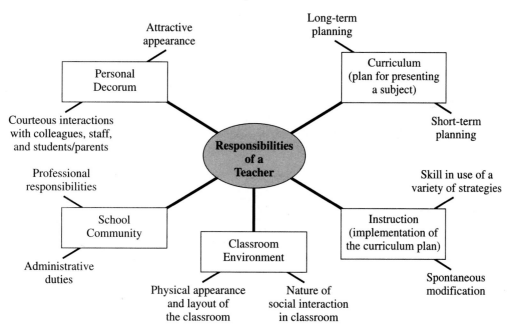

C h a p t e r 2

Learning

As you enter the world of the elementary school classroom, you are faced with an enormous task—how best to teach so as to foster student learning. A natural key to doing this as effectively as possible is to have a firm grasp of what learning really means. This chapter, therefore, will provide the understanding and insights about learning necessary to planning and carrying out a successful instructional program. The following topics will be discussed:

- Definition of learning
- The learning process
- Assessing learning
- Learning styles

Definition of Learning

Student learning is the goal of classroom teaching, but what is meant by *learning?* Put another way, When can one say that someone has learned something? Look at the following three statements that could well be made by a fourth-grader arriving home from school:

1. "Mom, I know that each state gets to have two senators."
2. "Mom, I can tell you how the country decided that each state gets to have two senators."
3. "Mom, I want to tell you why I think having just two senators here in California seems unfair to me."

A question needs to be asked here: Which statement indicates that this fourth-grader has learned something? The answer is that all three statements demonstrate that learning has occurred. What is different in each statement is the *level* of learning accomplished. In statement 1, the student is able to demonstrate recollection of a fact. In statement 2, the student is able to give some meaning to this fact. In statement 3, the student applies the understanding of this fact to form a personal judgment. One can clearly see three levels of learning: factual recall of information, understanding of information, and original application of information that has been understood. Not only has the student learned something at each level but also each higher level is made possible by accomplishing the prior one. For example, how could one develop understanding of a particular thing without first knowing some basic facts? Further, imagine how useless it would be to attempt creative application of information that is not understood. Although all three levels of learning are needed and important, it should be the teacher's goal to have the students reach the highest level possible. This is because once something is learned at this level, it is assimilated into one's life and retained.

Keeping these illustrations in mind, examine the following two definitions of learning. Each definition was collaboratively arrived at by teacher education students preparing to enter the classroom. In both cases, the prospective teachers attempted to look at learning in its highest sense:

1. Learning is the process of acquiring, applying, and retaining knowledge and skills through experiences that modify thinking and behavior in relation to the world around us.
2. Learning is the process of acquiring, expanding, and assimilating skills and knowledge in the form of information, concepts, and ideas through experience and application.

Both definitions look at learning as a process based on experience. Both also indicate that acquiring, retaining, applying, and assimilating knowledge and skills is the *sine qua non* of learning. These two definitions follow what is known as the *constructivist paradigm*. This is a view of teaching and learning that looks beyond rote memorization of information to "help learners to internalize and reshape, or transform, new information" (Brooks & Brooks, 1993, p. 15). If you want to know to what extent you are following this paradigm, ask yourself the following questions about how your classroom functions (Henderson, 1996, p. 110):

- Do you encourage your students to do most of the talking in the classroom?
- Do you design lesson activities that engage students in authentic, meaningful activities that are connected to the "real" world?
- Do you ask more than you tell so that your students' responses, ideas, and questions progressively lead them to construct meaning?
- Do you tend to ask questions that help your students focus on the relationship between what they already know (prior knowledge) and what they are learning?
- Do you help your students form a classroom community where meaning is constructed in a collaborative and supportive way?
- Do you guide students to recognize, understand, and control their own thinking processes and thus learn how to take responsibility for their own learning?

The more clearly defined the goal, the more possible it is to plan for and then work toward accomplishing that goal. Good teachers see the goal of student learning very much along the lines presented in the earlier two definitions. Having a clear idea of where you want to go, still leaves you with finding out how best to get there. For this, a solid understanding of how the learning process works is essential.

The Learning Process

The best way to understand anything is to identify with it personally. In the case of the learning process, this means a person has only to reflect on what he or she has gone through to learn something, in order to gain an insight into how the process works. In other words, each of us is a living emblem of the learning process. We merely have to rerun the tape, so to speak, concerning something we have learned, step by step, from the beginning onward to the point where learning in the highest sense was achieved.

Looking at an example of self-reflection on the learning process in Figure 2–1, notice that no matter who is doing this exercise and no matter what the "thing" learned is, the essential process will always be the same. (Do your own reflection on something you have learned to prove this.) This exercise demonstrates that a universal truth about the nature of the learning process has been discovered. This is tremendously valuable knowledge as one strives to create a positive classroom learning environment. The following discussion will examine this universal truth in terms of the three principal phases of the learning process. You will also see how the most highly regarded learning theories and effective instructional practices all follow these three phases.

FIGURE 2–1   Self-Reflection on the Learning Process

Content: An adult says, "I know how to play the clarinet."
 • Notice the steps that lead to this learning accomplishment:

Creating Interest	Building Background	Developing Understanding	Applying Creative Ability
How: Saw Benny Goodman play, liked it, wanted to play clarinet too.	**How:** Began taking clarinet lessons, read about the clarinet, watched other clarinetists play.	**How:** Practiced tone production, fingering, and music reading in preparation for weekly lessons and school performances.	**How:** Made personal interpretations of various musical pieces and improvised original melodies based on a solid understanding of how to play the clarinet.

Three Essential Phases of the Learning Process

By examining and reflecting on the example in Figure 2–1, you can see that the accomplishment of learning in the highest sense (i.e., when it becomes part of us) always begins with some interest. This interest can come as a positive force from within or as an imposed interest in that we need to learn something out of necessity or face certain consequences. The more positive the interest, the better, as far as sustaining effort and accomplishing learning. A person's interest puts him or her in the posture of wanting (or needing) to know—an essential condition for learning to take place.

This state of wanting to know first leads us to gather necessary information on what is to be learned. To do this, we read, observe, listen, discuss, ask, and do anything else that brings the information we need. This taking in of information in whatever way we can is an effort to build our background about what is to be learned. The more senses we use, and the better we use them, will measure how complete this background will be. This is called, appropriately, the *perception phase* of the learning process. Next, we seek to take the information obtained and find some use for it by putting the various facts together in ways that have meaning. To accomplish this, we try to solve problems, answer questions, and practice putting the information to use. In short, we employ that awesome ability of the human mind known as *thinking*. This search for meaning is the *conception phase* of the learning process. Finally, with the mind fully engaged and the information understood, we rely on ourselves creatively to use and apply what we have come to understand. This is the *ideation phase* of the learning process. Here, the full power of the mind, with its creative resourcefulness, comes into play.

One simple way to understand the nature of the learning process is that more brain power is needed and used with each succeeding phase. Equally important to note is the fact that effectively moving from one phase to the next one is based on success at the prior phase. For example, if a student's perceptions were poor due to lack of attention, interest, or the clarity of what was presented, then with what information will this student attempt to form an understanding? In life, people normally look on those who profess understanding based on limited or wrong information as being ignorant. Feeling racially superior is an example of such ignorance. In another area, consider a budding musician who knows his notes and fingerings (i.e., perception phase) but has not yet formed the essential concepts (conception phase) necessary to bring these smoothly together. When he attempts to take creative liberties with the music or to improvise (i.e., ideation phase), the results, not surprisingly, are less than satisfying. Being able to create in a certain area is based on a solid understanding of that area, and that solid understanding is based on having a background of essential information in that area. Put another way, the better a person perceives something, the greater will be the possibility of understanding it, and the better the understanding, the greater will be the possibility of creatively and originally applying it.

The Learning Process and Successful Teaching

The implication and utility of what has just been discussed above about the learning process is made clear in two recommendations. Following these recommendations will definitely help you reach the goal of effectively planning and carrying out classroom instruction.

Recommendation 1:   To accomplish the highest level of learning, students should be taken successfully through activities and experiences, addressing all three phases of the learning process.

Recommendation 2:   To realize student success at each phase of the learning process, the effective instructional characteristics listed in Figure 2–2 should be at the heart of planning and carrying out classroom instruction.

So that the suggestions in Figure 2–2 can be of practical use to you, they are presented according to what you need to do as you design instructional activities at each phase of the learning process. In addition to describing *what* you need to accomplish instructionally is a brief rationale stating *why* doing so is important to fostering student learning.

Knowledge of the learning process and attention to the recommendations in Figure 2–2 will be valuable as you create your daily lesson activities. In conjunction with this knowledge, one further point must be stressed here. Effective learning experiences are based on *what the students actually have to do to learn*, not simply on what they appear to be doing. With this in mind, notice how even a direct presentation (e.g., lecture) on

FIGURE 2–2   The Learning Process and Effective Instruction

Learning Phases	What the Teacher Should Do	Why the Teacher Should Do It
Perception Phase Activities	• Create interest by relating topic and instruction to students' backgrounds and interests. • Present information in several ways, using a variety of media.	• Gains students' attention and receptivity, opening their minds to more and better perceptions of material presented • Encourages students to use and take in presented material through several sensory modes
Conception Phase Activities	• Guide, faciliate, and monitor students' work. • Integrate enrichment resources with the textbook material. • Pose and encourage thought-level questions. • Make problem solving and discovery the focus.	• Increases students' development of understanding of the material • Provides students with additional insights, perspectives, and stimuli • Spurs use of mental abilities to fill in the gaps • Orients and requires students to find meaning in the information
Ideation Phase Activities	• Plan activities and assignments where students need to apply in original ways what they know. • Set up a portfolio system for students' work. • Encourage group projects.	• Provides students with opportunities to put their creative stamp on learning • Presents a living reality to students, parents, and teachers of students' creativity and accomplishments • Demonstrates to students that in the realm of ideas, people working together can achieve wonderful things

certain material done in a way that encourages students to integrate this material with what they have previously learned or experienced can be considered "meaningful learning" (Ausubel, 1963). However, a discovery learning activity (normally the highest of meaningful learning) in which students are mechanically following steps or formulas without understanding what they are doing is really little more than rote learning.

Major Learning Theories and Effective Instructional Practices

The universal truth—or what can be called the *generic theory* of the learning process in the form of perception, conception, and ideation—operates as the heart and soul of all credible theories and practices of learning and instruction. In Figure 2–3, parallels are drawn between this generic theory and those of Alfred North Whitehead (1929) and Jerome Bruner (1960), two of the greatest learning theorists. Similarly, parallels are drawn with three of the most respected and widely used teaching models: (1) Clinical, (2) Teach-Practice-Apply (TPA) (Reinhartz & Reinhartz, 1988), and (3) Preparation, Assisting Understanding, Reflection (PAR) (Richardson & Morgan, 1990) models of planning and instruction.

All of these learning and teaching models work because they follow the universal principle in the generic theory of the learning process. In fact, perception, conception, and ideation taken together are what is known as *cognition*. It is no wonder, then, that the components of any effective learning or teaching theory fit this chart according to the three phases. It will always work simply because for any theory or model of instruction or learning to be effective, it must relate to the universal process of how a human being learns something (i.e., cognition)—whether it be in the classroom or in life.

Concluding Insight on the Learning Process

As was stated previously, the person who relentlessly plans lessons and carries out instructional activities day after day is at a great advantage if he or she knows the inner workings of the learning process that you have examined here. Such understanding can provide a clear strategic focus to how lessons and activities should be designed in order to accomplish learning. There is, however, one further insight to share about the learning process, which, although seemingly obvious, is rather profound and offers reason for optimism by teachers. The more students learn by successfully going through the phases of the learning process, the more they are ready for additional learning. Noted developmental psychologist and educator Jean Piaget looked at readiness for learning in a similar way. He spoke of "conceptual frameworks" or "schemata" (Piaget in Wadsworth, 1971) to describe the mental process involved in linking past with present learning.

Students' existing conceptual frameworks, or the way they view information and ideas in relation, are important in determining when they are able to learn (i.e., take in new perceptions) and how they understand what they take in (i.e., form new conceptions). This denotes the cyclical nature of the learning process. The more a person per-

FIGURE 2–3 Parallels between Theory of Learning and Instruction

Universal Principles in Operation	Learning Theories			Teaching Models			Other
	Generic Theory	Bruner: Learning Episode	Whitehead: Three Stages of Learning	Clinical Model	Teach-Practice-Apply	Par	Any Learning or Instructional Theory That Has Proven Effective
To create interest and build necessary background	Perception	Acquisition	Romance	(Anticipatory Set and Objective) Direct Instruction	Teach	Preparation	
To facilitate comprehension and finding of meaning	Conception	Transformation	Precision	Guided Practice and Closure	Practice	Assisting Understanding	
To foster creativity and original application	Ideation	Evaluation	Generalization	Independent Practice	Apply	Reflection	

ceives, the more he or she understands, and then the more he or she can create. The point here is that the more a student creates, the wider his or her field of perceptions grows—and so continues the process over again, all at a higher level. It is a wonderful, ever-widening cycle that, if understood and strategically used by the classroom teacher, can lead to realization of not only instructional goals but also of larger ones, as Piaget (in Heck & Williams, 1984, p. 59) points out: "The ideal of education is not necessarily to teach the maximum but to help students learn to learn and to help them maintain the desire to continue to develop as lifelong learners."

Assessing Learning

To carry out effective classroom instruction, it is useful to examine the role that assessment of learning plays. The following discussion is relatively brief because later in the book Section V is devoted to evaluation in the elementary classroom. Therefore, for now, three issues will be discussed: (1) the phases of the assessment process, (2) the link between assessment and the learning process, and (3) assessment and the three aspects of human consciousness.

Phases of the Assessment Process

An overview of the assessment process is useful because, as with the learning process, it occurs over time in a series of distinct phases. Earlier, this chapter explained how learning takes place through a natural process inherent to all human beings. Thus, the assessment process should be thought of as having a flow and rhythm that addresses this natural process.

With this in mind, and to get a sense of the assessment process, think of a situation where a student has to learn a particular thing at school. First, you should determine how *ready* this student is for the learning that needs to be accomplished. Clearly, it would be frustrating and demoralizing for both you and the student if the child was pushed to attempt learning something for which he or she was not ready. The "readiness gap" must be determined and bridged if efforts to learn are to be successful. This is called the *diagnostic phase* of the assessment process. Once the student is ready and efforts are begun to learn the particular thing, it seems only natural that you monitor the *progress* being made by the student. Monitoring is a form of inquiry as you ask, Is the pace of instruction too fast? Should other strategies or resource materials be used? and so on. This period of monitoring and modifying learning experiences is aptly called the *formative phase* of assessment. Finally, after a certain period of time, you want to take stock and see how far the student is toward *accomplishing* learning of this particular thing. This is the *summative phase* of assessment. The information obtained from summative assessment tells you much about the student's readiness to go on to new learning. Notice here how the assessment process, like the learning process, is cyclical in nature. The phases of the assessment process keep recycling as the summative phase blends directly into the diagnostic phase, and so on.

The Link between Assessment and the Learning Process

Figure 2–4 shows the three phases of the assessment process according to their purpose and strategic use in relation to the learning process. Interestingly, an element of equity is seen in the assessment process. Considering the nature of the assessment process as outlined in Figure 2–4, fair assessment of a student is possible only if teachers take the time, have the skills, and use the varied means necessary to create or complete a profile of how and how much that student learns. Assessment of student learning is innately unfair and inaccurate if students' learning styles are not determined, if a variety of instructional activities addressing those learning styles is not employed, and if different types of instruments and activities (i.e., performance and on demand; see Chapter 5) are not utilized to obtain the data on which to make judgments. In short, since assessment is all about drawing a profile of each student's learning, it can only be accurate and useful if you know how and care to obtain as complete information as possible.

Assessment and the Three Aspects of Human Consciousness

In light of the need for equity and accuracy in assessment of learning, it is fitting to examine the three aspects of human consciousness that denote the "total person" who is involved in learning. Earlier, the three phases of the learning process—perception,

FIGURE 2–4   Phases of the Assessment Process

Phases of Assessment	Purpose	Relation to the Learning Process
Diagnostic Phase	To determine *readiness* for learning based on student's: • ability and skill levels • interest and backgrounds • prior learning accomplished	*Strategic Value:* Obtaining information and insights for connecting new learning with prior learning and for determining and building background (perception phase) as a foundation for understanding (conception phase)
Formative Phase	To monitor *progress* being made toward learning based on student's: • participation in class activities • completed assignments, classwork, and homework	*Strategic Value:* Obtaining information and insights for effectively designing and modifying instruction to help students understand information and concepts (conception phase) as the basis for creative application (ideation phase) of what has been learned
Summative Phase	To determine *accomplishment* of learning over particular time periods based on student's: • portfolios of completed work • test scores and other "on demand" performances • presentations and projects	*Strategic Value:* Obtaining information and insights into the degree learning has been assimilated so that further experiences can be provided for creative application of information and concepts, and as the basis for new and continued learning (recycling of the process)

conception, and ideation—were discussed. These phases represent the cognitive (knowing or mental) aspect of human consciousness. If you are aiming for as complete and accurate assessment as possible, it follows that the other two remaining aspects of human consciousness, the affective (feeling) and conative (willing or doing) aspects must be looked at, as well.

In whatever one does, these three aspects of human consciousness are operating and inextricably intertwined. If a teacher merely assesses a student's mental (cognitive) functioning without considering his or her interest (affective) and active involvement (conative) in the work at hand, then what is being measured? The teacher will perhaps wind up with some staggering numbers, but not much really to understand, and thus help, the student. Further, often only the perception level (i.e., recall or recognition of facts/information) of a student's cognitive functioning is measured. So even a true picture of the child's mental abilities is not obtained, let alone his or her entire human consciousness. The logic here is simple and clear—as human beings, students' minds, hearts, and wills are always involved to some extent in whatever they do. Assessment must address this self-evident truth. To carry out such holistic assessment of student learning as a means of both determining and fostering student learning and growth, Figure 2–5 provides a straightforward and readily usable profile based on the three aspects of human consciousness.

If we think of cognition as a student's understanding of subject material, affection as a student's interest in subject material, and conation as a student's will to take action toward learning the subject material, then Figure 2–5 can be used to obtain a relative measure of each area of functioning. By using such a holistic assessment of the three

FIGURE 2–5 Assessment Based on the Three Aspects of Human Consciousness

Aspects of Consciousness	Degree in Evidence			
	Low	Marginal	Moderate	High
Cognition (Knowing)				
Affection (Feeling)				
Conation (Willing)				

aspects of a student's consciousness, it becomes possible to discover essential under-lying causes for a student's failure or inability to achieve as expected or hoped. To see how this works, consider the following three scenarios concerning students who are not achieving well in class. In each case, the scale in Figure 2–5 for conducting a holistic assessment will be used to determine where the problem is.

Scenario 1

Student A is observed functioning in the classroom and the teacher determines that this student:

- Understands the material fairly well as it is presented (moderate in cognition)
- Has a healthy interest in the material (high in affection)
- Has poor work and study habits (*low* in conation)

Analysis and Solution.   The teacher realizes that if this student can be guided in developing a reasonably disciplined routine of study at home as well as in the class-room, his existing ability to understand and take an interest in the subject material will become a potent force toward accomplishing learning.

The teacher then works with the student to design a plan of study characterized by specific study times and work expectations. In the plan, both of these expectations are gradually increased over time as self-discipline and taste for success develop. As a result, this student becomes among the highest achieving in the class.

Scenario 2

Student B is observed functioning in the classroom and the teacher determines that this student:

- Understands the material very well as it is presented (high in cognition)
- Has disciplined work and study habits (high in conation)
- Has little interest or motivation to learn the material (*low* in affection)

Analysis and Solution.   The teacher realizes that by finding ways to create in the student an interest in the material, her existing ability to understand and work in a focused way on the material will then become a potent force in accomplishing learning.

The teacher then attempts to spark the student's interest in learning the material by using several approaches, including giving tangible rewards and praise, peer tutoring, using additional instructional resources, and relating the material to the student's life. As a result, this student becomes among the most successful learners in class.

Scenario 3

Student C is observed functioning in class and the teacher determines that this student:

- Has fairly disciplined work and study habits (moderate in conation)
- Has a healthy interest in the material (high in affection)

- Has considerable difficulty comprehending the information and concepts being presented (*low* in cognition)

Analysis and Solution.   The teacher realizes that by somehow modifying instruction so the student can understand the material, his existing ability to take interest in and work in a focused way on the material will become a potent force in accomplishing learning.

The teacher then modifies instruction by adjusting the pace at which information and concepts are presented, using activities and resources that allow for different learning styles, and employing greater use of cooperative learning structures.

Summary of the Three Scenarios

These scenarios depict simplified situations for the purpose of highlighting a clear deficiency in one of the three areas of human consciousness in each case. It can occur this way, but often the holistic profile will reveal a mix of strengths and needs across the three areas, especially as the content areas vary. By drawing basic profiles of how students function in the three areas of human consciousness, teachers can formulate specific steps that may have profound results in the students' classroom achievement as well as their growth as individuals.

Learning Styles

A crucial first step in making your instructional planning effective is to know how your students learn best. If you observe your students, other individuals, or yourself over time, it will soon become apparent that each individual has a consistent approach in how he or she tries to learn things. This consistent approach that each person uses defines his or her *learning style*. In fact, research and classroom observation over the past decades have clearly shown that there are several categories of learning styles into which individuals fit, rather than there being as many learning styles as there are learners. Knowledge of these categories provides the teacher with the necessary insights to promote and create an environment for student learning success by designing instruction that is consistent with students' strengths and tendencies.

To provide these insights so learning styles theories can be effectively applied in the classroom, the following pages will examine the most useful learning styles research and then present practical ways to assess students' learning styles.

Background

Just as each individual is unique and displays a set of characteristics not exactly like those of any other individual, each individual also learns in his or her own unique way. In the classroom, for example, students show differences in the ways in which they approach a learning task and in how they perceive and organize information. Students also display differences in terms of preferences regarding such variables as sound, light, temperature, working alone or in groups, and the type of learning task involved (e.g., worksheet as opposed to writing an essay). For many decades, educators have investigated these differences, looking for similar patterns of learning that could be identified as particular types of learning styles. The idea was to see how useful it would be to classify learners according to these types of learning styles.

Various researchers have looked at different aspects or characteristics of learning styles with the result that there are now a variety of different definitions of learning styles. For the sake of this discussion, however, the following broad definition is presented to encompass the various learning styles researchers have studied. "Learning styles are usually defined as cognitive, affective and physiological traits of learners as they interact in the classroom environment" (Orlich et al., 1994).

The contention of learning styles advocates is that students are more motivated and achieve greater learning when they are taught in a manner consistent with their learning styles. Critics of the learning styles movement, however, caution against the practice of clustering students according to their learning styles and instructing them accordingly. Since it is known that learning style differences do exist, it can only be to the teacher's advantage, in planning and carrying out classroom instruction, to make sure these differences are accommodated over time. This allows the teacher to build on students' strengths while addressing their weaknesses.

Learning Styles Research

The complexity and number of comprehensive learning styles theories can be confusing and intimidating to the new teacher who is trying to apply this knowledge to make his or her instruction more effective. This is due to the fact that each of these many theories has a unique view of learning and thus identifies and classifies learning styles in a different way. What, then, does the teacher do? A strong approach would be to examine a few of the most respected and used learning styles theories and decide which one (or aspects of these) provides you with the most practical guidance for designing instructional activities to foster student learning. Perhaps the single-greatest message and value from all the work and research on learning styles is that different students learn best in different ways. From this, it becomes clear that an inviting and successful classroom is one where a variety of teaching strategies is used on a regular basis so all students have opportunities to work in their areas of strength.

Dunn and Dunn (1978) and Witkin and associates (1977) have developed two of the most widely recognized learning styles theories. For purposes of planning and carrying out classroom instruction, these two learning styles theories will be examined as they provide particularly useful insights into how students function best. In addition to these two approaches to learning styles, Howard Gardner's work on Multiple Intelligences (1983) will be presented as a viable way of determining how and what your students learn best.

The Learning Styles Inventory
The work of Kenneth and Rita Dunn (1978) is the result of over 10 years of classroom research observing and studying individual students' preferences for various conditions and factors as they engaged in learning tasks. Dunn and Dunn developed an

instrument, the Learning Styles Inventory, to determine these learning preferences in four main areas:

1. *Environmental:* How the elements of light, sound, temperature, and physical room arrangements affect students' learning
2. *Emotional:* How responsible and persistent students are and the level of structure and supervision they need when involved in learning
3. *Sociological:* How students function in a large or small group, alone, or with adult assistance when involved in learning
4. *Physical:* How students use different sensory modes (i.e., visual, auditory, tactile, and kinesthetic) to learn and how they function with respect to need for movement, food intake, and time of day

Factors in these four areas have a major impact on student learning. For example, in the area Dunn and Dunn refer to as "physical stimuli," imagine a teacher trying to get a particular math concept across to a group of four students. It is possible that one student will take in the information best by listening to the teacher's verbal descriptions. Another student will perceive the concept best by seeing a diagram of it on the board. Yet another will get the most from reading what the textbook has to say about it, and the fourth student will be most at ease by manipulating plastic pieces to understand the concept. Although students tend to clearly manifest their physical preferences for taking in information and ideas, their interests are best served by designing instruction so that they come to feel more and more able to learn through all the sensory modalities. In short, build on their strengths (i.e., preferred learning styles) and slowly but surely address their weaknesses (i.e., nonpreferred learning styles).

Field-Dependent and Field-Independent Cognitive Styles
An excellent complement to the Dunn and Dunn Learning Styles Inventory is Witkin's Field-Dependent and Field-Independent Cognitive Styles (Witkin et al., 1977).

Cognitive Style.   A useful way to think of cognitive style, as with any learning style, is to look at it in terms of your students in the classroom. From this viewpoint, *cognitive style* refers to how the students tend to perceive and then form an understanding of the material presented to them. Witkin and associates (1977) conducted research for nearly 25 years that resulted in the notion of Field-Dependent and Field-Independent Cognitive Styles. Of the several ways to look at cognitive style, the simplicity and logic of Witkin's approach is the most readily applicable for classroom teachers. Figure 2–6 presents a chart describing the main characteristics to look for to determine students' cognitive styles.

How does this chart help? First, by describing characteristics of the two cognitive styles as it does, you can readily determine the degree to which students are field dependent or field independent. As opposed to rather elaborate learning styles inventories, checklists, and the like, you can actually gain important information about your students' cognitive styles in a relatively short period of time.

The question arises: What should be done instructionally once the students' cognitive styles are determined? The answer is straightforward: Build on the strengths and

FIGURE 2–6   Main Characteristics That Distinguish Field-Dependent from Field-Independent Students

Focus	Field Dependent		Field Independent	
	Characteristics	Classroom Examples	Characteristics	Classroom Examples
S t u d e n t s	Is global	During classroom instruction in general, develops an overall feeling or general idea of the material	Is analytical	During classroom instruction in general, develops a structure for categorizing the material and clustering concepts
	Is extrinsically motivated	Relies on peers for direction and motivation and prefers working in groups	Is intrinsically motivated	Develops a strong sense of personal direction and goals and prefers working alone
	Is socially oriented	Seeks to find social relevance of material presented in content areas	Is content oriented	Focuses on nature of concepts within and across content areas

preferences of the students and then be sure they acquire some measure of facility in the area where they are less adept. This advice sounds too general to be of value, but it is not. To demonstrate how useful it is, consider this example:

Ms. Jones's Classroom Observations

Ms. Jones has been observing her new group of third-graders for almost two weeks since the start of a new school year. She notices that Johnny seems to work better alone, is self-motivated, and shows a tendency to analyze things to find out what makes them tick. Being familiar with the concept of field-dependent and field-independent cognitive learning styles, Ms. Jones realizes that Johnny tends toward the field-independent style. With this simple insight about Johnny, she is able intelligently to make slight modifications in selected instructional activities, so that her classroom becomes a more inviting learning environment for Johnny and other field-independent students.

One of the modifications she makes is providing a daily menu of enrichment work for those who complete classwork assignments early. This is very effective with Johnny and others who tend to be self-motivated, because independent work is called for. In this regard, Ms. Jones is building on strengths and preferences. Another modification she makes addresses Johnny's need to widen his cognitive abilities by involving him periodically in cooperative learning activities where he must rely on peers for completing a task.

Ms. Jones also notices that Johnny is in the minority in terms of cognitive style. That is, most of her students seem to be field dependent. Realizing that these field-dependent students have considerable difficulty extracting main ideas from a general context as they read, listen to, or observe presentation of material, she wisely determines that she needs to make plentiful use of various graphic organizers to help them structure and focus their attention and thoughts.

The Cognitive Styles Survey in Figure 2–7 is an instrument that can help identify where students and teachers lie on a continuum between highly field dependent and highly field independent.

FIGURE 2–7   Cognitive Styles Survey

A = Field Independent   B = Field Dependent

Personal

1. Do you tend to look at:
   a. the whole to figure out how the part works?
   b. the parts to figure out what the whole is?

2. Do you tend to:
   a. create a structure as you read, listen to, or observe things?
   b. form an overall picture of things that you read, listen to, or observe?

3. Do you prefer to:
   a. have goals defined for you?
   b. define your own goals?

4. Do you tend to be:
   a. more internally motivated?
   b. more externally motivated?

5. Do you tend to focus on:
   a. the nature of content presented to you?
   b. the social relevance of content presented to you?

Teaching

6. Will you use questioning more:
   a. as an instructional tool (e.g., for inquiry learning)?
   b. as a device to check for student learning to follow instruction?

7. Will you use more:
   a. lecture and discovery learning?
   b. discussion and cooperative learning?

8. Will you tend to:
   a. correct student responses?
   b. give general reinforcement for all student responses?

9. Will you tend to stress:
   a. students applying principles?
   b. students learning factual information?

Processing

10. Look at the following list of words and take three minutes to treat them in any way you prefer.

    | water | weather | compass |
    | map | surplus | explore |
    | harvest | discovery | bushel |
    | hunger | crop | technology |

Note: Field dependence is indicated if the answers to questions 1 through 9 are all "a"s; field independence is indicated if those answers are all "b"s. Of course, a range of possibilities exists between these two poles. For question 10, field-dependent persons will tend to use the words to write a brief paragraph or thought, whereas field-independent persons will likely categorize the words into a few discrete lists.

Multiple Intelligences

While Dunn and Dunn look at students' learning preferences and Witkin looks specifically at students' cognitive functioning, Gardner looks at the different types of intelligence students tend to display predominantly according to seven discrete areas he has identified in his work on Multiple Intelligences. These seven areas of intelligence are listed in Figure 2–8, along with an operational description of each type of intelligence.

Gardner (1983) has shown not only great insight but also compassion by putting forth his notion of Multiple Intelligences. His insight is evidenced by his recognition of how unintelligent it is to confine the conception of human intelligence to a narrow area of academic performance. Rather, Gardner opens up the definition of intelligence to include and encompass various aspects of life itself. He shows compassion in that his notion of Multiple Intelligences includes and appreciates everyone and the diverse gifts, abilities, and attributes they have.

The information on Multiple Intelligences in Figure 2–8 can be used in two particularly effective ways. First, you can use it to help you assess where your students' tendencies and strengths lie. Second, you can use it as a guide to designing classroom activities so that, over time, your students have opportunities to experience working in

FIGURE 2–8   Description of Gardner's Multiple Intelligences

Intelligence	Operational Description
Logical/ Mathematical	• Sensitivity to and capacity to discern logic or numeric patterns • Ability to handle long chains of reasoning
Linguistic	• Sensitivity to the sounds, rhythms, and meanings of words • Sensitivity to the different functions of language
Musical	• Ability to produce, appreciate, and recognize pitch, rhythm, and timbre • Appreciation of the forms of musical expression
Spatial	• Capacity to perceive and represent the visual-spatial world accurately and creatively
Bodily/Kinesthetic	• Ability to control and coordinate one's body movement (fine motor and large motor skills)
Interpersonal	• Capacity and willingness to discern and deal with others' needs, desires, temperaments, and abilities
Intrapersonal	• Understanding of one's own feelings, motivations, strengths, and weaknesses as a guide to behavior and growth

Source: Description of Multiple Intelligences taken from *Multiple Intelligences* by Howard Gardner. Copyright © 1993 by Howard Gardner. Reprinted by permission of BasicBooks, a division of HarperCollins Publishers, Inc.

different areas of intelligence. Without such opportunities, you and they may never know what special talents they have.

Assessing Learning Styles

The key to making use of learning styles research lies in its thoughtful application to the actual classroom planning of instructional activities. The key for the teacher is in finding a practical way to assess the predominant learning styles of the students, especially those having difficulty achieving academically. To accomplish this, the Learning Styles Profile Continuum (LSPC) is presented next. The seven areas that make up the LSPC are derived, in large part, from the works of Dunn and Dunn, Witkin, and Gardner. So that this instrument can become a valuable and readily usable tool in the classroom, focus will be on three areas: (1) a description of the design of the LSPC, (2) the LSPC itself as it can be used in the classroom, and (3) a set of realistic guidelines for using the LSPC.

Design of the Learning Styles Profile Continuum

The LSPC is designed to allow the teacher considerable flexibility and focus in his or her efforts to determine students' learning styles. Taken together, the seven areas of the LSPC (i.e., environmental, sensory mode, sociological, affective, cognitive, intelligences, and generic) address a comprehensive set of factors related to learning style in the classroom. Each area, in turn, is divided into specific learning style attributes that are readily observable. This allows the teacher to construct a broad profile of how a student functions best in the classroom, or to focus in and obtain useful insights into just one or two very specific attributes of the student's learning style. A straightforward low-to-high continuum is used for measuring each learning style attribute to facilitate creation of a profile and to avoid the kind of complicated detail that would make the LSPC impractical to use.

The Learning Styles Profile Continuum

Figure 2–9 shows the Learning Styles Profile Continuum for each of the seven learning styles, followed by Figure 2–10, a summary record-keeping form.

Guidelines for Using the LSPC

First, the focus will be on how to begin using the LSPC in the classroom. Next, four effective ways to apply the information and insights obtained from its use will be discussed.

How to Begin Using the LSPC.   The following five-step sequence describes how to begin using the LSPC so that it serves as a practical and informative tool for planning and carrying out classroom instruction.

- *Step 1: Be Organized:* Set up a Learning Styles Notebook consisting of one LSPC page covering the seven areas for each student. Include at the end a Summary Record-Keeping Form providing a whole-class profile.

FIGURE 2–9   Learning Styles Profile Continuum

Student Name: Billy

Environmental

Low   *High*

Sound

Light

Temperature

Density
(seating design)

Affective

Low   *High*

Motivation
(interest)

Persistence
(determination)

Concentration
(attention span)

Responsibility
(thoughtfulness
& attitude)

Sociological

Low   *High*

Large Group

Small Group

Pair

Elder

Mixed

Alone

Sensory Mode

Low   *High*

Visual

FIGURE 2–9   *(Continued)*

Auditory   _____

Tactile   _____

Kinesthetic   _____

Cognitive

Low   *High*

Memory   _____

Field
Dependent   _____

Field
Independent   _____

Intelligences

Low   *High*

Logical/
Mathematical   _____

Linguistic   _____

Musical   _____

Spatial   _____

Bodily/
Kinesthetic   _____

Interpersonal   _____

Intrapersonal   _____

Generic

Time of Day	*Morning*	*Mid-day*		*Afternoon*
Pacing of Activities	Short activities	Mix of short & long activities	Long activities	Physical transitions	Restful transitions
Place	Own seat	Learning center	Library	Home	Media corner	Outside classroom
Type of Work	Directed worksheet	Independent study	Inquiry research	Thought-focused	Many-focused	Mechanical

FIGURE 2–10 LSPC: Summary Record-Keeping Form

Students' Names	Environmental				Sensory Mode				Sociological						Affective				Cognitive		Intelligences							Generic			
	Sound	Light	Temperature	Density	Visual	Auditory	Tactile	Kinesthetic	Large Group	Small Group	Pair	Alone	Elder	Mixed	Motivation	Persistence	Concentration	Responsibility	Field Dependent	Field Independent	Logical/Math.	Linguistic	Musical	Spatial	Bodily/Kines.	Interpersonal	Intrapersonal	Time	Pacing	Place	Work

- *Step 2: Start Small:* To get a feel for using the LSPC, develop a profile in just one or two of the seven areas for a few of the students having the greatest difficulty in the classroom.
- *Step 3: Analyze, Think, and Act:* Once you have completed your first profile, determine what this tells you about how that student learns, then think about what you can modify to address what you have found out. Finally, try one or two things and see what good it does.
- *Step 4: Widen Your Scope:* With the experience of using the LSPC with a few students as a guide to modifying instruction, you can productively use it with an increasing number of students as the school year proceeds. Eventually, you will get to a point where the whole class will be profiled. It is important to remember that there is no rush in widening your scope—go only as fast as your situation permits.
- *Step 5: Reflect As You Go:* As you reach the point of a wider application of the LSPC, consider whether you are finding the information and insights from profiles in particular areas (of the seven) useful and readily obtainable. It makes sense to focus on those profile areas or specific attributes within profiles areas that best serve you and your students. Also, reviewing the Summary Record-Keeping Form can help you notice general patterns that suggest certain instructional changes and practices that will be beneficial.

Productive Applications of LSPC Results.   The LSPC can be a valuable tool for helping you run an effective and successful classroom program. There are four particularly productive applications of the LSPC results:

- *Application 1: Planning Instruction:* The profiles of individual students and patterns of profiles for the class as a whole provide insights into the kinds of lesson activities, instructional resources, and classroom set-up that will lead to successful learning experiences for the students. Figure 2–11 gives an example of "Billy," an underachieving student. The Summary Profile Form indicates what his teacher found to be the most striking attributes (i.e., highs and lows) in each of the seven areas. The information on this summary form is critically important as the teacher strives both to determine and to plan for helping Billy experience learning successes. For the case in point, this teacher, after reviewing Billy's profile, could well have Billy do multiplication problems with a "math buddy" at the classroom media center using a math-tutorial computer program.
- *Application 2: Modifying Classroom Arrangements:* Once the teacher uses the LSPC and realizes how diverse students' learning styles can be, as well as how the class as a whole can have a few predominant learning style patterns or characteristics, he or she will know what variety of seating arrangements, learning stations or centers, wall and bulletin board displays, and resource areas to set up.
- *Application 3: Conferring with Parents:* Having the LSPC available to review with parents demonstrates that the teacher has taken the time intelligently to gain insights about the students' needs and ways of learning. It is also instructive to the

FIGURE 2–11   LSPC Summary Profile of Billy

Overall LSPC
Billy

	Factors with "Low"	Factors with "High"
Environmental	Sound and Light	Density
Affective	Concentration and Persistence	Responsibility
Sociological	Alone	Large Group and Elder
Sensory Mode	Auditory	Tactile and Kinesthetic
Cognitive (mental processing)	Field Independent	Field Dependent
Intelligences	Linguistic and Intrapersonal	Bodily / Kinesthetic and Interpersonal
Generic	Time = P.M.	Time = A.M.
	Work = Unstructured	Work = Structured

parents and is readily understandable so that they, too, can utilize these insights to provide positive experiences for their children at home.

• *Application 4: Reflecting on Teaching:* Ultimately, the applications in the classroom from what is learned by using the LSPC serve as a solid basis for *reflective teaching*. In other words, the teacher has the opportunity to perceive his or her classroom as a living laboratory where a scientific process of gathering data (i.e., observing and drawing up students' LSPCs) and employing interventions (i.e., these four and any other applications of LSPC information and insights) joins with creative and intuitive abilities to solve problems and promote learning.

References for Section I

Ausubel, D. P. (1963). *The psychology of meaningful verbal learning: An introduction to school learning*. New York: Grune & Stratton.

Brooks, J. G., & Brooks, M. G. (1993). *In search of understanding: The case for constructivist classrooms*. Alexandria, VA: Association for Supervision and Curriculum Development.

Bruner, J. S. (1960). *The process of education*. Cambridge, MA: Harvard University Press.

Dunn, K., & Dunn, R. (1978). *Teaching students through their individual learning styles: A practical approach*. Reston, VA: Reston Publishing.

Gardner, H. (1983). *Frames of mind: The theory of Multiple Intelligences*. New York: Basic Books.

Heck, S. F., & Williams, C. R. (1984). *The complex roles of the teacher: An ecological perspective*. New York: Teachers College Press.

Henderson, J. G. (1996). *Reflective teaching: The study of your constructivist practices* (2nd ed.). Englewood Cliffs, NJ: Prentice Hall.

Jarolimek, J., & Foster, C. O. (1981). *Teaching and learning in the elementary school*. New York: Macmillan.

Mullis, I., Owen, E., & Phillips, G. (1990). *Accelerating academic achievement: A summary of 20 years of NAEP*. Princeton, NJ: National Assessment of Educational Progress.

Orlich, D. C., Harder, R. J., Callahan, R. C., Kauchak, D. P., & Gibson, H. W. (1994). *Teaching strategies: A guide to better instruction*. Lexington, MA: D. C. Heath.

Reinhartz, J., & Reinhartz, D. (1988). *Teach-practice-apply*. Washington, DC: National Education Association.

Richardson, J. S., & Morgan, R. F. (1990). *Reading to learn in the content areas*. Belmont, CA: Wadsworth.

Tyler, R. W. (1987). *Predicting who will be a good teacher*. Presentation at American Educational Research Annual Conference, San Francisco.

Wadsworth, B. J. (1971). *Piaget's theory of cognitive development: An introduction for students of psychology and education*. New York: David McKay.

Whitehead, A. N. (1929). *The aims of education and other essays*. New York: Macmillan.

Witkin, H. A., Moore, C. A., Goodenough, D. R., & Cox, P. W. (1977). Field-dependent and field-independent cognitive styles and their educational implications. *Review of Educational Research, 47*, (1), 1–64.

Section *II*

Delivering Instruction

For the purposes of this book, *instruction* and *teaching* are interchangeable and are defined as activities specifically designed to bring about desired student learning. Many types of activities, of course, can bring about learning, and therefore classroom instruction takes place in many different ways. In order to examine this topic in an organized fashion, it is useful to classify all instruction that takes place in the classroom as being delivered in three essential ways: teacher-directed, student-directed, and interactive methods of instruction. In designing lessons, the teacher selects or creates activities that can be characterized by one of these methods. It is quite common to use activities from each of the three methods of instruction in a single lesson.

In the pages that follow, each of the three methods for delivering classroom instruction will be described. This section concludes with in-depth looks at study skills, questioning, and the role of technology in delivering classroom instruction. We will begin with the teacher-directed method of instruction.

$$Chapter \quad 3$$

Teacher-Directed Method of Instruction

The teacher-directed method of instruction involves the teacher presenting the material to the students. To examine the teacher-directed method, the following critical elements will be discussed:

- Use of advance organizers
- Use of lecture, demonstration, and questioning
- Accommodating different learning styles through the use of related resources
- Relating the lesson to the students' lives
- Limitation and repetition of new material
- Dynamic, enthusiastic delivery of the teacher presentation

Purpose

The main purpose of the teacher-directed method of instruction is the transfer of knowledge (facts, concepts, ideas, skills) from the teacher to the students. The means of this transfer of knowledge is through a planned presentation made by the teacher.

Form

The form of this instruction is basically of one type: the teacher positioned in front of the class delivering information directly to the students. This is the teacher presentation. Usually, it occurs as a whole-group instruction, although the teacher could give directed lessons to small groups of students, as well. The defining characteristics of this type of instruction are that the teacher is actively delivering information and the students are expected to absorb it. In other words, the teacher is doing most of the talking and the students are expected actively to attend to and remember what the teacher is saying.

Criteria

In order for the presentation to be effective in bringing about learning, it must hold the attention of the students and be understood by them. This does not happen automatically. One cannot simply stand up in front of a group of students and start talking or explaining something and expect to have their attention and understanding. Children do not attend to something that does not interest them or seem in some way relevant to them. They will also not attend to something they cannot understand. Figure 3–1 lists specific things a teacher can do to ensure that a presentation is interesting, relevant, and clear to the students. The teacher should follow these criteria while planning and/or delivering a presentation in order to maximize its effectiveness.

Use of Advance Organizers

Advance organizers serve the purpose of preparing students to receive the material to be learned from a presentation, a film, or a reading. The advance organizer consists of large concepts or propositions that are directly related to the material to be learned by the students. The concepts in the advance organizer, however, are of a more general and inclusive nature than the material to follow, which is more specific in nature. For example, an advance organizer for a presentation on the Civil Rights movement could focus on the concept of human rights within an organized society—what they would be and how they are protected or violated. Joyce and Weil (1996) have given the example of an advance organizer based on the concept of social stratification to organize a lesson describing the caste system in India.

The advance organizer is content in its own right that has to be taught to the students. That is, its central features have to be pointed out and carefully explained, and examples should be provided to facilitate understanding. Only when students have a clear understanding of the organizer can it serve to organize the learning material and thereby make it more meaningful to the students.

FIGURE 3–1   Planning and Delivering an Effective Teacher Presentation

1. Use *advance organizers* to aid student comprehension and retention.
2. Use all three *teaching activities* (i.e., *lecture, demonstration,* and *questioning*) in each presentation.
3. Use *related resources*—including *visuals, literature,* and *realia*—to engage interest and to accommodate various learning styles.
4. *Relate* new material to *students' lives,* experiences, and existing knowledge.
5. *Limit* the amount of *new information* and *repeat key information* frequently.
6. *Deliver* the presentation in a *dynamic* and *enthusiastic* manner.

It was the goal of David Ausubel (Ausubel & Fitzgerald, 1962), the developer of the advance organizer, to help teachers convey large amounts of information, meaningfully and efficiently, to students through the presentation method. According to Ausubel, students do not have to be passive while learning through listening if they are properly prepared for the material that will be presented to them. The advance organizer provides a mental framework that helps the students make sense of and internalize the new material.

According to Ausubel, as students learn, they build cognitive structures (i.e., the knowledge they possess regarding any particular phenomenon or subject at any given time *and* the extent to which that knowledge is organized and clear in the student's mind). How well new material will be understood and retained depends on how clear and strong a student's cognitive structure is regarding the topic to be presented. The advance organizer serves to clarify and stabilize the student's cognitive structure, thus facilitating his or her comprehension and retention of the new material.

Again, the advance organizer should consist of a concept or concepts that are more general than the concepts that will be presented in the new material. For a lesson on the farm industry in California, for example, the advance organizer might present the concept of natural resources and their use. Another advance organizer for the same topic could focus on the economic system of the state, especially in regard to production of goods. The advance organizer provides an intellectual foundation that helps students receive, understand, and remember the more specific material that follows as the main body of the teacher's presentation.

Use of Lecture, Demonstration, and Questioning

In any one presentation, the teacher should use all three teaching activities of lecture, demonstration, and questioning. However, depending on the needs and learning levels of the students, the nature of the material to be learned, and the availability of resources, the teacher may rely more heavily on one or two of the activities.

Older students are able to attend to straight lecture for longer periods of time than younger ones, and young children benefit greatly from a heavy dose of demonstration in the teacher presentation. All children of elementary school age, however, benefit from the use of examples, analogies, and questions integrated with lecture to make up the teacher presentation. The following discussion looks at each of these three teaching activities in more detail.

Lecture

Lecture is the verbal delivery of information. The teacher talks to the students, explaining facts, concepts, ideas, or skills. In this situation, the students learn by listening. The strength of lecture is that the teacher can reach many students at one time and the material to be learned can be organized in increments in accordance with what the teacher knows his or her students can absorb in a given period. By observing the students during lecture, the teacher can also monitor their interest and attentiveness, and thus make slight adjustments in his or her delivery.

While lecturing, it is important for the teacher to be aware of his or her voice modulation, and to make an effort to vary the tone and volume while speaking. Speaking in the same monotonous tone can have the effect of putting students to sleep! Part of the skill of maintaining the students' interest in the lecture, then, lies in the teacher's ability to use the voice effectively. Since most people are quite unaware of how they sound when speaking, it is a good idea for the teacher to tape classroom lectures and listen to them for the purpose of assessing voice modulation and to determine the necessity of making changes in the use of the voice while lecturing. This can go a long way toward creating more interesting presentations.

Even with good voice modulation, however, lecture cannot stand alone in a teacher presentation at the elementary school level—it must be enhanced with demonstration and questioning. Most students of elementary age are concrete learners. They learn best through active involvement with their environment, wherein the exploration of ideas takes place by beginning with the concrete and moving gradually to the abstract. Straight lecture—that is, just spoken words—takes place on the abstract level and may go over the heads of those needing concrete examples. For example, Mr. Ramirez explains the procedure for using several learning centers that have been set up in the classroom. After explaining what to do at each center, he divides the students into groups and sends them to do the activities at the centers. Mr. Ramirez is dismayed to see that many students do not seem to know what to do when they get to the centers. A more experienced teacher would know that it is more effective to have several students demonstrate the procedure at each center as the teacher explains it, then question the students as to what they need to do at each center even after it has been demonstrated, and finally have them repeat the procedure. Having the students demonstrate what is to be done gives them a concrete understanding of the procedure. Having them verbalize what is to be done takes them to the abstract level only after they have understood it in a concrete way. The younger the children, the more important it is to begin with the concrete and move to the abstract.

Demonstration

Demonstration is a description or explanation of a phenomenon, concept, or idea given with the aid of objects, experiments, or verbal examples. In a lesson on volume, for example, Ms. Andrews talks about various size containers (cup, pint, quart, half gallon, and gallon) as she demonstrates the size of each measure and its relationship to the other sizes. If Ms. Andrews tried to teach the students the concept of *quart* solely through a verbal description (i.e., straight lecture), it would be very difficult, if not impossible, for the students to have any idea of what she is talking about. The aid of life-sized pictures would help, but the use of actual three-dimensional containers is the best way to help the students conceptualize the various sizes.

Verbal or written examples (without objects) is also considered demonstration. Most teachers make frequent use of verbal or written examples in order to get concepts and ideas across to their students. An interesting way to use examples is by providing the students with exemplars and nonexemplars of the concept to be learned. In order to do this, the teacher must consider carefully what the essential characteristics of the concept are and then think of nonexamples of the concept. The teacher can list the exemplars and nonexemplars verbally or in written form for the students. Examples can be such things as a symbol, a word, or a phrase. Students can analyze the examples and nonexamples and then try to determine or identify the concept. The teacher guides the analysis by asking guiding or prompting questions.

Also included in demonstration is the relating of an analogy to the students in order to clarify a concept or idea. Use of analogy is a powerful teaching tool. For example, a first-grade teacher trying to explain the barter system may begin by asking the students if they have ever traded toys or food with their friends and why they did so. This helps the students understand the concept by comparing it to an experience they have had or can picture in their minds.

An analogy can be quite short and simple, such as the one just given, or it can be longer and more involved, such as the following analogy written by a teacher to help students understand the experience of U.S. citizens during the Civil War who found themselves having to side with either the Union or the Confederate states. The analogy in Figure 3–2 paints a picture that can be readily understood by students, thus providing

FIGURE 3–2   Example of an Analogy Used to Introduce a Unit on the Civil War

The following analogy will be read to the class. This will help the students understand how some of the people felt during the Civil War.

Imagine that it is the future. The West Coast of the United States and the East Coast of the United States have become very different. On the East Coast there are many factories and cities. There are more people on the East Coast. Therefore the East Coast has more members of Congress to make laws. On the West Coast there are many farms and orange groves. The workers on the big farms on the West Coast come from the planet called Venus. The Venusians are owned by the farmers and are worked very hard. Many of them die. Some people on the East Coast think that owning a Venusian is wrong and they want the big farms to let the Venusians go. Some laws have even been passed regarding the issues about owning Venusians. The people on the West Coast feel that the laws were passed unfairly because the East Coast has more representatives in Congress. You know little of this. Your family works its own farm in Arizona and people in Arizona do not own Venusians. Your family is kept busy just working on its own farm. Your best friend just moved to California a few weeks ago. You wonder if you will get to see him on your next vacation like your parents had promised.

Imagine that in Los Angeles a large convention takes place and the people of California decide that they no longer want to be part of the United States. In fact, Oregon, Washington, and Nevada have all decided to become another country. Nebraska, New Mexico, and Kansas are still trying to decide. Arizona, Utah, and Idaho have decided to stay a part of the United States.

A few weeks later you hear that the people of California ordered the United States Navy and Marines to leave the Naval Air Station at Miramar because California was part of a new country. The Commander of the air station refused to leave. A battle over the air station was fought. After this battle the United States declares war on California and the other states that also decided to leave the United States. Your father and older brother join the Arizona regiment of the Eastern States and march into California to fight against the very town where your best friend now lives.

The teacher will explain that this is similar to how many people experienced events during the Civil War. Students will then be asked to read the text to see if they can find similarities to the analogy.

Source: J. K. Fischer. Reprinted by permission.

a frame of reference from which they can empathize with the early Americans who had to make agonizing decisions with regard to the Civil War.

Questioning

Questioning is the most widely used activity by teachers to engage students in learning. Teachers regularly use questioning during all three methods of instruction. Questioning is an important teaching skill that requires some effort to acquire; it is covered in detail later in this chapter. However, at this point, the role of questioning will be considered as it relates to teacher-directed instruction—that is, how it is used during the teacher presentation.

Several different purposes are served by questions during the teacher presentation. Asked at the beginning of the presentation, questions activate schemata, or students' mental pictures or concepts related to the topic of the presentation. This is a very important function because it reminds the students of what they already know about the topic. Comprehension of new material is greatly influenced by how much an individual already knows about the topic in question.

Questions asked during the presentation also serve several purposes. They can be used to focus students on what is the most important material or information in the presentation. Just by the fact that the teacher is asking a question about a particular point of information cues the students that it is important. The teacher asks questions during the presentation to find out if the students are comprehending the presentation to that point. Madeline Hunter (1982) suggested three ways of posing questions to check for understanding: (1) signaled answers, (2) choral responses, and (3) sample individual responses.

In the first method, signaled answers, the teacher asks all the students in the class to simultaneously give a particular signal to indicate what they think is the right response to the teacher's question. For example, the teacher may say, "If the statement I'm about to make is true, then hold up the green card I have given you. If it is false, then hold up the red card. And if you're not sure, then hold up the yellow card."

A second way of ascertaining student understanding is to ask a question to the whole class and have the students respond verbally, all at once. In this method, the teacher would phrase a question in such a way that it asks for a choral response, such as, "Is the word *run* a noun or a verb in this sentence? Everybody respond either 'Noun' or 'Verb.'" If there is a very mixed response, it is safe to say many students in the class are still not clear on the difference between a noun and a verb and more examples are necessary. On the other hand, if a clear correct response comes, then the teacher can move on.

A third way of ascertaining students' understanding through questioning is to ask a question of the whole class and then call on an individual student who represents a particular ability level in the class and make a judgment about the class based on that particular response. For example, if the teacher calls on a high achiever and he or she is unable to answer the question, then the teacher can assume that most of the class will not be able to answer it. However, if a low-achieving student can answer a question correctly, then the teacher can assume that most of the class does understand and it is safe to move on. It is a good practice to ascertain student comprehension before the end of the presentation so that it can be modified if necessary. However, questions asked at the end of a presentation are generally meant to help the teacher determine student comprehension.

Questions asked at any point during a teacher presentation are important and useful to the teacher, for they provide information about the students in terms of interests, understandings, abilities, thought processes, and so on. Questions also open a way for students' direct participation during teacher-directed instruction. It is recommended that teachers plan the questions they will ask during lecture and that they take the time to study and practice the art of questioning. The webbing in Figure 3–3 depicts the three teaching activities that make up the teacher presentation and the purposes of each.

Accommodating Different Learning Styles through the Use of Related Resources

It cannot be stressed enough how important the inclusion of resources is for teacher-directed methods of instruction. In the Chapter 2 discussion of learning styles, one of the areas examined was that of modalities (i.e., the propensity of an individual to rely more heavily on his or her visual, auditory, or tactile mode of perception to take in new information). Through the use of visuals, literature, and realia, the teacher accommodates all three types of modality learning preferences. A visual learner is greatly aided by pictures, graphic organizers, diagrams, and so on in understanding ideas and con-

FIGURE 3–3   Teacher Presentation: Three Teaching Activities and Their Purposes

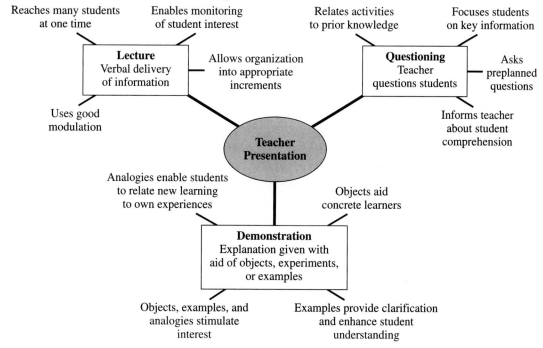

cepts. Literature greatly aids auditory learners, and realia stimulates interest and enhances memory of tactile learners. All students benefit from the variety of resources used in a presentation.

The weaving of a traditional story or folktale, beautiful pictures, webs or graphs, or special objects into the fabric of the presentation brings it alive for all students. This is not hard for adults to imagine, because those things that catch the attention and spark the imagination do so for all people, young and old alike. The resources discussed in this section include (1) visuals, (2) literature, and (3) realia.

Visuals

Visuals include pictures, drawings, photographs, graphs, charts, graphic organizers, webs, lists, graphic overviews, maps, and slides. Anything that is a visual representation of something—such as an idea, a concept, a series of ideas, a place, a geographic area, and so on—can be classified as a visual.

Visuals aid student learning in several ways. First, for those students who are visual learners, learning is enhanced when they can "see" the information being presented. Therefore, if a teacher is explaining three distinguishing characteristics of insects and while doing so puts a diagram on the board and labels the three distinguishing parts, then all the visual learners in the classroom are aided in their comprehension and retention of the information by that diagram.

Visuals such as graphic organizers and webs help students get a visual picture of the relationships of ideas and concepts. Consider the graphic organizer in Figure 3–4, which depicts a visual representation of the U.S. Civil Rights movement of the 1950s

FIGURE 3–4   Example of Graphic Organizer: Civil Rights

We hold these truths to be self-evident,
that all men are created equal . . . .

Source: Susan Aldrich. Reprinted by permission.

and 1960s. The substance of the Civil Rights movement is shown by names of important figures of the movement on the bus. The key concept of *justice* is moving in the direction of civil rights and equality and away from prejudice and discrimination.

In Figure 3.5 is a graphic organizer depicting key concepts and related detail regarding early humans. This graphic organizer relates descriptive detail to each of three types of early humans in a format that makes the information readily accessible.

It can be seen through these examples that such visuals aid in the mental organization of concepts and ideas by lifting key words and terms out of the narrative and showing how ideas are related to each other.

The usefulness of visuals extends beyond aiding only visual learners. Being able to "see" the concepts or information being described helps most students learn better, as most students comprehend more when they are using more than one channel (visual, auditory, and tactile) to take in information.

A picture, photograph, or colorful chart adds another dimension to a lesson. These visuals immediately catch the eye and the interest and make one more open to what is to follow. For example, Mr. Parker is doing a lesson on ancestors. To start off the les-

FIGURE 3–5   Example of Graphic Organizer: Early Humans

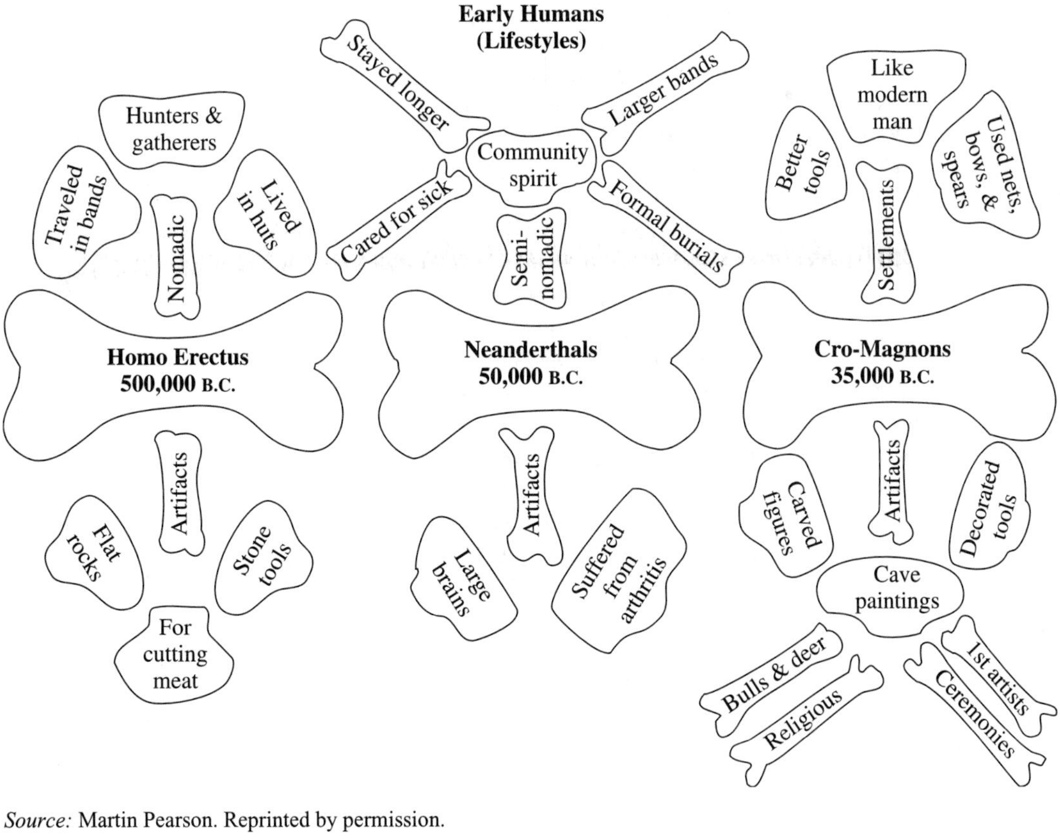

Source: Martin Pearson. Reprinted by permission.

son, he displays in front of the class his own family pictures, going back to his great-grandparents. The students are immediately curious about the pictures, especially the unusual "dress" of the people, who seem to have a whole different look about them. They are even more fascinated when they learn that all of these people are related to their teacher. (Typically, students love to learn about their teachers as "people" and really respond positively when teachers share some of themselves.) Thus, the students are hooked and are ready and eager to hear more. Mr. Parker has overcome one of the main barriers to learning—disinterest—and has motivated his students to learn through a simple use of visuals.

Richardson and Morgan (1990) have referred to a "visual literacy" that precedes oral literacy (listening and speaking) and written literacy (reading and writing) that all children possess. They have advocated the use of visuals in order to take advantage of this more basic and pervasive literacy to enhance understanding and retention. "Teachers discover that when they make use of visual aids such as graphs and pictures, they ensure a concomitant and reinforcing approach for many and an alternative for the learner who excels in visual but not traditional literacy."

The value of visuals to the teacher-directed method of instruction is very great indeed. There is no question that the teacher presentation is invigorated by the use of visuals and thus student learning is enhanced.

Literature

Literature is another resource that enhances the teacher presentation immeasurably. Literature is used here in the broad sense of the term, including such things as diary entries, newspaper articles, letters, historical fiction, folklore, fairy tales, biographies, autobiographies, poetry, song lyrics, documents, eyewitness accounts, interviews, and the like. Auditory learners are especially benefited by hearing stories, analogies, and diary entries read aloud as a part of a directed lesson. Most children enjoy listening to stories, even if they are not strong auditory learners.

Literature plays a special role in children's learning. It touches the heart as well as the mind, and thus personalizes learning for the student. A teacher's presentation of any kind of information in any subject area (including math) can be made more immediate and meaningful to the students through the incorporation of literature. For example, Mrs. DiLisio, in describing conditions in the United States during World War II, includes the fact that the government sent a large number of Japanese Americans to internment camps for the duration of the war, fearing that this particular group of Americans might somehow aid Japan. From a factual description of this event, it is difficult for students to gain an understanding of how people's lives were affected by this event, or what the flavor of the times was in which such happenings could take place. Mrs. DiLisio can help students more deeply understand the ramifications of this government action by reading accounts of people who were actually interned. A good account for the upper grades is an article entitled "Home Was a Horse Stall" by Jim Carnes (1995). For the younger grades, reading fiction such as *Blue Jay in the Desert* (Shigekawa, 1993) will help students understand how people were affected by this government action. The following excerpt from this story is an example of how literature can personalize the information.

> *A long time ago Junior and his family lived far away in California. Now they lived in a camp in Poston, Arizona, with thousands of other Japanese families. They were forced to leave their homes and belongings behind and move to this distant location. They called it an internment camp. Junior had been disappointed to find it wasn't anything like the camp he had imagined. There were no green forests, or tents, or singing around campfires. This camp had only dust and desert and more dust. Sometimes Junior would hear his mother and Grandpa sigh wistfully, and he would know they were missing their old home in California. Junior could hardly remember the cozy house they had left behind.*[*]

Teachers can make their presentations more immediate and interesting to students through the incorporation of literature. Both the students and the teacher will benefit from the regular use of literature in the classroom. It will open up new worlds for children, taking them beyond the constraints of textbooks. It will offer an ever-expanding array of information, ideas, stories, fantasies, and adventures. It will provide an avenue for the reader to feel and think about things beyond the purview of his or her own community and environment and thus offer the opportunity to go beyond the limitations of his or her regional, ethnic, or cultural borders. The authors have seen literature spark the interest of students who felt that school had nothing of value or interest to them, enticing those students to make self-initiated trips to the library to pursue, on their own, the pleasure they had experienced in the classroom due to their teacher's persistent incorporation of literature into daily instruction. Literature can and should be incorporated into instruction at all grade levels and in all subject areas.

Realia

The use of realia also enhances the teacher's presentation of information. Realia includes any type of three-dimensional objects that relate to the topic of instruction. Common everyday objects or more esoteric objects such as those brought from faraway places or objects from the past may be used.

For some children, learning is greatly facilitated when they can touch objects, use manipulatives, or take notes—all activities that require physical touch or involvement. For these students, touching things or being somehow physically involved with the material (including taking notes) enhances their ability to receive and remember information. For example, for a lesson on Japan, Mrs. Murray passes around various objects she had collected during a trip to Japan, including a doll, chopsticks, a kimono, and so forth. The students are fascinated by these objects and are eager to learn more about them and the people who use them. Another teacher begins a lesson on farming in the San Joaquin Valley by displaying various fresh and canned fruits and vegetables and

---

[*] Excerpt from *Blue Jay in the Desert* by Marlene Shigekawa, reprinted courtesy of Polychrome Publishing Corporation, Chicago, Illinois, © 1993.

asking the students what they think these foods have in common. Again, the students are interested in the objects and curious to learn more.

Three-dimensional objects can be touched, held, smelled, and sometimes tasted, and they appeal to a child's natural tendency to explore things, using all the senses. It is recommended that teachers use realia whenever possible to enhance student interest and participation during presentations.

Relating the Lesson to Students' Lives

In the beginning of the presentation, the teacher should link the new information to be learned to something the students already know or have experienced or is in some way familiar to them. An effective way to do this is through analogy. The teacher, knowing the interests of the students, can use an analogy to which the students can relate. The analogy is described to the students before the presentation of new material and provides a framework for understanding the unfamiliar information to come. When using analogy, the teacher must be sure that the students will easily relate to and understand the analogy. If they thoroughly understand the analogy, then they can transfer that understanding to the unfamiliar material. Analogies, examples, and advance organizers all allow students to transfer understanding in one situation to learn something new (but in some way related) in another situation, perhaps more detailed or complicated. This is called *transfer of learning*. Also, analogies arouse the students' interest and make them more receptive to what will follow.

An example comes from Mr. Anton's class as he introduces a lesson on the Civil Rights movement in the United States of the 1950s, 1960s, and 1970s. One of the topics he will discuss in his presentation is the injustices that African Americans suffered during this period. Before he relates this new information (which is now somewhat removed from the students lives), he presents the analogy in Figure 3.6 and asks the students to imagine themselves in the position of John.

Students can easily understand this analogy, which is based on events that are familiar to them (playing in a public park). Since they can picture the situation, it helps them understand the concept of *injustice* (i.e., why John had to face the denial of such a basic need).

FIGURE 3–6   Analogy: Regarding Injustice

John and friend Jerry had met in the park to play some softball. It was very warm that day, so they stopped often to get drinks of water to help cool off. Jerry and John did not drink from the same water faucet. The law said they couldn't. Jerry drank from a shiny, white porcelain fountain labeled "For Whites Only" and John drank from a rusty metal fountain labeled "For Negroes." After drinking their water, they would go back to playing; they were having a great time.

Pretty soon, they noticed that all the water they had been drinking was taking effect and they decided they needed to find a restroom. Jerry knew where a service station was with a restroom they could use, so off they went. When they got there, they were glad because their need was getting more urgent. When they rounded the corner by the door, John's eyes caught sight of a sign that said "For Whites Only." There was no other door labeled "For Negroes." What was he going to do? He knew it would mean big trouble if he ignored the sign.

Limitation and Repetition of New Material

At the elementary school level, it is unwise to present too many new concepts at one time. For the lower grades, one or two new concepts are all that should be presented in any one lesson. With each new concept, there are often related facts and ideas that must be understood and remembered. Young children cannot take in and learn too many things at a time. This is because short-term memory, where conscious thinking and processing of information takes place, is limited in the amount of information it can hold. If it is overloaded, some information drops out of short-term memory and is lost. In order to transfer information from short-term memory to long-term memory, young children rely on rehearsal or repetition. Therefore, it is wise to limit the amount of new information presented and to repeat it in various ways throughout the presentation. Even in the upper grades, where students are able to hold a little more in their short-term memories, it is still important not to overload the students with too much information and to be sure repetition of main concepts occurs in the lesson. Of course, exactly how much new information can be presented will vary with the ability of the students and the complexity of the material. Teacher judgment of these factors will be the key here.

Repetition, then, is an important way to enhance memory of material. Even adults often do not remember a new or unfamiliar name (of a person or a medicine) after having heard it just once. This is much more so for children, and many more things are unfamiliar to them. Therefore, the teacher should think of how to repeat main concepts and ideas in various ways during the lesson. The teacher can even have the students repeat main ideas themselves as they proceed.

Dynamic, Enthusiastic Delivery of the Teacher Presentation

Delivery of the presentation refers to the physical and affective demeanor of the teacher who is giving the presentation. For example, a teacher who delivers a presentation with enthusiasm and humor and whose body movements are energetic and crisp will be able to get and hold the attention of students much more readily than a teacher who has very flat presentation and less than positive body language. The former is an attractive figure, one that is enjoyable to watch and listen to, whereas the latter does little to inspire interest and respect.

Enthusiasm is catching. Strength, energy, cheerfulness, and optimism are positive forces that spread a positive message and atmosphere and are often communicated through nonverbal body language. The teacher sets the tone of the classroom and that tone affects all the members of the classroom for better or worse. In fact, Richardson and Morgan (1990) pointed out the following in regard to reading growth: "McDermott (1978) suggests that a child's progress in reading is less influenced by the nature of the reading activity than by the personal relationship the child has developed with the teacher. The argument is that children respond most often to the feelings the teacher displays when asking them to complete an assignment than to the activity itself."

Thus, the students' openness to hearing and absorbing the information may be more dependent on their relationship with the teacher than on the nature of the material itself. If the teacher projects a positive, encouraging, upbeat message through his or her demeanor, then the content of the presentation will be more readily received by the students. Therefore, the authors strongly encourage the new teacher to hold on to the enthusiasm and dedication that first brought him or her into the field of teaching.

For a summary of the method of instruction discussed in this chapter, see Figure 3–7.

FIGURE 3–7   Summary of Teacher-Directed Method of Instruction

Purpose:
Transfer knowledge from teacher to student

Form:
Teacher presentation

Criteria for Good Presentation:
1. Use lecture, demonstration, and questioning
2. Use visuals, literature, and realia
3. Relate new information to students' lives and experiences
4. Limit and repeat new information
5. Use dynamic and enthusiastic delivery

Chapter *4*

Student-Directed Method of Instruction

Student-directed methods of instruction involve the student working alone on a particular learning activity. To understand how these methods can be employed, the following areas will be examined:

- Individual classwork
- Individual study
- Criteria

Purpose

The purpose of the student-directed method of instruction is to enable students to learn independently. That means empowering them with the attitudes and skills they need to tackle and accomplish a learning task on their own. This gradual process occurs in stages over the course of a student's elementary school experience. The goal, however, is that the student becomes a self-directed independent learner who takes responsibility for his or her own learning and acquires the skills needed to learn inside and outside of school.

Students who take responsibility for their own learning know that they must see to it that they are, indeed, learning. For example, if they do not understand something the teacher has explained, they will ask the teacher or a fellow student for help until they do understand. When there is an exam coming up, they will study until they are sure they know the material. When homework is assigned, they take it as their responsibility to do the homework task to the best of their abilities. This attitude does not develop in most students without the conscious effort of the teacher (and hopefully the parents) to instill it. The training to take responsibility for learning must begin from the student's first day in school and must be emphasized at each grade level.

Besides instilling in students the attitude of taking responsibility for their own learning, it is of utmost importance to give students the study skills they need to learn individually. Having study skills allows students to use various strategies and techniques in order to comprehend, learn, and retain material; this can make the difference between success and failure in school. When students possess study skills, they are more able and more likely to take control of their own learning. Therefore, the teaching of study skills is one of the most important acts a teacher can perform during classroom instruction.

Since the topic of study skills is so important and requires a thorough examination, it is covered separately in Chapter 6. You should realize at this point that you cannot teach children to become independent learners without giving them the means to achieve this status, and doing so means doing two specific things: teaching them the study skills needed to understand and remember things and developing in them the attitude of being a responsible learner.

It is imperative that students learn how to learn independently as well as in groups. Besides preparing them for the more rigorous requirements of middle and high school, the ability and propensity to read and study enriches an individual's life in many ways. Such an individual has access to sources of information and enjoyment that will remain otherwise inaccessible to those who are not comfortable with or have facility in reading and studying for self-improvement, enrichment, or just plain enjoyment.

The types of learning activities or tasks (*learning activities* and *learning tasks* are used interchangeably here) students are engaged in during student-directed instruction are many and varied. They include such things as reading assignments, writing assignments, math problems and computations, memorization tasks, problem-solving activities, and experiments. Indeed, nearly any kind of cognitive activity can be included here.

Form

Student-directed instruction has two basic forms: individual classwork and individual study.

Individual Classwork

Individual classwork refers to the situation in which students are in the classroom working on learning tasks individually. The two distinguishing characteristics of this form of student-directed instruction is that it is done in class and teacher assistance is available. (Assistance from other students is also sometimes available.)

Individual seatwork takes place in various structured situations. One of these is the familiar scene in which all the students in the class are seated at their desks, working separately on the same assignment. This often follows a directed lesson in which the teacher has introduced and explained the task at hand. Another structured situation in which a student may be doing individual seatwork is at a learning center. Learning centers are small stations set up around the room that contain instructions for a learning activity, often associated with science or social studies. When a student is working at one of these alone, it is considered individual classwork.

Individual Study

Individual study is the other form of student-directed instruction. The two distinguishing characteristics of it are that it is done outside of class and teacher assistance is unavailable. Frequently, students engage in individual study at home while doing a homework assignment or preparing for an exam. The types of learning tasks students do during individual study is more or less the same as those they do during individual classwork, however, in this situation, students do not have the same support provided by the structure of the classroom and the presence of the teacher.

During individual study, the student rather than the teacher has the responsibility to decide when he or she will do the task, how much time to spend on it, and, often, how to go about doing it. Even if the teacher has explained how to do a homework assignment, it must be remembered that there is a time lapse between receiving the instructions and doing the task. Many students, in fact, experience frustration when they discover they cannot remember exactly what to do for the homework assignment or how to do it, even though they were sure they understood the assignment when they were in class. The classroom environment is supportive of the work students are expected to do in class, whereas the home environment cannot provide the same support and, for some students, may even be a hindrance to their efforts to study. Therefore, the situation for individual study is that the student has the major responsibility to accomplish the study task in a less supportive environment. The teaching of study skills plays a particularly crucial role here, as such instruction gives the students the strategies and attitudes required for successful studying and learning outside the classroom.

Criteria

In order for student-directed methods of instruction to be effective (i.e., result in student learning), there are several criteria the teacher must follow. When giving assignments for individual seatwork and outside study, the teacher can greatly increase chances for student success by attending to the following:

1. The assignments given for individual study must be meaningful and relevant for the students.
2. Assignments must be clearly explained and demonstrated.
3. Assignments must be consistent with the learning abilities of the students.
4. The students must get feedback on the work they produce during individual study.

In regard to the first criterion, a meaningful assignment is one that has value and from which students will benefit. Many kinds of assignments are meaningful and it is also true that judging the value of assignments can be subjective; in other words, what one teacher deems meaningful another may not. However, meaningful assignments tend to be related to a context of study, such as a unit of instruction in science or social studies, or to a lesson, such as a math lesson. Assignments such as randomly selected worksheets given as "busywork" lack meaning because students cannot relate them to a broader context, and they are quick to sense that they are just being kept busy. A teacher who assigns too much busywork will create a negative situation in which students fail to see the value of what they are doing. Gradually, the students will become resentful. Therefore, it is important that assignments do, in fact, have value for the students.

It is also important that assignments be relevant to the students. An assignment can be meaningful without seeming relevant to students. For example, students may not see the relevance of studying ancient civilizations—seeing no connection to their lives. In this case, the teacher needs to make the connection for the students through analogies or comparisons to show them the relationships that exist between the past and the present.

If students do not perceive the assigned task as meaningful and/or relevant to their lives, they will have little incentive to do it. The teacher must provide students with a reason to do their individual work by making them aware of how it is meaningful and relevant to them.

The second criterion, giving a clear explanation (and/or demonstration) of the work to be completed during individual classwork and study, is of utmost importance for students. It is a common experience of new teachers to find that students are quite unclear about what they are doing or that they hand in assignments that are totally incorrect. This happens because, lacking the experience, the new teacher does not realize how thoroughly an assignment must be explained. For example, when teaching how to multiply fractions and mixed numbers, a teacher may assume that after showing how to do this operation on the board, the students will now be able to complete a worksheet of these kinds of problems. A more thorough approach would include breaking the operation down into clear, numbered steps (Step 1: Multiply the numerators; Step 2: Multiply the denominators; Step 3: Write the answer in lowest terms), listing the steps on the board, and having students repeat the steps. After the teacher demonstrates the problem on the board, he or she has students come up and do problems on the board. Finally, the students practice one or two of the problems at their desks and the teacher checks their work before allowing them to begin their worksheets. If similar work is being given as homework, a guidesheet that enumerates the steps of the operation can be handed out. Such thorough explanation and demonstration of tasks assigned for individual classwork or outside study will avoid confusion and frustration for students and optimize chances of success.

Regarding the third criterion, it is important that the teacher assign work that is neither too difficult nor too easy for the students. In the former case, students will feel frustrated and defeated; in the latter, they will be bored and restless. Ideally, assigned tasks should be at the level that requires students to stretch themselves a little to complete the task, but never should the tasks require so much that they are out of reach. The task must be achievable. It is important, therefore, that the teacher ascertain student readiness for individually assigned work. This can be done through questioning or having students do a few sample problems, checking their understanding of those, and letting them continue only if they are on the right track.

Finally, the fourth criterion is to provide feedback. Individual study in class or outside of it will be important to students and be taken seriously by them only if the teacher collects their work, corrects it, and gives the students feedback within a reasonable amount of time (ideally, within a day or two.) This serves two purposes; namely, it informs the students about the quality and accuracy of their work and it shows the students that the teacher values their work.

Elementary students are not typically intrinsically motivated to do individual study. When they know, however, that their teacher is interested in their work and that what they produce will be checked and returned to them, they take a more serious attitude toward completing their assignments. In other words, when students see that their teacher values their work, then they, too, begin to value their own work.

Figure 4–1 provides a summary of the student-directed method of instruction and Figure 4–2 shows a summary comparison of the teacher-directed method of instruction and the student-directed method of instruction.

FIGURE 4–1   Summary of Student-Directed Method of Instruction

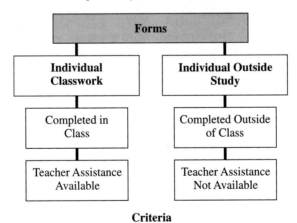

**Student-Directed Method
of Instruction**

Student Must:

1. Take responsibility for own learning.
2. Acquire study skills.

Forms

Individual Classwork	**Individual Outside Study**
Completed in Class	Completed Outside of Class
Teacher Assistance Available	Teacher Assistance Not Available

Criteria

Assignments Must Be:

1. Meaningful/relevant
2. Clear
3. Achievable
4. Checked and returned to students

FIGURE 4–2   Comparison of Teacher-Directed and Student-Directed Methods of Instruction

Methods	Purpose	Form	Criteria
Teacher Directed	Transfer knowledge from teacher to student	Teacher presentation	1. Lecture, demonstration, questioning 2. Visuals, literature, realia 3. Relate to students' lives 4. Limit new information 5. Enthusiastic delivery
Student Directed	Enable students to learn independently	1. Individual classwork 2. Individual study	1. Meaningful assignments 2. Clear explanation and demonstration 3. Consistent with student learning ability 4. Feedback to students 5. Study skills

$$Chapter \quad 5$$

Interactive Method of Instruction

Two of the most important goals of an elementary school program are to help students achieve academically and to foster in them a healthy attitude toward working with others. No method better accomplishes these goals than the interactive method of teaching. The following topics will be discussed in this chapter:

- Definition of interactive method
- Cooperative learning
- Cooperative learning structures
- Making the interactive method work

Definition of Interactive Method

Any activity that requires two or more students, or the teacher and student(s), to work together to complete a given task is an interactive method of instruction. This definition illustrates how wide ranging the interactive method of instruction is. It also shows that there is a standard to be kept if an activity is to be truly *interactive*. That standard is expressed and embodied in the words *work together*. For example, if the teacher presents a lesson where the second activity calls for a teacher/student discussion, and 90 percent of that discussion is conducted by the teacher, then the interactive method is not being used. The amount of teacher talk in this example clearly classifies this activity as a teacher-directed method. What you label an activity is of little importance compared with what actually takes place!

Cooperative Learning

Practical guidelines will be given here for making cooperative learning an integral part of a teacher's daily lesson planning and classroom activities. To accomplish this, three key questions will be answered: (1) What is cooperative learning? (2) What are the benefits of cooperative learning? and (3) What forms can cooperative learning take?

What Is Cooperative Learning?

The term *cooperative learning* has become overused and abused. Just throwing together a group of students, large or small, and having them do something is not cooperative learning. Slavin (1991, p. 88) pointed out that "cooperative learning usually supplements the teacher's instruction by giving students an opportunity to discuss information or practice skills originally presented by the teacher; sometimes cooperative methods require students to find or discover information on their own." If certain criteria are not kept firmly in mind and followed, the result will not be learning nor will it be cooperative. In fact, it is closer to the truth to call such ill-conceived attempts *inoperative learning*. What, then, has to take place and what criteria have to be followed so one can legitimately say a cooperative learning activity has taken place? Ellis and Whalen (1990) and Johnson and Johnson (1984) have provided useful guidelines for planning cooperative learning activities. An adaptation of their work is presented in Figure 5–1. Notice how cooperative learning is contrasted with relatively nondescript small-group activities.

What Are the Benefits of Cooperative Learning?

The best way to understand the benefits to be gained by using cooperative learning activities is by reflecting on instances where you have observed it being effectively used. You will notice that by having students work this way, three things occur: (1) students have an opportunity to develop *social and interpersonal skills*, since communication, accommodation, and sharing are called for to complete the task collectively; (2) students all have a part to play in accomplishing the learning objective, and thus *involvement is maximized* for the duration of the activity; and (3) students have first-hand experience seeing how several people's thinking and work can bring *superior results* to those of which a single person is capable. Cooperative learning activities that are well conceived and carried out contribute to three key goals of any successful classroom:

- Development of social and interpersonal skills
- Maximized student involvement in learning
- Attainment of superior results

Thoughtfully designed and executed cooperative learning activities that accomplish these three goals lead to an additional, overriding benefit—building students' self-esteem. "One of the most important aspects of a child's personality is self-esteem.

FIGURE 5–1   Cooperative Learning versus Small-Group Work

Cooperative Learning Activities (criteria and characteristics)	Small-Group Activities (comparisons)
1. *Group Accountability & Positive Interdependence* The accomplishment of the learning task is either through face-to-face interaction or division of labor. Ultimately, however, the students must collaborate to fashion the final product—the group's work.	1. *No Accountability & Interdependence* Students often work on their own with no sense of a group effort or product.
2. *Individual Accountability & Responsibility for Learning* Each group member has a well-defined role and assignment contributing to successful completion of the activity.	2. *"Hitchhiking"* Some students let others do most or all of the work.
3. *Monitoring and Facilitating Collaborative Work and Behavior* The teacher uses cooperative learning as opportunities to circulate and help students develop social skills and collaboratively accomplish common learning objectives.	3. *Laissez-Faire Approach* Limited direct observation of students' work, attention to students, and development of social skills and collaborative efforts are limited.

Many people have assumed that self-esteem is a relatively stable personal attribute that schools have little ability to change. However, several researchers have found that teams [i.e., cooperative learning] do increase students' self-esteem" (Slavin, 1991, p. 17). This makes sense because the interpersonal dynamic of cooperative learning provides children with opportunities to make friends and also to feel wanted and part of a successful learning venture. Further, children as well as adults always enhance what they already know by describing it to others and, even more so, by attempting to teach it to others. Cooperative learning is an excellent vehicle for affording your students with valuable sharing and coaching opportunities.

Considering the diverse abilities, levels of readiness, and cultural backgrounds found in any one class you might teach, the use of cooperative learning activities for heterogeneous grouping is an extremely valuable benefit. For example, by placing together students with different ability levels in math in a given activity, you create three positive possibilities. First, the more able students can serve as peer coaches for the less able. Second, a form of peer motivation can take place as those not achieving as much try to follow or model work habits, attitudes, and general approaches of their more engaged peers. Third, a sense of togetherness and self-esteem can be born since such heterogeneous activities minimize the segregation of students into "slow" and "fast" groups.

In a similar way, heterogeneous grouping for cooperative learning activities addresses the sensitive and critical issue of cultural understanding, tolerance, and harmony. A word of caution, however, must be made in using heterogeneous cooperative learning activities. Just placing mixed groups of students together will not work. You must thoughtfully design what work is to be done, how, and by whom so that the potential benefits can be realized. In addition, your careful guidance and coaching will help assure that things are proceeding in a productive manner. The directions and suggestions for using the selected cooperative learning structures below can be especially useful toward this end.

What Forms Can Cooperative Learning Take?

For the purpose of planning and carrying out lesson activities, it is best to think of cooperative learning as taking the form of various structures. Each cooperative learning structure is different in its own way and is best suited for particular learning situations. Whatever structures you may choose to employ, "all cooperative learning methods share the idea that students work together to learn and are responsible for one another's learning as well as their own" (Slavin, 1991, p. 89). In the following extensive discussion of useful cooperative learning structures, it will be seen that there are a number of factors to consider in determining which structure is most appropriate at a given time. Four of the ten cooperative learning structures are based on the work of Spencer Kagan (1992), one of the foremost experts on this subject.

Cooperative Learning Structures

To make this discussion of cooperative learning structures readily understandable and practical to use, each structure will be presented in the following manner:

1. Name of the structure
2. Brief introduction to the structure
3. Steps to carrying out the structure
4. Recommendations for using the structure

Numbered-Heads Together[*]

Introduction
Numbered-Heads Together is a very effective instructional activity to use for overcoming the chronic problem teachers have in getting full-class involvement in a review session that involves a series of questions posed orally. Usually, much of the class mentally goes on vacation while the few engaged learners do most of the answering. Numbered-Heads Together is a fun activity and it serves as an excellent strategy for building attentiveness, sharing, and academic success.

Steps to Carrying Out Numbered-Heads Together
1. Create a number of questions to present orally.
2. Divide the class into groups of five each (more or less, as you deem best).

[*] Adapted from *Cooperative Learning,* 1992 (Kagan Cooperative Learning), 1-800-WEE-COOP.

3. Give each group a name. (A nice touch is to relate the names to the topic being reviewed.)
4. Assign each student within each group a number from 1 to 5.
5. Ask all 1s, 2s, and so on, to raise their hands as you call their number. (This will confirm that everyone knows his or her number.)
6. Write each group's name across the top of the chalkboard for scorekeeping. Have your set of questions, bowl of group names, and number spinner all ready to go.
7. Give directions on how the questions will be answered, as follows:

   a. I will read a question to the whole class.
   b. I will then say "Numbered-Heads Together" as a cue for each group to confer for exactly one minute during which time you should make sure *everyone* in your group is ready to answer the question if called on. Remember, there is to be *no* conferring or prompting among group members after the one minute.
   c. I will then reach into the bowl and pull out an index card with one of the group's names on it. This group is first up.
   d. Finally, I will spin the number spinner to determine which number person in the group will have to stand and answer the question.
   e. Listen carefully to the answer given. If I decide it is not *completely* correct, I will pick another group's name out of the bowl and the same number person in that group will have a chance to capitalize by answering the question.

8. Proceed with the questions, making sure of the following:

   a. The one-minute (or however many minutes you set) time limit is strictly adhered to.
   b. No discussion or prompting occurs after the "Numbered-Heads Together" group conference takes place. (The integrity and value of this activity will be lost if this is not enforced.)
   c. Reserve a degree of flexibility in calling group names and student numbers so that everyone gets an equal chance.

Recommendations for Using Numbered-Heads Together
This cooperative learning structure is ideal for a review session where factual and convergent thinking questions are the focus. This is also an excellent team-building activity, as success depends on how effectively group members coach each other in preparation for answering the question.

Think-Pair-Share[*]

Introduction
Think-Pair-Share is probably the first cooperative learning structure a new teacher should attempt to employ because of its similarity to the questioning mode that is so familiar to students. In Think-Pair-Share, however, one new element is added to the typical question-and-response mode: sharing.

---

[*] Adapted from *Cooperative Learning*, 1992 (Kagan Cooperative Learning), 1-800-WEE-COOP.

Steps to Carrying Out Think-Pair-Share
1. Pose a question, factual or higher order, to the students.
2. Give directions on how they will answer this question, as follows:

   a. I want each of you to take one minute (vary this time allotment as you deem appropriate) to think to yourselves about this question.
   b. Now pair up with your neighbor and take two minutes to discuss your ideas, with the aim of agreeing on a single response to the question.
   c. Let's have each pair share their answers with the class.

Recommendations for Using Think-Pair-Share
Because all levels of questions can be used with Think-Pair-Share, it can be effectively used in any phase of a lesson or topic. It is just as effective a response mode for a series of questions as it is for just one question that happens to arise. In other words, the Think-Pair-Share mode can be moved in to and out of very quickly and smoothly. By employing Think-Pair-Share from the beginning, the students will understand that *involvement* and *sharing* are fixtures in your classroom. Once Think-Pair-Share becomes an established way of functioning in your classroom, you can try the following variation. During the "Pair" mode, have the two students web (diagram) their joint response to add visual and organizational elements to the activity.

Team Webbing[*]

Introduction
This cooperative learning structure focuses on developing students' abilities to think conceptually and analytically. As will be seen, the Team Webbing structure shows how a relatively visual and tactile activity can effectively promote the development of abstract, analytical thought processes.

Steps to Carrying Out Team Webbing
1. Divide the class into teams of five or six each.
2. Hand out sets of colored markers so that within each team students have different colors. Also furnish each team with a large sheet of chart paper (approximately 2 feet by 3 feet).
3. Give directions on how the Team Webbing activity will proceed, as follows:

   a. I am writing a word on the board (e.g., Community). I want one member in each group to write the word in the center of his or her sheet of chart paper and then draw a box around it. This word is our topic for today's lesson.
   b. The idea of the activity is for each group to think about the topic and create a web of related concepts and supporting details.
   c. Related concepts that define our topic (e.g., *people, occupations, transportation*) are to be placed in bubbles in orbit around the topic box. Attach the bubbles by long webbing lines. Supporting details that explain the related concepts (e.g., *people*—young, old; *occupations*—firefighters, teachers; *transporta-*

[*] Adapted from *Cooperative Learning*, 1992 (Kagan Cooperative Learning), 1-800-WEE-COOP.

tion—cars, trains) are to be written close to the concepts and attached by short webbing lines.

d. Each student is responsible for coming up with one related concept. For the supporting details, everyone is free to add as many as he or she can. Remember, I want to see different colors all over the sheet under the related concepts. Don't just stick to the concept you came up with. So I can know who is using what color, make a color code at the bottom of your sheet (e.g., Billy = blue, Mary = red, etc.).

Recommendations for Using Team Webbing

One effective way to lead into a Team Webbing activity is to have each team generate a list of concepts related to the topic. The key here is that team members need to reach consensus on each related concept. The analysis involved in differentiating and determining related concepts from supporting detail provides an opportunity for collaborative thinking. In this way, a hands-on activity for concept development, Team Webbing, makes an effective follow-up to the presentation of new material. After the teacher presents new material, the usual practice is to have students trudge through pages of their textbooks and answer some questions at the end. With Team Webbing, the text material, class notes, handouts, and students' memories and ideas all serve as resources as they work together to construct a conceptual framework for the topic that was just presented. Further, the teacher can readily go around to each group, facilitating and monitoring comprehension of the material.

Jigsaw*

Introduction

If there is one structure that has come to symbolize cooperative learning, it is Jigsaw. The name is used because in its most basic form, known as *Within-Team Jigsaw,* this activity places students on collaborative teams where each individual completes one aspect of the group's overall task or assignment. Each student has one piece of the "jigsaw puzzle" to complete, which, when put together with the work of his or her teammates, makes the total picture. In this sense, the Jigsaw structure places students in situations of total interdependence. To create assignments where the Jigsaw concept of task interdependence works, the teacher has to select or adapt the curriculum material to be covered in such a way that each part of the puzzle stands by itself as comprehensible to each student as he or she strives to complete the individual aspects of the task. Perhaps the greatest benefit from Jigsaw is that it gives students an opportunity to experience being a teacher as they teach the rest of their team about the aspect of the assignment they have come to master.

Steps to Carrying Out Jigsaw

1. Specially design the new curriculum material to be covered so that each team member can be assigned a different aspect of the topic on which to work.

* Adapted from *Cooperative Learning,* 1992 (Kagan Cooperative Learning), 1-800-WEE-COOP.

2. Prepare guidesheets for each team member to follow concerning his or her specific part of the overall group assignment.
3. Divide the class into teams of four each.
4. Give directions on how to proceed, as follows:

   a. I want each team member to review his or her guidesheet and use it while completing your part of your team's overall assignment on the topic we are covering today. Remember, for now, we are to work independently because once you are done, you each will be sharing what you have learned with your teammates.

   b. Now that our individual tasks have been completed, I want team members, one at a time, to relate what he or she has learned to the rest of his or her team. As your teammates share with you, briefly fill in the three spaces (one for each presenter) labeled What I Learned from My Teammates on the reverse side of your guidesheets.

   c. Place all of your completed assignments together, place them in your Team Folder, and hand them in.

Recommendations for Using Jigsaw

Jigsaw is an effective way to involve *every* student in the class in the presentation and learning of new material. First, students get to become mini-experts concerning their special aspect of the content, then they reinforce this learning by teaching it to their teammates, and, finally, they benefit by hearing their peers' presentations of what has been learned.

Jigsaw is an excellent way to familiarize students with new material, but it can also be used very well as a culminating project. The steps to follow would be similar to those just given, except that each team would prepare a coordinated presentation to the rest of the class on the topic (usually enriched by the aid of some visuals). In this regard, as a culminating project, it would be more interesting and useful if each team or, at most, two teams explore the topic from different vantage points.

Once the teacher and students become adept at Jigsaw, another variation can be added by forming Expert Groups. This can be accomplished by inserting one step after team members have independently completed their assignment and before they present what they have learned to their teammates. To form Expert Groups, the curriculum should be designed so all teams (or at least half of them if there are eight four-person teams) are working on the same four-part task. This allows the teacher to gather together all the students who have completed the same aspect of the overall team task (i.e., four or eight students) to form the Expert Groups. These "experts" on their aspect of the topic can then share with each other to broaden their understanding before going back to their respective groups to let teammates know what they have learned. Effective use of Expert Groups increases both the quantity and quality of student interactions.

Small-Group Think

Introduction

Small-Group Think is one of the most basic cooperative learning structures that can be used. It is an excellent strategy for obtaining each student's "mental investment" as a new concept is presented to the class. Too often, many students pay marginal attention during direct instruction of new material, and subsequently have to be dragged along to develop understanding. Wise use of Small-Group Think can be effective in avoiding this situation.

Steps to Carrying Out Small-Group Think
1. Select a concept to be presented to the class (e.g., *freedom, friendship, learning, sharing, estimating*).
2. Give directions how the students will define this concept, as follows:

    a. Everyone look at the word I have put on the board.

    b. I want each of you to take three minutes to write your own one-sentence definition for this word.

    c. Now that you have completed your individual sentences, I am going to count you off into groups of three. (A simple way is to team up those already in close proximity.)

    d. Using your individual sentences as the starting point, take five minutes this time to work together so your team can come up with a one *best* sentence that defines today's concept.

    e. As I walked around, I was impressed with the quality of each team's work and collaborative spirit. Let's all hear what each team did and use this to create a "best of the best" class definition of today's concept.

Note: At this point of bringing the activity to closure, the teacher plays the role of facilitator by listing key words or phrase segments on the board as each group reads its sentence. This list is then used to formulate the class's "best of the best" definition. Since the activity started with each student's own thinking (i.e., "mental investment"), all students will be interested and share in the final class product.

Recommendations for Using Small-Group Think
Small-Group Think will prove most effective as an instructional strategy when a concept (word) that is pivotal to a new topic is being presented. Not only does Small-Group Think gain maximum student involvement, but it does so by having students think about the concept presented at progressively refined levels. After a session of Small-Group Think, students will be well focused for subsequent instruction related to that concept.

Learning Lines

Introduction
Learning Lines is one of the simpler and, as you will see, quieter cooperative learning strategies to employ in the classroom. It is hard to think of a strategy that a teacher can use that is more efficient for determining the collective background of his or her class on a particular topic than Learning Lines.

Steps to Carrying Out Learning Lines

1. Pose a question to the class that has several possible answers (e.g., "Who were among the most important leaders during the colonial period of our country's history?").

2. Present directions to the students on how they will answer this question through an activity called Learning Lines, as follows:

   a. We are now going to form three learning lines (e.g, 10 students in each line) as I direct.

   b. Here is a sheet of paper with today's question printed at the top for each learning line.

   c. When I give the signal, I want the first student in each line who is holding a sheet to write one answer and then pass the sheet to his or her left for the next person to do the same. As I start the answer sheet going, each student in the rest of the line should be answering today's question in his or her own notebook so that he or she can immediately write it on the answer sheet when it is time to answer.

   d. When the answer sheet has passed through the entire line, it comes to rest.

   e. Let's look at the three lists of answers that were generated and see how we did. Designated line leaders, take turns reading your line's answers and I will write them on the board (or overhead transparency). Once our class list is up on the board, we will discuss what we have and will make any necessary modifications and additions. The end result will be a complete and jointly arrived at response to the question that is well worth being written into your notebooks.

Recommendations for Using Learning Lines

Learning Lines is a useful technique for reviewing material recently covered in class. It is also a productive and engaging way both to determine and to build students' backgrounds as a new topic is presented. For example, when introducing the topic Occupations in Our Community, this technique allows the teacher to obtain quickly a sense of the students' existing knowledge as that topic is about to be introduced. Because each student's knowledge will be shared as well as added to by his or her classmates and the teacher, the background of the entire class will be built at the same time. The key benefit here, as with the other cooperative learning structures, is that students will be actively participating. As you know, students learn when they are involved in activities, not when they are passive observers.

Reciprocal Teaching

Introduction

This cooperative learning structure is also simple in nature. Pairs team up to alternate the roles of teacher and student. For all its simplicity in design, Reciprocal Teaching is extraordinarily powerful as a tool for building reading comprehension skills. John McNeil, one of the nation's leading experts on reading and curriculum, has called this technique the "magic bullet" for developing reading comprehension.

Steps to Carrying Out Reciprocal Teaching

1. Tell the class you need a volunteer to help you demonstrate a new activity. Explain that Reciprocal Teaching will be done periodically to help them become great readers.
2. Have the volunteer sit by your side where everyone can clearly see both of you.
3. Hand out a sheet containing four paragraphs taken from a textbook or from some other source such as a newspaper, magazine, or book.
4. Give directions to the class by asking the students to watch you and your volunteer partner do the four steps of Reciprocal Teaching, as follows:

    a. We will both read the first paragraph quietly to ourselves. Class, you also read the paragraph so you can be in touch with what we are doing.
    b. I will play the role of teacher and you (i.e., the volunteer) play the role of student as we go through the four steps the first time. For the second paragraph, we will then switch roles. Class, for paragraphs three and four, you will be paired up to practice Reciprocal Teaching exactly as we did up here, so watch very carefully as we now do the four steps.
    c. *Step 1:* Johnny (the volunteer), in your own words, *summarize* what this paragraph is about.
    d. *Step 2:* Johnny, *pose a question* based on this paragraph that I could use on a test or quiz.
    e. *Step 3:* Johnny, is there anything in this paragraph about which you would like to *ask for clarification* (e.g., a word, thought, or concept)?
    f. *Step 4:* Johnny, *predict* what you think might happen next as we proceed to paragraph two.

Note: At this point, you should then switch roles, with Johnny playing the role of teacher and with you playing the role of student. Repeat the four steps of Reciprocal Teaching, this time for paragraph two.

5. Have the pairs of students do Reciprocal Teaching exactly as you just demonstrated for paragraphs one and two. Circulate to guide them and respond to any questions or difficulties as they practice the four steps.
6. Practice Reciprocal Teaching with the class on a regular basis. As they become well versed in the technique and as comprehension skills improve, do the following:

    a. Use longer reading passages.
    b. Ask that summaries be more concise (e.g., "Give me a headline for the excerpt we just read").
    c. Ask that questions created be thought level rather than just factual level.

Recommendations for Using Reciprocal Teaching

The key to using Reciprocal Teaching is effective modeling and regular, guided practice of the strategy in class. It is of greatest benefit to students who are able to decode words but fall short in comprehending what those words mean. All four steps are focused on having students develop the mental linkages necessary for understanding to be realized from a series of words. It gives students a mental strategy to process information in a meaningful way, and it provides invaluable assistance throughout their educational careers. It is also recommended that teachers try creative applications of the Reciprocal Teaching strategy other than with the written word, such as a follow-up to watching a video presentation or taking a field trip. The four steps will once again channel students' minds toward making those vital connections that bring about understanding.

Mystery Envelope

Introduction
Mystery Envelope is an effective way to gain student interest and participation in problem solving. It focuses the students on the task of either sequencing or matching information or ideas through a team-spirited, game-type activity.

Steps to Carrying Out Mystery Envelope
1. Divide the class into teams of three to seven students each.
2. Hand out a Mystery Envelope to each team. The envelope contains several slips of paper on which some information or ideas from a particular content area is printed.
3. Give directions on how Mystery Envelope will proceed, as follows:

   a. Teams, I want you to open your Mystery Envelopes and place the slips of paper you find inside in a vertical row on your tables.
   b. Look at the information on these slips and (1) rearrange them so that they are in what you all agree is the correct sequence (for example, events in a story) *or* (2) make two vertical rows matching the lighter-colored slips with the appropriate darker ones (for example, names of inventors matched to their inventions)
   c. Each team will now show us its sequencing (or matching) solution to the slips found in its Mystery Envelope and explain how it reached that solution.

Recommendations for Using Mystery Envelope
As a relatively simple, high-interest, and thought-provoking activity, Mystery Envelope can be used productively at three stages of the learning and lesson sequence. First, it can be employed as a way of determining students' backgrounds on a particular topic. For example, if the Mystery Envelopes contain four light-colored slips each with a season of the year written on it and four darker-colored slips with one weather characteristic written on it, then the teams are asked to lay these out and match the characteristics to the corresponding seasons. This particular application of Mystery Envelope can also be effectively used directly after the teacher's initial presentation on the topic The Four Seasons as a way of fostering understanding of the material. It is also easy to see how this same activity can be used to conduct an engaging review of the topic by simply increasing the type and number of characteristics slips.

Besides matching or sequencing information and ideas in specific content area topics—such as Life Cycles (science), Steps of a Proof (math), Events in a Story (language arts), or Historical Time Line (social studies)—the Mystery Envelope can be used in other ways. For instance, cut a comic strip into several separate panels and ask students to sequence the panels, or cut the headlines off several small newspaper articles and ask students to match the headlines with the articles. In other words, there are as many variations of Mystery Envelope as you or the students' can create.

Group Planning

Introduction
Group Planning focuses on student-directed cooperative learning. As you will see, the effectiveness of this activity depends not only on having several functioning learning centers in your classroom but also your students' ability to take responsibility for designing their own learning experiences.

Steps to Carrying Out Group Planning
1. Divide the class into groups of three students each.
2. Have each group confer to select the learning center it wishes to work at. Since you will want, at most, two groups working at the same center, it will be necessary to have at least five learning centers in your classroom. Those centers could include a reading center, current events center, writing center, geography center, art center, music center, graphic arts center, technology center, sports center, and listening center. (*Note*: Eventually, your students can suggest ideas for additional centers and modifications in existing centers.)
3. Present directions to the students on how they will do their work at the chosen learning centers through an activity called Group Planning, as follows:

    a. I want each group to take 10 minutes to fill out the "Planning Sheet" I have given you. You will notice that I ask you to tell me the center you have chosen to work at, the learning you expect to accomplish, and the specific things you will do to accomplish this learning.

    b. At my signal, each group is to go to its chosen center and begin carrying out the plan developed. We will work at the centers for half an hour.

    c. When I give the 5-minute warning, each group should begin to fill out its "What We Accomplished" sheet. I will then select one group to share briefly with us what it did today.

Recommendations for Using Group Planning
Group Planning provides your students with a refreshing break from the normal classroom routine. Well-designed learning centers are the key to employing Group Planning successfully in your classrooom. In this regard, it would be wise to obtain ideas about different types of learning centers and designs from your colleagues. Excellent learning center designs can also be found on the Internet and in books focusing on the topic of learning centers. Because Group Planning is child centered by its nature, excellent ideas for creating high-interest and user-friendly learning centers can be obtained right from your students themselves. To make sure students are benefitting properly from Group Planning, it would be a good idea to (1) monitor how they plan and then work together at the centers, (2) notice if certain students fall into a pattern of working at par-

ticular centers to the exclusion of others, and (3) have the students maintain a Group Planning file for periodic quality reviews. If used correctly, Group Planning can help make your classroom an inviting and adventurous place for students.

Team Review Tournament

Introduction
Team Review Tournament is an engaging, gamelike activity that helps create a non-threatening atmosphere as your class approaches a test. Because it maximizes student attention and participation concerning the material being reviewed, it also increases the likelihood of their doing well on the test.

Steps to Carrying Out Team Review Tournament
1. Divide the class into groups of four students each, identifying buddy pairs within each group.
2. Assign each group a different aspect of the material or chapter being reviewed.
3. Present directions to the students on how they will work on the content area material assigned through an activity called Team Review Tournament, as follows:

   a. I want each group to look over the material assigned and then have each buddy pair create two questions—one factual level and on thought level—for that material.
   b. Once you have created your questions, the buddy pairs in each group are to take turns quizzing each other on the questions they created until all four students in the group know the answers.
   c. I will then form the groups into two combined teams (consisting of three or four groups each, depending on class size), so we can begin our tournament.
   d. Each combined team is to assemble in a circle and then review all the questions created, with the task of selecting the best six questions for the tournament—three factural level and three thought level. (More questions can be included if a longer tournament is desired.) Write your selected questions on index cards and hand them to me.
   e. I will start the tournament by asking a question posed by one combined team to a randomly chosen student on the other team. If it is answered correctly, a point is awarded to the answering team. If it is not answered correctly, I will call on a student at random from the team that created the question. If it is answered correctly, that team earns the point. If we have a tie after all the questions are asked, I will pose my own question to break the tie. Each team will be allowed to confer briefly and then I will randomly select one student from each team to answer. The better answer will win.

Recommendations for Using Team Review Tournament
The relatively complex nature of Team Review Tournament suggests that it be used only after you have established a positive classroom routine and have had success implementing other cooperative learning structures.

Making the Interactive Method Work

The interactive method of teaching is a tremendous asset to any classroom program. It has the potential of simultaneously developing students' academic and social skills as no other method can. It works, however, *only* when planned and carried out intelligently. Just haphazardly throwing a group of students together to "work cooperatively" will prove futile. A guide to planning and carrying out cooperative learning activities is presented in Figures 5–2 and 5–3. By following the guidelines and through the experience of using various cooperative learning structures, you will be well on your way to creating a classroom environment characterized by active and positive student involvement and interaction.

Figure 5–4 provides a summary and comparison of the three methods of instruction—teacher directed, student directed, and interactive—that have been discussed.

FIGURE 5–2   Planning Cooperative Learning Activities

What to Do	How to Do It	Why to Do It
1. *Review curriculum content.*	Look over the material to be covered and see where in the lesson and learning sequence it fits in; that is: • present new material (perception) • practice for understanding (conception) • creative application (ideation) • review	Analyzing curriculum content in this way allows you to decide which cooperative learning structure will be most suitable to use, since some are clearly more effective than others for certain phases of the learning and lesson sequences.
2. *Select cooperative learning structure.*	Look over your bank of cooperative learning structures and select one that: • best suits the curriculum content (as determined above) • best fits into the overall scheme of the lesson plan	Selecting a cooperative learning structure in this manner ensures that students will feel invited to participate and learn instead of being bored.
3. *State objectives.*	Having analyzed the content and selected an appropriate cooperative learning structure, determine the specific learning outcomes to be reached as far as: • what students will be able to do academically • what students will be able to do interpersonally	In planning any instructional activity, the objective(s) should be stated so you and the students alike know what they are trying to accomplish. The need for clearly stated objectives is especially important when venturing to use cooperative learning because of the additional complexity involved, such as differentiated tasks and increased student movement and interaction.

(continued)

FIGURE 5–2   *(Continued)*

What to Do	How to Do It	Why to Do It
4. *Determine group work.*	Consider the content to be covered, your class size, the cooperative learning structure chosen, and the students' ability levels to plan: 1. the specific work each student in each group is to do and be accountable for 2. cooperative groups in terms of size and makeup 3. seating and desk arrangements corresponding to the structure chosen	The beauty and value of cooperative learning is that it allows you to address the diversity of cultural backgrounds, ability levels, and personalities in the classroom. Deciding on who will work with whom and what they will be doing is a pivotal step in planning cooperative learning activities.
5. *List steps to follow.*	Once the group work is formulated, a practical guide to carrying out the activity must be created by: • thinking through the activity in terms of what the students and you are actually going to do • listing, in a sequence of steps, what is going to happen from the beginning to the end of the activity	By writing out the sequence of steps, you move from a more theoretical conceptualization of the activity to a very real and practical "order of battle." Creating the sequence of steps, then, is the vital link between theory and practical application.
6. *Diagram the activity.*	With the sequence of steps listed, a visual map of the activity should be drawn, depicting: • the actual seating and grouping patterns from step to step • student and group names and numbers	At all costs, confusion must be avoided. With so many moving parts (i.e., students, furniture, and materials), it is easy to quickly lose control. A diagram of the activity provides a readily usable map to follow while everything is happening. This is especially important if you are new to using cooperative learning activities.
7. *Prepare materials.*	As the final preparation for carrying out the cooperative learning activity, all the materials needed should be: • organized for distribution at the appropriate time (i.e., printed, copied, labeled) and available	By having all your materials ready to go, every aspect of the group's work can flow smoothly.

FIGURE 5–3   Carrying Out Cooperative Learning Activities

What to Do	How to Do It	Why to Do It
1. *Have room and materials ready.*	• List on the board the steps to be followed. • Position the seats and desks as needed	• Students are provided with a visual sequence of actions. • Movement is facilitated and confusion and disruptions are minimized.
2. *Give directions.*	• Explain what (curriculum) is to be done, how (collaborative approach) it will be done, and the time allotted for doing it. • State the criteria for measuring success of the group and of each individual student.	• Students will know exactly what to do. • Students, in groups and individually, are accountable for their work and behavior.
3. *Circulate.*	• Walk around periodically, observing and facilitating each group's efforts.	• You will know how well the students are doing, provide direction and guidance when needed, and determine the efficacy of the plan and activity.
4. *Recognize accomplishments.*	• Bring work back to a whole-class focus to see what has been accomplished (i.e., presentations, reports, displays) and to summarize main ideas.	• Learning across groups will be reinforced, and the value and effectiveness of working and sharing together will be demonstrated.

Grading: The most effective way to grade cooperative learning work is to look at and assess several things:
1. The final group product
2. Each student's contribution to his or her group's work
3. The collaborative effort within each group

FIGURE 5–4   Overview of Three Methods of Instruction

Methods	Purpose	Form	Criteria
Teacher directed	Transfers knowledge from teacher to student	Teacher presentation	1. Lecture, demonstration, questioning 2. Visuals, literature, realia 3. Relates to student's lives 4. Limited new information 5. Enthusiastic delivery
Student directed	Enables students to learn independently	1. Individual classwork 2. Individual study	1. Meaningful assignments 2. Clear explanation and demonstration 3. Consistent with student learning ability 4. Feedback to students 5. Study skills
Interactive	Fosters collaborative effort	1. Students working together 2. Student(s) and teacher working together	1. Review and design curriculum content 2. State objective(s) 3. Plan for positive interdependence and accountability 4. List steps to follow 5. Prepare materials 6. Monitor and facilitate work

$$Chapter\ 6$$

Study Skills

It is difficult to find an aspect of learning that is so crucial to student success in school and at the same time so noticeably absent from the elementary school curriculum as study skills. Direct training in *how* to study effectively is typically only begun in middle school or even high school. By this time, attitudes and habits are formed and, for many students, it is too late to develop the determination and mental discipline needed for the more rigorous demands of the higher-grade curricula. Therefore, many students never acquire the study skills, strategies, and discipline needed to study and learn the content and information presented in school. This has dire consequences, as the research indicates that "75 percent of academic failure is caused by poor study and examination strategies" and "these are teachable skills which 75 percent of high school dropouts could learn; if they did they could do passing work" (Richardson & Morgan, 1990).

The acquisition of good study habits must begin at the elementary school level—in fact, it should start in kindergarten, at the very start of a student's schooling career. Only when students learn the responsibility and skills associated with good study habits as an integral part of their elementary school experience will they be well prepared for the academic rigors of middle school, high school, and college. The importance of systematic instruction in study skills to academic success cannot be overemphasized.

During the course of their elementary school experiences, students are required to read and comprehend material, to memorize facts and information, to do research, and to write coherent explanations and essays regarding various academic subjects. The teacher's responsibility in preparing students to be successful in their study efforts is to create a classroom environment that focuses students' attention on the importance of study skills and how their use leads to improved academic performance.

How can teachers create classroom environments that foster the attainment and regular use of study skills? They can do so by having an awareness of, and scheduling regular instruction time for, the following:

- Teaching responsibility for learning
- Teaching, modeling, and reinforcing the various study strategies and techniques

- How to teach study skills
- Time management and organization skills
- Information location skills

The following pages will examine each of these teaching activities and provide suggestions for their implementation into classroom instruction.

Teaching Responsibility for Learning

Teaching children that they are responsible for their own learning goes hand in hand with the development of good study habits, and both should begin in kindergarten. Doing so provides the optimum opportunity for students to develop the behaviors that eventually lead to the capacity to do serious, sustained study. The acquisition of study skills and good work habits is a gradual process that progresses in accordance with the developmental abilities of the students and the escalating academic and intellectual demands of each higher elementary grade. The basis of success in this progression is the student's sense of responsibility for his or her own learning. The feeling that "I am responsible to understand and complete my assignments; no one else can learn for me" gives students the emotional fortitude and will to sustain daily study routines.

How does the teacher foster this attitude of responsibility in students as well as help students develop good study habits? Figure 6–1 lists teaching behaviors that lead to student responsibility and the development of good study habits. These activities are meant to be implemented at each grade level in accordance with the needs, interests, and ability levels of the students. Some examples are given here of how to implement these behaviors at the lower and upper elementary grade levels.

1. *Discuss Responsible Behaviors:* The teacher may begin by explaining the importance of responsibility and good work habits for success in school. The students should understand that the goal is for them to become independent learners and that this will benefit them not only while they are in school but also for the rest of their lives. Then, the teacher should lead a discussion with the students about what it means to be responsible for one's own learning (i.e., what some responsible behaviors are). The teacher should invite students to name responsible behaviors and together they develop a list of these behaviors on the board. Figure 6–2 shows some examples of what this list might look like at lower and upper grades. These lists made up by the teacher and the students together can be made into wall charts that are prominently displayed where they can be referred to as needed.

FIGURE 6–1   Teaching Responsibility for Learning

- Discuss responsible behaviors.
- Provide opportunities to practice responsible behaviors.
- Provide academic choices.
- Share progress reports and self-evaluations.

FIGURE 6–2   Lower- and Upper-Grade Lists of Responsible Behaviors

Lower-Grade List	Upper-Grade List
1. Carry my homework safely to and from school. 2. Study every night in a quiet place. Ask when I don't understand something.	1. Set and prioritize my goals for daily study. Devote adequate time to achieve study goals. 2. Keep a homework notebook. 3. Keep a notebook for each subject.

2. *Provide Opportunities to Practice Responsible Behaviors:* Along with discussion of what responsible behaviors are, the teacher needs to provide opportunities for students to practice them. Figure 6–3 shows how this can be done, for example, in conjunction with the lower-grade list of responsible behaviors. Figure 6–4 suggests ways the teacher can provide opportunities for students to practice responsible behaviors developed for the upper-grade level. A form designed to help students set and prioritize study goals is given in Figure 6–5.

Figures 6–4 and 6–5 offer suggestions for providing students with opportunities to practice responsible behaviors. It is anticipated that these activities will be added to and modified to suit the needs of individual classrooms.

FIGURE 6–3   Behavior List with Examples of Practice: Lower Grades

Lower-Grade List of Responsible Behaviors	Opportunities to Practice Responsible Behaviors

1. Carry my homework safely to and from school.	1. Teacher does the following:
	    a. Discusses with students how to carry homework safely:
	        (1) Put homework in folder
	        (2) Put folder in backpack
	        (3) Don't put homework down an dirty place
	    b. Provides pocket folders
	    c. Provides homework sheets
	    d. Recruits parent help (for reminders)

2. Study every night in a quiet place.	2. Teacher does the following:
	    a. Recruits parent support to provide student with a quiet place and time for homework
	    b. Asks students periodically if they are using their study place each night

3. Ask when I don't understand something.	3. Teacher does the following:
	    a. Invites questions during lessons
	    b. Explains it is perfectly okay not to something
	    c. Reinforces student questions

FIGURE 6–4   Behavior List with Examples of Practice: Upper Grades

Upper-Grade List of Responsible Behaviors	Opportunities to Practice Responsible Behaviors
1. Set and prioritize my goals for daily study.	1. Teacher does the following: a. Models to students how to set and prioritize goals in context of their actual homework b. Provides a form (see Figure 6–5) for setting goals c. Reviews goal setting and prioritizing
2. Devote adequate time to achieve study goals.	2. Teacher does the following: a. Assigns meaningful homework b. Discusses with students how much time is enough c. Has students self-evaluate d. Recruits parent support to require student to study for a specified period of time each night
3. Keep a homework notebook.	3. Teacher does the following: a. Requires notebook for homework b. Demonstrates how to organize the homework notebook c. Reminds students to write homework assignments in notebook as teacher dictates it ("I'm going to give you your homework assignment now for the social studies chapter. Be sure to enter the assignment in your homework notebook–get it out now.")
4. Keep a notebook for each subject.	4. Teacher does the following: a. Requires notebook for each subject b. Demonstrates how to organize notebook c. Reminds students to use notebooks during instructional time ("Take notes on this information and put them in your notebook," "Get out your science notebooks and review notes from yesterday.")

3. *Provide Academic Choices:* When teachers provide opportunities for students to select from among several options which activity they will work on for a given period of time, they are giving students practice in taking responsibility for their own learning. They are also helping students become more independent in their learning. Providing academic choices to students can be structured in various ways and at all grade levels. The following discussion shows how this can be done at the kindergarten level and at the grade 4/5 level.

Academic Choices, Level K: Math Instruction: Ms. McClean has five math stations set up around the room. This week, her class is working on learning the number 5. At each station is an activity designed to help students internalize the meaning of the

FIGURE 6–5   Form for Setting and Prioritizing Study Goals

DAILY STUDY SCHEDULE

Date _____   Name _____

Priorities	Subject or Assignment	Goal for Tonight	Time Needed
First priority	**1.** Spelling test	Spell all 12 words perfectly	25 min.
Second priority	**2.** Book report	Write outline for the report	20 min.
Third priority	**3.** Schoolwide Reading Rainbow contest	Read 20 pages in *Black Beauty*	15 min.
		Total Time Needed for Homework	<u>1 hour</u>

symbol 5 through the use of manipulatives. For example, Station 1 is set up with kidney beans that are white on one side and red on the other, a recording sheet that shows numerous groups of five beans, and red and white crayons. Students are instructed to take five beans, shake them up, and let them fall on a flat surface. They then record the number of white and red kidney beans. By continuing the process, they eventually see all the possible combinations of five (2 + 3, 1 + 4, 4 + 1, 3 + 2, 5 + 0, 0 + 5). The other four stations also have activities that are related in some way to the number 5. Each child has a card that has his or her name on it and a picture of each station. When called on, each child takes his or her card and puts it in the pocket holder at the station he or she chooses. Each day, different children have the early opportunities to make their choices so everyone gets a chance to be wherever he or she wants to be. There is a set limit of five children to a station. Figure 6–6 provides an example of an individual child's card. Ms. McClean has the children mark their cards each day according to which center they chose so she can see how they are spending their time.

Academic Choices, Level 4/5: Extra Student Time: Mr. Pearson has a rule in his classroom that when students finish their assignments early, they are allowed to choose from several learning centers and desk activities that he has set up (and changes periodically). His learning centers include the following:

- Electronic game on history facts
- Giant puzzle depicting a historical scene
- Computer station
- Multicultural center featuring brain teasers from different cultures

FIGURE 6–6   Example of Individual Child's Card: Academic Choices

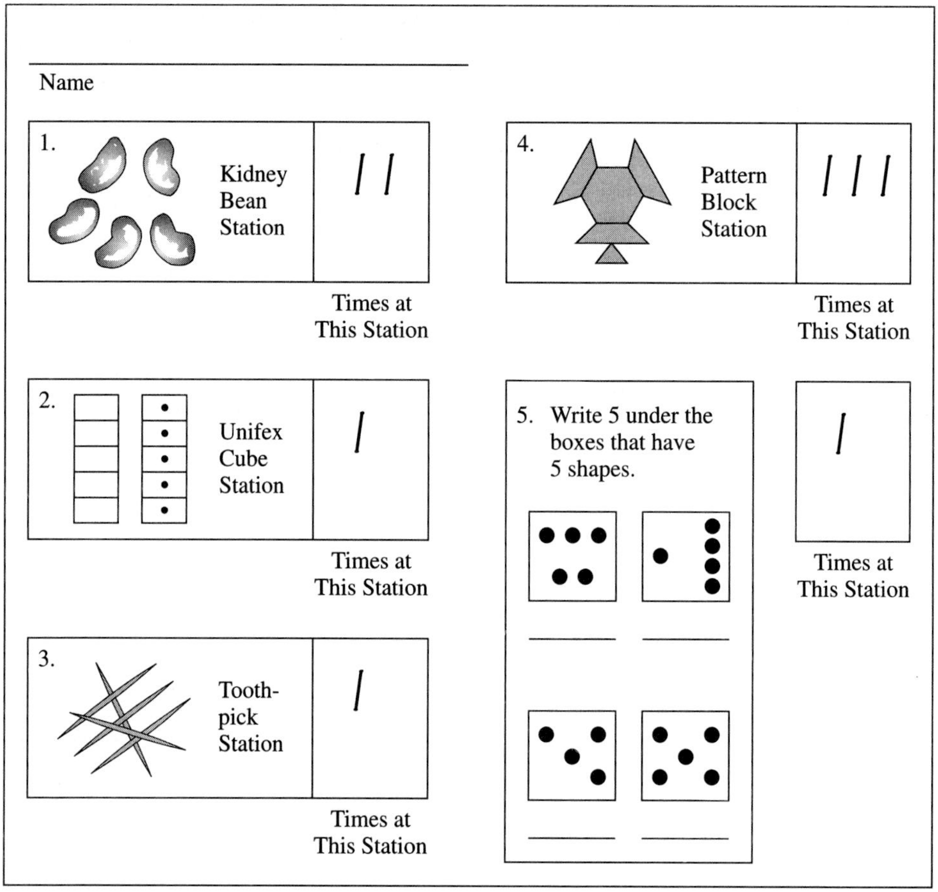

His desk activities include:

• Worksheet activities
• A selection of books and magazines from which students may select

Mr. Pearson has instructed his students regarding their conduct at the centers and desk activities. His students know that there can be no more than three at each learning center, they must use soft voices to communicate, and they must be on task. They also know that violation of conduct rules leads to loss of the privilege of using the centers. This system works very well in giving students the responsibility of choosing how they will use their study time and in providing practice in carrying out their activities with minimum disturbance to others, thus increasing awareness of how their actions affect their fellow students.

4. *Share Progress Reports and Self-Evaluations:* Another way to help students develop responsible study behaviors is to make them aware of how they are doing in this area. This can be done by having them evaluate themselves on the various behaviors and by sharing the teacher's progress report with them and their parents.

Self-evaluation logs are a good way to keep the issue of responsibility alive and fresh for students. Figure 6–7 is an example of a lower-grade self-evaluation log and Figure 6–8 is for the upper grades. Student evaluation logs should be done at least once a week. The teacher can check them to be sure students have a fairly realistic idea of how they are doing and have a conference with the student if there appears to be any major inconsistencies or problems. The teacher should also fill out monthly progress reports regarding responsible behavior and share them with students and their parents. Students need to know that both the teacher and their parents expect them to be responsible regarding their school work. Figure 6–9 suggests a form for the teacher's evaluation.

Thus, it is easy to see that a lot can be done by the classroom teacher to foster responsibility and good study habits. These efforts may not get every student to the 100

FIGURE 6–7   Example of a Weekly Self-Evaluation Log: Lower Grades

Name: _____

Week: _____   Parent Signature: _____

Check the Correct Answer

1. I finished my homework each day of the week.

I handed in completed homework:

5 days this week	4 days this week	3 or less days this week
_____	_____	_____

2. I brought my homework to school each day.

I brought my homework to school:

5 days this week	4 days this week	3 or less days this week
_____	_____	_____

3. I studied every night in my quiet place.

I studied in my quiet place:

5 days this week	4 days this week	3 or less days this week
_____	_____	_____

4. I asked questions when I did not understand.

I asked questions:

Everytime I did not understand	Most times when I did not understand	Very few times when I did not understand
_____	_____	_____

FIGURE 6–8   Example of a Weekly Self-Evaluation Log: Upper Grades

Name: _____

Week: _____   Parent Signature: _____

Check the Correct Answer

1. I set and followed my homework plans   *I set and followed my homework plans:*
    daily.

5 days this week	4 days this week	3 or less days this week
_____	_____	_____

2. I devoted adequate time to study.   *I devoted adequate study time:*

5 days this week	4 days this week	3 or less days this week
_____	_____	_____

3. My notebooks are in order and up to date.   *My notebooks are in order and up to date:*

All the time	Most of the time	Part of the time
_____	_____	_____

FIGURE 6–9   Monthly Progress Report Completed by Teacher

Monthly Progress Report

Name _____ Date _____	100%	Most of the Time	Half of the Time	Rarely
1. Completes homework on time.				
2. Organizes study time and set goals and priorities.				
3. Follows directions.				
4. Asks for clarification when needed.				
5. Keeps notebook up to date.				

percent level, but they will certainly reach many more students than the alternative, which has been a lack of focus on this area. To reiterate the first step in study skill acquisition, that is—responsibility and work habits—and to connect the "how to" aspect for the teacher, a summary is provided in Figure 6–10. The summary is meant to be a handy reference for teachers to use when planning their approach to teaching responsibility and good work habits. It should be noted that, at first, this process is teacher directed so that students are able to form study habits. However, the expectation is that the students will become more and more self-directed in regularly planning and following a productive study routine.

FIGURE 6–10   Summary for Teaching Responsibility and Good Study Habits

Fostering Responsibility and Good Study Habits	Specific Activities
1. Teach and discuss responsibility and good study habits.	• Teacher explains why responsibility and study habits are important. • Teacher and students create a list of responsible behaviors. • Display the list in a prominent place and refer to it often.
2. Provide opportunities for students to practice responsible behaviors and good work habits.	• Teacher assigns homework daily. • Teacher provides homework folders and/or form for setting goals and priorities. • Teacher recruits parents' support for quiet time and a place for student to do homework. • Teacher requires notebooks and demonstrates how to organize them, and refers to notebooks during class instruction. • Students participate in cooperative group activities that provide them with the chance to perform responsible behaviors.
3. Provide opportunities for students to choose what they will work on in class.	• Teacher provides work stations during content area instruction from which students may select. • Teacher provides alternative activities and learning centers for students who finish class assignments early.
4. Provide progress reports and self-evaluations.	• Teacher provides self-evaluation forms and has students/parents fill out once a week. • Teacher does progress report once a month and shares with students and parents.

Teaching, Modeling, and Reinforcing
Study Strategies and Techniques

Using study strategies does not come naturally to many students; in fact, most children will not use them at all unless these skills are taught and reinforced in the classroom (Rafoth, Leal, & DeFabo, 1993). Yet, when they do use study skills, students improve their academic performance, and for some students, it can mean the difference between passing and failing. Typically, training in study skills starts at the middle school level as the academic rigors of schooling increase; however, it is often too difficult for students at this stage to break set habits and to find the determination and mental discipline needed for serious study. The attitudes, work habits, and skills needed for effective study cannot be acquired overnight. Rather, study skill attainment is a gradual process; it takes time and repeated practice to acquire the various skills and to strengthen the will and capacity needed for sustained mental effort. The perfect time to begin to build these capacities is during the elementary school years. This is why it is so important that *elementary* school teachers be committed to study skill training, incorporating it into content area instruction where the strategies and techniques can be modeled and practiced in a relevant context.

Study skill attainment is a developmental process; that is, the capacity to learn study skills is limited in young children (due to limitations in short- and long-term memory) and gradually increases as they grow and gain experience. Basic study skills training in some areas, such as teaching responsibility and good work habits, should begin at the kindergarten level, as discussed earlier. Some other kinds of skills can be started in a very simplified manner in the lower elementary grades. As children mature and move to higher grade levels, these skills are taught at a more sophisticated level.

How to Teach Study Skills

Study skills are best taught within a context of content area instruction. This means they should be taught concurrently with the regular instruction that occurs in the classroom. Richardson and Morgan (1990) have presented an excellent paradigm for teaching study skills within the context of content area instruction. The paradigm includes the following seven steps:

1. Explain the skill to be taught.
2. Introduce the lesson.
3. Develop structured practice using the skill.
4. Have students report on their use of the skill.
5. Summarize how the skill was used in the content lesson.
6. Review and reinforce the skill.
7. Continue practice with the skill.

Each step of the paradigm will be looked at in the context of a social studies lesson on Growth in California, 1870–1900. The study skill to be taught is two-column note taking.

1. *Explain the Skill to be Taught:* When explaining the skill to be taught, be sure to include the following elements in the explanation:

    a. Describe the skill.

    b. Explain the purpose of the skill.

    c. Explain how the skill will benefit the student.

Possible Teacher Script: "Today we are going to learn a very useful system for taking notes called *two-column note taking* or the *Cornell System.* You will be taking notes in a specific way that is meant to help you keep track of information and locate things in your notes quickly. In this system, you will draw a line down your notebook paper, not down the center, but one-third of the way from the left margin. (The teacher demonstrates on the board.) On the left side of this line you will write down main words, ideas, and events. On the other side of the line, the right side, you will write descriptions of the ideas and events.

"Taking notes in this manner benefits you in several ways. First of all, when you want to go back over your notes to find something in particular, it will be easy to locate, by looking over the left column of the paper where you have the main words or key terms listed. Second, when you take notes in this format, it is perfect for studying for a test, as you can cover the detailed side (right side) and use the left side with key terms as a cue to test yourself. You can also reverse this process by covering the key terms and seeing if you can remember them by their descriptions."

2. *Introduce the Lesson:* When introducing the lesson, the following elements should be included in the introduction:

    a. Connect new material to previous learning.

    b. Relate new material to the students' experiences.

    c. Focus students on new learning.

Possible Teacher Script: "Today we're going to learn about how California grew in population and industry from 1870 to 1900. We've already seen how the Gold Rush affected the population of our state. We've also seen that many of the would-be miners turned to farming as they realized that very few actually got rich panning for gold and that they could make more from farming than they could from mining.

"How many of you have noticed that our school has grown in the last year? Our school has grown because more people have moved to our town and our town has grown. Why do you think this has happened? (The teacher is looking for the answer that a main highway was built connecting the town to a major city.)

"In today's lesson, I want you to look for important things that caused California to grow so rapidly in the last half of the nineteenth century."

3. *Develop Structured Practice Using the Skill:* Two important things should be done in this step:

    a. Model the skill.

    b. Provide a form (worksheet) for students to use that has partial notes.

Possible Teacher Script: "Let's read page 191 in your social studies book together and see how the two-column note-taking system would work. Remember that key words and main ideas go on the left and details go on the right. (The teacher and students read a text selection aloud.) Now, what's the main idea of this section? What is a key term I can put on the left side of the line on my paper? What detail should I put on the right side to explain the key word?" (The teacher works through a few pages of text in this manner, asking key questions and soliciting student input. Figure 6–11 shows how the model the teacher and students create could look.)

This technique is what is meant by *modeling* the skill. The teacher is showing the students, step by step, how to use the note-taking system. Next, the teacher provides students with a partially filled note-taking form and has the students read the next page of text on their own and fill in the blanks on the form. This is the *structured practice* wherein the students have a guide in the form of the partially filled note-taking worksheet. An example of how such a worksheet could look is provided in Figure 6–12.

After the students have completed the structured worksheet, the teacher goes over it with them to be sure they have grasped the concept and done their notes correctly. The amount of information provided is gradually lessened until students are eventually doing all the note taking themselves.

4. *Have Students Report on Their Use of the Skill:* The teacher can ask questions such as the following to elicit students' comments about their use of the skill:
- How did you use the skill?
- How did it help you?
- Did you have any problems with the note taking?
- Did you add any helpful steps of your own?

5. *Summarize How the Skill Was Used in the Content Lesson:* The teacher reiterates the purposes and benefits of two-column note taking, such as:
- The two-column note-taking system helps you identify the main ideas of the reading (or lecture).
- It also helps you understand and remember the material you read or hear.
- When you take your notes in this way, it is easy to find specific information in your notes.
- The two-column format is ideal for studying for a test.

6. *Review and Reinforce the Skill:* In the following days and weeks, the teacher reviews how to use the skill, provides opportunities to use it again, and reiterate its usefulness. Student attempts at using the skill should be praised.

FIGURE 6–11   Example of Two-Column Note Taking Modeled by Teacher for Students

Key Words, Main Ideas and Concepts, Your Comments	Supporting Detail
Orange Industry	The business of growing and selling oranges.
Luther Tibbet	1875: A Californian who buys first navel orange trees for planting in California. Soon, thousands are growing oranges.
Two Reasons for Growth in California	Oranges Railroads (advertise)

FIGURE 6–12   Structured Practice Worksheet for Two-Column Note Taking

Instructions: Read page _____ of your text. Where key terms are given, write the supporting details or definitions. Where details or definitions are given, write the appropriate key terms.

Key Terms	Details, Definitions
Santa Fe Railroad	California's only railroad until 1885.
Competition	
	A period of fast growth.

(1/3)	(2/3)

7. *Continue Practice with the Skill:* This is an extremely important step because without continued practice, the students will probably forget about the skill. Only through the continued practice that refocuses the students on the use of the skill can the students internalize the skill and feel the competence and familiarity needed to use it on their own. Continued practice should involve reteaching steps 1 through 5 at least 10 additional times with lessons from other subjects such as math and science so that the skill transfers to different kinds of subject matter. The teacher should keep reminding the students to use the skill throughout the year.

When teaching a study skill, it is important to model how to use the skill (demonstrated in step 3). The teacher more or less thinks out loud with the students, showing how he or she thinks about the material at each step, such as, How did I know this was an important point to write down? Why do you think I am putting a question mark next to this term? How do you think I can write a shorthand version of this information? This provides valuable insights for students who are at the stage of developing their thinking processes.

Another important step in teaching study skills is to provide opportunities or practice of the skill. This should be done the next day and several times over the next week (besides periodic practice over the school year). Research has shown that students forget information most quickly just after they have learned it (Gagne & Driscoll, 1988).

Providing structured practice aids students in learning the skill. As they get more practice at it, they can be given less and less structure, so that gradually they become independent in their ability to use the skill. They may even have their own modifications or additions that work for them.

Finally, it is important that the teacher make the connection between the use of the skill and how it affects the students' understanding and memory. For example, with the two-column note-taking system, the teacher should be sure to point out that the method will help them understand and remember the material. From observation of high school classes in which a large percentage of the students cannot take notes in class or from readings, and are at a loss as to how to organize and keep track of information, it is apparent that many students are handicapped academically because they have had little or no training in *how* to study. "Knowledge of appropriate study strategies, and the ability to choose them appropriately and judge their effectiveness, may in fact separate successful from unsuccessful students more so than ability" (Rafoth, Leal, & DeFabo, 1993). A few lucky students may receive some study skill training from their parents, but most students are totally dependent on the classroom teacher for knowledge about how to study. Without this knowledge, they are severely hampered in their ability to learn in school.

Many different kinds of activities fall under the umbrella of *study skills*. In order to discuss these activities in a systematic way, they are grouped into four categories:

1. Memorization techniques
2. Study and comprehension strategies
3. Time management and organization skills
4. Information-finding skills

Figure 6–13 enumerates the strategies and techniques that are grouped into each of these four main categories. Also indicated is the grade level in which training can begin.

Memorization Techniques

Children are required to memorize various kinds of information at every grade level in the course of their schooling. Having a good memory is a decided asset not only for success in school but also it is very helpful in functioning in day-to-day living. The more an individual can remember, the less dependent he or she is on looking things up and the better able that individual is to solve problems and think on his or her feet. As

FIGURE 6–13   Study Skills for the Elementary School Grades

Category	Skill	Introduce	Continue to Develop in Sophistication
Memorization Techniques	Rehearsal	K 6	
	Rhymes and Rhythmic Activities	K 6	
	Association	2/3 6	
	Mnemonics	2/3 6	
	Self-Testing	3/4 6	
Study and Comprehension Strategies	Previewing	K 6	
	Reading Visual Aids	K 6	
	Study Systems	4 6	
	Reciprocal Teaching	3/4 6	
Time Management and Organization Skills	Outlining	4 6	
	Note Taking	4 6	
	Personal Organization	K 6	
Information Finding	Dictionary	1/2/3 6	
	Encyclopedia	4 6	
	Parts of Book	K 6	
Responsibility (Foundation)		K 6	

the amount of information stored inside grows, so does an individual's ability to function more efficiently in various circumstances because there is more to draw upon from within. Memory capacities vary from person to person; however, very few people have photographic memories and most can benefit greatly from memory training.

For school children, memory is especially important because they are asked to memorize many things. Remembered information is the basis of many mental activities. For example, remembering sums and products of numbers makes it easier (and faster) to solve math problems. Reading phonetically is based on having learned (and remembered) the sound/symbol relationships of letters. Remembering information in a social studies chapter facilitates writing a report on the chapter or giving an oral presentation. When memory skills are strong, individuals can work faster and with more facility, and many cognitive activities in school become easier for them, including taking and passing tests. While children are in elementary school is the ideal time to teach them memory strategies, for they are at an optimum age for absorbing information through memorization.

This section will examine five different types of memory strategies: rehearsal, rhymes and rhythmic activities, association, mnemonics, and self-testing strategies. Figure 6–14 lists the five strategies and gives a brief definition and an example of each.

FIGURE 6–14   Memorization Strategies with Examples

Strategy	Definition	Examples
Rehearsal	Using rote repetition to remember something	Writing a spelling word five times. Repeating aloud the characteristics of an insect.
Rhymes and Rhythmic Activity	Using rhymes, songs, chants (rap), and/or movement to remember things	Singing the "ABC" song. Repeating "Thirty days hath September, April, June and November."
Association	Using a variety of techniques that rely on associating what has to be remembered with something familiar or easily recalled	Remembering the name "Carianna" because it has "car" in it, "i" in Spanish means "and," and my mother's name is Anna: *Car-i-anna.*
Mnemonics	Aiding memory through associational techniques such as acronyms and acrostics	Acronym: *PEN*: To remember parts of an atom—proton, electron, neutron. Acrostic: **E**very **G**ood **B**oy **D**oes **F**ine: To remember notes of treble clef line notes.
Self-Testing	Testing one's ability to remember specific information through various methods	Multiplication flashcards. Turning all headings in a text chapter into questions and seeing if one can answer them. Answering questions at end of chapter.

Rehearsal

Rehearsal is defined as the use of rote repetition to aid memory. Teachers frequently weave rehearsal into lessons for the purposes of enhancing the students' memories of key terms or concepts. It is not unusual to hear dialogue such as the following in any elementary school classroom:

Teacher: What did I say we call an animal that eats only meat?

Students: Carnivorous.

Teacher: What's that again?

Students: Carnivorous.

Teacher: One more time.

Students: Carnivorous!

Although it is not unusual for teachers to provide their students with opportunities to use repetition to remember information, it *is* unusual for teachers to take the next very important step, and that is to make the connection for students between the act of repeating and the resulting benefit to the memory. "All teachers enable their students to remember information by providing opportunities for repetition, however, research shows that they rarely include the important step of making the connection between an activity and its value as a study strategy or its relationship to effective memory and learning" (Rafoth, Leal, & DeFabo, 1993). When students understand this connection, they can have more control over the learning process. To make this important connection, the teacher could add a statement to the preceding dialogue such as:

Teacher: I'm having you repeat "carnivorous" because repeating words *helps us remember* them.

Rehearsal strategies are profitably used at all grade levels in elementary school; however, they are particularly useful in the early grades. Young children are not usually developmentally ready for more sophisticated strategies such as those based on meaning and association.

Rhymes and Rhythmic Activities

Rhymes, songs, chants, and rap are all *very powerful* strategies for memorizing information. Elementary school students at all levels are enchanted by the play of rhyme and rhythm in songs and poetry. Generally, they find these kinds of activities very pleasant, so much so that you will find students singing the songs or repeating the rhymes on their own time, such as on the playground.

There are many primary teaching materials available, such as records and tapes that use song and rhyme to aid memory of such things as numbers (counting order), days of the week, months of the year, colors, shapes, letters, and so on. There are also memory songs for middle and upper-elementary grades, such as songs for remembering all the states of the United States. Using rhymes and rhythmic activities to enhance memory is highly recommended because they are very powerful techniques.

Association

There are many kinds of associative techniques for remembering information; in fact, many people regularly make up their own associations to remember information. A typical associative technique for remembering an unfamiliar name or term is to break the word up into smaller chunks to which an individual attaches an association that has meaning for him or her. For example, to remember the name *Carianna,* one student broke the name into *car-i-anna. Car* is a familiar object, *i* (pronounced *ee*) is *and* in Spanish, and *anna* is the name of the student's mother.

Mnemonics

Another kind of associative technique is called mnemonics. Acronyms and acrostics are both examples of mnemonics. An example of an acronym is the word *HOMES* used to remember the names of the Great Lakes (Lakes Huron, Ontario, Michigan, Erie, and

Superior). Each letter of an acronym stands for something such as a term, object, place, person, or phenomenon.

Acrostics are sentences such as *My Very Educated Mother Just Served Us Nine Pizzas* used to remember the names of all the planets (Mercury, Venus, Earth, Mars, Jupiter, Saturn, Uranus, Neptune, and Pluto). In this case, the first letter of each word in this unusual sentence is also the first letter of one of the planets. Sentences that are somewhat outlandish are good acrostics because they are more memorable.

Associative techniques are very helpful in remembering all kinds of information, and the elementary school teacher should model them frequently. As with all study skills, students are not likely to use mnemonics unless the teacher focuses on the skill and provides frequent opportunities for students to practice the skill.

Self-Testing Strategies

Self-testing strategies are "methods of knowing when one can terminate studying" (Rafoth, Leal, & DeFabio, 1993). Many times, students will express surprise at a low grade on a test because, they say, "I studied a long time for that test." What they failed to do was test themselves in some way to be sure they knew the information. Ways of self-testing can include using flashcards, such as for a multiplication test. Flashcards can also be used for science and social studies by writing a question on one side of the card and the answer on the other. Flashcards for science and social studies are shown in Figure 6–15.

FIGURE 6–15   Examples of Self-Testing Cards in Science and Social Studies

Self-Testing
Flashcard—Science

Describe the "dark zone" of the ocean.

Flashcard—Science

• Between 1,000–4,000 meters deep • Dark—no sunlight • Cold—2° to 4° C • Enormous pressure of water above you • Scarce food • Inhabited by viper fish • Only light comes from viper fish who use it to catch prey

Self-Testing
Flashcard—Social Studies

When did California become a state?

Flashcard—Social Studies

September 9, 1850

Again, as with any study skill, it is necessary that the teacher model the skill in class for the students and provide many opportunities to use the skill. A few days before a scheduled test (in any content area) would be a good time to have a lesson on the use of this skill. Although the study skill teaching paradigm described earlier in the chapter provides an excellent general format to use in teaching this skill, a little more detail is seen in this possible teaching script for introducing and modeling the skill.

Introducing the Self-Testing Study Skill—Possible Teacher Script: "Several of you told me that you were disappointed about your grade on the last social studies test. You said you had studied a lot and still did not get the grade you wanted. I know how bad it feels when you put in the time to study and still don't do that well. Well, today I'm going to show you a special study technique that will help you get the grade you want. It's called the *self-testing technique.* You are going to learn a great way of testing yourself before you take a school test."

Modeling the Self-Testing Study Skill—Possible Teacher Script: "We have been studying about the first Californians for the past three weeks; that's Chapter 2 in your textbook. Your test on this chapter is scheduled for Friday. Let's look at the chapter and see how you could test yourself on the information. Here are the steps I want you to follow—write them down in your notebook.

1. Look at each lesson in the chapter. Decide what are the main ideas and key terms you need to remember.
2. Make flashcards for the important information. (We'll practice making flashcards; you take down all the steps.)
3. Test yourself with the flashcards.
4. Keep studying until you get all the answers correct. (It may take more than one study session.)
5. You can stop studying when you get all the flashcards correct. You can ask a parent or brother or sister to quiz you.

"I want you to follow these steps tonight when you study the flashcards we are going to make in class today. Here is how you make the flashcards. I've given each of you index cards. You can also cut up paper if you don't have cards. To make the cards, you write a key word or a question on one side and then the definition or answer on the other side of the card. Now look at Lesson 1 of Chapter 2. What are some key terms or important ideas you should remember?"

Student: The first people arrived in California 12,000 years ago.

Teacher: Good. How can we make a flashcard for that fact?

Student: Write on one side of the card: When did the first Californians arrive in California? Then on the other side, write: 12,000 years ago.

Teacher: Correct. Now I want you to get in your study pairs and make up flashcards for the rest of Lesson 1.

As the students make their flashcards, the teacher circulates around the room and checks to see that they are doing it correctly. Then the teacher has the students quiz each other with the cards. For homework that night, they are to make and study flashcards for the next two lessons in the chapter. In class the following day, the teacher puts the students in study pairs again and has them quiz each other with the cards they made the night before. In order for students to internalize the skill and use it on their own, the lesson must be repeated 6 to 10 more times and plenty of opportunities must be provided for practicing the skill. Even after all this, the teacher still needs to remind students periodically to use the skill. This is what it means to *focus* on study skills as part of classroom instruction (i.e., it is the direct focus of many lessons and it is also applied when learning the facts and information of the classroom pedagogy).

For some students, making flashcards may be too tedious, especially when there are a lot of facts or terms to learn. In this case, students can use a format similar to the two-column note taking in which they write key terms on the one-third side of their paper and the definitions on the two-thirds side of the paper, then cover one side and practice remembering the other. They can switch which side they cover for further practice. Here is an example of this format filled in with facts from a science lesson:

Example of Notes for Self-Testing Technique

Evaporation	Change from liquid to a gas
Water vapor	Water in the form of gas
Condensation	Water vapor changes to liquid water
Dew point	Temperature at which water vapor condenses
Water cycle	Evaporation and condensation of water
Jet stream	A fast-moving stream of air high in the atmosphere
Fronts	Places where cold and warm air masses meet

In both of these self-testing formats, students give themselves a cue or question to which they respond. When all of their responses are correct, they know they can terminate studying.

Study and Comprehension Strategies

This category includes strategies that help students understand and remember reading material, especially with regard to content area textbooks. Experienced teachers are familiar with the inability of some students to read and comprehend textbook material. An example comes from a sixth-grade class where students are doing a cooperative reading activity in groups of five or six. Each student in the group is responsible for reading one column on a page in a social studies text and summarizing it to the others in the group. The students read their short sections to themselves but are unable to summarize it for the other members of their group. They were unable to organize the material into "meaningful chunks" for presentation to their peers, so most of the students resort to reading the whole of their sections aloud to the others in the group.

Another example comes from a fifth-grade class where students are assigned to answer questions at the end of a social studies chapter after they read the selection and discuss it in class. In observing the students' written responses to the chapter questions, it is obvious that they were unable to grasp the meaning of the questions; their responses were insufficient and, in some cases, did not make sense.

Unfortunately, these occurrences are neither rare nor unusual. There exists a very definite lack of study and comprehension strategies among school children today. Figure 6–16 lists the strategies that will be discussed in the category of study and comprehension strategies: previewing, reciprocal teaching, outlining, note taking, and SQ3R.

These five strategies are meant to help students comprehend material by requiring them to think about the material in meaningful ways. A by-product of this type of thinking is that memory is also enhanced.

Previewing

Previewing is a means of acquiring information about the nature of the material to be read in terms of its genre, subject matter, main subtopics, and level of reading difficulty. The person ascertains this information by following a series of steps prior to reading:

1. Note the title and the author of the reading selection.
2. Look at any pictures included in the selection.
3. Read all charts/tables/graphs/maps.
4. Read all headings and subheadings.
5. Read the questions at the end of the chapter.

FIGURE 6–16 Study and Comprehension Strategies

Strategy	Definition
Previewing	A method of ascertaining information regarding the nature of the material to be read (content, reading level, genre, level of academic rigor) through a series of prereading steps
Reciprocal Teaching	A cooperative learning strategy combining four study skills (summary, questions, clarification, and prediction) to create a powerful comprehension tool for students
Outlining	A general plan or structure that has a systematic format and contains main ideas or points and related detail
Note Taking	A systemized way of recording relevant information from a lecture or a reading selection
SQ3R	A method of improving reading comprehension skills and retention of information through a series of steps that involve surveying the material, asking questions, reading to answer those questions, writing main ideas in own words, and reviewing one's own outline and notes

Gleaning information about the selection in this way serves several purposes for the students, including:

1. Students are well informed regarding the nature of the material in terms of genre (i.e., technical, fiction, current/historical, etc.).
2. Previous knowledge is recalled regarding the subject of the selection.
3. Students have an idea of what aspects of the topic will be covered.
4. Students are informed about the level of difficulty, which allows an estimation of how much time and effort the reading will require.
5. Students will be more focused for reading.

The teacher should model previewing in a way appropriate for his or her grade level. For example, at the kindergarten level, the teacher guides students through a preview of a book in the following way:

Teacher: Look at the picture on the cover of the book. What do you think the book will be about?

Student: Something friendly.

Teacher: What makes you think it will be friendly?

Student: He has a smile (referring to an imaginary animal on the front cover).

Teacher: Let's look at the name, or title, of the book. *Huggles Has Breakfast.* Now what do you think the story will be about?

Student: What Huggles eats for breakfast.

Teacher: Let's read and find out if you guessed right.

At the upper-level grades, the teacher would model a more sophisticated version of previewing, the final goal being that the students learn to use previewing on their own.

Reciprocal Teaching

Reciprocal teaching is a cooperative learning strategy meant to enhance comprehension of written materials. Once students have learned to use this excellent strategy cooperatively, they can adapt the same steps of the strategy to their independent study. The skills they gain in reciprocal teaching are especially effective in helping them comprehend reading assignments in content area textbooks. This strategy is a powerful one that benefits students instructionally in several key ways.

Reciprocal teaching as a cooperative learning strategy combines four study skills (summarization, questioning, clarification, and prediction) to create a total comprehension strategy. Each of the four study skills that make up the steps of reciprocal teaching can stand alone as a useful study strategy, and when the four are combined, it makes for an effective means to comprehend reading material.

To teach this skill, the study skill paradigm should be followed. When modeling the skill, the teacher should use a short, high-interest segment of a selected text to maximize student interest and successful application of the strategy. Figure 6–17 suggests a procedure for modeling this strategy and the instructional purpose of each step.

As always, continued practice of the skill is most important in order for students to learn and subsequently use the skill on their own. Those working with the reciprocal teaching method have ascertained that a minimum of seven complete practice opportunities are needed for students to be able to use this strategy independently. (See a thorough discussion on reciprocal teaching as a cooperative learning structure on page 72.)

Outlining
In Figure 6–16, outlining was defined as creating a general plan structured in a systematic form that contains main points and related detail. Outlining is a time-honored study skill that helps students organize reading material into chunks of meaning (i.e., main ideas with supporting detail). It helps students rank the importance of ideas and information and see relationships among them. Once a student grasps these hierarchical relationships, his or her comprehension is enhanced, and what was a jumble of facts and information will then take on meaning for him or her.

Outlining can be used by students for the following purposes: (1) to understand text material, (2) to plan and write reports, (3) to study for tests, and (4) to prepare

FIGURE 6–17   Procedure for Teaching Reciprocal Teaching as an Independent Study Strategy

Steps of Procedure	Instructional Purpose
1. Teacher reads short segment of high-interest selection to students.	Provides motivation and built-in success
2. Teacher asks students how they would retell the reading selection in their own words. Teacher records what students say.	Indicates understanding or lack of it
3. Teacher asks students to reduce their summaries to a concise sentence or two in which they include the important information.	Disciplines students to identify and select most important and relevant information only
4. Teacher asks students to think of a question they could ask about the reading segment.	Promotes critical thinking
5. Teacher has students write down anything they may not quite understand. Teacher clarifies any confusion they may have.	Helps students to know when they don't know
6. Teacher asks for predictions about what they think the next section of the reading selection will be about.	Helps students make inferences with information at hand

for oral presentations. Upper-elementary teachers are urged to teach and reinforce this skill. Criteria for creating an outline fall into two categories: structure and content. Figure 6–18 enumerates these criteria.

Teaching Outlining.   An effective way to teach outlining is through an interactive webbing exercise. The webbing acts as a working model in which thoughts about the rank or importance of text ideas and information can be tentatively tried and changed if needed. As a working model, it is less intimidating to students than going directly to the more formal outlining. Visually, the webbing is more accommodating to students—that is, it makes it easier for them to see the ideas and linkages. An example of a webbing and the resulting outline is provided in Figures 6–19 and 6–20, respectively. The source of information is a section of text on the Makah Indians from a Houghton Mifflin fifth-grade social studies text.

The webbing is done as an interactive activity with the teacher incorporating student input but guides the ranking of ideas. After the webbing is complete, the teacher explains the rules for making the outline and again solicits student input and guides the ranking of ideas through questions and suggestions. Structured practice can be done by

FIGURE 6–18   Criteria for Outlining

Content Rules	Structure Rules

Outlines Include:
 	
Main ideas
Supporting detail
Terms
 	
Outlines Provide:
 	
A visual picture of relationships of ideas in a hierarchical fashions
	I. Roman numerals (I, II, III, IV, etc.) mark off the major divisions of ideas in the paper.
	  A. Capital letters (A, B, C, etc.) are used to subdivide ideas within each roman numeral group.
	    1. Arabic numerals (1, 2, 3, etc.) subdivide the ideas within each capital letter group.
	      a. Lower-case letters (a, b, c, etc.) form the subgroups within the arabic numeral divisions.
	• It is not necessary to subdivide each topic. No topic, however, should have an A subhead without also having a B subhead. Similarly, if there is a 1, there must be a 2; if there is an a, there must be a b. In other words, there should be at least two subdivisions within a category.
	• The subdivisions within an outline should be balanced. All topics should be as important as II and III topics. Within each further division, there should also be a balance.

Source: The Vest-Pocket Writer's Guide, 1987, Boston: Houghton-Mifflin.

FIGURE 6–19   Web: Makah Indians

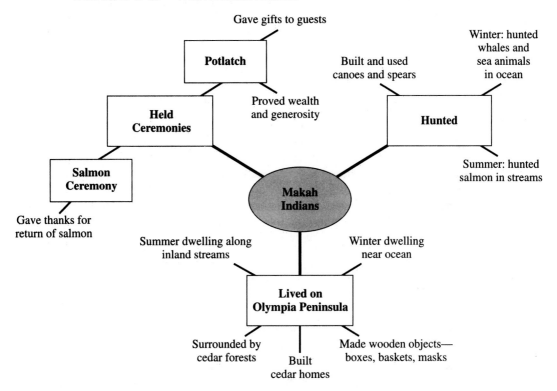

FIGURE 6–20   Outline Made from Webbing

Makah Indians

I. Lived on Olympia Peninsula
  A. Surrounded by cedar forests
  B. Built cedar homes
  C. Made cedar objects—boxes, baskets, masks
  D. Summer dwelling near inland streams
  E. Winter dwelling near ocean
II. Hunted
  A. Summer: hunted salmon in streams
  B. Winter: hunted whales and sea animals in ocean
  C. Built and used canoes and spears

III. Held Ceremonies
  A. Potlatch
    1. Gave gifts to guests
    2. Proved wealth and generosity
  B. Salmon ceremony
    1. Held every year
    2. Gave thanks for return of salmon

Note: In an instance where there is an A but no B under a roman numeral, then the A should be included as part of the roman numeral.

providing the students with partially completed webbings that they must fill in as they read and then convert to outlines. As they get more practice, the teacher can provide a partially filled outline, skipping the webbing step. Eventually, the students will be expected to create the entire outline on their own.

Note Taking

Note taking is a systemized way of recording relevant information from a lecture or a reading selection. Note taking is, of course, a necessary tool for any student. It aids students in accumulating information from lectures and books, understanding text and written material, generating ideas, and studying for tests. Note taking is a kinesthetic activity, and for those students who are strong kinesthetic learners, it also aids thinking and memory. That is, these learners think more clearly and efficiently when they can write their thoughts down.

How to teach note taking has been described in the earlier discussion of the teaching paradigm. The only thing that needs to be added here is that without note-taking skills, students are severely hampered in their access to the information their teachers provide in lectures and assigned readings. This is increasingly true as students progress to middle and high school, where they are expected to be more independent in their learning. Therefore, note taking should be a well-acquired skill before students leave elementary school.

SQ3R

Another helpful study and comprehension strategy is the SQ3R, which is appropriate for the upper-elementary grades. SQ3R stands for survey, question, read, recite, review. Because it is a somewhat sophisticated strategy, students should be expected to be able to use the SQ3R only if they have had practice applying each of the individual steps to reading material in previous lessons.

In the *survey* step, students do a preview of the material. That is, they read headings of sections (these are usually in bold type), look at pictures/charts/graphs and read the captions under them, and read the questions and/or summaries at the end of the chapter. The mental activities done in this step familiarize the students with the material, focus them on major ideas of the chapter, and organize the information in the chapter.

In the *question* step, the students turn all of the section headings into questions and write them in outline form. This gives them a guideline of what specifically to note or focus on as they read.

As they *read* the material, the students do so with the purpose of answering the questions they had formed from the section headings. This fosters an active search for answers as they read, which enhances both understanding and memory.

For the *recite* step, the students close their books after reading a section and write the answer to the heading questions on the outline they made during the *question* step, putting the answer in their own words. Putting the essence of the reading into their own words forces them to engage with the material in a meaningful way, as opposed to reading the material mechanically without thinking about it. It also helps them evaluate their own understanding of the material, because if they cannot put it into their own words, they do not understand it.

In the final step of SQ3R, the *review* step, the students study the outlines they have made. In this process, they try to see how various concepts and points are related to each other as well as use the outline to test their memories of main points. This prepares them for a classroom discussion of the material.

According to Rafoth, Leal, and DeFabo (1993), the SQ3R is effective because it conforms to how individuals process information. In the first two steps, it facilitates selective attention and ensures that important information enters short-term memory. In the last three steps, it enhances the understanding of material in meaningful ways, which increases the likelihood that the information will enter long-term memory.

Teaching the SQ3R.   As mentioned earlier, it is preferable that students have already had practice with the individual steps in the SQ3R during previous classroom instruction, both in cooperative and whole-group activities as well as in individual study. This way, when the steps are put together and modeled as a system for the students, it will not seem overwhelming to them. As with the other study skills, the teacher needs to model the use of the system for the students and provide structured practice.

A summary of the five study/comprehension strategies is provided in Figure 6–21.

Time Management and Organization Skills

Time management skills involve the student in determining his or her own study needs in terms of what needs to be done, how much time is required to do it, and in what order to do it. These are decisions most students make in connection with their independent study at home. Making these decisions helps students set study goals and formulate a general plan of accomplishing these goals. It helps students organize their study time and study efforts.

Time management skills are very important. Setting goals gives the student a point of reference and having a plan to follow helps the student know when he or she is on schedule or falling behind. Setting priorities tells students what to tackle first. When used properly, time management skills give the student more control over his or her learning, which results in greater success in school and in consequent gains in self-confidence.

Organization skills go hand in hand with time management skills, and the combined use of both provides students with a powerful means of achieving efficiency and effectiveness in their personal study habits. With regard to organization skills, the discussion will focus on keeping notebooks and keeping track of one's personal possessions such as pencils, pens, erasers, and so on.

Most students will not organize themselves on their own, so unless they learn this much-needed skill in school, they are unable to locate what they need when they need it. This renders them ineffectual, and they more or less fumble through school at a low level of functioning, but this can all be turned around with organization training.

Ideally, training in organizing oneself should start in kindergarten. It can, however, be effectively introduced at any grade level, although the earlier it is begun, the better

FIGURE 6–21   Summary of Study/Comprehension Strategies

Strategy	Definition	Instructional Purposes	How to Teach
Previewing	A method of determining nature of material to be read	• Stimulates recall of previous knowledge • Determines genre • Determines topics • Determines level of difficulty	• Model what is appropriate for grade level through interactive methods like questioning.
Reciprocal Teaching	A cooperative learning strategy combining four study skills (summary, questions, clarification, prediction) to create a total comprehension strategy	• Requires student to determine his or her own understanding of the material • Disciplines student to be concise and precise • Promotes critical thinking • Teaches student to make inferences from information at hand	• Use high-interest, short passages to begin. • Learn first in cooperative groups. • Model how to adapt for independent study. • Remind and reinforce its use for independent study.
Outlining	A general plan structured in a systematic form that contains main points and related details	• Promotes comprehension • Provides plan for written reports and oral presentations • Provides a means to study for an exam	• Model by using an interactive webbing exercise. • Make transition to outline. • Provide structured practice.
Note Taking	A systemized way of recording relevant information from a lecture or reading selection	• Aids in accumulating information • Promotes comprehension • Fosters generating ideas • Aids in studying for exams • Fosters thinking and memory • Promotes use of selective attention.	• Use high-interest passage when modeling skill. • Model main concept and supporting detail on 2-column page. • Solicit student participation in writing ideas on 2-column page.
SQ3R	A method of improving reading comprehension skills and retention of information through a series of steps that involve surveying the material, asking questions, reading to answer those questions, writing main ideas in own words, and reviewing one's own outline and notes	• Facilitates selective attention of reading material • Enhances comprehension • Increases retention of material read	• Give previous experience with individual steps of the process. • Model the system as a process series of steps. • Provide structured practice for use of the strategy.

for the student. In the lower grades, organization skills involve getting homework safely to and from school and keeping school papers safe until they are no longer needed. For the upper grades, teaching organization skills involves teaching students how to keep a tabbed hardcover binder notebook for all classroom papers and how to keep supplies handy and ready for use. Figure 6–22 enumerates steps for teaching these skills at the upper-grade level.

One of the most common interruptions to classroom instruction is students who do not have a pencil with which to take notes or do their assignment. Students will not make an effort to keep track of their pencils if they are constantly supplied with new ones by the teacher. This also gets to be expensive. What can the teacher do with the child who has no pencil with which to do his or her work? One teacher described her solution to this problem as follows:

> *In the beginning of the year, I give all my students several pencils and pens to start them off. I explain to them how to keep from losing their pencils by always putting them away in the pencil holders in their notebooks. If a student tells me he has no pencil to begin his work, I ask the class if anyone will lend him an extra pencil. Then it is the lender's responsibility to get the pencil back from the student when that student finds or replaces his own. If no one will*

FIGURE 6–22   How to Teach Organization Skills: Upper Grades

Teaching Steps	Materials

1. At the beginning of the year, each child is supplied with:
  • 3-ring hardcover binder
  • plastic pencil holder
  • pens/pencils
	Supplied by school or parents:
	  • 3-ring binders
	  • pencil holders
	  • pens/pencils

2. Teacher introduces organization skills by explaining school policy that every child be "ready to learn" everyday.
  • Have all supplies (notebook, pencils, pens, erasers) at school and ready for use.
  • Teacher explains school policy for students who fail to come to school "ready to learn."
  • Teacher explains benefits of being organized.	

3. Teacher demonstrates how to organize the 3-ring binder, labeling the tab sheets by subject and inserting them in binder.	Tab sheets
4. Teacher sends home letter to parents, explaining the "ready to learn" policy of school.	Form letter to parents
5. Teacher periodically reminds students to use notebooks and have pencils and pens ready for use. Teacher conducts spot checks of notebooks.	

lend the student a pencil, he must do his work in crayon. All work done in crayon must be copied over in pencil before it is handed in to me. I also explain to students that they must be ready to learn. This means that their pencils have to be sharpened and ready to use. I do not allow students to sharpen pencils during instruction time. This eliminates the incentive to break the pencil points to delay getting down to work. (Shelley Woodruff, Euclid School, San Diego, 1995)

Information-Finding Skills

Being able to locate information is an essential skill in today's fast-paced society, where new advances in science, health, and technology make it imperative to know how to find the information one needs. It is also relevant to students as they do research and write reports or prepare oral presentations. Although students' need of this skill increases as they pass into the higher grades, it is beneficial to begin information-location training in the lower elementary levels in a simplified form and increase the substance of that training as students get into the upper elementary grades.

Figure 6–23 provides a sequenced enumeration of teaching activities for information-finding skills. As can be seen in the figure, the information-locating skills for the

FIGURE 6–23   Sequence of Information-Location Training

Grade Level	Teaching Activity
Lower Elementary Grades 1 & 2	1. Teach use of picture dictionary—create class dictionary. 2. Teach students to alphabetically file their sight-reading words—each child keeps a file box in which to file his or her words. 3. Teach alphabetical filing of pictures—or create class picture file. 4. Teach parts of book—author, title, illustrator.
Middle Elementary Grades 3 & 4	1. Teach location and use of primary book parts—table of contents, index, glossary, chapter headings, subtitles, maps, graphs, charts, picture clues. 2. Teach how to locate information in dictionary by using guide words. 3. Teach how to locate information in encyclopedia.

Upper Elementary Grades 5 & 6	1. Teach more detail in use of dictionary:
	  a. Locating root word
	  b. Locating derivations of root words
	  c. Using pronunciation key
	2. Teach how to use encyclopedia and other sources such as magazine and newspaper articles to glean information for a written report or oral presentation.

lower-elementary grades (1 and 2) are simplified but form the basis of further training. Since children begin reading in first grade, they are ready to learn how to file information (pictures) alphabetically by the first letter of the object pictured. A class picture file can be created in which pictures related to various activities can be filed over the year. First- and second-graders can also be taught how to file their sight-reading words alphabetically by the first letter of the word. Each child should have his or her own file box and file new words in them. Each day, they go through the file box to see if they can read all the words in it. Children of this age can also be introduced to dictionary skills with a picture dictionary and they can be taught to note the title, author, and illustrator of books they read in class.

In the middle grades, students are ready to learn all the primary parts of content area reading books such as the table of contents, index, glossary, chapter headings, subtitles, maps, graphs, and charts. This training should be integrated into content area instruction. Students can be instructed to look up in the glossary those words relevant to the lesson. They can also be asked to find out what topics they will be covering in a particular chapter by checking the table of contents. When students are asked to use these skills in a way that is related to their lessons, they will see the usefulness of mastering the skills. At this stage, they can also begin using a dictionary to look up word meanings and referring to encyclopedias to find out specific information.

At the upper-grade level, more detailed instruction can be given regarding use of the dictionary and encyclopedia. In fact, at this level, students should start using various reference materials to write reports.

All of this information-finding training can easily be integrated into content area instruction and will form the basis of the students' future capability to succeed in the more rigorous academic requirements of middle school, high school, and college.

Giving Feedback and Reminders to Students

For all of the study skills examined in this chapter, it is very important that the teacher reinforce the students' use of the skills through praise and recognition. Periodically, the teacher should ask the students which study skills they have been using. Also, when making an assignment that lends itself to the use of a particular study skill, the teacher should remind the students that this is a good opportunity to use the note-taking technique or to make self-testing flashcards.

Finally, teachers should point out to students the improvements they have accomplished through the use of study skills. For example, if the teacher sees an improvement on content area tests due to use of self-testing flashcards, the teacher should be sure to mention to the students how the study skill helped them. It is important to make the connection between the particular skill and academic improvement. Through feedback and reminders, the teacher keeps the focus on study skills alive for the whole year.

Summary

Study skill training has been examined in terms of three broad areas: (1) teaching responsibility for learning; (2) teaching, modeling, and reinforcing study strategies and techniques; and (3) providing feedback and reminders to students.

Teaching responsibility for learning should begin in kindergarten and be continuously stressed through all the elementary grades. Four teaching activities were presented as ways of fostering responsibility in the students: (1) discussing responsible behaviors, (2) providing opportunities to practice responsible behaviors, (3) providing academic choices, and (4) giving students feedback through progress reports and self-evaluations.

Related to the second broad area of teaching, modeling and reinforcing study strategies and techniques, study skills were categorized into four areas: (1) memorization techniques, (2) study and comprehension strategies, (3) time management and organization skills, and (4) information-finding skills. Several strategies or techniques in each of the categories were discussed and specific suggestions and examples of how to teach them were given.

Finally, the chapter highlighted the importance of providing reminders to students to use their study skills and giving them feedback on their progress or academic improvement due to their use of the skills. By maintaining the focus on study skills throughout the academic year, the teacher creates a classroom environment that fosters independent learning and self-directed study behaviors in students.

Chapter *7*

Questioning

Now that each of the three methods of instruction has been explored in detail with some mention of the role questioning plays in each one, it will be helpful to examine in more depth this most pervasive of activities. Questioning is an extremely important activity that teachers engage in frequently and continually. It is estimated that teachers ask as many as 300 to 400 questions a day (Levin & Long in Wilen, 1987, p. 13).

The ability to ask good questions—that is, questions that enhance the effectiveness of instruction—must be developed through study and practice. It is an crucial skill to develop, as questioning guides student thinking and determines how students will process material presented to them. Given the impact questioning has on student thinking and learning, Hilda Taba described questioning as "the single most influential teaching act" (Wilen, 1987, 13). Because questioning is such an important teaching act, it will be covered in detail in the following pages.

The examination of questioning will include a consideration of the purposes of questioning, the nature of various questions, approaches to questioning, and effective practices related to questioning. The examination of questioning will include a consideration of the following:

- Purposes of questioning
- The nature of questioning
- Approaches to questioning
- Effective practices related to questioning

Purposes of Questioning

Teachers use questioning to:

- Motivate and interest students.
- Draw out prior knowledge related to a topic.

113

- Stimulate thinking.
- Pace and orient cognitive processing.
- Check for understanding.
- Maximize student involvement.
- Build communication skills.

Questions can be strongly motivating to students, especially when the questions are of a nature that provide students with an opportunity to share personal experiences with the class. These kinds of questions are often asked at the beginning of a lesson or just before reading a passage on a particular topic in order to stimulate interest in that topic. For example, Ms. Chang's class is about to read a story involving cats. Before beginning the reading, Ms. Chang asks the students if any of them have a cat or have known a cat well. She asks: What was the cat like? What were its traits? Has anyone ever known a cat who did something outstanding or amazing? These questions create interest in the topic.

Questions asked before the reading of new material or before a new learning experience also serve another very important function. They activate the students' prior knowledge related to the new material to be covered. Student comprehension of any topic is greatly influenced by how much the student already knows about the topic or something related to it. Therefore, questioning is an excellent practice to help students tap into what they already know about a topic before they read or hear about it. The same questions that Ms. Chang asked about the cats, besides creating interest, remind students of what they already know about cats. Relating what they know about cats and hearing what other students know about cats will enhance the students' understanding of the reading material on cats.

A well-placed question will activate the students' minds and make them think more deeply about the material being presented. Good teachers have always instinctively relied on questioning as a means of activating student thought. An example of using questioning to stimulate student thinking can be found in Mr. Meyer's class where, during instruction about the 13 colonies, he raises the following thought-provoking question: Now that you know some essential facts about each of the 13 colonies, which one would you have preferred to live in and why? In order to answer this question, students must analyze the material they have been given and, at the same time, make value judgments.

Questions can also serve a structural purpose when used both to orient students as to what is of particular importance and to let them consolidate their thoughts at various intervals during their reading or during the teacher's presentation. Mr. Armand's class provides a good example of this as he conducts his lesson on occupations in the community. About one-fourth of the way through his presentation of the material, Mr. Armand asks the following question: What would your community be like without police officers and fire fighters? By doing this, he helps the students understand the important aspects of these occupations as well as allows them to focus on a couple of occupations before the list gets too long. Thus, he has helped the students focus on what is important for them to learn and he has given them an opportunity to absorb the information about these two occupations before moving on to others.

Teachers often ask questions during or after instruction to see whether students are comprehending the concepts or ideas presented in the instruction. It is important for a teacher to ascertain whether the students are "with" him or her at various intervals during the instruction because often students will not let the teacher know when they are confused or just not understanding. After explaining the concept of ecology to her fourth-grade class, for example, Mrs. Snyder asks the students to write, in their own words, a definition of ecology before moving on with the rest of the science lesson in which they will explore further the concepts and phenomena related to ecology. These kinds of checks for understanding can occur in all settings in the classroom, not just during a formal lesson. For example, Mr. Griffin reads to his students every day after lunch. Whenever he reads a passage that contains vocabulary he thinks his students may not be familiar with, he stops reading and asks if anyone knows the word or words he suspects they may not know. Mr. Griffin clears up any misunderstandings or ambiguities before moving on. An observant teacher can often sense when students are not grasping the meaning of what he or she is saying, and, by asking the right question at the right time, he or she can clear up confusion and misunderstanding.

The magic of questions is that they have a way of "pulling the audience in"—that is, getting them more involved in the proceedings of a presentation. Why is this so? For elementary school children, questions hold out the possibility of direct participation in the lesson, which is exciting. As discussed earlier, questions pique students' curiosity and make them think, and thinking about what the teacher is saying heightens their involvement.

Finally, questions both in written and oral form help children build their communication skills. In a discussion, questions get the ball rolling and are an impetus for oral exchanges among students. In these kinds of exchanges, they must listen as well as speak. While answering written questions, students are practicing their writing skills, and by sharing their written responses, they practice reading and listening skills. One of the most important things children can do in school is to learn good communication skills. These skills will serve the student well in all areas of his or her present and adult life. Teachers, therefore, need to make sure that the lessons they design for their students include plenty of opportunities to practice the four communication skills of listening, speaking, reading, and writing. Because of a widespread obsession of teachers for maintaining silence in the classroom, *speaking* has typically been minimized or omitted from classroom practice of communication skills. This is unfortunate, since the ability to speak well is an important skill. Indeed, teachers should provide students with opportunities to speak about what they are learning in the classroom. By planning questions ahead of time, teachers can prepare lessons that give students ample opportunity to practice all their communication skills, including speaking.

Teachers have many good reasons to ask questions. Taking the time and effort to become a skilled questioner is a very wise investment for any teacher.

The Nature of Questions

It is critical to understand that different kinds of questions elicit different thought processes. By understanding the nature of questions—knowing what type of thought processes are activated by a particular question—teachers can provide students with opportunities that invite them to use their minds in different ways. The following discussion will focus on what the different questioning possibilities are, along with examples and descriptions of when best to use various types of questions.

Questions can be characterized according to two general categories: low level/high level and convergent/divergent, which can be further analyzed according to four types: (1) low-level convergent, (2) high-level convergent, (3) low-level divergent, and (4) high-level divergent. In the remainder of this chapter, it will be shown how each of these four types of questions exercise different mental processes in the students and how each type plays a role in accomplishing learning.

Convergent questions require the student to go on a mental search for the single correct answer to the question posed. For example, the teacher asks, "Who was the sixteenth president of the United States?" Given this question, the student would normally have to go through his or her storehouse of information and come up with the single correct response of Abraham Lincoln. Therefore, convergent questions are those to which there is one single correct response. The following are all convergent questions:

1. What is 5×9?
2. What is the state capital of Illinois?
3. Look carefully at this bug. Based on the characteristics you see, is it an arthropod or an arachnid?
4. Identify each of the following as either a screw or a wedge: (a) nail, (b) fork, (c) ax, (d) needle, and (e) winding staircase.
5. A pet store owner has three display windows where he can put animals for people to see as they walk by on the street. He has seven puppies and he puts two in each of the three display windows. How many puppies does he have left over?
6. What is the name of the science that deals with the recovery and study of artifacts, ruins, bones, and fossils remaining from the past?

Divergent questions cause the students' minds to have recourse to the realm of their imaginations and to processes of exploration, where different possible acceptable answers are generated in response to a question. A divergent question, then, is any question for which many different possible answers are appropriate. The following are examples of divergent questions:

1. What is an example of an inclined plane?
2. What are some reasons that living things die?
3. What is the name of an insect?
4. What do you think is the most significant scientific discovery of this century?
5. What is your favorite period of American history?
6. Name a famous person that you admire and tell why you look up to that person.

Divergent questions are very useful in promoting student involvement, as many students can respond to the same question. Other purposes served by divergent questions will be examined in the following discussion of how both convergent and divergent questions coincide with high/low-level qualities.

The other category for characterizing the nature of a question is its level—namely, low level/high level. A *low-level question* is a question that requires only mental recall in order to be answered. In other words, in order to answer a low-level question, the student has only to remember something he or she already knows. The following are some examples of low-level questions:

1. In what ways are all insects alike?
2. What is your birth date?
3. What were some of the forces that influenced the rise of civilization in ancient Greece?
4. Name two foods eaten by homo erectus.
5. List two differences between a predator and a prey.
6. What are the states that make up New England?

A *high-level question* is one that requires more than mere recall to be answered. This means that the student must do some kind of processing of information in order to answer the question. This mental processing could be at various levels of complexity and can include such processes as comparing, describing, inferring, hypothesizing, analyzing, and making judgments or evaluations. The following are examples of high-level questions:

1. Which do you think is a more interesting city: New York or Paris?
2. In your opinion, which animal has a better life: a predator or a prey?
3. Compare the sense of community of the Neanderthals to that of homo erectus.
4. What do you think will happen to this paper clip when I drop it into the cup of water: Will it sink or float?
5. If you were president of the United States, what kinds of changes would you try to bring about for the country?
6. What do you think makes a person turn to a life of crime?

Both low-level and high-level questions are very valuable and effective in promoting student learning; each is appropriate for different purposes. For example, if a teacher wishes to have the class practice times tables for the purpose of memorization, then the low-level question, What is 9×8? is the obvious choice.

Low-level questions are not inferior to high-level questions just because they are called *low level*. The term merely refers to the fact that to answer a low-level question, one needs only to *recall* information. It must be remembered that the information that one can recall makes up the basic material one has to work with in order to engage in higher-level thinking. Low-level thinking (recalling information) is the foundation for higher-level thinking and gives students opportunities to respond to both types of questions.

Basically, one type of thinking is stimulated by low-level questions: recall of information. High-level questions, on the other hand, can stimulate a variety of types of thinking, depending on the question. In order to formulate higher-level questions that foster a specific type of thinking, many people have relied on Bloom's taxonomy (Bloom et al., 1956), which classifies thinking into six categories ranging from the most basic level (recall level, or what has been termed here as low level) to successively more complex levels of cognitive activity. Bloom's taxonomy is hierarchical; that is, the attainment of each level depends on having mastered the knowledge and skills of the lower levels. Figure 7–1 shows the six levels of cognitive activity included in Bloom's taxonomy.

As can be seen from the figure, what Bloom terms the *knowledge* level corresponds to the type of thinking that would be stimulated by low-level questions. The other five levels of cognitive behaviors identified by Bloom—*comprehension, application, analysis, synthesis*, and *evaluation*—all correspond to types of thinking that would be stimulated by high-level questions. In order to use the taxonomy to formulate specific questions meant to stimulate one of the specific levels of thinking, it is useful to list verbs that could be used in the questions to be asked for each level. Therefore, Figure 7–1 also provides a list of verbs associated with each level of cognitive activity and gives sample questions that would encourage the type of thinking required at that level.

Bloom's taxonomy is "the most widely used classification system for analyzing educational objectives in the cognitive domain" (Orlich et al., 1994) and is widely used in connection with writing educational objectives. It is also used as a guide to formulate questions that encourage higher-level thinking, as demonstrated in Figure 7–1. Research indicates that teachers tend to ask primarily low-level questions and that they neglect high-level questions (Durkin in Richardson & Morgan, 1990, p. 214). Thus, students lose the opportunity to learn to think critically. If we want our students to be able to reason soundly, see inconsistencies, identify causal relationships, distinguish fact from opinion, detect propaganda techniques, find creative solutions to tough problems, and make informed decisions, then we must provide them with opportunities to do so in the classroom by asking high-level questions. Students will not automatically become adept at analyzing and evaluating information and situations, and if they are given only low-level questions, their thinking will remain trapped at the "literal" level. It is necessary to have a balance between low-level and high-level questions; that is why teachers not only need to recognize the different levels of thought triggered by different questions but also to *plan* questions for classroom instruction so that both low-level and high-level questions are regularly included in daily lessons. The four types of questions discussed here, with their definitions, are shown in Figure 7–2.

Based on what you now know about low-level and high-level questions, discussion will now go back to the convergent/divergent questions, combining the two categories and identifying both low-level and high-level convergent questions and low-level and high-level divergent questions. To do this, return to the earlier lists of convergent and divergent questions and see if you can find both low-level questions and high-level questions among both groups of questions. As you read each question, take a moment to decide for yourself whether it is high or low level before reading the following discussion of the question.

FIGURE 7–1   Bloom's Taxonomy of Cognitive Behaviors with Verbs and Sample Questions

Level	Verb	Sample Questions
Knowledge Knowledge questions encourage students to recall information in the form that they learned it.	Name Tell List Repeat Count Identify Point to State Remember Recall Write	Name those things you can do to make your home safer during an earthquake. Who remembers why the Sierras are called fault-block mountains? Write the definition of *a fraction in lowest terms.*
Comprehension Comprehension questions encourage students to communicate an idea or phenomenon in a new or different form.	Describe Restate Reword Retell Explain Account for State in your words Translate Change	Explain erosion and how it can be stopped. Describe two clues that show that the continents moved. Describe three types of clouds and the kind of weather related to each type.
Application Application questions encourage students to apply ideas or skills to new situations or to use the knowledge they possess to solve a problem.	Apply Solve Demonstrate Illustrate Use Utilize Dramatize Relate	Imagine you are an archaeologist working at a dig. You find a piece of wood used in building an ancient house. What are two techniques you might use to find out how old it is, and how would you apply them? (From *A Message of Ancient Days*, Houghton Mifflin, 1994.) We have seen how this section in your text is organized in the compare/contrast pattern and how to organize our notes for that pattern. Now find another section in your text that uses the same organizational pattern and make notes that demonstrate the compare/contrast pattern.
Analysis Analysis questions require students to break down something, such as an idea, into its constituent parts or to uncover the unique characteristics of a "thing."	Analyze Break down Uncover Look into Dissect Examine Inspect Study Separate Scrutinize	Examine the written material I have given you and decide which organizational pattern it follows. Study the amphibian in the aquarium at your table. Based on its characteristics and behaviors, decide if it is a frog or a toad.

(continued)

FIGURE 7–1   *(Continued)*

Level	Verb	Sample
Synthesis Synthesis questions encourage students to think in imaginative and/or original ways.	Create Design Build Plan Make Construct Develop Invent	Make up a board game; create rules for playing and winning. Design a logo for our school. Design a floor plan for your ideal room. With your group, create a television commercial for the product on your group table. Invent a sign language.
Evaluation Evaluation questions require students to judge something by determining a standard and comparing it to the standard.	Rank Judge Evaluate Determine Decide Critique Measure Recommend Choose Assess Support	Decide which candidate would make a better president and tell why. Is experimentation on animals justified? Why or why not? Do you think the character in the story did the right thing? Why or why not? Recommend three rules for our classroom.

FIGURE 7–2   Four Types of Questions and Their Definitions

Convergent Questions	Those questions to which there is one single correct response
Divergent Questions	Those questions for which many different possible answers are appropriate
Low-Level Questions	Those questions that require only mental recall in order to be answered
High-Level Questions	Those questions that require thought to be answered

Beginning with the list of convergent questions, Question 1 was: What is 5×9? To determine the level of this question, you need to identify the thought process that must be used to answer it. Assuming that the student who answers this question has memorized the times tables, then he or she would need only recall information in order to give the correct answer. Suppose, however, that the student had not memorized the operation, but understood what the operation of multiplication meant (that is, 5×9 means five groups of nine), and suppose that the student arrived at the answer to the problem by applying that knowledge (understanding what the operation means) and proceeded to add 9 five times. In this case, the student has not relied on recall to answer the question, but rather has applied general knowledge (what the operation of multiplication means) to a particular problem. Thus, the same question can be low level or high level, depending on the mental process the student uses in order to answer the question. For present purposes, assume that the student has memorized the times tables and is able to answer the question from memory; thus, Question 1 is a low-level question.

Question 2 in the convergent group was: What is the state capital of Illinois? Assuming that the teacher expects students to answer the question from memory, this can be classified as a low-level question.

Question 3 was: Look carefully at this bug. Based on the characteristics you see, is it an arthropod or an arachnid? In this case, the student must observe and analyze the characteristics of a particular bug and then apply what he or she knows about the characteristics of arthropods and arachnids in order to place the bug in the correct class of animals. Therefore, the student uses the mental processes of observation, analysis, and application, and so, Question 3 is a high-level question.

Question 4 was: Identify each of the following as either a screw or a wedge: (a) nail, (b) fork, (c) ax, (d) needle, and (e) winding staircase. This is also a high-level question for the same reason as given for Question 3. That is, the student must use information he or she has acquired regarding the nature of a screw and a wedge, analyze the nature of each of the objects in the list, and determine whether its characteristics qualify it to be classified as a screw or a wedge. Therefore, the student has to observe characteristics of a new set of objects, analyze these characteristics, and apply his or her knowledge of the qualities of screws and wedges to each object. Obviously, this is a higher-level question requiring several mental processes in addition to recall.

Question 5 was: A pet store owner has three display windows where he can put animals for people to see as they walk by on the street. He has seven puppies and he puts two in each of the three display windows. How many puppies does he have left over? This question is typical of word problems students encounter in their basal math texts. In order to solve this problem, the student must determine what is the crucial information and arrange these facts in a specific kind of relationship to each other— that is, determine how they fit into a mathematical operation. The student knows that two puppies will go into each of the three windows, which can be represented by $2 \times 3 = 6$. The student also knows that there was a total of seven puppies and that he or she has accounted for six of them, which is represented by $7 - 6 = 1$. What the student has done is taken information given to him or her on the abstract level and transformed it to the representational level in order to do the mathematical operations involved. The student could also have solved the problem by making a drawing of three windows with two puppies in each, counted the total puppies in the windows, and subtracted these from the original total of seven. In that case, also, the student has made a representational form of the information so that he or she can understand how the facts relate to each other. The student has started with basic facts, analyzed them to determine the essential from the unessential, transformed the essential facts from an abstract to a representational form, and then proceeded to carry out the mathematical operation involved. The student has thereby exercised mental processes above and beyond recall, and so Question 5 is a high-level convergent question.

Question 6 was: What is the name of the science that deals with the recovery and study of artifacts, ruins, bones, and fossils remaining from the past? This question could be posed either before instruction to determine what the students already know, during instruction to determine if the students are attending to the pertinent information, or after instruction to see if the students have comprehended and absorbed the information. In each of the cases, the students would be answering the question from memory. Either they can recall the word *archeology* or they cannot; therefore, the question is a low-level convergent question.

Low-level convergent questions are the types of questions asked most frequently during a commonly used method of questioning called *recitation*. Here, the teacher asks recall questions in rapid succession, allowing for only very quick exchanges between teacher and student for the purpose of determining whether students have mastered the material of a lesson. Recitation helps students rehearse material they have studied, thus increasing their ability to remember it. Figure 7–3 provides a summary of the low/high-level classification of the convergent questions.

Now that you have looked at convergent (one correct answer) questions in terms of their level (high or low), discussion will move to the divergent questions, or those for which many different answers are appropriate, and determining their nature in terms of high or low level. Again, it is suggested that, after reading each question, you take a moment to make your own judgment before continuing to read the analysis of the question.

FIGURE 7–3   Convergent Questions: Low Level and High Level

Low-Level Convergent Questions	*High-Level Convergent Questions*
1. What is 5×9? 2. What is the state capital of Illinois?	1. Look at this bug carefully. Based on its characteristics, is it an arthropod or an arachnid? 2. Identify each of the following as a screw or a wedge: (a) nail, (b) fork, (c) ax, (d) needle, and (e) winding staircase. 3. A pet store owner has three display windows where he can put animals for people to see as they walk by on the street. He has seven puppies and he puts two in each of the three display windows. How many puppies does he have left over?

Divergent Question 1 was: What is an example of an inclined plane? This question could be high level or low level, depending on the process the student goes through to answer it. For example, if the student has just read about inclined planes in the science text, remembers that the text mentioned that a staircase is an inclined plane, and thus volunteers *staircase* as an answer to the question, the student is using recall to answer the question. Thus, it is a low-level question. Supposing, however, that the student thinks back to the science text and remembers the properties of an inclined plane, looks around the room and sees an object that he or she determines has those properties, and then concludes that the object is an inclined plane. The student has then applied the information about the inclined plane to a new situation, and, in that case, the question is a high-level question. Remember, a high-level question is any question that requires more than recall to be answered. High-level questions range a good deal in their level of complexity or difficulty, so even as a high-level question, Question 1 is still a fairly simple one.

Question 2 was: What are some reasons that living things die? This would most likely be answered from memory, either by recalling the reasons read in the text or a personal experience, such as the death of a pet. Therefore, it is classified as a low-level question.

Question 3 was: What is the name of an insect? Again, this is a low-level divergent question because students would use recall of previously learned information to answer the question.

Question 4 was: What do you think is the most significant scientific discovery of this century? This question requires the student to engage in several mental processes. First, the student must recall several scientific discoveries, then analyze them in terms of their effects, and, finally, evaluate those effects in terms of their importance. This requires a fairly involved level of thinking; thus, Question 4 is a high-level one.

Question 5 was: What is your favorite period of American history? The student is asked to recall several periods in American history, compare them in terms of their characteristics, and then make a judgment as to which he or she most prefers. In this case, the question is a high-level question. However, this question lends itself easily to being *either* high or low level because there are students who are experts of a certain period of history, such as Civil War buffs, and therefore do not have to think for a second about their response to this question. Again, the level of the question is determined by the process the student engages in to answer it.

Question 6 was: Name a famous person that you admire and tell why you look up to that person. This requires the student to recall someone that he or she admires and then to analyze what it is about the person that is admirable. Thus, it is a high-level question because it requires the student to analyze a person's traits and/or actions and then to evaluate them. Figure 7–4 provides a quick overview of how these divergent questions were classified.

By knowing the nature of a question, a teacher can purposefully use questions to engage the students' minds in various kinds of thought processes. It is important not only to understand what kinds of questions trigger what kinds of thought processes but also to use that knowledge to plan lessons that will include a balance of low-level/high-level and convergent/divergent questions. This way, the teacher can be sure that the

FIGURE 7–4 Divergent Questions: Low Level and High Level

Low-Level Divergent Questions	*High-Level Divergent Questions*
1. What is an example of an inclined plane (answered from memory)? 2. What are some reasons that living things die? 3. What is the name of a type of insect?	1. What is an example of an inclined plane (answered by applying characteristics to an object)? 2. What do you think is the most significant scientific discovery of this century? 3. What is your favorite period of American history? Why have you chosen this period? 4. Name a famous person that you admire and tell why you look up to him or her. 5. Read this newspaper article and create as many interesting titles for it as you can. 6. Should Christopher Columbus be regarded as a great man despite the fact that his cruel policies resulted in complete genocide of the Arawoks in Haiti?

students are getting the opportunity to learn to think in various ways, such as to analyze, solve problems, compare and contrast, evaluate, describe, interpret, and apply principles. Figure 7–5 depicts the four types of questions possible by combining the two categories that make up the nature of questions.

FIGURE 7–5 Four Types of Questions and Thought Processes Elicited

Type of Question	*Thought Processes Elicited*
1. Low-level convergent: Example: What is 5×9?	Recall, attention to detail
2. High-level convergent: Example: Look carefully at this bug. Based on its characteristics, is it an arthropod or an arachnid?	Problem solving, using clues to solve a mystery, classification, categorization, using examples and nonexamples to identify a concept, analysis, observation
3. Low-level divergent: Example: What are some reasons that living things die?	Recall, attention to detail
4. High-level convergent: Example: What do you think is the most significant scientific discovery of this century? If you could invent anything, what do you think would help humankind the most?	Recall, analysis, synthesis, evaluation, observation

Approaches to Questioning

This section will discuss four different approaches to questioning that a teacher can use to enhance the success and quality of student responses. The four approaches are (1) wait time, (2) redirection, (3) prompting, and (4) probing. Each will be discussed in terms of its definition, purpose, and results.

Wait Time

Wait time is the amount of time the teacher waits for the student to answer a question before redirecting the question to another student or answering it directly. It is the amount of time, then, that the teacher gives the student to begin answering the question. Mary Budd Rowe (Wilen, 1987, p. 95), who has done major research in this area, has given a further analysis, calling it "wait time 1." Her "wait time 2" is the amount of time a teacher waits for further explanation or elaboration once the student has given an answer to the question. For both wait time 1 and wait time 2, teachers typically allow one second or less.

Simply by increasing wait time 1 and 2 to three seconds or more, teachers can greatly enhance student responses, causing replies to be longer and richer. The purpose of using wait time, then, is to enable students to answer more questions and to give fuller, richer answers.

According to Rowe, employing wait time 1 and 2 is effective at all grade levels and the resulting benefits are many. Some of these benefits include:

1. The length of student responses is increased 300 to 400 percent.
2. Students increase their use of evidence, or of logic based on evidence, to support their statements.
3. The failure to respond to questions decreases.
4. The necessity for disciplinary measures decreases.
5. The variety of students participating in discussions increases.
6. Students gain confidence in their ability to construct responses to questions.

Furthermore, it is the personal experience of the authors that wait time not only increases student participation in discussion but it also builds a sense of community in which students are willing to share personal concerns as they arise in relation to the topic under discussion. This is abundantly illustrated in the following anecdote.

> Ms. Berman has decided systematically to employ wait time during her small-group reading time in her kindergarten class. She works with each group of seven to eight students for a period of 20 minutes, during which time she reads fairy tales to them and asks them questions related to the plot or characters in the stories. She has two rules for herself (which she follows faithfully) regarding how she conducts her questioning. First, she makes sure that she calls on all students, even those whom she perceives as less willing or able to answer questions. Second, when she asks a question, she counts six seconds before prompting the student or redirecting the question to another student.

It took Ms. Berman's students a few sessions to get used to the long pauses after her questions, especially when she called on those students who typically did not respond in the hopes that they would be soon passed over. Although at first there were long and what seemed to be awkward silences, the students soon began to respond more eagerly, apparently beginning to enjoy interchanges with Ms. Berman and each other.

What is more, Ms. Berman was pleased to see the changes in her students, who not only became eager to respond but also began to challenge each other's responses and to have free and heated debates regarding the characters or events in the stories. Ms. Berman speculated that the students perceived that she really cared to hear their answers and that she, in fact, fully expected them to answer. The students gained confidence in their ability to respond, became more interested in hearing each other's responses, and began to talk to each other even without waiting for Ms. Berman's next question. As a sense of sharing and community began to build, a remarkable incident occurred.

While discussing the plight of the princess in the story of Rumpelstiltskin, who, faced with the prospect of giving up her first child as she had promised, pleaded desperately with Rumpelstiltskin to release her from her promise, one of the students piped up very seriously with, "I don't think that my mother loved me when I was a baby." Ms. Berman, totally taken aback, asked, "What makes you think that?" The student, a child to whom approval seemed to be very important, had taken note of the determination of the princess in the story to keep her baby daughter at all costs, and she compared it with her own mother who, when the student was a baby, had given her over to the grandmother for several years after her marriage broke up. The student had harbored feelings of rejection for a long time and was finally able to voice them because of the sense of community that had developed in her reading group.

By using wait time in the small groups, Ms. Berman had slowed down the whole teacher/student exchange pattern, and it had evolved into a shared adventure rather than "I am teaching you" kind of activity. So, the student felt free to reveal something that was deeply troubling her. Ms. Berman was then able to confer with the school counselor and the mother of the child to help the mother understand what her daughter was going through and to help her find ways to reassure the daughter that she did, indeed, love her daughter very much. Ms. Berman got much more than she had bargained for when she began her experiment with wait time. She was, though, thoroughly convinced of the value of the technique and the many benefits that resulted from it as she observed affective as well as cognitive gains in her students.

Redirection

Redirection of questions refers to the technique of asking the same open-ended (divergent) question to several students in a sequence uninterrupted by the teacher's comments. Such questions as What is your favorite color? Who do you think is the single most influential political figure in American politics today? and What can you tell me about cats? are the kinds of questions that can be asked of several students. Because there is no one right answer, each student who is called on can make a different contribution from that of the previous students.

By redirecting questions, the teacher can include more students in direct participation in the lesson than would otherwise be possible. For example, if a teacher asks the class, What type of animal is a cat? and the first student called on responds that it is a mammal, the exchange has ended with the active participation of only one student. However, if the teacher phrases the question as What can you tell me about cats? then the teacher can call on six or seven students, all of whom can make a unique comment. By the time the exchange is over, quite a few students will have actively participated in it. The purpose of redirection, then, is to engage the active participation of several or many students at a time in the lesson. To use the technique properly, it is important that the teacher not comment on or make evaluative statements regarding various students' responses. Each student response is accepted neutrally as a contribution to the discussion as the teacher continues to redirect the question.

The result of the redirection of questions is that students become more attentive and involved in the lesson. They realize that they will be called on more frequently and therefore have a greater chance to participate directly in the lesson. The types of questions used in redirection are not threatening because many different answers are appropriate. Thus, another result of redirection is that students gain confidence in their ability to answer questions. The use of question redirection to increase student interest and participation in classroom instruction is highly recommended.

Prompting

Prompting is the technique of leading a student to the correct answer of a convergent or divergent question by a hint or a series of hints that provide the student with the means eventually to verbalize the correct answer. Prompting is used when the student has given an incorrect answer to a question or simply says, "I don't know."

The purpose of prompting is to guide the student to the correct response to a question, as opposed to calling on another student to help out the first student. Many times teachers do not realize the fragility of a student's confidence or willingness to answer a question for fear of being wrong and looking foolish in front of the other students. After one or two such experiences, many students will no longer take the risk of venturing an educated guess to a teacher's question, and will only be willing to answer questions to which they are absolutely sure they have the correct answer. This discourages students from thinking of possibilities and hypothesizing answers and, of course, from sharing their "guesses" with the class. Students often need to be encouraged to take risks and make educated guesses, thus learning how to use various thought processes to find answers to questions and problems. Prompting is a way to help students do this.

Consider the following exchange observed by the authors in a fourth-grade social studies lesson. Ms. P., a student teacher, makes the following observation to her students:

Ms. P.: Sacramento has been the state capital of California since 1854. Before that, between 1850 and 1854, five other cities—Monterey, San Jose, Vallejo, Benicia, and San Francisco—served as temporary capitals. If you'll notice, all of these cities are in the northern part of the state. Why do you think that all of the cities that were chosen to be capitals were in the northern part of the state? Steve?

Steve: Because the northern part of the state is closer to Washington, DC, which is the capital of the whole country?

Ms. P.: No, I'm afraid you're really way off there. Anybody else have an idea? Melissa?

Instead of moving on to the next student, leaving Steve with a definite taste of failure in his mouth, which is likely to dampen his enthusiasm for volunteering an educated guess again, Ms. P. could have prompted Steve, or given him hints to lead him to the correct answer. The interchange could have gone like this:

Ms. P.: Why do you think that all of the cities that were chosen to be capitals were in the northern part of the state? Steve?

Steve: Because the northern part of the state is closer to Washington, DC, which is the capital of the whole country?

Ms. P.: I see your reasoning—that distance to the national capital played an influential part. However, remember that California was quite cut off from the rest of the nation in the 1850s. Can you think of a reason that has to do with the characteristics of the state itself?

Steve: Not really.

Ms. P.: When California became a state in 1850, were there more Californians or Americans living in the state?

Steve: There were more Americans.

Ms. P.: And where did the Americans live, for the most part, in the northern or southern part of the state?

Steve: In the northern part of the state.

Ms. P.: So where was the greatest concentration of population at that time, in the south or the north?

Steve: In the northern part of the state. Oh, I see, so they made the state capitals where more people lived, and in the southern part mostly there were big rancheros and not so many people or cities.

Ms. P.: That's right.

By providing hints in a series of questions, Ms. P. has led Steve to the correct answer, which he then is able to verbalize himself. This process helps build Steve's confidence in his ability to answer questions and it allows Ms. P. to model for Steve and the whole class how logically to think through an answer to a question by considering the relevant circumstances.

Some teachers find prompting a difficult skill to acquire because one cannot plan the "hint" questions ahead of time; rather, one has to think on one's feet, so to speak, in order to do prompting. However, many opportunities will present themselves to the teacher to practice the skill, as all teachers encounter the incorrect answer or the "I don't knows" frequently enough. With practice and persistence, it is possible to master this very useful questioning technique. It is perhaps the most subtle and complete form of education.

Probing

Probing is a technique to get a student to elaborate on an incomplete or minimal response to a question. In this case, the student gives a correct but very minimal answer and the teacher seeks to draw more information out of the student. Questions such as Why do you think that? or Could you tell us a little more? are frequently used when the teacher suspects that the student is actually able to contribute more information than he or she has chosen to mention. Following is an example of probing:

Teacher: During the California Gold Rush, many new mining towns sprang up very quickly near the mining sites. What were these mining towns like? Jerry?

Jerry: They were crowded.

Teacher: What else can you tell us about them?

Jerry: There was a lot of crime, like stealing and fighting.

Teacher: How did the miners deal with the crime problem?

Jerry: They formed vigilante groups and took law into their own hands. They went out and took people that they thought were guilty and hanged them. Sometimes those people that got hanged weren't guilty.

Teacher: Anything else you can tell us?

Jerry: Well, it was not too much fun to live in a mining town. The buildings were shabby and there were no sidewalks or streets, and when it rained everything turned to mud and you couldn't walk in it without sinking really deep. And most people never did find the gold, so there were a lot of depressed people walking around.

Teacher: Given Jerry's description of a mining town, how many of you think you would have chosen to join the Gold Rush if you had lived at that time?

Probing is a means of getting students to elaborate on their initial responses to questions, particularly when the initial response to a question has been minimal. Because of the common practice of recitation (rapid-fire questioning with short-answer responses expected), many students are conditioned to the short-answer response and may not even respond in complete sentences. When the teacher regularly uses probing, students will begin to respond in a more complete manner on their own.

Figure 7–6 provides an overview of the four approaches to questioning and includes a definition of each approach. Thus far, discussion has focused on the purposes of questioning, the nature of questions, and the approaches to questioning. Next, several effective practices related to questioning will be considered.

Effective Practices Related to Questioning

Questioning is one of the most frequently practiced teaching activities in elementary classrooms today. Gall (1970, pp. 40, 707–721) stated that elementary teachers typically ask about 150 questions per hour in science and social studies lessons. According to Dunkin and Biddle (1974), questions constitute one-tenth to one-sixth of all classroom interaction time. Teachers use questioning with great frequency, but frequency does not guarantee effectiveness. In order for questioning to be effective—that is, to enhance student learning—several guidelines must be followed. These guidelines include:

1. *Plan* the questions that are to be asked during a lesson.
2. *Clarify* the purpose of questions.
3. Use a *balanced combination* of low/high convergent/divergent questions.

Planning Questions

Although teachers do make substantial use of questioning in their instruction, they tend to overemphasize low-level, or recall, questions. This tendency denies students the opportunity to practice higher-level thinking skills. By planning questions ahead of time, the teacher can ensure that there will be a balance of different types of questions asked of the students. Planning a variety of types of questions (i.e., low/high level and convergent/divergent) will engage students in various levels and types of thinking in their responses.

FIGURE 7–6   Four Approaches to Questioning

Wait Time:	The amount of time the teacher waits for the student to answer a question before he or she directs the question to someone else or answers it directly
Redirection of Questions:	The technique of asking the same open-ended question to several students in a sequence uninterrupted by the teacher's comments
Prompting:	The technique of leading a student to the correct answer by a hint or a series of hints that provide the students with the means eventually to verbalize the correct answer
Probing:	The technique to get a student to elaborate on his or her own incomplete or minimal response to a question

A very good resource and aid for teachers who wish to become skilled at writing questions that require different types of thought processes is a book called *Classroom Questions: What Kinds?* by Norris M. Sanders (1966). Sanders uses Bloom's taxonomy as a basis for identifying seven categories of thinking—memory, translation, interpretation, application, analysis, synthesis, and evaluation—and proceeds to demonstrate questioning for the various levels.

Clarifying Purpose of Questions

Various types of questions are valuable for different reasons. For example, low-level questions serve several important functions: They help students remember important facts, they help students acquire a body of knowledge deemed necessary by society, and, most importantly, they help students acquire knowledge that will serve as the building blocks for any kind of higher-level thinking. At various times, the teacher's instructional aims will be related to one or all of these purposes. It is during planning that the teacher identifies the objectives of a lesson and can thus design questions in accordance with those objectives. Of course, in any one lesson or unit of instruction the teacher will have identified several purposes or types of objectives and thus will include more than just one type of question in the lesson. In fact, for most lessons (not including skills drills), the teacher will deliberately plan the questions so there is a balance of types of questions.

Balancing Types of Questions

Teachers need to incorporate both low and high, convergent and divergent questions into unit plans and daily lessons. This way, the teacher gives the students an opportunity to engage in and practice various types and levels of thinking. Without attention to this guideline, there is a tendency to concentrate on low-level questions to the exclusion of high-level questions. This deprives students of the chance to become independent thinkers, able to evaluate information critically and make thoughtful decisions. It is, of course, this very type of individual, one able to think and reason so as to make informed decisions, that is needed in a democratic society. It is imperative that students acquire these important thinking skills in school. Low-level questions are also important because we want our students to acquire information—that is, facts, concepts, and generalizations—so that they will have a storehouse of knowledge within. This acquired knowledge provides the foundation for their critical thinking and creative problem solving. Both are important; a balance is needed.

This is also true for convergent and divergent questions. Convergent questions are needed to help students sharpen their focus and attention to detail and accuracy, whereas divergent questions help students delve into imagination and creativity while at the same time build their confidence. By using a balanced combination of low/high level and convergent/divergent questions in classroom instruction, the teacher can provide the students with opportunities to acquire knowledge and various types of thinking skills.

Summary

Because questioning is such a vital teaching skill, it has been covered in some detail in this chapter. There are four broad areas related to questions: (1) the purposes of questioning, (2) the nature of questions, (3) approaches to questioning, and (4) effective practices related to questioning.

In the discussion of the purposes of questioning, the following were described as worthy purposes of questioning: (1) to motivate and interest students, (2) to draw out prior knowledge related to a topic, (3) to stimulate thinking, (4) to pace and orient cognitive processing, (5) to check for understanding, (6) to maximize student involvement, and (7) to build communication skills.

Regarding the nature of questions, four basic types of questions were identified: low-level cognitive, high-level cognitive, low-level divergent, and high-level divergent (based on combining the two broad categories of low/high level and convergent/divergent). Low- and high-level questions are distinguished by the level of thinking required to answer them. Low level requires recall alone; high level requires mental processing of information. Convergent/divergent questions are distinguished by the specificity of the answer required. Convergent questions require one correct answer, whereas divergent questions are more open ended and can be correctly answered in several or many different ways. The four types of questions were related to the types of thinking they foster during classroom instruction.

In the discussion on approaches to questioning, four useful approaches designed to enhance the quality of student responses were described: (1) wait time, (2) redirection, (3) prompting, and (4) probing. Wait time is the amount of time the teacher waits for the student to answer a question before moving on to another student. Typically, wait time is one second or less; however, there are numerous benefits of increasing wait time to three seconds or more. These include an increase in length of student responses, an increase in student use of logic and reasoning, a decrease in failure to answer questions, a decrease in the necessity of disciplinary measures, an increase in the variety of students participating in discussions, and an increase in student self-confidence.

Redirection of questions is the technique of asking the same question to several students in a sequence uninterrupted by the teacher's comments. The benefit of question redirection is an increase in the number of students participating directly during instruction time.

Prompting is the technique of leading a student to the correct answer to a question by giving him or her a hint or series of hints that enable him or her eventually to verbalize the correct answer. Prompting is a valuable questioning skill because it allows the teacher to enable the student to experience success rather than failure in responding to the question and, at the same time, it models a thinking process for the students.

Finally, probing is a technique to get students to elaborate on incomplete answers to questions. This questioning technique has the effect of teaching students to give fuller, more thoughtful responses to questions.

In the general discussion regarding effective practices related to questioning, the importance of planning questions ahead of time, clarifying the purposes of questions, and using a balance of high- and low-level, and convergent/divergent questions were emphasized.

Teachers who use questioning skills effectively will greatly enhance student learning. Questions determine how students interpret and evaluate information, events, and situations, as well as determine their willingness and ability to solve problems with imagination and creativity. Different questions foster different types of thought processes, and the effective teacher must know what the types of questions are and what type of thinking they promote. It is the hope of the authors that aspiring teachers and those already practicing will devote the time and study needed to learn this most valuable teaching skill.

C h a p t e r 8

Technology for Delivering Instruction

The goal of classroom instruction is to promote learning. As noted in the discussion of learning in Chapter 1, learning cannot even begin to take place if students are not paying attention to or involved in your lesson activities. With this in mind, this chapter will examine the increasingly important and changing role technology is playing in the elementary school classroom. To do this in a way that is both informative and practical, technology for delivering instruction will be looked at from three perspectives:

- Types of technology (hardware and software) available for delivering instruction
- Productive uses of technology in the classroom
- Setting up the classroom to facilitate the use of technology

Types of Technology Available for Delivering Instruction

Sometimes you will hear the word *multimedia* as a general reference in regard to technology used to aid instruction. The reason for this is straightforward: Multimedia simply means the presentation of material through any combination of media such as video, computer, spoken word, written word, still images, and various hands-on materials. The beauty and effectiveness of multimedia for delivering instruction is that it brings different students' sensory modes into play. Remember, learning starts with sensory input, which is then transformed into memory, understanding, and creative thought by that master sense, the mind. The more vivid and varied the sensory input, the greater the likelihood that memory, understanding, and creative thought (i.e., learning) will occur. Intelligent use of technology provides you with the means for delivering and enriching instruction so as to achieve such high-quality and varied sensory input.

In Figures 8–1 and 8–2, the various types of technology are listed along with brief descriptions of their main characteristics. Notice that Figure 8–1 looks at hardware and Figure 8–2 looks at software. These are the two categories into which all technology is divided. The simplest way to understand these two terms is that *hardware* is the mechanical devices that are needed to access the instructional material contained on the *software*. For example, you need a computer monitor, hard drive, and keyboard to

FIGURE 8–1   Types of Technology: Hardware

Hardware	Main Characteristics
Computer	• Processes input data • Provides output on screen • Transfers output onto paper
Laserdisc (Videodisc) Player	• Plays laserdiscs (looks like VCR player) • Can be operated by remote control • Can be operated by bar code reader • Can be set up to be controlled via computer
CD-ROM Player (Drive)	• Plays CD-ROM disks • Transfers data from CD-ROM disk to computer • Can be built into a computer as an all-in-one design or be external as a peripheral device
Modem	• Links computers through phone lines • Translates computer (digital) and phone (analog) language in both directions • Creates, endless possibilities for networking and accessing information on the Internet
LCD Panel	• Projects material from computer screen onto a large screen • Does not require any software and is solely a projection/viewing device • Provides color and black and white images
Scanner	• An external device from a computer • Allows for taking pictures outside the computer and then sending these images back through the computer • Solely for scanning and transferring two-dimensional (i.e., flat) images
Digital Camera	• Same as a scanner except that it can just as well take pictures of three-dimensional objects
VCR	• Plays video tapes
Cassette Tape Recorder (Audio)	• Plays audio cassette tapes

FIGURE 8–2   Types of Technology: Software

Software	Main Characteristics
Word Processing	• A tool for creating, editing, formatting, and printing documents • Keyboard is used to carry out all the functions • Can be integrated with graphic and multimedia (see below)
Integrated Word Processing	• Includes *data bases* for organizing, sorting, depositing, and retrieving sets of information • Includes *spreadsheet* for organizing information, especially where numerical calculations are needed • Includes communication for two-way networking with other computers through a modem
Desktop Publishing	• Does all functions of word-processing software, but, by using special page layout software (several on the market), can achieve a professional typeset look (i.e., with a high-quality printer)
CD-ROM (Compact Disk Read Only Memory)	• Stores information digitally, allowing for hundreds of times more information to be on one disk than can be fit on a typical floppy disk (e.g., a 20-volume encyclopedia on one disk) • Has capability for interactions and multimedia presentation of material through a CD-ROM drive
Laserdisc (Videodisc)	• A compact disc that holds large amounts of various forms of information (e.g., music, movies, live recordings) • Allows for accessing information by chapter and frame or by time (widely used in schools) • Information is retrieved by using a bar-code reader, remote control, or special software
Multimedia	• Computer presentation of video, animation, or sound • Often educational multimedia software is interactive in that students can control what they see, hear, and do • Specially designed software and a more powerful computer (i.e., greater memory and hard disk storage) is necessary
Hypermedia	• Mainly used for creating multimedia projects • Hypermedia software allows information to be reviewed and created in a nonlinear format • Computer must be hooked up with other hardware (e.g., CD-ROM and laserdisc) to achieve multimedia effect (sometimes referred to as *tutor program*)
CAI (Computer-Assisted Instruction)	• Programs used for practicing and drilling skills that have already been taught • Designed for independent learning • Can be a drill and practice simulation, or game format

access information from a program (software) concerning the 13 original colonies. What you want to do is become increasingly conversant with which types of hardware play various types of software and what the different instructional benefits are from these various technologies.

Productive Uses of Technology in the Classroom

Given the numerous forms of hardware and software available, the task is to figure out how to utilize this technology in ways that increase and enrich student learning. In essence, there are three main ways technology can be used for instruction:

1. *Resource Use:* Accessing a wealth of information
2. *Activity Use:* Individual or small-group activities and teacher presentations
3. *Skills Use:* Personally paced skills practice

Figure 8–3 presents a matrix on which the various types of software are cross-referenced according to their resource, activity, or skills use for instruction (as indicated by the words *Primary Use*). Examples and suggestions are also provided to demonstrate the practical use of each type of software.

In addition to an instructional focus, technology can also be helpful in managing the enormous amount of paperwork and information that will come your way as you run your classroom program. Software used for such purposes is often referred to as *teacher tools*. For example, Grade Machine, created by Misty City Software, allows you to computerize your entire grading system and maintain readily accessible student and class progress files.

Setting Up the Classroom to Facilitate Technology Use

Described here are three basic orientations for designing your classroom to facilitate technology-delivered instruction. Following these descriptions, Figures 8–4, 8–5, and 8–6 are presented to show ways you can set up your classroom, depending on which orientation you wish to emphasize. The broken lines in these figures indicate paths for easily flowing into the other computer uses (i.e., orientations) when needed.

1. *Presentation Orientation:* Using technology for student and teacher class presentations and cooperative learning activities. The emphasis here is on group dynamics and needs for viewing and interacting with the material presented.
2. *Work Station Orientation:* Using technology for individual research, skills practice, and long-term projects. The emphasis here is on individual work in the practice or exploration of various skills, concepts, or information.
3. *Information Management Orientation:* Using technology for maintaining grading and other related information and for generating correspondence and curriculum materials (e.g,. tests, activity directions, etc.). The emphasis here is on helping you

FIGURE 8–3   Matrix of Technology Uses for Instruction

Types of Software	Resource/ Reference Use	Activity Use	Basic Skills Use	Examples/Suggestions
Word Processing	--	Primary Use	--	• Students use word processing in a Writer's Workshop to create writing samples, including the editing, proofing, and revising process.
Integrated Word Processing • Data base • Spreadsheet • Communication	 Primary Use -- --	 -- Primary Use Primary Use	 -- -- --	• Teacher and students keep track of key demographics for selected countries in the world. • Students work with basic algebraic principles by charting and calculating batting averages of selected star baseball players. • Students become electronic pen-pals with students in another school, state, or country.
Desktop Publishing	--	Primary Use	--	• Students engage in a whole-class project to create a period newspaper from the Civil War era.
CD-ROM	Primary Use	--	--	• Students do research by reading, listening, and watching information about selected world leaders of the twentieth century in the Macmillan Dictionary for Children CD (Resource use). • Students interact with literature they are reading by creating word lists, adding their voices in reaction to text, and keeping running notes (Activity use).
Laserdisc	Primary Use	Primary Use	--	• Students work on a research project in the classroom interactive laserdisc library accessing photos, films, and video clips concerning the Gold Rush (Resource/ Reference use). • The teacher enriches presentation of a new topic by strategically accessing laserdisc material at certain points in the lesson (Activity use).
Multimedia and Hypermedia	--	Primary Use	--	• Students create a group multimedia project containing a variety of photos, graphics, and film footage to bring alive their culminating class presentation on Dr. Martin Luther King, Jr.
Computer-Assisted Instruction (CAI) • Drill • Simulation • Game	-- 	 Primary Use Primary Use	-- Primary Use 	• Students work on two-digit multiplication drill and practice exercises using a math tutorial software program. • Students are placed in the driver's seat of a covered wagon as they problem solve their way across the frontier in search of gold. • Students reinforce their grasp of phonics skills by playing Clue in on Phonics, a detective game approach created by GAMCO.

FIGURE 8–4   One-Computer Classroom with a Presentation Orientation

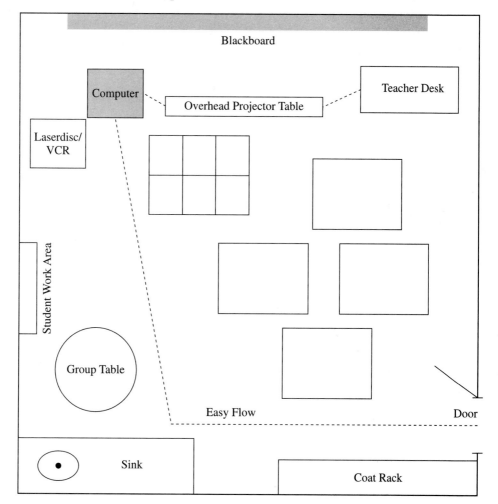

Source: From #517—*Managing Technology in the Classroom.* Published by Teacher Created Materials, Inc., © 1995. Reproduced by permission.

create and organize the myriads of information that normally have to be dealt with in the elementary classroom.

If you are fortunate enough to be teaching in a school that provides you with several computers for your classroom, then the design shown in Figure 8–7 for a classroom computer pod can be useful. With a classroom computer pod, you can do all the things that are possible in a one-computer classroom plus provide students with more

FIGURE 8–5   One-Computer Classroom with a Work Station Orientation

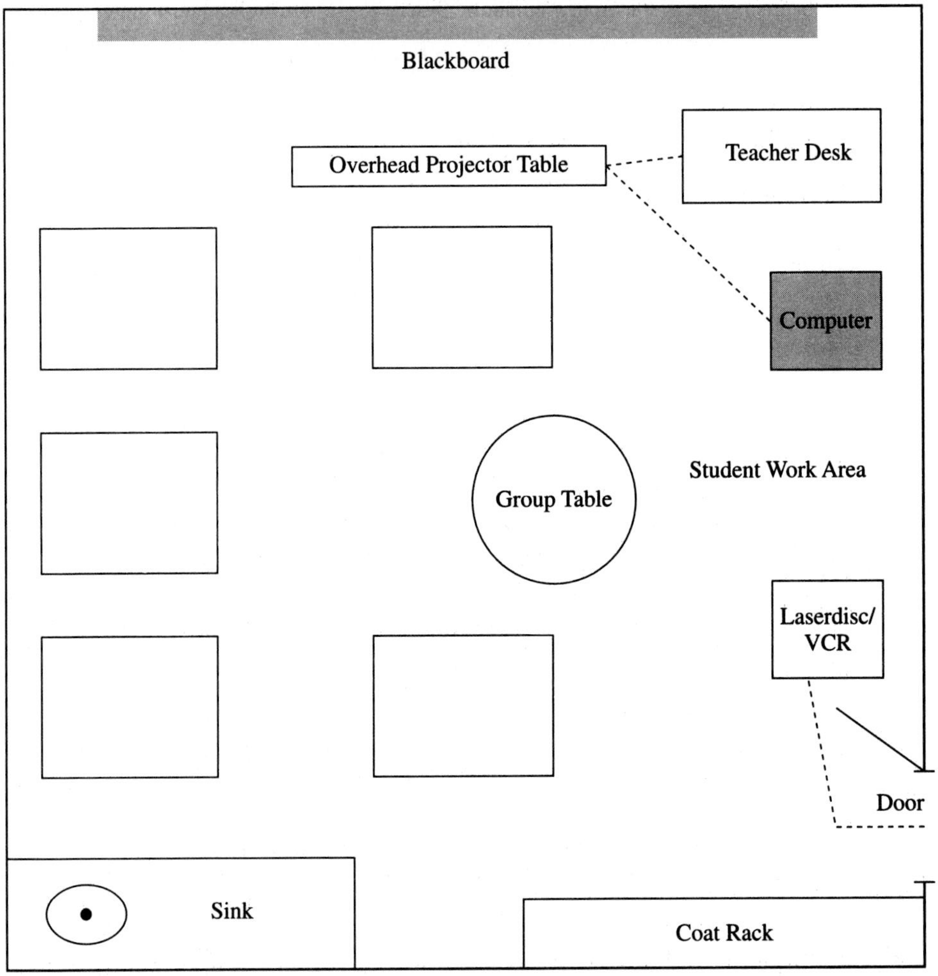

Source: From #517—*Managing Technology in the Classroom.* Published by Teacher Created Materials, Inc., © 1995. Reproduced by permission.

opportunities to spend time on the computer for skill building, problem solving, research, and individual or group projects.

Final Note on Using Technology for Delivering Instruction

From the preceding discussion and from an increasing number of elementary teachers' experiences, it is easy to recognize the potential of various types of technology for enriching instruction and promoting student learning. Chris Dede, an expert on educa-

FIGURE 8–6   One-Computer Classroom with an Information Management Orientation

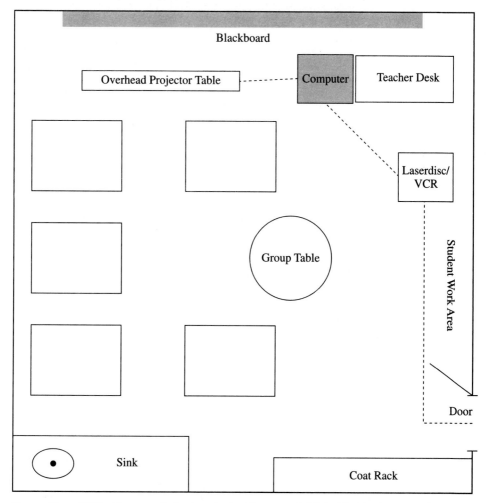

Source: From #517—*Managing Technology in the Classroom.* Published by Teacher Created Materials, Inc., © 1995. Reproduced by permission.

tional technology, has cautioned that new technologies, although opening vast vistas of information, will be effective only if they are used to support effective models of teaching and learning.

> *Classrooms right now are not information-poor environments. Many teachers feel overwhelmed by how much information they're already supposed to convey. If anything, the curriculum is too crowded now. We teach a wide array of things very superficially through presentation, which we then have to reteach a couple of years later because students don't remember it…. Again, the ques-*

FIGURE 8–7   Classroom Computer Pod

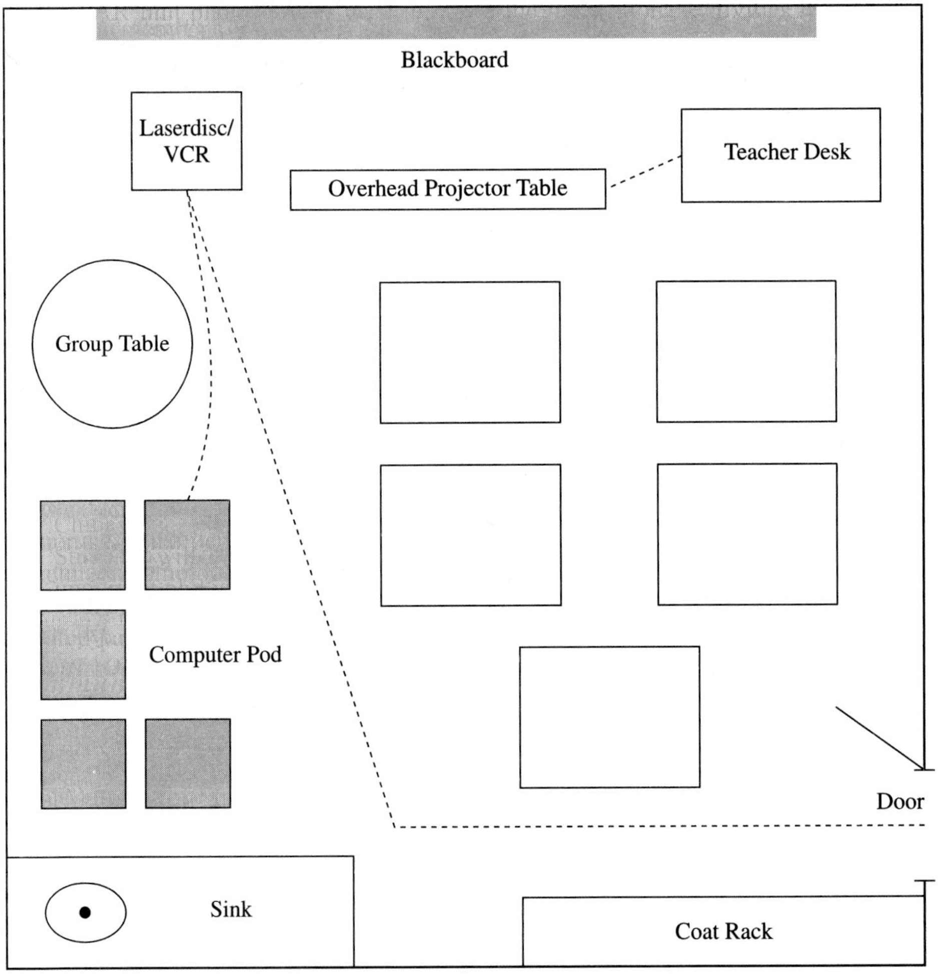

tion of whether this access to information that technology affords us is a good thing depends on what model of teaching and learning we're striving for. One way of looking at it is to distinguish between inert knowledge—which is something you know but that doesn't make any difference in your life—and generative knowledge, which changes your mental model, your whole perspective on how you view the world. (1995, p. 8)[*]

---

[*] *Source:* O'Neil, J. "On Technology and Schools: A Conversation with Chris Dede." *Educational Leadership* 53, 2: 8. Reprinted by permission of the Association for Supervision and Curriculum Development. Copyright © 1995 by ASCD. All rights reserved.

Dede's words of caution must be taken to heart if using new technologies is to be a boon rather than a boondoggle. More information, more time in school, more textbooks, more homework, more of any kind of intervention or resource is not the main problem in the classroom. In fact, more of something that is already not being designed, carried out, or utilized effectively will detract from, not add to, student learning. For example, teachers who are unimaginative in their choices and uses of instructional strategies will be equally unimaginative in their uses of technology. It is found that those who emphasize lecture and worksheets virtually ignore the array of technologies available and relegate the computer to a machine for providing drill-type exercises.

The goal, as Chris Dede has pointed out, is to use resources to supplement and enrich instruction so they help students create *generative knowledge*. Accomplishing this goal is directly related to how much you care and are able to design learning experiences that engage students in increasingly higher levels of the learning process. Also, it depends on your ability to utilize whatever resources you can to light your students' imaginations to the wonder of discovering knowledge and understanding the amazing world in which they live. Technology used with such care and capability is a powerful tool for helping your students grow and explore the world around them. In short, technology, no matter how sophisticated or creative, will not make you a good teacher. Rather, a good teacher will find ways to use technology to enhance already effectively designed and delivered classroom instruction.

References for Section II

Armento, B. J., Klor de Alva, J. J., Nash, G. B., Salter, C. L., Wilson, L. E., & Wixson, K. K. (1994). *America will be*. Boston: Houghton Mifflin.

Armento, B. J., Nash, G. B., Salter, C. L., & Wixson, K. K. (1991). *Oh, California*. Boston: Houghton Mifflin.

Ausubel, D. P., & Fitzgerald, J. (1962). Organizer, general background, and antecedent learning variables in sequential verbal learning. *Journal of Educational Psychology, 53*, 243–249.

Bloom, B. S., Engelhart, M. D., Furst, E. J., Hill, W. H., & Krathwohl, D. R. (1956). *Taxonomy of educational objectives. The classification of educational goals. Handbook I: Cognitive domain*. New York: David McKay.

Carnes, J. (1995). Home was a horse stall. *Teaching Tolerance, 50*, Spring.

Dede, C. (1995). Technology & schools: A conversation with Chris Dede. *Educational Leadership, 53*, (2).

Dunkin, M. J., & Biddle, B. J. (1974). *The study of teaching*. New York: Holt, Rinehart and Winston.

Elliot, D., & Wendling, A. (1966). Capable dropouts and the social milieu of the high school. *Journal of Educational Research, 60*, 180–186.

Ellis, S. S., & Whalen, S. F. (1990). *Cooperative learning: Getting started*. New York: Scholastic Professional Books.

Gagne, R. M., & Driscoll, M. P. (1988). *Essentials of learning for instruction*. Englewood Cliffs, NJ: Prentice Hall.

Gall, M. D. (1970). The use of questions in teaching. *Review of Educational Research, 40*, 707-721.

Hayes-Shepard, D. (1995). *Managing technology in the classroom*. Huntington Beach, CA: Teacher Created Materials, Inc.

Hunter, M. (1982). *Mastery teaching: Increasing instructional effectiveness in elementary, secondary schools, colleges and universities*. El Segundo, CA: TIP Publications.

Johnson, D. W., & Johnson, R. T. (Eds.). (1984). *Structuring cooperative learning: Lesson plans for teachers*. Minneapolis, MN: Interaction Book Co.

Joyce, B., & Weil, M. (1996). *Models of teaching*. Boston: Allyn and Bacon.

Kagan, S. (1992). *Cooperative learning*. San Juan Capistrano, CA: Kagan Cooperative Learning.

Levin, T., & Long, R. (1981). *Effective instruction*. Washington, DC: Association for Supervision and Curriculum Development.

McDermott, R. P. (1978). Some reasons for focusing on classrooms in reading research. *Reading: Disciplined inquiry in process and practice*. Clemson, SC: 27th Yearbook of the National Reading Conference.

Orlich, D. C., Harder, R. J., Callahan, R. C., Kauchak, D. P., & Gibson, H. W. (1994). Lexington, MA: D. C. Heath.

Rafoth, M. A., Leal, L., & DeFabo, L. (1993). *Strategies for learning and remembering: Study skills across the curriculum*. Washington, DC: National Educational Association.

Richardson, J. S., & Morgan, R. F. (1990). *Reading to learn in the content areas*. Belmont, CA: Wadsworth.

Sanders, N. N. (1966). *Classroom questions: What kinds?* New York: Harper and Row.

Shigekawa, M. (1993). *Blue jay in the desert*. Korea: Dong-A Publishing and Printing.

Slavin, R. E. (1991). *Student team learning: A practical guide to cooperative learning* (3rd ed.). Washington, DC: National Education Association of the United States.

Taba, H. (1966). *Strategies and cognitive functioning in elementary school children*. Cooperative research project #2404. San Francisco, CA: San Francisco State College.

Wilen, W. W., ed. (1987). *Questions, questioning techniques, and effective teaching*. Washington, D.C.: ASCD.

Strategic Classroom Planning

The complex responsibilities and physical and emotional demands on the new teacher are great. Anything that helps in dealing with these demands in a positive and productive way is indeed valuable, if not life or career saving. The need to plan for instruction every day of the school year as the basis for carrying out engaging learning activities places the most relentless demand on the new teacher. Section III provides a structured, logical system to use so that creative planning can be done in a realistic amount of time.

New teachers never cease to be amazed by how much time and effort go into planning for classroom instruction. In order to maximize your effectiveness in planning, discussion will focus on specific strategies for carrying out the two basic types of planning: long-term and short-term planning. It cannot be emphasized enough how important it is to your success as a teacher that both types of planning be carried out. All efforts at short-term planning will be more difficult and less successful if not guided by the overview of the long-term plan. The long-term plan tells you where you are going to go and the short-term plan tells you specifically how you are going to get there.

For the purposes of this book, long-term planning will be considered as the *macrostep* and short-term planning as the *microsteps* that the teacher needs to take to remain organized for creative and effective instruction to occur regularly. Both the macrostep and microsteps are designed to encourage reflection as the process goes forward. It is important to realize that without thoughtful and organized planning (both short and long term), self-evaluation of your efforts in the classroom is an empty exercise. After all, if there is no plan in place that you are working from, what is it that you are evaluating? For example, you might ask yourself: Did that math lesson work? You can answer this question only if you taught the math lesson from a thoughtfully prepared plan from which you can reflect on later concerning the value of the specific activities, resources employed, and pacing you used. Indeed, you can answer the question fundamental to all evaluation: Did I follow the plan itself? If there is no coherent plan, if you are more or less winging it or improvising, no basis exists for determining what worked or not. You will find yourself totally lost about what can be done better next time.

The successful elementary teacher views all aspects of the planning process as one grand and continuous opportunity for overall professional renewal. This is why, in the following pages, you are introduced and oriented to the various aspects of planning by *key questions*. In this sense, planning is seen as a process of inquiry and discovery. As you look at the world around you, you can ask: What scientist in any field is involved more in live action research day after day where the mental, emotional, and spiritual well-being of impressionable young lives hangs in the balance than the elementary teacher? There is enormous responsibility on your shoulders to conduct this search for answers to what will help your students. Planning is where this search starts. It is the necessary foundation to the process of professional growth and renewal.

Section III is divided into two major chapters. The first chapter provides a systematic strategy for carrying out the macrostep of planning; the second chapter provides a variety of strategies for carrying out the microsteps of planning. Since the designing of instructional activities takes up the overwhelming portion of any elementary teacher's planning time, it is not only logical but necessary that the microsteps to planning will take up a considerably larger portion of Section III. The steps to planning in Chapter 10 are divided into two parts: (1) block-type approaches that involve the planning of sequences of learning activities over an extended period of time and (2) daily approaches that involve the creation of a plan to be delivered in one lesson.

The following outline describes the order in which the major topics of Chapters 9 and 10 will be presented and the purpose of each.

Macrostep

To provide a systematic way to create an overall curriculum outline in each content area

Topic 1: Orientation to Long-Term Planning

Topic 2: Major Elements of Long-Term Planning

Microsteps

To provide a variety of detailed strategies for creating learning experiences

Topic 1: Block-Type Planning Approaches

Topic 2: Daily Planning Approaches

$$C \; h \; a \; p \; t \; e \; r \quad 9$$

Macrostep:
Long-Term Planning

Two essential questions come to mind here: (1) What is long-term planning? and (2) How is long-term planning carried out? To answer these questions, a brief orientation to the nature and purpose of long-term planning is presented here, followed by what can be called a "windows" approach to understanding the macrosteps that constitute long-term planning. Each step will be examined as to how it works in the context of the entire planning process.

Orientation to Long-Term Planning

The what and why of long-term planning is described well by way of an analogy. If you are going to set out on a journey by car across the United States, you would naturally want to plan a few things before taking off. You would probably ask: (1) Where do I expect to wind up at the end of the trip? (2) What will be the major legs of the trip as I proceed on my way? (3) What will be the pace at which I will travel? (4) What route (approach) will I take to get there? and (5) What kinds of resources will I need to see me through the trip? A close examination of these questions reveals that a venture of this magnitude demands an overall or long-term plan—a plan that, at the least, addresses these five questions. Notice, too, that for the overall plan to be of any use, the right questions need to asked. Furthermore, the ability to answer some of the questions is dependent on answering certain ones first.

Why would a teacher, especially a new teacher, want to begin a school year without asking similar-type questions concerning the curriculum in each content area? The fact is that many, if not most, new teachers do not ask or answer these questions, thus adding much stress and uncertainty to what is already a very difficult job.

In relation to long-term planning for a first-grade social studies curriculum, notice how these five questions are addressed in Figure 9–1. Of particular importance in this figure is the listing in the right column—that is, the benefits to the teacher in addressing each of the five questions.

Major Elements of Long-Term Planning

If you were to sit down in an effort to develop a long-term plan in one of the content areas, you would first determine the major elements involved in creating such a plan. One thing that would come to mind is your *goals*. After all, wouldn't you be developing this plan to accomplish something? Of course you would. And that "something" is the growth of your students through learning. In this regard, the goals, as expressed in your long-term plan, will be spoken of as your *standard of learning*. Next, as you set

FIGURE 9–1   Essential Questions for Long-Term Curriculum Planning

Content Area: Social Studies   *Grade Level:* 1

Question	Answer	Benefit
1. Where will we wind up?	We will cover all the units and topics concerning "My Community."	This lets you know exactly what the children must study to appropriately begin second-grade social studies.
2. What will be the major legs (divisions) of the curriculum over the year?	We will list the units and topics to be covered within those units concerning "My Community."	This provides a specific road map in terms of both the *scope* of the material to be covered and in the *sequence* it will be covered.
3. What is the pace at which material will be covered?	Using a school calendar, approximate the number of days that can be assigned to each unit and its constituent topics based on their relative breadth and importance.	This relieves a great deal of stress due to uncertainty and unbalanced coverage of material. Now, not only has a road map been created (i.e., scope and sequence) but a clear time frame is also established.
4. What approaches will we take?	Note that next to the scope and sequence and pacing time frame are indications of which units or topics will be possible to cover theoretically, using PAR, inquiry, or any other particular approach.	This lets you consider and indicate the best places to use different and creative approaches in context and with the security of knowing what needs to be covered and when.
5. What resources will be needed?	By examining the above responses to the first four questions, lists of general resources and specifically targeted resources can be indicated right next to other information.	This allows for that most valuable of elements—the ability to intelligently prepare resources or to procure them in advance so what is needed and desired is there at the right time.

out on this long-term planning venture, it is quite natural to determine the nature of the actual *content* that is to be covered over the span of the school year. Thus, the two principal macrosteps in long-term planning are:

1. Determining your goals (standard of learning)
2. Determining the nature of the content to be covered

Determining Your Classroom Goals: Standard of Learning

One way to grasp the notion of a standard of learning is to consider how the phrase *standard of living* is commonly used. If one is asked what denotes a high standard of living, the typical response will be a list of things such as income level, bank account, size and location of house, model of car, and so on. Notice how this list equates one's standard of living with material affluence. This perspective on standard of living ignores the quality of life of a person. For example, regardless of material circumstances, aren't questions such as the following more suitable: How stable and happy is a person? How accepting and understanding is a person of people and situations? How healthy and well adjusted is a person? and How loving and loved is a person? If this set of questions is examined honestly, compared with the more materially oriented viewpoint, it becomes clear that the answers to these questions provide a much deeper insight into a person's growth and condition as a human being.

A similar comparison needs to be drawn as you embark on your efforts to determine your classroom standard of learning. What should you look at to obtain a deep insight into your students' growth? The more materially oriented view would look almost exclusively at test scores (especially the standardized variety) and grade-point averages. On the other hand, a perspective comparable to the one that looks at the quality of life would consider students' abilities to think, take responsibility for learning, appreciate fellow students and life in general, respect the value of knowledge, maintain disciplined study habits, develop broad interests, and so on.

Development of ability in these areas can arguably be said to denote learning in the highest sense. This is learning that not only prepares students for achievement in school but also prepares them to be productive citizens and well-adjusted human beings. Interestingly, and not surprisingly, if students were to make progress in these areas, test scores and grade-point averages would be high as a natural consequence. It is all too possible, however, to find students who learn to "work the system" early on, getting reasonable test scores and grade-point averages without accomplishing much in these other important areas. The most revealing fact of all is that such students come to define and strive for a standard of living based on accumulation of material possessions. In other words, these students lose on both fronts—in school and in life. The goals they have been trained to strive for are limited as far as the realization of higher and finer human potentialities.

This all points out the importance of setting classroom goals. The goals you set largely determine what you will be trying to accomplish over time on a daily basis. They shape the kind of activities you plan, resources you use, and interactions and expectations you have. Try to remember the good elementary teachers you had and you will notice that what remains foremost in your mind, to this day, is the attributes they strove to foster in the children—perhaps the goals were self-discipline, love of reading, respect for others, or a sincere interest in discovering knowledge. These goals would have directly influenced how those teachers conducted instruction and ran their class-rooms. As you reflect on this, notice that specific facts, although necessary for under-standing of the content being taught, are a vehicle for learning these larger lessons essential for carrying a person through the rest of his or her education and life.

Before going any further in this book, take a moment and think about your Class-room Standard of Learning. Write down a short list of goals you hope to reach with your students. Tape the list to the inside cover of this book so that you can add to or modify your goals as needed.

Because all teachers have individual perspectives on life, education, teaching, and students, a personal standard of learning is always operating and motivating a teacher's efforts in one way or the other. It seems, however, so much more productive to take the initiative and consciously determine these goals, making them an integral part of an overall and creative classroom instructional plan.

In setting the Classroom Standard of Learning for your classroom, it is wise not only to make personal reflections but also to consider the district's and school's goals, parents' input, and the nature of your students. In addition, fellow teachers who are doing an effective job can offer valuable guidance in selecting goals that are of partic-ular relevance to the students at your school. The point of creating your Classroom Standard of Learning is not to make an abstract philosophical statement; rather, it is meant to serve as a guide for the practical day-to-day operation of your instructional program. To demonstrate how this can be accomplished, look at Figure 9–2, in which one particular goal (Appreciation of the World Around Us) a teacher hopes to foster in her students is given a practical reality through one of her social studies activities.

Figure 9–2 provides a glimpse of this teacher's *modus operandi*. See how this one specific social studies lesson activity is in a small way fostering one of this teacher's goals for the students. By designing and carrying out numerous activities in the various content areas in like manner, her goals can become a practical reality. Remember, the school day, in essence, is a series of instructional activities. Over time, if you have in mind the larger goals you are trying to foster (e.g., taking responsibility for learning, respecting others, developing disciplined study habits, thinking critically and care-fully) as you plan daily lessons, your instructional activities will have in them some element of reaching these goals. In the aggregate, the effects of these daily learning experiences so developed will go a long way toward fostering the goals you have set for your Classroom Standard of Learning.

Determining the Nature of Content to Be Covered

The life of an elementary teacher is hectic, and with all the time and scheduling demands, life can become stressful. Skill in time management, both at school and home, is extremely valuable. With this in mind, imagine the advantage gained by knowing how to do long-term planning in a way that:

FIGURE 9–2   Practical Application of Classroom Standard of Learning

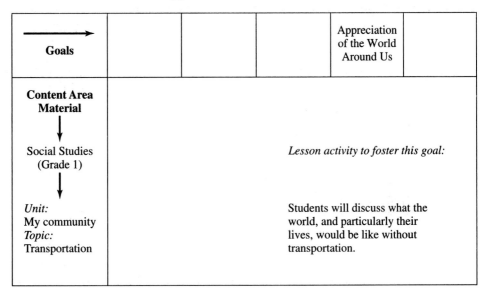

Goals ⟶				Appreciation of the World Around Us	
Content Area Material ↓ Social Studies (Grade 1) ↓ *Unit:* My community *Topic:* Transportation				*Lesson activity to foster this goal:* Students will discuss what the world, and particularly their lives, would be like without transportation.	

1. Greatly facilitates your weekly and daily planning
2. Allows you to use your vacation periods as superproductive planning times

The following section describes a system for breaking down any content area into a series of units and topics and then setting up a pacing schedule for covering that material.

Breaking a Content Area into Units and Topics

Before getting to the *how* of this operation, it would be good to think of the *why*. The answer is straightforward. You want to know how each content area is divided into its constituent units and topics so that you can have a clear and relatively detailed picture of what the students are required to learn in that content area for that year. It is a lot more useful to have this picture at the very beginning of the school year, rather than trying to piece it together as you go. There is ample opportunity in elementary teaching for spontaneity, but not when it comes to long-term planning. To do so is to flirt with chaos. The following six steps and accompanying examples provide a process for generating content area units and topics that meet state, district, and school requirements, yet leave scope for your creative input as long-term planning is begun.

Step 1: Own Ideas
To begin the process, take a few minutes to write down what you think the major divisions (i.e., units) of a particular content area should be at the grade level you are teaching. During any aspect of planning, it is wise to jot down your own ideas initially and then make modifications based on reference to various resources. Functioning in this

way makes you think more carefully and encourages original, creative ideas. Once your mind sees a printed word from some authoritative source, it tends to close down in its consideration of other possibilities.

Example of Step 1:

Content Area: Social studies

Grade Level: Fifth grade

Own Ideas

Unit 1: Geography of North America

Unit 2: American Government

Unit 3: Culture

Unit 4: American History

Unit 5: Economy

Step 2: State Guidelines

Now that you have made a list of units based on personal insights, experiences, and perspectives, look up the guidelines your state has developed for the content area being planned. These guidelines are usually the principal source for publishing companies as they seek to determine what to cover in their various content area textbooks at each grade level. Of further value is the fact that these state guidelines (sometimes called *frameworks*) are created by a cross-section of experts in each content area. For example, the California Social Science/History Framework was designed by selected K–12 teachers, university professors, and state and county resource persons—all having special expertise and experience in the social studies.

Example of Step 2:

Content Area: Social studies

Grade Level: Fifth grade

State Guidelines

Unit 1: The Land and People before Columbus

Unit 2: The Age of Exploration

Unit 3: Settling the Colonies

Unit 4: Settling the Trans-Appalachian West

Unit 5: The War for Independence

Unit 6: Life in the Young Republic

Unit 7: The New Nation's Westward Expansion

Unit 8: Linking the Past to the Present

Step 3: District/School Guidelines

Although your district's and school's curriculum guidelines (i.e., local guidelines) are heavily influenced by the state's guidelines, you will usually discover some important differences. Also, it is essential that you know what your district and school expect you to cover in the content areas at the grade level you are teaching. Failure to cover this material can have serious repercussions on student articulation from one grade to the next, as well as on students' ability to pass grade-level or districtwide tests. Your ability to follow and address these local guidelines is part of the professional evaluation of your competence as a teacher.

Example of Step 3:

Content Area: Social studies

Grade Level: Fifth grade

District/School Guidelines

Unit 1: The Land and People before Columbus

Unit 2: The Age of Exploration

Unit 3: Settling the Colonies

Unit 4: The New Nation's Westward Expansion

Unit 5: The American People Then and Now

Step 4: Your Textbook's Contents

Even though textbook publishers pay close attention to state guidelines, they can be found to offer a somewhat unique presentation of the content at each grade level through the various content areas. This is due to the fact that a particular textbook may be attempting to address the guidelines of several states, or even a national perspective. Also, the authors of a particular content area textbook may have a creative and original way of covering the material, albeit within state guidelines. Finally, since you are given the textbook you must use, a general initial review and understanding of what it contains is a vital part of the early stages of your long-term planning effort.

Example of Step 4:

Content Area: Social studies

Grade Level: Fifth grade

Textbook Contents

Unit 1: The United States Past and Present

Unit 2: Exploring and Settling America

Unit 3: Life in the English Colonies

Unit 4: The Struggle for Independence

Unit 5: Life in a Growing Nation

Unit 6: A Nation in Conflict

Unit 7: Finding America's Future

Step 5: Your "Best" List of Units

Up to this point, you have gained considerable insight into the scope and nature of the curriculum in a particular area at one grade level. To put a final, creative touch to this endeavor, you should place these four lists side by side and review them to generate a single "best" list of units (see Figure 9–3). What will be the value of this "best" list? First of all, it will be based on respected expert sources. These are sources that you are expected to be mindful of as you proceed with planning throughout the year. Second, by generating this one "best" list, you retain a measure of creative control over the broad conception of the curriculum in the content area examined. Rather than blindly following one source or being confused by many sources, you have availed yourself of several valued perspectives in order to create what is likely to be the most useful overall curriculum design for your classroom. Indeed, personal experience with dozens of teachers has shown that the "best" list they have created has *never* been identical to *any* of the lists from the four previous steps. There is always some measure of originality and creative input on the teacher's part. You can see an example of this in Step 5. This "best" list of units was arrived at by an elementary teacher after completing Steps 1 through 4. (This teacher's work is reflected in the accompanying examples for each step.) The beauty of the result is that the "best" list is original, but within the scope of what the knowledgeable and authoritative sources to whom you are accountable say is required.

Example of Step 5:

Content Area: Social studies

Grade Level: Fifth grade

Best List of Units

Unit 1: The Geography of the Land

Unit 2: The Struggle for Independence

Unit 3: Westward Expansion

Unit 4: Life in a Growing Nation

Unit 5: Finding the Future

Step 6: Breaking Units into Topics

Using your "best" list of units, it is now time to determine what topics will be covered in each of those units. The resulting list of units and topics gives what is commonly known as the *scope and sequence* of the particular content area being planned. Scope

FIGURE 9–3   Review of Lists from Steps 1–5

Own Ideas	State Guideline	District/School Guideline	Textbook	Best List

and sequence merely means the extent of what is to be covered (scope) and the order in which it will be presented (sequence). How, then, should you go about determining appropriate topics for each unit? A solid start would be to refer to the sources you have just used for creating the lists of units. This time, however, your aim is to glean more detail from each source. It is very likely the state guideline will offer useful ideas and the textbook you will be using will provide what you are looking for in detail. Because you want this to be the finest possible effort at long-term planning, you need not stop at these sources for "topics" ideas. Wonderful ideas for topics within specific units can be obtained from fellow teachers, other textbooks your school or district does not use, subject area experts, and, of course, your own creative perspective.

Example of Step 6:

Content Area: Social studies

Grade Level: Fifth grade

Units and Topics

Unit 1: The Geography of the Land
    Topic 1: Understanding Geography
    Topic 2: Regions of North America
    Topic 3: Studying Globes and Maps
    Topic 4: Stories Maps Tell

Unit 2: The Struggle for Independence
    Topic 1: Crisis with Great Britain
    Topic 2: War Breaks Out
    Topic 3: Searching for Unity

Unit 3: Westward Expansion
    Topic 1: The Moving Frontier
    Topic 2: Changes on the Great Plains
    Topic 3: Settling the Great Plains

Unit 4: Life in a Growing Nation
    Topic 1: Southern Society
    Topic 2: Industrial North
    Topic 3: A Divided Nation

Unit 5: Finding the Future
    Topic 1: Cultural Diversity
    Topic 2: Linking the Past to the Present

Experience with hundreds of teachers has demonstrated that this strategic method of determining units and topics for a particular content area can be effectively completed in about two hours at a county office of education or a district professional materials (reference) center. The quality and value of the resulting curriculum outline make this an extremely wise use of a few hours.

The next section shows just how helpful it can be to have a well-developed list of units and topics (i.e., curriculum outline) for the content areas you will be teaching.

Utilizing Your Curriculum Outline Productively

After you have completed the six steps just described, you will essentially know where you are going with the content area material. With the *where* clearly delineated, you can now address three critical questions concerning the *how* of getting there so student growth and learning are accomplished. These three critical questions are presented in Figure 9–4, which includes a brief statement concerning the value of finding answers to them. The following discussion will show you how to go about systematically answering these questions.

Addressing the Three Critical "How" Questions

Question 1:   In what order should the various units and topics within those units be presented?

The decision on the sequence for presenting the content curriculum material is made for you to some extent by the textbook you have been given. Certainly, if your school or district prescribes a particular curriculum sequence for purposes of alignment with certain grade articulation needs or testing plans, your flexibility here is limited. Even when this is the case, there is still latitude for making your own determination concerning the order in which some or all of the topics within each of the units are presented. Also, when a school or district prescribes a particular curriculum design, it is indicating the minimum that you must cover. Nothing stops you from expanding specific units and topics or addressing topics you feel will enrich student learning of a unit. The only limitations in enriching the curriculum in this way are available time, resources, and ideas. These limitations can be overcome by having a systematic and creative approach to planning. The following discussion and criteria will guide you in planning an effective curriculum presentation sequence.

How to Plan an Effective Sequence for Presentation of Units and Topics. Accomplishing this task mirrors, to a degree, what you have done in Steps 1 through 6 for developing your overall curriculum outline. The difference is one of detail. Here,

FIGURE 9–4   Questions Concerning How to Present the Curriculum

Questions	Value of Resulting Answers
1. In what order should the various units and topics within those units be presented?	Provides a degree of security that a strategic scope and sequence design is in place.
2. How much time should be spent on the various units and topics within units?	Provides a pacing schedule to maintain indicating the extensity and intensity accorded units and topics.
3. What special approaches or enrichment activities are anticipated for particular units or topics within units?	Provides a clear picture and manageable plan to pinpoint where particularly creative experiences will fit best and be most productive.

you are going to examine more closely the nature and scope of your list of units and topics and the essential concepts and skills students need to learn from them. Of particular use in making this examination will be your textbook, state curriculum framework, school or district curriculum guide, and the advice of fellow grade-level teachers. The following three criteria should be used as guides when reviewing these sources so your resulting sequence of units and topics has a solid strategic basis.

Criterion 1:   Take into account readiness for learning.   The resulting unit and topic sequence should take into account students' learning readiness by serving as a well-designed series of building blocks. It is a shame to present certain material first that is beyond the grasp of students because the textbook presents it first, when other material would be more accessible to them conceptually.

Criterion 2:   Take into account the students' and your interests and backgrounds. Because of the particular interests, experiences, and strengths of you and your students, it makes good sense to use certain topics as "lead-ins" or "hooks" to other topics. Remember, your textbook does not know your students, you, your school, or your community. You have the advantage of knowing these things in ever-increasing measure.

Criterion 3:   Take into account the availability of resources.   While giving precedence to learning readiness and interests and backgrounds, the availability of certain enrichment materials (e.g., related literature, videos, computer software, manipulatives, field trips, guest speakers, etc.) may reasonably influence when certain topics should be presented for optimal results. Just thinking about this criterion as you develop your long-term plans effectively puts you in touch with the world of curriculum enrichment possibilities that exist beyond your textbook.

Question 2:   How much time should be spent on the various units and topics within units?

Unfortunately, this question often arises well into the school year as the teacher becomes anxious, saying, "At this pace, how will I ever cover all the material I am supposed to cover?" Multiply this anxiety by a couple or all of the content areas, and you can understand why attention to this question during long-term planning is a wise move.

How to Plan an Effective Pacing Schedule for Units and Topics.   As you set out to create a pacing schedule for presenting the material in each content area, realize that this schedule will serve as a starting point and a guide. As the year unfolds, you will modify this schedule for various reasons. The fact remains, however, that by having created the discipline of such a starting point, you are in a position of control, so that necessary changes can occur in a calm, intelligent manner as the year proceeds. The less clear your picture of the curriculum is, the more the need to be flexible and make changes will be done haphazardly and be fraught with stress. The following criterion should be used as a guide as you develop a workable curriculum pacing schedule.

Criterion: Take into account your school calendar.   To meet this criterion, a simple method consisting of five steps is recommended. Have in front of you your overall curriculum outline, which now has the units and topics in proper sequence. Right next to this, have the textbook you will be using and a copy of the school calendar. From this point, the five steps can be completed. The first four steps are quantitative in nature and the fifth one is qualitative.

Step 1:   Review the school calendar to accurately determine the actual number of teaching days, taking into account shortened days, standardized test days, beginning and end of the year special activities, and so on. Interestingly, many teachers are often surprised that they do not have the number of teaching days available that they thought they would. This increases their anxiety about "getting through the curriculum." By completing this step, you can avoid such needless stress.

Step 2:   Divide the number of units for a particular content area into your number of teaching days. For example, if you have five social studies units to cover and 165 teaching days available, that computes to 33 days for each unit. As you will see, this initial mathematical computation gets adjusted as the succeeding steps are completed.

Step 3:   Using your textbook and any other relevant sources, adjust the number of days planned for teaching each unit arrived at in Step 2, noting the size (number of textbook pages gives a good ideas of this) and scope (number of topics to cover) of each unit. You may find that Unit 1 is covered by 30 pages of text and consists of three topics, whereas Unit 2 has double the number of pages and topics. For purposes of this step, adjust the number of teaching days to reflect this ratio. Thus, you will schedule Unit 1 for 22 days and Unit 2 for 45 days at this point.

Step 4:   Perform a computation similar to the one in Step 3 for topics within each unit. These computations are fairly clinical. If one topic is covered by 5 pages of text and another by 10 pages, allot double the number of days to the latter—for now. For example, if you determine a particular unit should be covered in 45 days and it consists of three relatively equal-sized (in terms of text pages) topics, figure each should take about 15 days. For the topics within the other units, simply allot the number of days proportionately according to their size.

Step 5:   A qualitative adjustment can now be made to fine-tune the computations arrived at in Steps 1 through 4. To do this, keep two things in mind: (1) the students' and your interests, strengths, and backgrounds; and (2) the special approaches and enrichment activities you anticipate using.

For example, a teacher may be quite an expert on the Civil War and have particularly wonderful artifacts to share with the class. If one of the topics within one of the units in social studies is the Civil War, this teacher could well decide to add a few days in covering this topic. Similarly, if a teacher anticipates using a thematic approach to teaching a particular topic in math by integrating it with aspects of the social studies and science curricula, it is reasonable that a few days might be added for covering that topic. Sometimes, it is the students' interests or backgrounds that prompt a teacher to lengthen the period for covering a particular topic, or even an entire unit. If students demonstrate a fascination with some aspect of a content curriculum, you may want to seize the opportunity to explore it with them in more detail and from more perspectives. On the other hand, if you find that students have little or poorly built background in a particular topic, if may be necessary to extend the time they work on it to remediate what is lacking.

Creating pacing schedules for the different content areas provides solid and structured foundations for planning. Having these pacing schedules will provide a sense of being on top of things and allow you to calmly make necessary changes as external demands and your own experiences dictate.

Question 3:   What special approaches or enrichment activities are anticipated for particular units or topics within units?

The curriculum outline you have developed to this point represents a well-thought-out scope and sequence of the units and topics to be covered, along with a pacing schedule that indicates approximately when and for how long they will be covered. The last aspect to put in place to complete the macrostep of planning is a determination of the special approaches and enrichment activities you can effectively use.

How to Determine Use of Special Approaches and Enrichment Activities.   A process consisting of two main steps can be used to determine, and then indicate on your Overall Content Area Curriculum Plans, the special approaches and enrichment activities you will employ.

Step 1:   Assemble relevant materials.   These relevant materials include: (1) each of your content area curriculum outlines, (2) a list of the special approaches and enrichment activities you can think of to select from (see Figure 9–5), (3) the teacher's edition of your content area textbooks, and (4) any other materials obtained from your school (e.g., fellow teachers), district (e.g., inservices), county office, or professional associations

Step 2:   Review your materials and make notations on the content area curriculum outlines.   With your content area curriculum outlines in front of you, scan both within and across each one in a systematic fashion to determine where special approaches and enrichment activities seem useful and practical. By *systematic* is simply meant to ask yourself: Based on my understanding of the possible ways to employ a thematic approach, are there any ideal places to use it either within a particular content area or across two or more content areas for specific units or topics?

Next, ask yourself the same question about the possibilities of using PAR, Inquiry, and so on, concerning "special approaches." Following this line of self-questioning, you would ask similar questions about the strategic use of various enrichment activities. A word of caution: As a new teacher, consider carefully what you can successfully handle as far as frequency and complexity of special approaches and enrichment activ-

FIGURE 9–5   Special Approaches and Enrichment Activities

Special Approaches	*Enrichment Activities*
• Thematic approach	• Field trips
• PAR approach	• Guest speakers
• Inquiry approach	• Group projects
• Original (other) approach	• Original (other) ideas

ities go. There is no mechanical answer to knowing how much is too much. This will vary according to each teacher and his or her particular classroom situation. There is one thing of which you can be sure. By completing these two steps, you will have infused a strategic and dynamic element into your already well-structured content area outlines: strategic, in that you will have thoughtfully pinpointed places where it looks feasible and productive to go above and beyond the regular mode of instruction and textbook coverage, and dynamic, because you will have stepped back to get a view of the living and integrated nature of all the content areas.

As the school year proceeds and you learn about new possibilities, your original plans will naturally be modified for the better. Such positive modifications are possible because you started with an organized plan to serve as your blueprint. With the macrostep of the planning process completed, you are well prepared to turn your attention to the essence of an elementary teacher's existence—the microsteps of block (weekly) and daily lesson planning.

Microsteps:
Short-Term Planning

This chapter will examine the two essential aspects of short-term planning: block and daily approaches. These two aspects represent the microsteps of planning in that they involve the detailed view of what the teacher and students will actually do on a day-to-day basis in the classroom. In block-type planning, activities are conceived of in an over-all framework covering a period anywhere from a few days to several weeks or even months. In daily planning, activities are designed for one specific lesson on one day.

The goal of the first part of this chapter is to give you an effective guide for using the following four block-type approaches:

- PAR approach
- Thematic approach
- Inquiry approach
- Generic approach

After a thorough examination of the block-type approaches, the second part of this chapter will discuss how to design effective daily lesson plans. The following models for lesson planning will be detailed:

- Clinical model
- Generic model

Block-Type Planning Approaches

Block-type approaches are employed where the nature of the material involved, either within or across content areas, lends itself to conceiving of a series of lessons at one time. Rather than writing several detailed lesson plans at one sitting, a broad sketch is made of where instruction will begin, how it will develop, and when to reach a point of culmination. The four block-type approaches presented in this section—PAR, thematic, inquiry, and generic—have been chosen to provide you with flexibility in the way you do such planning. Each approach emphasizes a different purpose, as can be seen in Figure 10–1. As you review the ins and outs of each block-type approach, begin to think of when and where any, or a combination, of these approaches will fit best with your classroom situation and needs.

PAR Approach to Planning

The Preparation, Assisting Understanding, Reflection model (PAR) framework for planning, developed by Richardson and Morgan (1990), is an effective means to plan integrated units of instruction for all subject areas. The framework works well for weekly planning; it can, however, easily be applied to longer periods of time. In addition, once the purposes of the phases of the PAR are grasped, the plan lends itself particularly well to the useful application of your imagination and creative ability that often are obscured by the drier methodical mindset of daily planning. The PAR framework is a *guide* for planning—it fosters creativity and the teacher's ability to respond to the specific needs of his or her students.

In using PAR, it is important that one has a grasp of the instructional purposes of each of the three phases of the framework. Once these are understood, it becomes clear not only how to use various instructional *activities* in accordance with the framework but also how to create one's own activities for the different phases (Preparation, Assistance, and Reflection) of it. In order to present the PAR in a clear but efficient manner, discussion concerning PAR is arranged in the following three sections:

1. Part 1 provides a discussion of the design and characteristics of the PAR.
2. Part 2 provides an exemplary sample PAR unit so you can see how a complete plan looks in written form (the entire unit plan appears in Figure 10–4).
3. Part 3 is a discussion of the sample plan with explanations of the activities presented therein.

FIGURE 10–1   Focus and Purpose of Block-Type Planning Approaches

Approach	Purpose
PAR	To present an extended sequence of activities at progressively higher levels in the learning process
Thematic	To integrate information, concepts, and ideas within or across content areas
Inquiry	To foster the development of thinking, research, and study skills through guided and independent discovery learning
Generic	To facilitate daily lesson planning by creating a strategic weekly planning continuum (outline) for each content area

The PAR model of planning is a framework consisting of three phases. At each phase, a specific instructional purpose is meant to be achieved through the use of instructional activities. There are many different types of instructional activities that can be used to achieve the goals of each phase. In the example of a PAR unit (Part 2), some of these activities are demonstrated. In their text, *Reading to Learn in the Content Areas*, Richardson and Morgan have demonstrated a great many kinds of activities to use with each phase of the PAR. Many of these have been adapted by various teachers and student teachers for use in their classroom instruction. The appendix at the end of this book provides a rich resource of activities. Although the activities are discussed in terms of the PAR, they can be used in any lesson plan to achieve the instructional purpose for which they are designed.

Part 1:   Design and Characteristics of the PAR

The PAR framework is a three-part process for instruction intended to ensure that students have successful and meaningful reading experiences in the content areas of instruction (social studies, science, math, and language arts). To have successful reading experiences, students must be able to comprehend what they are reading. Each of the three steps of the PAR provides instructional activities that aid comprehension in different ways.

The PAR framework is based on three assumptions about what is necessary for the successful comprehension of written material:

1. Students must have some background knowledge of the concepts or ideas being presented in the reading.
2. Students must be guided through their reading of new, unfamiliar material.
3. Students must reflect on newly learned material so it can be internalized, retained, and applied in future learning situations.

The first assumption—that students must have background knowledge in order to successfully comprehend new material—is considered of prime importance. The PAR framework provides ample scope for the development of such knowledge in the Preparation step. During the P step of PAR, the goal is to *determine* and *build* the students' backgrounds for the new material that will be read by the students.

During the Assistance step of PAR, the second assumption is accomplished; that is, the students must be guided through their reading of new material. The goals in the A step are twofold: to provide a purpose for learning and to develop comprehension of the new material. It is important at this point that students are given the utmost opportunity to process new information (with the help of guiding activities) before they are evaluated on the new learning.

Finally, in order to help students internalize, retain, and apply newly learned information, the Reflection step of PAR is designed to cause students to *think critically* or *reflect* about what they have read. It is only at this R step of the PAR process that students should be evaluated. This three-stage process is pictured graphically in Figure 10–2.

FIGURE 10–2   The PAR Framework

P	A	R
Preparation	**Assistance**	**Reflection**
Determine Background	Provide Purpose	Think Critically about the Reading
Build Background	Assist Comprehension	

The PAR framework will guide you in planning and delivering classroom instruction. It is applicable to any content area and any grade level, and it is specifically designed for content reading instruction. In other words, it is meant for planning instruction in which students *read* to gain knowledge or information, and it is designed to help students experience the maximum learning and thinking with regard to their reading. It is meant to be used with both narrative and expository writing and it is intended to help students eventually become independent in their abilities to comprehend reading material of all sorts. By helping students become confident in their ability to comprehend reading material through the PAR, you will be helping them become independent learners—that is, individuals who are motivated to learn through reading.

Many of the activities presented in conjunction with the PAR are metacognitive; they allow the students to identify and use various mental strategies as they read and study various kinds of material. The whole aim of the PAR is to help students become more and more independent in their abilities to select and comprehend reading material to further their own learning objectives. In this sense, it is a very child-centered approach because it aims at providing the child with the training, skills, knowledge, and attitudes necessary to be a self-motivated learner.

The time period required for the PAR will vary, depending on how much the teacher wants to cover and to what depth; however, the framework lends itself readily to weekly planning. For this reason, it is regarded as unit planning, or *block planning*, as opposed to daily planning.

All three methods of classroom instruction—teacher directed, student directed, and interactive—can be appropriately used at any phase of the PAR. The PAR could begin with an interactive instructional activity, a student-directed instructional activity, or a teacher-directed activity, depending on the teacher's discretion. It is also possible for the teacher to invite the students to share in decision making about which learning activities to do, or even in what topic they would like to study. Again, the aim is that the students gradually acquire the thinking skills and mental attitudes fostered by the PAR activities so that they become capable of learning on their own and are motivated to do so.

Another characteristic of the PAR is that it allows the teacher a great deal of flexibility in responding to the instructional needs of the students. For example, suppose you have planned a particular activity to build the students' background for a particular topic. Suppose further that as you observe the students doing the activity, you realize that additional background building will be needed before they are ready to read. At this point, you can simply add another activity to the P phase to further prepare the students for the reading. As another example, suppose you notice that the students have a good deal of interest in and enthusiasm for a particular topic they are reading about and so you decide to extend exploration of the topic. In this case, you may add on further reading and research activities in the R phase of the PAR. Figure 10–3 depicts the characteristics of the PAR. See the appendix at the end of this book for activities that are appropriate for each phase of the PAR.

So far, each step of the PAR has been described, its purpose has been stated, and general characteristics have been discussed. Next is a demonstration of how the PAR works and a description of how to accomplish each step. A complete PAR unit plan is shown and discussed.

Part 2:   Example of a Complete PAR Unit Plan

The PAR unit plan shown in Figure 10–4 was developed by Susan Aldrich for a sixth-grade social studies lesson from the Houghton-Mifflin text, *A Message of Ancient Days* (1994). The topic of the unit is the Han Dynasty of ancient China.

(text continues on page 174)

FIGURE 10–3   Characteristics of the PAR

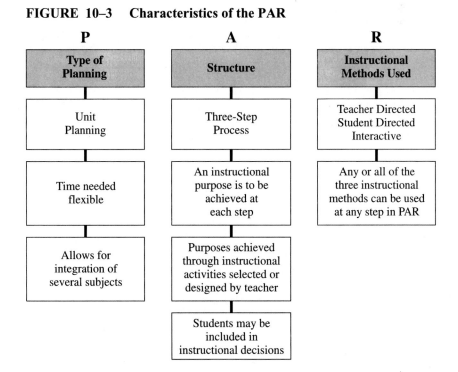

FIGURE 10–4   PAR Unit Plan on the Han Dynasty

State Overall Goals

1. To have students gain an awareness of part of the rich history of the Chinese people
2. To have students have an understanding of how the Han Dynasty fit into the overall history of China
3. To have students develop an understanding of the concept of Yin and Yang as an important philosophical component of the history of China

State Specific Objectives

1. Students will be able to list three contributions made during the Han Dynasty that continue to benefit us today.
2. Students will be able to define the philosophical concept of Yin and Yang.
3. Students will be able to identify the Han Dynasty as being a balance of previous historical government types—Legalism and Confucianism.

First Step of PAR: Preparation

Determining Background

1. *Determining Background: Self-Inventory Sheet.* A self-inventory sheet will be completed by students individually the day prior to the lesson and returned to the teacher to consider. It will include concepts and vocabulary from the target lesson. (See page 169.)
2. *Determining Background: PreP.* (Done as a total class activity.) The teacher will inform students that they are continuing in their study of Ancient China and that today they will be studying the Han Dynasty.

   Phase 1:   Teacher will ask: "What comes to mind when you hear the term *Han Dynasty*? Teacher will write down student ideas on the board.

   Phase 2:   Teacher will ask: "What made you think of _____? (paper, Yin and Yang, Confucianism, silk road, etc.).

   Phase 3:   Teacher will ask: "Based on our shared ideas and before we study the lesson, have you any new ideas about the Han Dynasty?"

Building Background

1. *Building Background: Prewriting.* Teacher will read a short story to students to develop interest and background.

Short Story

The Story of Lu

Lu was a young boy, just 11 years old. He lived with his family in a village not far from the city of Beijing. On this particular day, Lu was very excited as he talked to his friend Li. "Li—this is such an important day. I can hardly wait until the afternoon comes. Imagine the emperor visiting our humble village and walking among our mud houses."

"I think this is an important day, too," said Li. "Father promised me that if I carried the water to the fields fast enough, I could go wait alongside the road and watch the emperor's arrival. I don't even care that water sloshed out of my buckets and made my itchy old shirt wet, and today not even the weight of that heavy yoke bothered me."

Lu agreed. "Nothing could make me sad today. Today, my father has told me I am old enough for a special honor. I get to present the glazed tile my family made to honor the

FIGURE 10–4   *(Continued)*

Self-Inventory

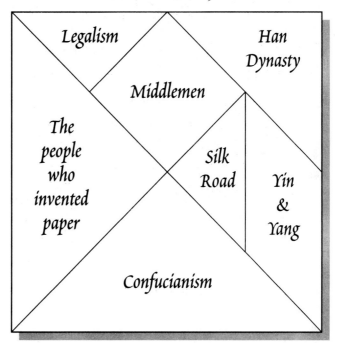

The terms in the tangram above will be helpful in our next social studies lesson. Please help your humble teacher by filling out according to these most honorable instructions:

- Color in the shapes according to the following key.
  (This is not a test!)

Green	**Yellow**	**Red**
I know this!	I think I know.	I don't know this yet.
(I can tell about this.)		

(continued)

FIGURE 10–4   *(Continued)*

emperor. My father is really proud to show off the new glazing process we use on our pottery and I get to carry the tile. Father says we should be happy to honor our emperor who has helped make our country such a happy place to live."

Just then, the boys heard the sound of men approaching on the road. Li said, "Hurry, Lu, I think the emperor is approaching. Run get your tile—tell your family!"

Lu ran toward his mud house. He could see his father holding back the rough hemp curtain and looking out. Lu called out, "The emperor is coming. I must get the tile!"

Lu ran inside and carefully picked up the beautiful tile. The glazing was so amazing to him. He hurried outside, holding the tile so carefully. He moved quickly toward the road to where the big clearing was. He clutched the tile tightly. He could see Li ahead. What Lu didn't see was a branch from a mulberry tree laying in the path. Too late, he fell and the tile went sailing from his hands. He ran to where it fell, but fell to the ground in horror as he saw the pieces, all seven of them, lying there.

Just then, he saw the emperor's party come into the clearing. A man dressed in a fine silk robe addressed him, "You must be the boy who had a gift for me."

Lu, too afraid to speak, just held out the pieces. He didn't even look up to see the expression on the man's face. The man began to laugh. *"*What a wonderful gift," he said. "You must be proud of your family for making such a fine puzzle. I shall have fun with this."

2. *Building Background: Graphic Organizer.* Students will be given a copy of a graphic organizer (see below). Teacher will ask: "Why do you think I chose a representation of a scale as the graphic?" "Why do you think the terms *legalism* and *Confucianism* are in the plates of the scale?" "Why do you think that *middlemen* is in the center of the scale?" "What do you think the terms around the center of the scale represent?"

Graphic Organizer

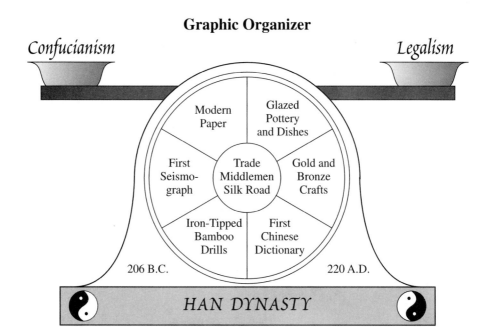

FIGURE 10–4   *(Continued)*

Second Step of PAR: Assistance

Setting a Purpose for Reading

1. *Setting a Purpose for Reading: Mystery Clue Game.* The students will be put in groups of seven students. In keeping with the Chinese theme, the clues for the Mystery Clue Game will be contained in fortune cookies.
   a. Students will be told that they cannot show one another their clues; however, each student may read his or her clue out loud to the group. (This way, everyone must participate.)
   b. Students will be told that they need to use the clues to solve the mystery.
   c. They will have five minutes to work on the mystery.
   d. The group will choose a secretary whose job it is to report their solution to the class.
   e. Students will read the lesson and determine which group came closest to guessing the mystery. (The Mystery Object is silk.)

Mystery Clues

1. It was woven.
2. It was important for trade.
3. It was made on foot-pedaled looms.
4. Middlemen helped protect its secret.
5. Cocoons were important for it.
6. Only the Chinese knew how to make it.
7. It was a type of strong cloth.

2. *Developing Comprehension: Mapping.* Teacher will write *Han Dynasty* on the center of the board and circle it. Students will contribute facts learned in the lesson and suggest how they would fit together. See below for possible outcome.

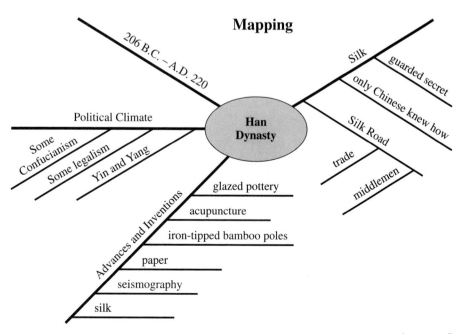

(continued)

FIGURE 10–4 *(Continued)*

3. *Developing Comprehension: Synthesizing.* Students will do a writing excercise using the concept of Yin and Yang. See below.

Writing Exercise

Yin and Yang

 Our book discusses Yin and Yang as a way that Chinese thinkers explained the opposing forces of life. Yin is said to be dark, calm, weak, and mysterious. Yang is thought to be bright, active, strong, sunny, warm, and positive.

 Some animals might be thought of as dark, weak, and/or mysterious. A gopher, for example, sneaks around at night in dark, cool tunnels, so we might think of him as a yin creature. Think of four animals that you would classify as Yin and four that you would classify as Yang. You must give reasons why you classified each animal in the way you chose.

Third Step of PAR: Reflection

1. *Reflection: Semantic Web.* Students will be shown a partially filled in semantic web (see below). Students will work in cooperative groups to fill out copy of the web, in each group, using only facts found in the lesson.

FIGURE 10–4   *(Continued)*

Semantic Web

Decide which of the entries are fact and which are opinion. Circle the opinions. Fill in the rest of the web with facts from the lesson.

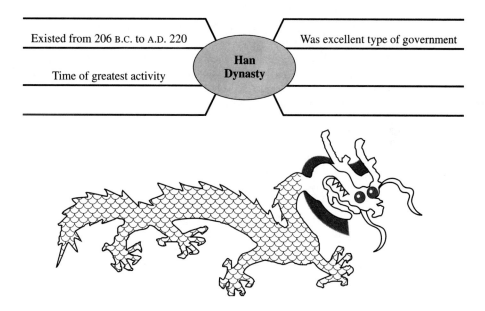

Existed from 206 B.C. to A.D. 220

Was excellent type of government

Han Dynasty

Time of greatest activity

2. *Reflection: Synthesizing.* Students will be asked to prepare a letter. They are to imagine that they live during the Han Dynasty and are part of a family who farms silk worms. The letter is to be written to an uncle who is away, traveling to other countries to sell the silk products. Students are instructed that the letter should include references to certain political and social happenings of the times. The exercise will require students to use their knowledge of the period to create an original letter that is plausible in terms of its factual information. It is a wonderful exercise to encourage students to use synthesis in their thinking. See instructions to students below.

Instructions to Students

Write a Letter

1. Imagine that you live during the Han Dynasty and are part of a family who farms silk worms.
2. This letter is to be written to an uncle who is away, traveling to other countries to sell the silk products.
3. The letter should include mention of the following:
   a. Your feelings about the new political climate
   b. A new invention and its use and value
   c. Where your uncle is at the time you are writing him
4. Base your letter on reliable sources. You may be asked to justify your descriptions.

Source: Susan Aldrich. Reprinted by permission.

Part 3:   Discussion of the Sample PAR Unit

In the PAR unit plan, Aldrich used many of the instructional activities described in Richardson and Morgan (1990), modifying the format of the activities in a creative way to fit the theme of her lesson. Part 3 will look closely at the plan to provide an example of how to create a PAR unit.

As she begins the planning process, the first thing Aldrich does is to examine the content of the lesson and decide what she wants her students to learn from the lesson. She identifies several major concepts in the reading to form the basis of her goals and objectives. (For detailed instructions on how to write effective instructional objectives, see the discussion of the clinical model and the generic lesson-planning later in this chapter.)

Overall Goals

1. Students will gain an awareness of part of the rich and colorful history of the Chinese people.
2. Students will understand how the Han Dynasty fits into the overall history of China.
3. Students will develop an understanding of the concept of Yin and Yang as an important philosophical component of the history of China.

Specific Objectives

1. Students will list three technological contributions made during the Han Dynasty that continue to be of benefit today.
2. Students will define, in writing, the philosophical concept of Yin and Yang.
3. Students will describe, in writing, how the Han Dynasty was influenced by two previous historical government types—Legalism and Confucianism—so that it became a balance of both.

First Step of PAR: Preparation

The Preparation phase of PAR has two instructional purposes: to *determine* the background students have for the material they will be reading and to *build* their background for that reading. These purposes are accomplished through learning activities selected or designed by the teacher. With the use of computers, teachers can design their own instructional activities, making them specifically appropriate for the topic of study and the learning levels and needs of their students. Aldrich's first instructional activity for determining background is an excellent example of how a teacher can modify a standard activity to fit the specific theme of the lesson at hand.

Determining Background.   To determine the background of her students regarding the Han Dynasty, Aldrich decides to use an activity called a *self-inventory*, which she intends to give a day or two prior to beginning the unit so she can look over the students' responses.

In a self-inventory, students are asked to indicate their familiarity (e.g., I know this, I think I know this, or I don't know this yet) with key words and/or concepts that will be found in the lesson to come. Figure 10–5 is an example of a standard format for a self-inventory exercise.

With the use of her computer, Aldrich modifies the format of the self-inventory exercise to conform to the theme of her unit. Figure 10–4 shows the self-inventory she designed to give her students an opportunity to indicate their familiarity (or lack of it) with some of the key concepts they will encounter in the material they will be reading. Notice how the modification Aldrich makes creates a very interesting activity for the students.

Aldrich decides to use one more activity to help her determine the level of background knowledge her students bring to the lesson about the Han Dynasty: a PreP activity (Prereading Plan). By listening to and observing her students during this whole class PreP activity, Aldrich can determine whether the students have very little, some, or much knowledge about the Han Dynasty. Since the PreP is a total group activity, as the students hear each other respond, they will be building their backgrounds as well.

FIGURE 10–5   Self-Inventory: General Example

The following words will be used in the selection you are about to read. In order to give me an idea of your vocabulary background, please check the appropriate category for each word. **REMEMBER:** This is not a test, and it will not be graded.

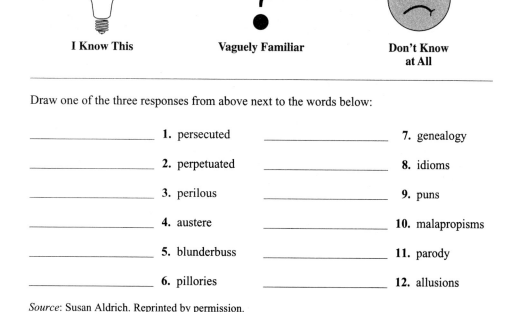

| I Know This | Vaguely Familiar | Don't Know at All |

Draw one of the three responses from above next to the words below:

_____ **1.** persecuted	_____ **7.** genealogy
_____ **2.** perpetuated	_____ **8.** idioms
_____ **3.** perilous	_____ **9.** puns
_____ **4.** austere	_____ **10.** malapropisms
_____ **5.** blunderbuss	_____ **11.** parody
_____ **6.** pillories	_____ **12.** allusions

Source: Susan Aldrich. Reprinted by permission.

In the PreP exercise, the teacher questions students in three different phases to elicit three different types of thought processes. First, the teacher asks for *initial associations* with the topic at hand. For example, prior to a science unit on ecology, the teacher would say to the class, "Tell me anything that comes to mind when you hear the word *ecology.*" The teacher writes student responses on an overhead or on the board. This level of questioning activates students' prior knowledge on the topic through *association.*

For the second phase of PreP, the teacher asks students what made them think of the responses they just gave. Here, the teacher is asking them to reflect on how ideas and words are connected in their own network of associations. Suppose one child responded to the question with *tree.* When that child thinks of why tree came to mind, he may realize that for him, ecology has something to do with environment, which reminds him of planting and saving trees as an effort to maintain a healthy environment. Perhaps another child would think of an event, such as a schoolwide observance of Earth Day because ecology was mentioned in association with the events of that day. Each child's path of associations will be different, but this step will help the students see how they associate words and ideas. At this point, it may occur to a student that although he or she has some vague associations with the word *ecology,* a knowledge of the precise definition is lacking in his or her personal store of information.

In the third phase of the PreP activity, the teacher asks, "Based on all the ideas we have written on the board here, have any of you formed any new ideas about ecology?" This gives students a chance to incorporate other students' ideas with their own and develop a broader or deeper understanding of the term *ecology.* Figure 10–6 shows the PreP Aldrich prepares for her unit on the Han Dynasty.

FIGURE 10–6   Ms. Aldrich's PreP (Prereading Plan)

Phase 1: Initial Associations with the Concept:
Ms. Aldrich: "What comes to mind when you hear the term *Han Dynasty?*"
Teacher writes student responses on board (students activate prior knowledge through the associations).

Phase 2: Reflections on Initial Associations:
Ms. Aldrich: "What made you think of (that response)?" (e.g., paper, Yin & Yang, Confucianism, silk road, etc.)
This phase helps students develop awareness of their networks of association and to interact with other ideas and change their own ideas about the Han Dynasty.

Phase 3: Reformation of Knowledge:
Ms. Aldrich: "Based on our shared ideas and before we study the lesson, have you any new ideas about the Han Dynasty?"
This allows students to verbalize associations, probe their memories, and refine responses.

Source: Susan Aldrich. Reprinted by permission.

Building Background.   Next, Aldrich thinks about activities designed to build background and decides to write a story for her students based on a legend of how the tangram puzzle was discovered. Stories or literature selections are an excellent way to build background, as they bring life to the subject and are motivating to students. Aldrich reads "The Story of Lu" (Figure 10–4) to her students.

To further build background, Aldrich chooses to design a graphic organizer. Graphic organizers are created by highlighting key words and phrases that represent concepts and ideas (from a reading selection) and by putting them in a pattern that shows how they are related or interconnected. These organizers are visual representations of information, ideas, concepts, and/or events (such as what students might encounter in the content of a reading selection). As we saw in Figure 3–5 in Chapter 3, the main ideas from a reading selection about early man are depicted graphically. This kind of graphic organizer is referred to as hierarchical because it depicts main ideas or concepts and then shows how the supporting detail is related to the main concepts and subconcepts. Thus, the information is ranked, showing a hierarchical relationship.

Graphic organizers come in a wide array of formats, including webs, semantic webs, time lines, story maps, structured overviews, and more—all of which organize information into visual patterns that show how ideas, concepts, and/or events are related. Further examples of these various types of graphic organizers are provided later in the chapter.

Figure 10–4 shows the graphic organizer that Aldrich created to fit the theme of her unit. The pattern in this particular organizer makes it a conceptual graphic organizer; that is, it depicts a central concept (Han Dynasty) with supporting detail (characteristics of the dynasty such as trade, middlemen, silk road, gold and bronze craft, first Chinese dictionary, etc.). Aldrich also makes use of symbolism in the graphic organizer by presenting the information within the drawing of a scale that depicts how the Han Dynasty incorporated aspects of both Legalism and Confucianism into its social organization, becoming a balance of both. Pictorial graphic organizers such as this one are user friendly to children, and the picture seems to increase students' interest and ability to remember the information.

Each student receives a copy of this graphic organizer to examine as Aldrich asks the following questions:

1. Why do you think I chose a representation of a scale as the graphic?
2. Why do you think the terms *Legalism* and *Confucianism* are in the plates of the scale?
3. Why do you think that *middlemen* is in the center of the scale?
4. What do you think the terms around the center of the scale represent?

Research has supported the fact that graphic organizers help students understand and remember information. Dunston (1992), who did a review of 10 years of research on graphic organizers, found that when they were presented to elementary students before reading, graphic organizers aided comprehension and memory. Another interesting finding of Dunston is that when students were instructed in the use of graphic organizers and taught to construct their own, the effects of the graphic organizers were greater.

Graphic organizers are a wonderful way to help children see organizational patterns in written material and to make the information therein more accessible to them. Further examples of graphic organizers are presented in the appendix at the end of this book. Through the visual stimulation provided by the graphic organizer and the discussion created by Aldrich's questions, the students are exposed to the main ideas of the lesson and are given a picture of how they are related. Graphics are immensely valuable to students in helping them to pull out the main ideas of a selection from the field or context in which they are embedded, and they are particularly helpful to field-dependent learners.

Considering that Aldrich's students have participated in a total of four learning activities related to the material to be read (all during the P step of PAR), they have been exposed several times and in different ways to the major ideas and vocabulary they will encounter in the reading selection. It is now time for the students to read the selection, which they will do during the A part of PAR, with the help of guiding activities. Aldrich has one more activity planned for them to do before they actually read their textbooks. Since this activity is part of the A phase of PAR, it will be discussed in the following section.

Second Step of PAR: Assistance

Activities for the A part of PAR are geared to do two things: provide a purpose for reading the selection and develop comprehension of the material. Aldrich is now ready to give the students a purpose for reading the lesson, and so she designs a *Mystery Clue Game*, a group activity in which students collectively try to solve a mystery with clues the teacher provides for them. Aldrich has chosen the important product *silk*, made and used in trade by the Chinese during the Han Dynasty, to be the mystery word. She puts the students into groups of seven and provides each student with one of the following clues:

1. It was woven.
2. It was important for trade.
3. It was made on foot-pedaled looms.
4. Middlemen helped protect its secret.
5. Cocoons were important for it.
6. Only the Chinese knew how to make it.
7. It was a type of strong cloth.

A very creative touch at this point is that Aldrich has put the clues in fortune cookies (in keeping with her Chinese theme), which will further increase the motivational factor of the activity. She gives the following directions to the students for playing the game:

1. I am giving each of you a clue. You can read it but do not show it to anyone else.
2. All of the clues will be needed to solve the mystery, so each of you can read your clue out loud when it is your turn.
3. After *all* the clues have been read, you may begin discussing the identity of the mystery word.
4. Choose a representative whose job it will be to report your solution to the class.
5. You will have five minutes to work on the mystery.

6. Each group's solution to the mystery will be listed on the chalkboard. You will then "pair-read" the lesson to find out which group(s) came closest to solving the mystery.

The students are now ready to read the lesson with the added motivational factor of finding out which group came closest to solving the mystery.

After giving the students a purpose to read, the next step for Aldrich in the Assistance part of the PAR is to select activities that will help ensure comprehension of the reading selection. In fact, she chooses two activities for the students to do after they have read the text to help develop their understanding of it.

The first activity is an interactive activity (teacher and students do together) called *mapping*, which is a form of a graphic organizer. Like the hierarchical graphic organizer, it will provide the students with a visual representation of the relationship of major and supporting ideas. Seeing these relationships is the key to understanding any reading selection. Once students are practiced at creating maps, the activity can be done in cooperative groups or even individually. Steps for designing a mapping and an example are given in Figure 10–7.

Figure 10–4 shows what Aldrich's mapping lesson about the Han Dynasty looks like. In order to do the mapping, the students will have to look back at their books and

FIGURE 10–7   How to Implement a Mapping Activity in the Classroom

1. Select a *portion* of a chapter to map. (Mapping a whole chapter is usually too time consuming.)
2. Write the main concept (idea) of the written selection down on a blank sheet of paper (or on chalkboard) and circle it.
3. Ask students for related information. Guide them to major subheadings related to main concept topic. Add subheadings to circle with lines.
4. Ask students for supporting detail for each subheading. Add on with lines.

Example:

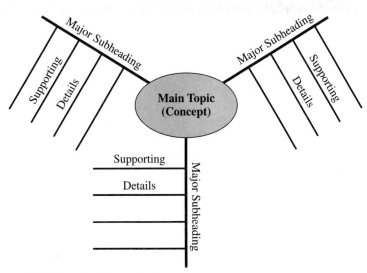

Source: Susan Aldrich. Reprinted by permission.

reread to find specific information. As they do so, their attention will be focused on ideas and relationships between them. Mapping is appropriate at all grade levels.

The second activity Aldrich has chosen for Assistance is a writing activity in which students classify animals as either Yin or Yang (based on their habits and characteristics). By requiring the students to state why they classified an animal either way, Aldrich is fostering their analytical thinking skills and thus enhancing their understanding of the concept of Yin and Yang. This writing activity is presented in Figure 10–4.

Aldrich decides to relate this activity to the "flourishing of the arts" that occurred during the Han Dynasty. After viewing many examples of the artwork of the period, she has the students create pictures of the animals they wrote about, with the goal of making their pictures look like the artwork of the time. By becoming Chinese artists, the students will experience an aspect of ancient Chinese culture in a very direct way. An art activity such as this involves students affectively as well as cognitively. Research has shown that affective learning (activities involving the fine arts, such drawing, painting, singing, dancing, listening to music, etc.) supports cognitive learning, increases memory, and actually enhances intellectual achievement (Hom, 1990).

Students can then make a presentation of their pictures and explain why they chose to classify them as Yin or Yang. By the time they have heard each other explain their Yin/Yang choices, they will have a very good understanding of the concept of Yin and Yang and how it fit into Chinese culture. The artwork and written exercises can be displayed on a bulletin board for all to enjoy.

By now, the students have read the lesson through a first time to get the whole picture and then have gone back to reread it with a particular focus generated by the A activities. Rereading is usually necessary for comprehension, and doing so with a focus or perspective in mind further enhances understanding. See the appendix at the end of this book for more A activities.

Third Step of PAR: Reflection
During the Reflection phase of PAR, the goal is to have the students think critically about what they have read. Thinking about what has been read is an essential part of reading comprehension. Until the individual ponders the implications of what he or she has read and reflects on the significance of it for his or her own life, the material remains distant and irrelevant. In this case, the information or knowledge remains not only meaningless to the individual (as much of what is memorized in school does, which is why much of it is forgotten) but it also remains inapplicable to solving problems or making decisions.

It has been said that for every one hour of reading, one should do two hours of thinking. In the modern way of life, most people have time constraints that would prohibit this ideal kind of study. It is notable that in most U.S. classrooms, provision for *any* time or opportunity for just thinking or reflecting is virtually unheard of. The typical organization of elementary instruction (i.e., having specific curricula that must be covered in each grade in a set amount of time) is antithetical to a reflective curriculum. The R part of PAR provides the opportunity for critical thinking and reflection by the students within a framework or structure that can be realistically implemented on a regular basis within the confines of the set curriculum.

The activities used in the Reflection step are geared to provide students with the skills, opportunities, and time necessary to engage in what Richardson and Morgan (1990) call *effective thinking*—"that multifaceted and complex process… which deals with the ability of students to gather data, test hypotheses, and reflect in a skeptical disciplined manner." This process is the basis of decision making. All individuals, in the course of their lives, must make many decisions that have important consequences to themselves and others. Therefore, systematically providing students with exercises and activities that foster effective thinking is essential; PAR is designed to ensure the inclusion of this important process in classroom instruction.

Now the question is, What kinds of activities will foster effective thinking? The answer is that there are many and varied ways to engage students in this process. Such activities could include an individual writing assignment, a cooperative problem-solving activity, an inquiry activity, debates, simulations, various kinds of fine arts projects, and so forth. There is no limit to the types of activities that can be used here. The teacher can get very creative in designing them, as long as the activities serve the purpose of extending the students' learning by making them think more deeply and/or from different perspectives about what they have read.

For example, doing a simulation of a historical event would require students to do research beyond the textbook (such as using primary sources and other secondary sources) to ascertain all the details of the event, including what exactly has happened, who was involved, what was said by whom, what the customs and dress of the period were, and so on. Decisions will have to be made when sources present conflicting information, and students will have to justify their conclusions. This kind of activity engages students in analysis and synthesis as they strive for authenticity and creativity in their presentations.

A Reflection activity does not have to be so elaborate, however, to cause students to think and reflect and to practice what McPeck terms *reflective skepticism* (Richardson & Morgan, 1990). This refers to the ability to weigh evidence carefully and with skepticism before making decisions. Students should be taught to "read between the lines" or to analyze material in terms of specific criteria, such as differentiating fact from opinion, detecting propaganda techniques, seeing causal relationships, and evaluating consequences of an action. Whatever type of activity the teacher chooses to use, it should be a structured activity that guides the students through a process that ensures accuracy, rationality, and justification of conclusions.

Aldrich selects two activities for Reflection, the first of which is called a *semantic web*. This activity is designed to give students practice distinguishing fact from opinion. Aldrich follows the basic structure of the traditional semantic web, but she adds a few touches with her computer to make it fit in with the theme of her unit. Figure 10–4 shows the semantic web designed by Aldrich.

Aldrich decides to make this a cooperative group activity in which each group is provided with a partially filled web containing both facts and opinions about the Han Dynasty. The students are to discuss the webbing, decide which statements are fact and which are opinion, fill in the rest of the web with facts only, and, finally, present their finished product to the class.

The next activity is an individual writing activity that requires the students to construct a plausible personal letter of that period based on what they learned from the text and other sources provided by the teacher and trips to the library. Figure 10.4 depicts instructions students receive for the activity.

This activity will require students to think again about the Han Dynasty and to research further into the period. In addition to deepening and broadening their knowledge of the period, the students will be using their knowledge plus their imaginations to create something entirely different from, though based on, their knowledge of the period. Putting themselves in the place of a person of the times, and imagining how that person felt about the social, economic, and moral realities of the period, will require the students to synthesize the information they have and to create a product based on that information. See the appendix at the end of this book for more R activities.

In the discussion of Ms. Aldrich's PAR unit, it can be seen that at each phase of the PAR, there were specific instructional purposes to be achieved. In the P phase, she chose activities to *determine* and to *build* the backgrounds of her students. For the A phase, she selected activities that would provide students with a *purpose* to read and *assist their comprehension* of what they read. For the R phase, she selected activities that would require her students to *think critically* about what they had read. Figure 10–8 shows in telegraphic form the purposes of each phase of PAR and the activities Aldrich used for each of those purposes.

Knowing the instructional purpose of each phase of the PAR enables the teacher to use the same basic activity at any phase of the PAR, with slight modification. For example, in the sample lesson, it was seen how a graphic organizer could be used to build the students' background. By leaving some of the supporting detail out of the graphic and having the students fill it in as they read, it becomes an activity that assists comprehension. By having the students construct their own graphic organizer depicting the main ideas of the chapter and the supporting detail, it becomes an excellent reflection activity. Most instructional activities can be modified to fit any phase of the PAR. The teacher can also create his or her own activities for the three phases of the PAR, and this process becomes easier as he or she becomes more familiar with each

FIGURE 10–8   Three Phases of PAR: Instructional Purposes with Activities

Preparation Determine Background Build Background	*Ms. Aldrich Used:* • Self-Inventory • PreP
	• Short Story • Graphic Organizer
Assistance Provide a Purpose to Read	*Ms. Aldrich Used:* • Mystery Clue Game
Develop Comprehension	• Mapping • Writing Exercise with Art Activity
Reflection Think Critically about the Reading	*Ms. Aldrich Used* • Semantic Web • Create a Personal Letter

phase of the PAR and its purposes. The key is knowing and understanding the instructional purpose at each phase; it then becomes possible to select or create activities that fulfill those instructional purposes and that meet the needs and interests of the students.

By consistently using the PAR framework to plan instruction, the teacher will not only be helping his or her students to acquire knowledge, thinking skills, and confidence in their ability to learn but will also be providing them with the opportunity to become independent, self-motivated learners. Gradually, the classroom will become a community of learners.

Thematic Approach to Planning

Whereas PAR can be considered an extended learning sequence consisting of many activities to be presented in several days, thematic planning focuses on the integration of information, concepts, and ideas around a central theme. Much has been written from numerous perspectives on thematic approaches to planning. Often, thematic approaches are presented in such complex ways as to create, rather than solve, a new teacher's planning problems. The focus here, then, is to make thematic planning a practical reality by answering the following questions:

- What is the nature and essence of thematic planning?
- Why does thematic planning work?
- How is thematic planning done?

What Is Thematic Planning?

The most uncomplicated and direct way to understand the nature of thematic planning is to look at the thematic planning approach grid presented in Figure 10–9. Thematic planning can be short or long term, using either an integrated curriculum model or a relevant theme model. Essentially, your choices when using a thematic planning approach correspond to the four quadrants of the thematic planning approach grid. It will be useful here to look at examples of each of the four choices. As you review these examples, keep two things in mind:

1. In the *integrated curriculum model,* two or more content areas are concurrently linked through a topic from one of those content areas. This topic can then be thought of as an "organizing hub" theme.
2. In the *relevant theme model,* curriculum material in one or more content areas is related to an external theme.

Example for Quadrant I

Short-term thematic approach emphasizing an integrated curriculum model

> *Content Areas:*   Social studies and language arts
>
> *Grade Level:*   First grade
>
> *Topics:*   Transportation (social studies)
> "Story of the Big Red Train" (language arts)

FIGURE 10–9   Thematic Planning Approach

Model / Time	Integrated Curriculum Model	Relevant Theme Model
Short Term	Quadrant I	Quadrant II
Long Term	Quadrant III	Quadrant IV

Time Frame: 1 day

Analysis: The teacher planned it so that on this particular day, information, concepts, and ideas being presented in one content area would directly link with those being taught that day in another content area. Thus, the curriculum material and objectives of two content areas were aligned to complement and reinforce one another.

Example for Quadrant II

Short-term thematic approach emphasizing a relevant theme model

Content Areas: Social studies and science
Grade Level: Fifth grade
Relevant Theme: The Future
Time Frame: 3 days

Analysis: The teacher sought to find a relevant theme on which to focus for three days that would help make the content being covered particularly interesting and useful to the students. Because of the nature of the topics being covered at this time in social studies and science, she thought that looking at this material as it relates to what things may be like in the future would work as an effective theme.

Example for Quadrant III:

Long-term thematic approach emphasizing an integrated curriculum model

> *Content Areas:*   Social studies, Language arts, mathematics
>
> *Grade Level:*   First grade
>
> *Units*:   My Community (social studies)
>
> Communication Skills (language arts)
>
> Counting (mathematics)
>
> *Time Frame:*   5 weeks
>
> *Analysis:*   The teacher reviewed her curriculum outlines in the content areas and realized that if she regarded this particular social studies unit as her "organizing hub," it would be possible to link information, concepts, and ideas across three content areas. For example, various pieces of literature, spelling words, and writing exercises would center around "My Community" over this five-week period. Similarly, many of the activities for developing counting skills over this five-week period would utilize things found in the community (e.g., counting houses, people, schools, supermarkets, parks, etc., by 1s, 2s, and 3s).

Example for Quadrant IV:

Long-term thematic approach emphasizing a relevant theme model

> *Content Area:*   Mathematics
>
> *Grade Level:*   Sixth grade
>
> *Relevant Theme:*   Classroom Economic System
>
> *Time Frame:* Entire school year
>
> *Analysis:*   The teacher has helped the students maintain a cohesive, well-organized environment by setting up a classroom economy, including a bank, supply store, and various related jobs. Many of the topics covered in math are related to the operation and needs of their economic system. Through this approach, the students are eager to master math concepts and skills in order to solve the day-to-day problems of keeping their economy running smoothly. Such ongoing hands-on application of the material being covered greatly increases their learning in math.

Why Does Thematic Planning Work?

The integrated curriculum model works because students are afforded the opportunity of having information, concepts, and ideas reinforced by the dynamic linking of two or more content areas. The time and thought spent in planning such lessons is well worth it as the integrated presentation of the content reflects the reality of how students experience everyday life. For example, through this approach, spelling is not just an exercise concerning a list of words. Rather, the words chosen may be directly related to a theme taken from a topic being studied in social studies or in the literature currently being read. Just as you have a much fuller and lasting impression by seeing something in three-dimensional form rather than in two dimensions (i.e., in person as opposed to in a picture), so, too, do the students gain a richer and multifaceted impression of content area material by experiencing it through the unifying thread of a theme. Memory and understanding are greatly increased when such integrated and "living" connections are made in the mind.

The relevant theme model is also effective in promoting student learning because of the dynamic mental connections it allows students to make. In this case, these connections center around things that are of particular interest to the students, hence the name *relevant theme*. From day to day, teachers can often be seen searching for student-relevant examples as an effective way to explain concepts and ideas in the different content areas. These spontaneous moments of trying to relate instruction to students' interests and lives are fine. Planning, however, by using a relevant theme model is much more effective because whole lessons and series of lessons are consciously designed so students can perceive and explore content area material through familiar and engaging themes. All people have "mental road maps" called *schemata* that, in large part, determine how they perceive and understand new things. By using relevant themes, teachers are effectively tapping into the students' existing schemata, and thus facilitating the comprehension of new information.

How Is Thematic Planning Done?

Now that you have an understanding of the types of thematic planning that can be used and why they promote student learning, it will be useful to have a set of steps to follow so the actual planning can be accomplished. Figure 10–10 lists a set of sequential steps for each of the four types of thematic planning approaches as shown in Figure 10–9 according to quadrants I–IV.

In attempting the use the steps listed in Figure 10–10 for carrying out thematic planning, the following four points should be considered:

- *Point 1:*   Whichever of the four types of thematic planning you choose, it is crucial that you start by reviewing your overall content area curriculum plans. If the overall plans have been crafted with thought and care, a solid basis exists for completing the remaining steps in the thematic planning process. In short, thematic planning is done best in the context of a clear framework indicating what is to be taught and when.
- *Point 2:*   It will be helpful as you do thematic planning to follow the steps listed in Figure 10–10, and to refer to the narrative examples given for Quadrants I–IV as guides.
- *Point 3:*   Long-term thematic planning, whether the integrated curriculum or relevant theme model, requires the additional step of creating a working outline. This

FIGURE 10–10   Steps to Planning the Four Types of Thematic Approach

Quadrant I	Quadrant II
Using a Short-Term Integrated Curriculum Model	*Using a Short-Term Relevant Theme Model*
Step 1: Review overall content area curriculum plans.	Step 1: Review overall content area curriculum plans.
Step 2: Select a topic in each of two or more content areas that come at the same time on the planning schedule and have good potential for being aligned.	Step 2: Select a theme that has good potential for fitting with a topic in one or more content areas, and for being relevant and engaging to the students.
Step 3: Review the text material for the selected topics.	Step 3: Review the text material for the selected topics.
Step 4: Design the thematic lesson plans in which information, concepts, and ideas in the selected content area topics are linked so as to complement and reinforce each other.	Step 4: Design the thematic lesson plan(s) in which information, concepts, and ideas in the selected content area topic(s) is linked to the relevant theme being explored.
Quadrant III	**Quadrant IV**
Using a Long-Term Integrated Curriculum Model	*Using a Long-Term Relevant Theme Model*
Step 1: Review overall content area curriculum plans.	Step 1: Review overall content area curriculum plans.
Step 2: Select a topic in each of two or more content areas that come at the same time on the planning schedule and have good potential for being aligned.	Step 2: Select a theme that has good potential for fitting with topics in one or more content areas, and for being relevant and engaging to the students.
Step 3: Review the text material for the selected topics.	Step 3: Review the text material for the selected topics.
Step 4: Draft a working outline indicating advantageous places and general ideas for linking the content areas over the desired long-term period.	Step 4: Draft a working outline indicating advantageous places and general ideas for linking the relevant theme to topics being covered over the desired long-term period.
Step 5: Design the thematic lesson plans in which information, concepts, and ideas in the selected content area topics are linked so as to complement and reinforce each other.	Step 5: Design the thematic lesson plans in which information, concepts, and ideas in the selected content area topics are linked to the relevant theme being explored.

makes perfect sense because when you are attempting to carry a theme through several weeks or more, it is necessary to have laid out a road map for yourself that indicates the most advantageous and likely places for certain linkages and activities to take place. The more complex, creative, and long-term the type of planning you use, the more you will be grateful for having a structured working outline to guide your efforts all along the way.

- *Point 4:*   A strong recommendation: Start small and simply in your first attempts at thematic planning. In practical terms, this means it is best to use the short-term approaches first. Perhaps you can find a theme to carry through one particular lesson (i.e., relevant theme approach) or use a theme from a lesson in one content area to link with another content area on the same day (i.e., integrated curriculum approach). As you get the feel for how this type of planning is done, then your thematic plans can cover longer periods and be more complex. Just as you always want to build for student success over time, you should do the same in your efforts to employ this creative and relatively complex form of block planning.

Inquiry Approach to Planning

Think if you will. This admonition is so appropriate for this age, and especially for children in school. The human mind is a most precious instrument. If it is used consistently and correctly, it becomes ever more effective and sharp. If it stays relatively unused or misused, it becomes dull and relatively useless. It is hard to imagine a greater waste than the failure to develop the human mind. From the preceding discussion, it is clear that proper development of students' abilities to think and effectively use their minds is of primary importance. Although no single teaching method will ensure such development, the *inquiry approach*, which can be thought of as a student-directed journey through the learning process, focuses specifically on this.

Inquiry as an approach to learning is at the heart of the constructivist paradigm for teaching, as discussed in Chapter 1. It focuses on discovery and meaning-centered activities in which students take responsibility for learning and have opportunities to relate what they are learning to their own experiences. If planned for and used properly, inquiry can provide students with direct experience in using their minds in a disciplined and a thoughtful way to solve problems and understand and deal with situations. This skill will not only increase students' learning in the content areas but it will also, more importantly, set them on the path for successful learning for the rest of their school years and beyond. To examine the inquiry approach to planning, the following topics will be examined:

- Types of inquiry
- How to use inquiry
- Two models of inquiry
- Why inquiry works

Types of Inquiry

As with thematic planning, inquiry can be done on a short- or long-term basis. This means you can range from one particular lesson in the inquiry mode all the way to using this as the *modus operandi* for covering an entire year's curriculum in a specific content area. To look at the types of inquiry you can use, the open and closed approaches will be examined through several examples and then two specific models of inquiry that can be employed will be outlined—namely, the scientific model of social inquiry and the Ws of inquiry.

Open and Closed Approaches.   Whether planning for short-term or long-term use of inquiry, you have the choice of using an open or closed approach or a combination of open and closed approaches. Figure 10–11 presents a grid that graphically depicts these possibilities.

It is useful to understand the nature of open and closed inquiry approaches and then determine how these can be accomplished over short and long periods of time. There are two aspects to any inquiry approach: (1) the thing to be inquired about (i.e., problem) and (2) the method of inquiry to be used. With this in mind, a brief description of the possible inquiry approaches, as depicted in Figure 10–12, is provided to help in determining what works best in a given circumstance. Note that the four possible approaches shown are arranged from the least to the most difficult to carry out, for reasons stated in the descriptions of each approach.

1. *Closed/Closed Approach:*   This is clearly the way to begin using inquiry as a new teacher. In the closed/closed approach, you *define the problem to be investigated* and *decide what specific mode of inquiry to use.* Remember, you not only want to encourage your students to think but you also want to build their confidence (as well as your

FIGURE 10–11   Types of Inquiry

Type Time	Closed/ Closed	Open/ Closed	Closed/ Open	Open/ Open
Short Term				
Long Term				

FIGURE 10–12   Continuum of Inquiry Approaches

Aspects	Possible Approaches			
Problem for Inquiry	Closed	Open	Closed	Open
Mode for Inquiry	Closed	Closed	Open	Open

own!) in their ability to successfully carry out inquiry. It is wise, therefore, to make the initial attempts structured and straightforward. This gives the students a clear sense of direction and security that they know what they are doing. It is then in context of this purposefulness and security that they make inquiry, using their minds to discover information, make decisions, and attempt to solve problems.

2. *Open/Closed Approach:*   Once the students have had successful experience conducting inquiry into problems that you have placed before them, and they also understand how to follow a particular mode of inquiry, *they can be given the opportunity to choose their own problems to investigate and solve.* Again, so as to build for success all around, it would be wise to have them use the mode of inquiry with which they are already familiar. It is much easier for them to formulate or select a problem to inquire about than to create their own mode of inquiry. As you can predict by now, having them create their own mode of inquiry is the next step in order of difficulty among the four inquiry approaches. Before moving to that step, however, the following three ways should be considered when trying to determine how to go about having your students formulate or select their own problems to investigate:

a. Present students with a menu of problems from which they can choose. (This allows for element of choice while still providing direction.)

b. Have students generate a menu of problems from which to choose as the focus of their inquiry. (This has an inherently higher student-interest potential.)

c. Have individual or small cooperative groups formulate its own problems for investigation. (This places greater responsibility on individual students.)

3. *Closed/Open Approach:*   In keeping with the progression from the least to most difficult of the inquiry approaches to use, the closed/open approach logically fits here. Students, having had positive results using the first two approaches, are now ready to attempt a more difficult step. *They are ready to be asked to determine or create their own mode of inquiry as the means to exploring and solving a given problem.* Experience will show that it takes some time and much guided effort before students feel completely comfortable doing this. The encouraging thing to note, though, is that students can be made to enjoy this opportunity to be "learning detectives" as they set out, either in small groups or individually, to investigate and solve a problem.

4. *Open/Open Approach:*   Finally, after much practice and guidance using the other three approaches, students are ready to take *full responsibility* for the inquiry process. In short, *they can now determine what problem to solve and how best to solve it.* Of course, you are never far away and are available to facilitate their efforts. This is a natural consequence, as one of the students' responsibilities here is to access whatever resources are necessary to understand and solve the problem. Having been ushered progressively up to this point, the students' natural desire to know is given scope to operate fully in the context of a thoughtful and disciplined process.

How to Use Inquiry

The five sequential steps (outlined in Figure 10–13) for using the inquiry approach to planning are examined next, including examples of some of the decisions a new teacher made at each step.

    Step 1:   Review your overall content area curriculum plans.

The value of having a set of overall content curriculum plans is that it puts before you the blueprint of the year's work. As you proceed to build for student learning, it is quite natural that you will need to refer to this blueprint. Knowing that inquiry will require students to investigate and solve problems, you will want to scan these plans to see which topics in the different content areas are best suited to such an approach. Also, you will have to think about the need to make reference resources readily available to your students as they conduct their inquiry.

Example of Step 1

    Content Area: Social studies
    Grade Level: Fourth grade
    Topic: Chumash Indians

FIGURE 10–13   Steps to Planning for Using the Inquiry Approach

Steps	Why to Do It
Step 1: Review your overall content area curriculum plans.	To provide a holistic view for seeing where the most advantageous places are for inquiry in context of curriculum material over the short and long term
Step 2: Determine the type of inquiry approach to use.	To choose a framework that is workable for the students considering their readiness and the nature of the problem being investigated
Step 3: Identify the problem to be investigated.	To establish a clear and relevant focus for the investigation
Step 4: Prepare materials to be used.	To create a ready resource area where students can refer to in their quest for knowledge and answers
Step 5: Guide the inquiry process.	To facilitate the students' investigation and build for understanding of the process and success

Analysis: This new teacher made the following decisions concerning use of inquiry upon reviewing his overall content area curriculum plans:

a. The first attempt at inquiry should be in social studies because of the students' demonstrated interests and the teacher's subject area knowledge.

b. The second month of the year is a good time to begin using inquiry, as the students' needs and abilities are known and classroom routines and procedures have been established. Also, this is when the unit on Native Americans comes in the curriculum sequence.

c. The indigenous Chumash Indians is a good topic to use for inquiry because there is a wealth of resources readily available at the district's Instructional Materials Center (IMC).

Step 2:   Determine the type of inquiry approach to use.

The decision to use anything from a closed/closed to an open/open approach depends on where you are with your students as far as ability and successful experience using inquiry are concerned. Other factors to consider in deciding which inquiry approach to use include: (1) the nature of the problem to be investigated, (2) the availability of reference resources, and (3) the students' prior experience or background with the topic out of which the problem is generated.

Example of Step 2

Content Area: Physical education

Grade Level: Fifth grade

Topic: Playground Games

Approach: Closed/Closed

Problem: The need to resolve conflict over disagreements concerning rules that apply to different playground games

Analysis: This new teacher made the following decisions concerning the type of inquiry approach to use:

a. The continuing conflict over disagreements about the rules for different playground games makes this a timely and relevant problem for the students to look into solving.

b. A closed/closed approach makes sense here because the students have used inquiry only once before and still need much structure and direction.

c. The mode of inquiry used here can be generalized and adapted by the students for solving similar class problems that may occur.

Step 3:   Identify the problem to be investigated.

The key to identifying the problem for the students to investigate is relevance and clarity. This is why it is wise to begin using inquiry only after you have a fairly good reading of your students' interests and abilities. Remember, you want to build for success. The last thing you would want to do is turn them off from this mode of discovery learning that will serve them well for the rest of their lives.

Example of Step 3

Content Area: Science

Grade Level: First grade

Topic: Pets

Approach: Closed/Open

Problem: The need to care for the class's pet hamster

Analysis: This new teacher made the following decisions in identifying the problem the students were to investigate:

a. The need to figure out how best to care for the class's pet hamster is a natural problem to select, because the students love the animal, do not know how to care for it, and are very interested in its well-being.

b. This problem provides for students' varying learning styles to come into play, as there will be opportunities to read, write, listen, observe, touch, and use motor skills in finding and implementing a solution.

c. The investigation and eventual solution of this problem, through questions the students will collaboratively generate, will reinforce classroom routines, as the care of the class pet will be an ongoing daily feature of the students' lives in the classroom.

Step 4: Prepare materials to be used.

Inquiry means a search for information, concepts, and ideas in order to understand and solve a problem. To accomplish this, students need to refer to various resources related to the problem being investigated.

Example of Step 4

Content Area: Physical education

Grade Level: Fifth grade

Topic: Playground Games

Approach: Closed/Closed

Problem: The need to resolve conflicts over disagreements concerning rules that apply to different playground games

Resources: Poster board, colored markers, pamphlets, books, articles

Analysis: This new teacher made the following decision concerning the resource materials to prepare for this inquiry endeavor:

a. Five large pieces of poster board are needed to list the names (and eventually the agreed-upon rules) of the five games students play.

b. Pamphlets, books, and articles on setting game rules and collaboratively resolving conflicts are to be placed under the Current Materials sign in the classroom library.

   c. Students are to be given clear directions about how and when to use the Current Materials, what these materials have to offer, and how they can contribute additional materials for a particular problem being investigated.

Step 5:   Guide the inquiry process.

The best way to know how students are learning and what they are learning is to be among them, monitoring and assisting them as they are working. This is all the more true for inquiry learning experiences that require students to think at a more sophisticated level than usual in an attempt to understand and solve problems.

Example of Step 5

Content Area: Science

Grade Level: First grade

Topic: Pets

Approach: Closed/Open

Problem: The need to care for the class's pet hamster

Resources: Sheets of paper, books and pamphlets, pocket chart

Guiding Mode: Facilitate small-group work and guide use of Current Materials section of classroom library

Analysis: This new teacher made the following decisions concerning guiding the inquiry process:

   a. There needs to be close monitoring and facilitation of the students' efforts as they work in their small-group inquiry, because this will be their first attempt at solving a problem using their *own method* of investigation.

   b. The problem to be investigated, caring for the class's pet hamster, has been purposely chosen because much discussion has already gone on about this issue and because of the hands-on nature of trying to deliver such pet care.

   c. The students seem amply primed to tackle this problem, with close monitoring and guidance.

Two Models of Inquiry

In principle, there are as many modes of inquiry for solving problems as there are individuals attempting to do so. As individuals, teachers and students look at the world from unique perspectives, and thus it is not surprising that they may ask different questions, have different interpretations of data, and reach different conclusions as they investigate problems. As noted earlier, depending on the type of inquiry approach you use—from closed/closed to open/open—there is scope for accommodating these unique perspectives.

    Two particular models can serve as highly structured, logical, and effective guidelines as you begin to orient your students to the nature and benefits of the inquiry process:

- The scientific model of inquiry
- The Ws model of inquiry

Both of these models will be examined with examples to demonstrate how they work.

The Scientific Model of Inquiry.   Although the name *scientific model of inquiry* sounds somewhat forbidding for the elementary level, it really is nothing more than the application of commonsense to solving a problem. To understand better the formal sequence of steps in the scientific method of inquiry and the terminology used, look at Figure 10–14 for a commonsense perspective.

This sequence of events is what one normally experiences when attempting to solve a problem. The steps to the scientific model of inquiry are *exactly* parallel to this; the only difference is the terminology. Notice how this terminology is applied in Figure

FIGURE 10–14   A Commonsense Perspective of the Scientific Model of Inquiry

Commonsense Approach to Solving a Problem			Steps of Scientific Model of Inquiry
You have a concern about something—	leading you to ask…	"What is the problem here?" and "What are some questions I need to ask?"	Problem Formulation
You raise some key questions concerning the problem—	leading you to ask…	"What is my preliminary best guess about answers to these questions?"	Hypothesis Formulation
You look into the problem more deeply—	leading you to ask…	"What information do I need to answer these questions and get a grasp on understanding and solving the problem?"	Data Collection
You go about finding the information you need—	leading you to ask…	"What does this information tell me about my questions, guesses, and solving the problem?"	Data Analysis
You look over and think about the information you have found—	leading you to ask…	"What do my findings tell me I should do to solve the problem?"	Conclusions & Recommendations
You see how effective the action you take is in solving the problem—	leading you to ask…	"What, if any, part of this process do I need to go back to, to come up with a better solution to the problem?	Recycling the Inquiry Process

10–15 as a first-grade class went about solving the problem of how to care for its pet hamster. From this example three main points can be understood:

- *Point 1:*   Something as sophisticated as the scientific model of inquiry can be used productively by a first-grade class.
- *Point 2:*   The scientific model of inquiry, being a commonsense approach to understanding and solving problems, can be used in all content areas to deal with an unlimited range of problems.
- *Point 3:*   The amount of teacher direction needed for any or all of the steps in the scientific model of inquiry should be based on the students' experience, abilities, and needs, and on the nature and complexity of the problem itself.

The Ws Model of Inquiry.   As with the scientific model of inquiry, the Ws model is rooted in common sense and human experience. Both, for instance, can be used effectively to buy a car or solve a host of other day-to-day problems that occur. The Ws model

FIGURE 10–15   Application of Scientific Model of Inquiry in a First-Grade Class

Inquiry Steps	Description of What Students Did
Concern/Doubt/Need	The students in a first-grade class were given a pet hamster and expressed a need to figure out how to care for it.
Problem Formulation	The students raised five main questions that seemed important to solving their problem: 1. What do hamsters eat? 2. How often and how much do they eat? 3. What do they need besides food? 4. What kind of house do they live in? 5. What kind of things need to be in the house?
Hypothesis Formulation	The students were given an opportunity during Rug Time to guess at what the answers to the questions would be.
Data Collection	The students gathered information from different prearranged sources to find answers to their questions. This was accomplished at the Classroom Inquiry Center.
Data Analysis	The students reviewed and discussed the information they found to answer their questions.
Hypothesis Testing (conclusions/ recommendations)	The students took their findings and set up "Hamster City" for the ongoing care of their pet hamster.
Recycling the Inquiry Process	The students recognized that new questions needed to be answered, new sources referred to, and new solutions tried as their experience running "Hamster City" continued.

is a most straightforward way to approach understanding and then solve a problem. The Ws model is actually a set of individual questions, which, when answered, fit together like the pieces of a puzzle to give a composite picture of the thing being investigated.

Questions Constituting the Ws Model of Inquiry

- Who?
- What?
- When?
- Where?
- Why?
- How?
- What If?

This probably looks familiar to you because either you heard of this approach before or you have naturally used it, or a version of it, to explore some problem or topic.

Not all seven questions need to be, or logically should be, used in every situation. Much depends on the content area and the nature of the problem and topic being investigated. The key is that by getting the students to ask these questions about a specific problem or topic, their minds are being actively focused. No longer are they empty vessels waiting to be filled. Rather, they are inquiring minds seeking information, analyzing and evaluating that information, and then applying it thoughtfully. Crucial to using this approach to inquiry is the generation of related questions under each *W*. For example, there are often many *Who? What? When?* and so on, questions that can be asked when investigating a problem. The number of questions the students can generate is limited only by their imaginations. For the students, the very act of coming up with these questions to look into provides the process with built-in student interest and personal investment of thought, from beginning to end. Figure 10–16 provides an example of how students generated a series of questions in their search to solve a problem.

Why Inquiry Works

Inquiry is effective in the elementary classroom because of its inherent value to student growth and because it naturally follows the learning process.

The Value of Inquiry.   Inquiry has a special place of importance among block-type planning strategies because it helps students develop skills that not only build for classroom achievement but that also are applicable to the situations they will face throughout their lives. It helps them to become thoughtful, aware, and productive citizens who are able to use their mental abilities to solve problems. Because it is so valuable and sophisticated a planning strategy, it is important to introduce it simply and in a progressive manner. You can be sure that once you and your students have reached the point where an open/open inquiry approach is taken to with enthusiasm and skill, you have made a significant difference in their lives.

Inquiry and the Learning Process.   As stated earlier, inquiry is a student-directed journey through the learning process. As you know now from the discussion in Chapter

FIGURE 10–16   Example of Ws Inquiry Model

Ws	Questions Generated
Who?	will feed the hamster? will buy the hampster's food and supplies? will clean the hampster's house?
What?	will the hamster eat? will be the best kind of house to put the hamster in? will be the hampster's name?
When?	will the hamster be fed? will we get to play with the hamster? will the hamster get a friend of his own (another hamster)?
Where?	will "Hamster City" (his house) be kept? will we buy the hampster's food and supplies? will we store the hampster's food and supplies?
Why?	(These questions will be generated over time as "Hamster City" is in operation.)
How?	will we know if the hamster is healthy and happy? will we deal with any illnesses or injuries?
What if?	the hamster has a baby? the hamster gets too fat? the hamster gets lonely at night and on the weekend?

2, the learning process has three essential phases: perception, conception, and ideation. Here is a brief example of how students' self-directed journies during inquiry relates to these phases of the learning process.

At the first stage of inquiry, the students must determine which facts are needed to answer their questions and solve the problem. They must go about gathering these facts from appropriate sources. This accords with the *perception phase* of the learning process where information is taken in. Next in the inquiry process, students must sift through, categorize, analyze, and piece together the facts (data) they have gathered. This is where a clear understanding of the problem in its various aspects is achieved. This development of understanding accords with the *conception phase* of the learning process. Finally, with a good background (perception) and understanding (conception) of the problem, the students are ready to draw their own conclusions and make recommendations for solving the problem being investigated. This effort to originally apply the understanding gained through their search accords to the *ideation phase* of the learning process.

Generic Approach to Planning

Each block-type approach examined in this chapter has its own characteristic conceptual design and purpose. The generic weekly planning approach presented next serves more as an organizational approach to handling the various needs for preparing each week's lessons. These lessons can be theme oriented, inquiry oriented, skill and drill oriented, or any other type of orientation. The generic weekly planning approach shows you how to systematically structure your objectives, curriculum materials, and related resources materials so all your creative energies can be poured into designing the learning experiences your students will be involved in.

The Need for an Organized Weekly Planning System
As any new teacher knows, the need to be prepared with lesson plans places a substantial demand on one's time, both at school and at home. All effective teachers have in common the fact that they have worked out some system and routine for planning so that they know *how, when,* and *where* this task will be accomplished on a regular basis. This represents your discipline—and a most necessary discipline it is—for there is no surer way to fail as a teacher than to be poorly planned as you come to school each day. The intent of this section on weekly planning, and the following section on daily planning, is to provide you with a practical system for planning that can be accomplished on a routine basis.

Setting Up Your Weekly Planning System
The weekly planning system presented in Figure 10–17 is considered a block-type approach, because in it you are projecting in outline form the material to be covered for a coming week. In essence, you are preparing for yourself what can be called *A Week at a Glance* in the content areas. It is also called a generic approach because it is not based on any specific method of planning, and, as such, it can be related to and used to support any method.

Having at hand a generic outline of what needs to be done for the coming week greatly facilitates your daily lesson planning. It provides you with an advanced organizer that lets you look in one place at all the content areas over a week's time. Natural linkages across subjects and areas where reinforcement and recycling of concepts can be best accomplished are readily noticed when you have your week's planning outline in front of you. Perhaps most importantly, in drawing up this outline as depicted in Figure 10–17, you will have "broken the ice," so to speak, by having thought about and noted key planning information. This places you in the strong position of being ready to use all your time and energy designing creative sequences of instructional activities once you begin to write your daily lesson plans. These five recommendations should be followed to gain maximum benefit from your efforts at weekly planning:

Recommendation 1:   Establish Your Planning Routine.   Planning on a regular basis through the entire school year is a discipline that is critical to learn. Therefore, set a day, time, and a place for carrying out your weekly planning. One particularly effective approach that is known to work well is to set aside three hours on Saturday for drafting your weekly planning outline.

Recommendation 2:   Establish Your Planning Workshop.   Set aside an area where you keep the essential materials for planning, including:

FIGURE 10–17   Weekly Planning Continuum

Content Areas		Monday	Tuesday	Wednesday	Thursday	Friday
Social Studies	Topic:					
	Focus Today:					
Unit #	Main Objective:					
( )	Text Pages:					
	Reminders:					
Language Arts • Reading • Writing • Spelling • Vocabulary	Topic:					
	Focus Today:					
Unit #	Main Objective:					
( )	Text Pages:					
	Reminders:					
Math	Topic:					
	Focus Today:					
Unit #	Main Objective:					
( )	Text Pages:					
	Reminders:					
Science	Topic:					
	Focus Today:					
	Main Objective:					
Unit #	Text Pages:					
( )	Reminders:					

- Textbooks and related materials
- State and district curriculum guidelines
- Writing materials and computer
- Various district, county, and professional resource materials
- Weekly and daily planning blanks

Keep this area organized and user friendly so that your work is pleasant and productive.

Recommendation 3:   Use Your Overall Content Area Curriculum Plans.   By having a well-crafted set of overall content area curriculum plans available, your task of outlining plans on a weekly basis is greatly facilitated. You simply need to look at the sequence and calendar of units and topics already laid out for each content area to fill in the Unit and Topic portion of the weekly planning blank. A word on the notion of flexibility is needed: At times, you will want to rearrange aspects of your overall curriculum plans or weekly plans. This is natural and very easily done in the context of the thoughtfully developed structure already in place. Attempts at flexibility without this core structure as the basis can lead to chaos.

Recommendation 4:   Systematically Review Your Essential Materials.   A preliminary systematic review of the relevant pages of your content area textbooks (and related materials) will allow you to determine and fill in the Focus Today for each day in each content area on the weekly planning blank. For example, if the social studies unit is Westward Movement and the topic for the week is The Gold Rush, after looking over the textbook pages on this topic, you might decide that on Monday the Focus Today is going to be Routes West. You would then make a similar decision for the remaining days of the week and in the other content areas as well. This review of the textbook pages will also allow you to fill in the place on the weekly planning blank that indicates the text pages to be covered each day. Further, by this preliminary review and selection of the Focus Today, you are in a position to state what you expect to accomplish each day. Thus, you can also fill in the Main Objective for each day in the content areas on the weekly planning blank. For example, after reviewing the textbook pages for Routes West, you may determine that your Main Objective for that day will be: "Students will compare the types and difficulties of three principal routes west that were used." Notice that by determining this Focus Today and Main Objective, you are ready and primed to apply all your creative attention to designing a set of activities that will best involve the students and accomplish learning of the material.

Recommendation 5:   Use Your Completed Weekly Planning Outline for Daily Planning.   If you spent two to three hours on Saturday drafting your outline of the coming week's plans (following the first four recommendations), then it will be very workable to spend a few hours on Sunday creating the actual daily lesson plans. This combination of Saturday and Sunday to do your planning is a strong routine to maintain. Sometimes, however, it becomes necessary to write your lesson plans even the night before they are to be presented. At such times, the value of having put thought into drafting a weekly outline pays off in a big way. There is nothing more tiring or stressful than coming home dead tired from teaching all day and having to create a set of lesson plans for the next day *from scratch* at 10:00 or 11:00 at night. Using the weekend to fill out the weekly planning blank and to focus some strategic thought will make your late-evening lesson planning during the week relatively easy. You will find that by having determined the Unit and Topic, Pages to Cover, Focus Today, and Main Objective, you are ready and primed with all your creative and strategic thought to design sets of instructional activities for each day's lessons that will best promote student learning of the material to be covered.

The next section, Daily Planning Approaches, will provide you with effective ways to create and write your lesson plans.

Daily Planning Approaches

Daily lesson planning is where it all happens—the lesson plan is the detailed blueprint that tells what the students will actually experience in the classroom. However, there are a number of planning steps that are extremely important and helpful for building the foundation so that creative and effective lesson plans are a possibility. The building of this foundation (i.e., *all* the planning done up to this point) is not seen by the students. They do benefit, or fail to benefit, directly from how well this has been done. If you conduct a survey of elementary teachers, you will find that there are numerous ways and formats used for writing lesson plans. Upon being hired by a particular school district, it is essential that you find out whether it prefers or requires a specific lesson planning style. In this section, two ways of planning have been chosen for their general applicability to most any teaching situation in which you may find yourself:

- The clinical model
- The generic model

The clinical model is one of the most widely accepted and used lesson planning formats. The generic model is a practical format that can be readily adapted to address any particular requirement for daily planning placed on you by your school or district.

The Clinical Model

One of the most well-known and widely used lesson plan formats for daily planning of classroom instruction is the clinical model. Based on the teaching techniques described by Madeline Hunter in her 1982 book, *Mastery Teaching*, the model has been developed as a series of sequenced steps that are intended to be completed in a specified time period (an hour is typical) for a single lesson. Each step has an instructional purpose and must be executed in a set order in relation to the other steps. The clinical model is designed as a series of five, six, or seven steps; for the purposes of this book, it will be examined in the form of a six-step lesson plan. Figure 10–18 provides an outline of the six-step lesson plan.

It is important that teachers not only be familiar with but also be able effectively to use the clinical model, for three reasons:

FIGURE 10–18   Outline of Clinical Model: Six-Step Lesson Plan

1. *Anticipatory Set:* (Opening activity—link to previous learning day or student experience; prepares student for lesson. Often this is a three- or four-sentence statement given by the teacher at the beginning of the lesson).
2. *Objectives:* (What will the student be able to do as a result of the lesson [i.e., "Student will state three reasons why railroads came to California."])?
3. *Instruction:* (What does the teacher do to get across concept, information, knowledge, thinking, etc.?)
4. *Guided Practice:* (What are the students doing? How is the teacher helping them?)
5. *Closure:* (How does the teacher help students summarize and internalize the new learning?)
6. *Independent Practice*: (Does the teacher provide an opportunity for students to practice the new learning on their own?)
7. *Materials:* (What is needed for the lesson?)

1. Used properly, the model is the basis of effective teaching (i.e., students learn).
2. It is frequently the model of choice required by principals when they observe teachers for the purposes of evaluation.
3. It is part of the knowledge of the profession that all teachers should possess.

In order to present this model in a clear and efficient manner, the characteristics of the model will be described, an example of a well-designed six-step lesson plan will be examined, and criteria for effectiveness for each step of the plan will be identified. Several more six-step lesson plans will be discussed to show a variety of ways in which the model can be designed.

Characteristics of the Clinical Model

The clinical model is considered a form of direct instruction, and the first three steps of the six-step lesson plan are delivered as teacher-directed instruction. The last three steps involve student-directed and/or interactive forms of instruction. The six steps are:

1. Anticipatory set
2. Objectives
3. Instruction
4. Guided practice
5. Closure
6. Independent practice

To get an overview of how the clinical model works, it is useful to observe the teacher's role and the student's role as the six-step sequence proceeds. For the first three steps, the teacher's role is one of presenter and the students' role is like that of an audience attending to the presentation. During this phase, the students are expected to be listening to the teacher, absorbing the information the teacher is presenting. The teacher may, however, entertain or encourage some minimal direct student participation at this point in order to keep students engaged in the proceedings (by asking students to respond to questions or by having a student come up to point to something on a map, etc.). As presenter, the teacher is the main show and does most of the talking.

During the fourth step of the model, the teacher's role changes to one of a facilitator as the students carry out their role of active learners. Now, the students are the main show, as they perform a task assigned by the teacher and the teacher circulates among them to offer assistance and monitor their performance. At this step, instruction is no longer teacher directed; it is either student directed or interactive, depending on what kind of activities the teacher has decided to have the students do.

In the fifth step of the model, a summary or review of what has been learned in the lesson takes place, and the teacher may employ teacher-directed, student-directed, or interactive instruction to achieve this goal, again depending on the type of activity he or she decides will take place.

Finally, in the sixth step, the students' role is to perform an assigned task independently and the teacher's role is to subsequently provide feedback to the students regarding the accuracy and quality of their work.

As can be seen from this sequence, there is a natural progression to where the students' responsibility for active learning continues to increase throughout. Notice, however, that the teacher makes *all the decisions* regarding what the students will learn and how they will learn it. Figure 10–19 provides a summary of the characteristics of the clinical model.

FIGURE 10–19   Characteristics of the Clinical Model

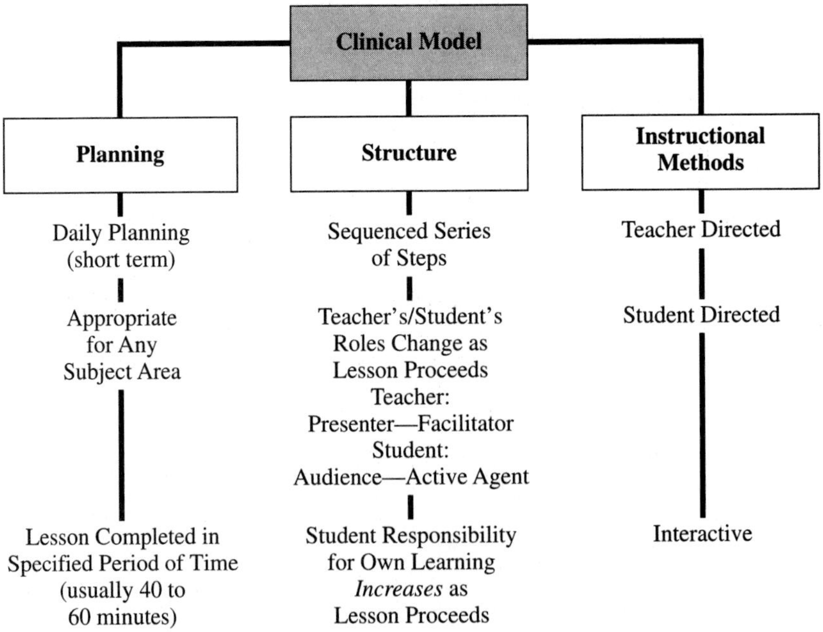

The clinical model is a tool that you, as a teacher, can use to plan and deliver effective instruction. It is the goal of the authors to present the model in such a way that it can be most readily grasped and applied for classroom instruction, as seen in the following:

1. A complete six-step lesson plan will provide an overview of the model.
2. The instructional purpose of each step of the plan is examined.
3. The criteria for effectiveness for each step of the lesson plan is described.

Sample Six-Step Lesson Plan
Coming to America: The Immigrant Experience
Topic: Immigration
Grade Level: Upper elementary grade

Anticipatory Set

"Yesterday, we discussed some reasons why people left their native countries to come to America. We classified them into three categories. Can anyone remember what those three categories were?" (The teacher will refresh the students' memories by referring to a chart made earlier that depicts three distinct categories.) "They were economic, political, and social. Today, we will be learning about how these people, or immigrants, actually came to America. Today, we will embark on a journey, just as our ancestors before us did.

"Today's objectives are listed on the overhead. I want you to pay specific attention to the word *steerage* during this lesson, as it will be a vocabulary word for this unit. In addition, each of you will need to identify the differences and similarities between *steerage* and *cabins*. Pay close attention as we embark on a journey to a new land—America."

Objectives

1. "By the end of today's lesson, you will be able to define the word *steerage* in writing."
2. "You will also be able to compare and contrast, both orally and in writing, the conditions of *steerage* versus *cabins*."

"Knowing these things will help you understand the hardships endured by European immigrants who came to America and settled here in the mid-1800s. Life was not easy for immigrants then and may not be for today's immigrants, as well. Let's find out why."

Instruction

"Before we go any further, I am going to read you a story called *Watch the Stars Come Out* by Riki Levinson." (The teacher discusses the story with students upon completion.)

"Can anyone tell me what method of transportation the immigrants used to come to America?" (The teacher solicits responses from the students and writes them on the overhead.) "What type of boat do you think it was? Was it like a present-day cruise liner? Was it like an oil tanker? What are some of the characteristics that the vessel possessed? Remember, we're talking about the mid-1800s. Most of the boats were old tobacco sailing boats. Tobacco would be shipped to Europe and immigrants would ride the ships back to America.

"There were two types of passage aboard these sailing ships. If you were rich and were willing to spend the money, you could buy yourself and your family a ticket in first class. Has anyone ever flown in first class on an airplane or been in first class on a train? What kind of treatment do you receive?" (The teacher discusses with the students what present-day first class may consist of and compares it to the first class of the sailing ship of the mid-1800s.) "This usually meant you had a private cabin as well as a private bed to sleep in. The location of your cabin was up near the deck so that you had access to fresh air and the outside." (The teacher shows a picture of the location of a cabin.) "You would also eat your food in a dining room.

"But most of the immigrants traveled in the least expensive way—that is, in 'steerage.' What does *steerage* mean? This will be a vocabulary word for this unit, so you will need to recall the meaning of the word *steerage*." (The teacher writes the word *steerage* on the board with the meaning. He or she then displays a diagram of the immigration ship that depicts the various areas of the ship, and continues to describe the traveling accommodations.)

"The steerage area was far below the deck, on the lowest level of the ship. Several hundred passengers were crammed into steerage with no fresh air. This is where our journey begins." (The teacher asks several students to come to the front of the room and sit in a taped-off area. As the lesson progresses, the teacher will ask more and more students to join the marked-off area until all students are within its confines. This is a mini-simulation of steerage.) "Passengers slept in narrow bunk beds, sometimes three high. Many got frostbite from the cold. Usually, there was only one bath area for all the steerage passengers, with sink faucets that frequently did not work. The steerage area was often filthy.

"The food for steerage passengers wasn't much better than their sleeping accommodations. Cold soup, boiled potatoes, and stringy beef were often the only items on the menu. Many immigrants reported that all they ate was herring, bread, potatoes, and tea. One reporter who wanted to see what it was like to travel in steerage boarded a ship in 1906. He wrote: 'How can a steerage passenger remember that he is a human being when he must first pick the worms from his food ... and eat in his stuffy stinking bunk, or in the hot atmosphere of a compartment where one hundred and fifty people sleep?'

"The ocean voyage was very dangerous also. How many days do you think it took in the mid-1800s to travel the Atlantic to America?" (The teacher writes estimations on the board.) "It took anywhere from 42 days to six months to cross the Atlantic. The immigrants had to endure these conditions for a long time. Not only were there severe storms to worry about but ship conditions were so crowded and unsanitary that diseases spread rapidly. Thousands died from typhus, called 'ship fever,' and cholera. Often, the ocean voyage was so bad that people committed suicide. A fatality rate of 10 to 15 percent was not uncommon. So many people died from disease and suicide that some newspapers called the ships 'swimming coffins.'

"This is the end of our voyage aboard the *Red Star*. When the immigrants arrived in America, each passenger was given a landing card. Today, I am going to give each of you one and you must remember to bring it back to our social studies class tomorrow, because tomorrow we will be discussing what happened when the immigrants first arrived. If you forget to bring your landing card, you will not be permitted to enter America and you will be sent back to your native land. So please remember to bring them. You can all go back to your seats now."

After the children have returned to their desks, discussion is continued by asking, "Do we still have immigrants coming to America today?" Discussion might focus on possible current events that correlate to the journey taken in the mid-1800s.

Guided Practice

Put students in cooperative groups of four. Each student is numbered off and assigned a role (speaker, recorder, illustrator, organizer) within the group. The students must compare and contrast *steerage* versus *cabins* by using a graphic organizer. They will create their own graphic organizers in the form of a sailing ship. The differences will either be listed on the *cabin* floor or the *steerage* floor. The similarities will be listed on the main deck, where everyone dwelled. Children must also decorate and color their graphic organizers. Their products will be presented to the class and displayed around the room.

Closure

Each child will have a KWL (What I Know, What I Want to Know, What I Learned) chart within his or her own immigration portfolio. Individually, each student will write one item that he or she learned and will add some of the responses to the class KWL chart.

Independent Practice

The students will be required to interview someone who has immigrated to this country. They will create a little 4" × 4" book about this individual, including a photograph, if they can obtain one. They will be required to answer the following questions: Why did this person leave his or her country? How did he or she get to the United States? What method of transportation did he or she use? Under what conditions did he or she travel? Did he or she leave behind any family or friends? Did he or she travel by *cabin* or by *steerage*?

You have just read a complete six-step lesson plan. Each step of the plan has a *specific* and *unique* instructional purpose as an integral part of the whole plan. In order to write an effective six-step lesson, not only must you know the instructional purpose of each step of the plan but also how to write each step so that this instructional purpose is achieved. To do so, certain criteria must be followed in the writing of the plan. Figure 10–20 states the instructional purpose and the criteria for writing each step of the plan. Next, the purposes and criteria for each step of the plan will be examined in detail.

FIGURE 10–20   Instructional Purpose(s)/Criteria: Six Steps of the Clinical Model

Six-Step Plan	Instructional Purpose(s)	Criteria
Anticipatory Set	• Make connection between new material and what is already known. • Motivate students to learn. • Focus students on new material.	• Short/concise • Relates directly to objectives
Objectives	• Inform students of what they will learn and how they will demonstrate that learning.	• Describes what students will do, not what teacher does • Must be measurable in terms of how students demonstrate learning • Realistic in terms of time and resources • Includes a purpose-setting statement
Instruction	• Impart information/knowledge and/or skills to students.	• Uses lecture, demonstration, questioning • Uses visuals, literature, realia • Relates new material to students' lives & experiences • Delivers in dynamic way
Guided Practice	• Students perform learning task or practice skill.	• Learning task supports objective(s) • Requires students to use communication and/or thinking skills • Monitored by teacher
Closure	• Help students summarize and internalize new learning.	• Completed in short period of time (10–15 minutes) • All students participate • Requires students to review what they learned in the lesson
Independent Practice	• Students practice newly acquired skill or apply new knowledge *independently*.	• Requires students to practice skill or apply knowledge • Helps students solidify learning (achieve lesson objectives) • Done by students without help of teacher

Anticipatory Set

Instructional Purpose.   The purpose of the anticipatory set is threefold:

1. To make a connection between the new learning that will take place and previous learning or experiences that the students have had
2. To motivate the students to want to learn the new material
3. To focus the students on the new learning

The teacher usually accomplishes these purposes by making a brief (two to five minutes) direct statement to the students. Looking at the earlier sample lesson, notice that the first instructional of the anticipatory set has been accomplished within the first five sentences, wherein the teacher makes the connection between today's topic and previously learned material. *Note*: It is important to make this connection for the students because it gives them a context within which to understand the new material. In fact, research by cognitive psychologists has shown that connecting new material to previously learned material enhances learning and memory.

> *Information in long-term memory appears to be stored on the basis of meaning. In fact, the brain encodes information in meaningful ways alongside related concepts and material already known and understood. Thus, it is easier to remember new, meaningful information when we can understand and store it in relation to other previously encoded knowledge. Teachers can facilitate this type of meaningful learning in the classroom by presenting new information in the context of material that students already know. (Rafoth, Leal, & DeFabo, 1993)*

Thus, there is a strong rationale for connecting new information to knowledge the students already possess. As the teacher, you must be conscientious about making this connection.

The second instructional purpose of the anticipatory set, to motivate students to want to learn the new material, is addressed in the statement "Today we will embark on a journey, just as our ancestors before us did." *Embarking on a journey* is a phrase that hints at possible adventure or excitement and it invites students to participate in the day's lesson.

Regarding the third instructional purpose of the anticipatory set, to focus students on the new learning, it is accomplished in this lesson in the sentence "I want you to pay specific attention to the word *steerage* during this lesson, as it will be a vocabulary word for this unit." This alerts students to an important concept in the lesson and prepares them to focus on it when the time comes.

Criteria for Effectiveness.   In order to write an effective anticipatory set, the following criteria must be observed:

1. The three instructional purposes of the anticipatory set (connecting new and already learned knowledge, providing motivation to learn the new material, and focusing attention on the material to be learned) must be accomplished by the narrative.
2. The narrative of the anticipatory set must be concise so that it can be delivered in a limited amount of time (three to seven minutes).
3. The anticipatory set must relate to the objective(s) of the day's lesson.

Here is how the anticipatory set of the sample lesson plan used these criteria.

Criterion 1:   Connect new and already learned knowledge, provide motivation to learn new material, and focus attention on new material.

How the anticipatory set of the sample lesson accomplishes the three instructional purposes included in Criterion 1 has already been discussed.

    Criterion 2:   The narrative should be concise and short.

The anticipatory set of the sample lesson takes less than one minute to read out loud, so even with the added time to take responses from the students to the question regarding the previous lesson, it would still be within the time limit of three to seven minutes.

    Criteria 3:   The anticipatory set must relate to the objectives of the day's lesson.

The teacher clearly links the anticipatory set to the objectives by referring directly to them, alerting students to their importance.

    Within the confines of these criteria, the variety of ways in which the anticipatory set can be set up is limited only by your own creativity. Questions, visuals, auditory stimuli, and surprise demonstrations are all appropriate activities to include in the anticipatory set.

    The anticipatory set establishes the tone for the rest of the lesson. When it is designed carefully (meeting all criteria), it prepares students for the upcoming lesson by creating in them the prerequisite desire to learn. The anticipatory set is also important for another reason. Madeline Hunter (1982) has described a phenomenon of learning: Students are better able to learn and remember information introduced at the beginning of any sequence than they can material of equal difficulty encountered later in the sequence. This holds true for any type of sequence (e.g., lists of facts, concepts, a six-step lesson plan, a unit of instruction, etc.). Hunter has emphasized the importance of using this "prime time" to the fullest advantage through the teacher's use of an effective anticipatory set and by letting the students know the objective(s) of the lesson and its importance to them. Next, attention is focused on the second prime-time activity: letting the students know the objective(s) of the lesson.

Objectives

Instructional Purpose.   Objectives are statements that indicate what students will be able to do at the end of, and as a result of, a lesson. Educators strongly disagree as to whether to communicate objectives to students at the beginning of the lesson or let them "discover" (discovery learning) the objectives during the course of instructional activities. For the purposes of the clinical model, objectives should be stated directly for the students at the beginning of the lesson. In this way, students will know what they are expected to learn and how they will demonstrate what they have learned. The objectives should also be displayed in written form in a prominent place so students can refer to them during the course of the lesson. The positive impact of announcing objectives while learning is enhanced when a purpose-setting statement is added to the objectives that tells students why the objective is important to them. According to Hunter (1982), "Students usually will expend more effort and consequently increase their learning if they know what it is they will learn today and why it is important to them."

Criteria for Effectiveness.   The criteria for writing clear and effective objectives are as follows:

1. Objectives describe what the students will do—not what the teacher will do.
2. Objectives should be measurable in terms of how the students will demonstrate the expected accomplishment.
3. Objectives should be realistic in terms of the students' ability levels and time available.
4. Objectives should include a purpose-setting statement.

Here is how the sample lesson plan used these criteria.

Criterion 1:   Objectives describe what the students will do—not what the teacher will do.

The two objectives for the sample lesson clearly meet this criterion: The teacher is telling the students that they will be able to define *steerage* and compare and contrast *steerage* versus *cabins.*

Criterion 2:   Objectives should be measurable.

The two objectives do state how the learning will be measured. For the first objective, the students will be able to *write* the definition of *steerage*, and for the second objective, the students will be able to *write and describe orally* the similarities and differences between cabins and steerage.

Criterion 3:   Objectives should be realistic in terms of the students' abilities and time available.

This criterion cannot be evaluated in terms of students and time available, as that is dependent on the actual classroom situation. Based on the authors' experience, however, these objectives would be achievable in most middle-grade classrooms, as they are simple and straightforward.

Criterion 4:   Objectives should include a purpose-setting statement.

This criterion has been met by the purpose-setting statement that applies to both of the objectives, namely: "Knowing these things will help you understand the hardships endured by European immigrants who came to America and settled here in the mid-1800s. Life was not easy for them and may not be for today's immigrants, as well. Let's find out why."

This statement appeals to the students' curiosity about the hardships of ocean voyages—a topic that has interest for most students. It is perfectly acceptable to use extrinsic as well as intrinsic motivation—for example, to say something like, "It is important that you learn these objectives because this information will be on Friday's test." It is good to vary purpose-setting statements so that sometimes they appeal to the students' desire to learn and sometimes to their desire to get a good grade on a test or quiz.

To develop objectives, the teacher must first look over the material to be learned and then decide what two or three concepts or skills he or she wants to get across in that day's lesson.

In the case of the sample lesson plan, the teacher decided to focus on the traveling conditions endured by the immigrants, specifically on the sailing vessels' accommodations called *steerage* and *cabins*. The teacher felt this would give the students an appreciation of the sacrifices made by people hungry for freedom and a better life. Figure 10–21 summarizes the process for writing effective objectives.

Following are some examples of objectives that meet the preceding criteria.

Examples of Effective Objectives

1. Today, you will be able to name the European countries involved in early exploration of the Western Hemisphere and you will be able to tell why this exploration took place.

   This exploration is important to you because without it, you may not even be here today, and if you were, you may be leading a very different kind of life.

2. By the end of today's lesson, you should be able to define, in writing, the terms *sanctuary, tragedy*, and *comedy.*

   It is important to know the meanings of these key terms in order to understand some of the customs and religious beliefs of the ancient Greeks. Don't forget, your Moment in History simulations are due next week and you will need this information to create accurate simulations.

3. Today, we are going to learn about transportation. At the end of today's lesson, I want you to draw three different ways that transportation affects your life.

   It is important for you to know about transportation because it touches your life in many ways. Many of the things you are used to having and doing would not be possible without transportation. Let's find what some of these things are.

4. Today, we are going to find out what life was like for the Native Americans who lived on the California Missions.

   It is important for everyone to understand what happens when people are forced to live as slaves, being forced to forsake their own culture. At the end of this lesson, I want you to write a letter to a friend of yours who lives in another country and does not know anything about U.S. history. I want you to describe to this friend what life was like for the Native Americans on the Missions and how you think they were affected by their circumstances on the Missions.

5. Today, in math, we are going to practice problem-solving skills. Having these skills can help you with everyday problems in your own life. In fact, after I show you some examples, I will ask you to think of a problem in your house that could be solved using math.

   You will describe, in writing, the problem and how to solve it.

6. By the end of today's lesson on fuels for heating homes, I will ask you to write down three ways to conserve fuel.

   This is important to you because at the rate fuels are being used, they will soon be gone. And when they are gone, there will be no way to heat your home.

FIGURE 10–21   Procedure for Writing Objectives

1. Read over material to be learned by students.

2. Note the main idea or concepts contained in the narrative.

3. Organize the main ideas/concepts with supporting detail graphically.

    Example:

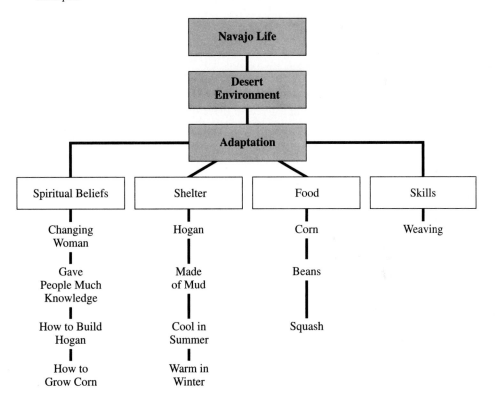

4. Decide to what depth you want the class to study the material. (You may want to go into more detail than the text offers by bringing in extra resources.)

5. Based on your decision concerning depth of study, decide how many ideas can be covered in a lesson.

6. Write objectives for those ideas based on the criteria described above.

These examples are meant to provide some insight into writing objectives that will be clear and inviting to your students. Once you know your students and have some practice writing objectives, you will be able to identify and write your objectives quickly and easily.

Instruction

Instructional Purpose.   The instructional purpose of the lesson is to impart information and/or skills to the students that will prepare them to do the learning task they are assigned in the Guided Practice section. During the instruction, the teacher is building the backgrounds of the students and providing information that will help the students achieve the objectives of the lesson. The teacher does this through the teacher presentation described in Chapter 2 as the method of teacher-directed instruction. The teacher presentation consists of lecture, demonstration, and questioning. Figure 3–3 in Chapter 3 presents the important aspects of these three teaching activities of the teacher presentation. The instruction can take anywhere from 10 minutes to a half hour, depending on the age and attention spans of the students.

In the sample lesson, the teacher decided to write out everything she wished to say during instruction. Many teachers, especially as they become practiced at delivering instruction, merely jot down an outline for the instruction and speak from that. This is a matter of personal preference. It is, however, a good idea to write out your script the first few times you deliver instruction as a new teacher, keeping in mind the criteria for an effective teacher presentation discussed in Chapter 2. The following is a brief reiteration of these criteria. Also shown is how the sample lesson plan employed the criteria.

Criteria for Effectiveness.   The criteria for creating an effective teacher presentation (i.e., instruction) include the following:

1. Use all three teaching activities (i.e., lecture, demonstration, and questioning).
2. Use related resources, including literature, visuals, and realia.
3. Relate new material to students' lives and experiences.
4. Limit the amount of new information and repeat key information frequently.
5. Deliver the presentation in a dynamic and enthusiastic manner.

Here is how the sample lesson plan used these criteria.

Criterion 1:   Use lecture, demonstration, and questioning.

Reading over the paragraphs of the instruction, it is apparent that the teacher has met this criterion very effectively; that is, lecture, demonstration, and questioning are woven skillfully to form the fabric of the presentation. Lecture is the backdrop of the presentation, with questions and demonstration integrated variously.

Lecture.   Lecture, the bulk of this presentation, is straightforward, clear, and logical. The teacher also uses much colorful description, which makes the lecture interesting.

Demonstration.   Demonstration is used especially effectively in this lesson by having the students sit on the floor in a taped-off area while the teacher is talking. Squeezing together for the duration of the lecture gives the students a feeling of empathy for the immigrants.

Questioning.   Questions are used effectively for several different purposes in the presentation. In the second paragraph of instruction, questions are used for two purposes: (1) to activate related prior knowledge of the students and (2) to emphasize certain information. The teacher activates students' prior knowledge by asking such questions as the type of transportation immigrants used to come to America, what the immigrant ships were like, including specific characteristics, and so on. Note the question "Was it (the immigration ship) like a present-day cruise line?" This question helps students get a better understanding of what the ships were like by giving them a reference with which to make a comparison. By asking specific questions about the characteristics of the ships before describing them, the teacher has set the stage for that description; that is, she has prepared the students to listen closely to the description.

Later, by asking students if they have ever traveled first class in an airplane or train and what kind of treatment they received, the teacher is helping them relate the information about steerage versus cabins to experiences they have had in their own lives.

In paragraph five, by asking "What does steerage mean?" the teacher is focusing the students' attention on key information and cuing them to pay attention as she gives the definition. Before telling how long crossing the Atlantic took for the immigrants, she asks students how long they think it would take. Again, this prepares them to pay special attention to that information, like putting it in **boldface** on a verbal level.

Finally, at the end of the presentation, the teacher asks about present-day immigrants, relating the history lesson to the present and to present-day experiences of the students.

Criterion 2:   Use related resources: literature, visuals, realia.

Related resources are used effectively in the presentation.

Literature.   The teacher begins her presentation by reading *Watch the Stars Come Out* by Riki Levinson, an appropriate work of literature for the subject matter of the lesson. Beginning her instruction with a story has the advantage of creating interest and getting the students hooked right away. It also helps build background for the information to be presented later in the presentation.

The teacher uses literature once more in the presentation when she reads the quote from a reporter who took the journey in steerage accommodations. The quote is very short, but it is all that is needed to help the children understand the reality of the situation. Using personal diary or eyewitness accounts is a wonderful way to bring the past alive and make it more real and immediate.

Visuals.   The teacher uses visuals in several ways during the presentation. In the beginning of the lesson, when she asks the students questions about the transportation of the immigrants, she writes their responses on an overhead. This enables them to see as well as hear each others' responses. Also, adding another sensory mode for information intake (seeing as well as hearing) increases perception and memory of the information. In addition, writing down the responses of the students confirms for them that the teacher values what they have to say.

The teacher uses a visual later in the lesson when she shows the diagram of an immigrant ship, depicting the locations of the steerage and cabin accommodations. Using a diagram is an excellent way to give students a visual picture of the teacher's description.

Realia.   A clever use of realia is employed by giving each student a "landing pass" (in the same way that the immigrants received landing passes before they could enter America). These passes must be brought to class the following day so that the students can continue the "immigrant journey"—that is, find out what happened to the immigrants as they actually entered the country. This gives the students something concrete to remind them of that day's lesson and to pique their curiosity about the following day's topic.

Although this teacher did happen to use all three of the resources discussed—literature, visuals, and realia—it is not necessary to use all three in every lesson. Not all lessons lend themselves to the use of realia and it is not always possible to find the appropriate literature for a particular topic, especially in technical subjects such as math. However, literature can be used very effectively in math lessons, although it probably would not be possible for every math lesson. There are also limitations of the teacher's time and available resources. Math lessons, on the other hand, lend themselves to the use a manipulatives, a form of realia.

Criterion 3:   Relate new material to students' lives.

The teacher does this several times during the presentation. In paragraph four, the teacher asks the students if any of them have ever traveled first class on a plane or train. She then asks them what it was like, and discusses how it might compare to first class on the sailing ship in the mid-1800s. This gives the students a direct comparison to an example from modern times that they can relate to.

By giving the students the experience of being crowded together in a confined space during the lesson, the teacher is helping them relate the information about the traveling accommodations of the immigrants to their own experience.

Finally, in the last paragraph of the instruction, the teacher asks the students if there are still immigrants coming to America today. Again, the students can think of their own experiences (they may have school friends who have recently immigrated, they may have seen many examples on the news, etc.) and relate it to the information about the immigrants of the mid-1800s.

This particular question helps them see the connection between the past and present so that the past becomes more familiar and relevant.

Criterion 4:   Limit new information and repeating new information.

The teacher has done an excellent job of limiting the amount of new information and repeating the new information frequently. The new information introduced in this lesson centers around two main ideas: (1) the formal definition of *steerage* and (2) the description of the conditions of steerage.

The information about steerage is discussed thoroughly and the word *steerage* is repeated many times. When the teacher first mentions steerage, she alerts students to the importance of the word, that it will be a vocabulary word for the unit, and that they will need to recall its meaning. She then defines it, describes conditions related to it, and then reads an actual eyewitness account of steerage. The vocabulary word is heard many times by the students. By the end of the instruction, the students have heard about steerage many times and have had an experience of the conditions of steerage, which will make a lasting impression on their minds.

Criterion 5:   Give a dynamic and enthusiastic delivery of presentation.

Since the teacher was not actually *observed* during the sample lesson, this criterion cannot be evaluated as the others were. It suffices to comment on the importance of the teacher's enthusiasm for a topic as he or she talks about the topic.

When the teacher presents information in an enthusiastic and dynamic way, it holds the attention of the students and creates interest in the topic or information being presented. The enthusiastic teacher provides a role model for the students that sends the message that learning is something that one can enjoy and get excited about. One of the goals of all teachers is to inspire their students to become self-motivated learners who seek to learn things on their own. The teacher's own enthusiasm helps in this regard.

Guided Practice

Instructional Purpose.   The instructional purpose of the guided practice is to have the students actively engage in a specific learning task for which they have been prepared by the teacher's presentation during the instruction. The students now become the main actors, as they work on a task assigned by the teacher. The teacher's role shifts from presenter to facilitator, as he or she moves among the students to ensure that they are on task and that they are performing the task correctly, and to provide general guidance and feedback to the students as they work.

The type of tasks the students can be doing in guided practice varies greatly and can include individual seatwork (such as filling a worksheet, writing a paragraph, or drawing a picture) or group work (such as a cooperative learning activity, a game, role-playing, etc.).

Criteria for Effectiveness.   In order for the guided practice activity to be effective, three criteria must be met:

1. The guided practice activity should be something that supports the objectives, which means it should be a task or activity that helps the students achieve the objective(s).
2. The guided practice activity should be a task that requires students to use all or some of the communicative arts (listening, speaking, reading, and writing).

3. The guided practice activity should be closely monitored by the teacher so that students receive feedback as they work.

When planning the guided practice, the teacher needs to make certain that the activity does, indeed, enable the students to achieve some or all of the objectives of the lesson. That may seem obvious, but the authors have seen many lesson plans where the guided practice activity had nothing at all to do with the stated objectives of the lesson.

Regarding the second guideline, the guided practice is an ideal place to work in student use of the communicative arts, since they are supposed to be actively working on a task at this point. Cooperative group activities work very well here because they require students to communicate with each other, especially emphasizing speaking and listening. (This is valuable, since students do not get to do much talking during instruction.)

It is important that the teacher take care to design opportunities for students to use their *verbal* communication skills—that is, to give them many opportunities to speak about the concepts and ideas they are studying. Not only will they remember more of what they say and do than what they hear, read, or write but they will also be able to communicate clearly and well when they speak. This, in turn, will enhance their effectiveness as they function in the community, at their jobs, and even in family life. All too often, students have little or no opportunity to speak and discuss ideas with each other during class time. They will not develop these skills unless they are given time and opportunity to use them *in class*. It is incumbent upon teachers who are striving to create meaningful learning experiences for their students to design lessons that require their students to communicate verbally with each other.

During the implementation of the guided practice, it is important that the teacher walk among the students to make sure they are on task and to give them guidance and feedback. Teachers who sit at their desks (grading papers or whatever) do their students a great disservice, as the students will note the teacher's lack of interest and may deviate from the task.

Here is how the sample lesson plan used these criteria.

Criterion 1:   The guided practice activity should support the objectives.

For the guided practice activity, the teacher chose a cooperative learning activity that requires the students to create a pictorial graphic organizer in which they are to list the similarities and differences of conditions in steerage and cabins. The activity directly supports the second objective, which calls for a comparison of *steerage* and *cabins* and indirectly supports the first objective in that they must know what steerage is to compare it to cabins.

Criterion 2:   The guided practice activity should require students to use all or some of the communicative arts.

In this activity, the students will be using all four of the communicative arts: listening, speaking, writing, and reading. They will be discussing what they will write on their graphic organizer, which means they will be speaking and listening to each other. Then they must actually write down their ideas and read them to each other before putting down their final list on the organizer. When they present their graphic organizers to the rest of the class, they will be reading and explaining their ideas (from the organizer) to the class. This is excellent practice in using communication skills.

Criterion 3:   The guided practice activity should be closely monitored by the teacher.

With regard to this criterion, it is necessary that the teacher move among the students to see what they are doing and how they are doing it. This keeps the students on task and informs them as to the correctness of their work. For example, the teacher may say, "Yes, you are doing it correctly; keep going," or "Wait a minute, you missed a step here; try so and so." This intervention by the teacher can save a student from frustration and failure, whether the activity is a group one or an individual one. The success of the clinical model depends, in part, on the close monitoring of the students' performance during the guided practice.

Closure

Instructional Purpose.   The instructional purpose of the closure activity is to help the students summarize and internalize the new learning that has just occurred. Students do not typically go over (on their own) what they have learned in the day's lesson nor do they have an awareness of what it is they can do after a lesson that they could not do yesterday. This must be pointed out to them and made a part of their awareness. The closure activity should require the students to think back over the lesson and review major concepts in order to encode the information into long-term memory— that is, in order to internalize the information.

There are a multitude of ways in which the closure activity can be designed. One very simple way is for the teacher to ask the students to think about what they have learned in "today's lesson," write it down, and share what they have written with a classmate.

The closure activity could be a cooperative activity such as creating a list of key vocabulary from the lesson, writing a brief summary of the lesson, or making a diagram or drawing a picture that represents key ideas from the lesson. It could also be an individual activity, such as a short writing assignment or an art activity.

An important consideration to keep in mind when designing a closure activity is that it should involve *all students*. For example, if the teacher asks the students what they have learned today, and then calls on a few students to respond, only those few students have been involved in the closure. In order to have *all* the students summarize and internalize the lesson, all must be participating in the closure activity.

Criteria for Effectiveness.   To design an effective closure, the following three criteria should be followed:

1. The closure activity should be one that can be completed in a short period of time, such as 10 to 15 minutes.

2. The closure activity should be organized in such a way that all students are activity participating in it.
3. The closure activity should in some way require students to review and summarize what they have learned.

Here is how the sample lesson plan used these criteria.

Criterion 1:   The activity is completed within 10 to 15 minutes.

The closure activity—which involves having students write down one thing they have learned, taking students' responses, and adding them to the class chart—is one that can easily be completed in 10 to 15 minutes. The teacher can control the time limit by giving the students a specified amount of time in which to write their information (such as 3 to 4 minutes) and by limiting the number of students he or she calls on to share responses. If the teacher finds there is a full 15 minutes left for closure, then more students can be asked to contribute their information; however, if there is less time left for the closure, the teacher can limit how many students participate.

Criterion 2:   All students actively participate.

For the closure activity in the sample lesson, each child writes down one thing they have learned on their KWL chart. Figure 10–22 shows an example of a KWL chart.

Since each child must write something they have learned on their chart, all the students are involved in the activity. The teacher then calls on students to share what they have written and he or she adds responses to the Class KWL Chart, so all can see the information and add it to their own individual charts. Even though the teacher cannot call on all the students to share, all still participate by making an original entry on their KWL charts and then by adding other students' responses to their own KWL charts. So even if they do not get called on to share verbally, all children are still actively involved

FIGURE 10–22   Example of a What-I-Know (KWL) Sheet

Topic: Immigration to America

Purpose for Activity: To create knowledge of and empathy for immigrants of the late 1800s and early 1900s

What I Know	What I Want to Know	What I Learned

by the written requirement. If the teacher had depended on the verbal responses alone (e.g., if the closure activity consisted merely of asking the students what they had learned and taking a few responses), then the activity would not be very productive because it would not involve all the students. A cooperative group activity such as Numbered Heads Together (described in Chapter 2) would be another way of involving all of the students.

Criterion 3:   The students review and summarize what they learned.

The closure activity should require the students to think back over what has transpired in the lesson, to focus on main points or concepts, and to summarize the information. In the sample lesson, the students do have to think back over the lesson to recall what they learned so they can make the entry on their KWL charts. In addition, they will hear what other students remembered and they will be adding that information to their charts also. In this way, they will thoroughly review what has transpired. As they make the written entries on their charts, they will also have to summarize the information, as they cannot write everything that took place in the lesson.

The closure activity of the sample lesson is designed in such a way that it will be meaningful to the students and still be fairly brief. Closure activities can include a wide range of tasks and can be quite simple. For example, having students draw a picture of what they have learned, and then explaining it to one other person in the class, is an effective activity that can be completed in the short period of time allotted for closure. The time factor is partly a matter of training the students to complete tasks in a set amount of time. For instance, the teacher can say, "You have five minutes to make a drawing of what you have learned. Then, you and your partner have three minutes each to explain your drawings to each other." By setting the timer and enforcing the time limits, the teacher can get students used to working quickly and efficiently.

Independent Practice

Instructional Purpose.   The purpose of the independent practice is to give students an opportunity to practice their newly acquired skills or apply newly learned knowledge independently (without the teacher's guidance). It is very common for the independent practice to be a task given as homework, although it can also be done during class time, as long as the students do it independently.

The types of activities that are suitable for the independent practice are varied and depend on the subject area as well as what the teacher wishes to accomplish. In math, for example, the teacher may want the students to practice a newly learned algorithm and may assign problems similar to those done in the lesson for the independent practice. In this case, the students are practicing the same skill they worked on in the lesson, solving the same type of problems. However, for a lesson in social studies, the teacher's goal for the independent practice may be to get the students to practice using higher-level thinking skills, rather than have them solely involved in reviewing content. In this case, the assignment may involve having the students answer open-ended questions that require them to use such thinking skills as hypothesizing, comparing, analyzing, evaluating, and so on.

Both kinds of activities are useful for student learning. At times, students need to practice skills, engage in drill activities to aid memorization of math facts or spellings of words, and similar activities. At other times, it is important that they learn how to think critically, apply learned knowledge to a new situation, solve a problem, or create something original. By assigning various kinds of tasks for independent practice, the teacher can give students the opportunity to engage in these various kinds of learning activities.

Criteria for Effectiveness.   The following criteria will help in developing an effective independent practice:

1. The independent practice should help students practice a skill or apply knowledge learned in the lesson.
2. The independent practice should help students achieve the objective(s) of the lesson.
3. The independent practice activity should be done by the students without the direct guidance of the teacher.
4. Student work produced in the independent practice activity should be checked by the teacher and feedback should be provided to students in a timely fashion.

Here is how the sample lesson plan used these criteria.

Criterion 1:   Practice a skill or apply knowledge.

The sample lesson independent practice requires students to interview someone who has immigrated to America and to find out from them what type of travel accommodations they had, cabin or steerage. The activity allows students to apply knowledge they have gained in the lesson to a new situation. The activity is such that it will involve the students in action, talking to real people about real situations. This is a valuable experience for students, as well as a memorable one.

Criterion 2:   Achieve objective(s).

The activity will further emphasize the meanings of *steerage* and *cabin,* as the students will be comparing them to the travel accommodations experienced by the person they interview.

Criterion 3:   Accomplish the task without the teacher's guidance.

The students must go out on their own in order to interview someone who has immigrated to this country. They will not have the direct guidance of the teacher as they accomplish this task, nor will they have direct guidance as they create their book about the individual.

Criterion 4:   The teacher checks and provides feedback.

It is very important for the teacher to provide feedback to students about the accuracy and quality of their work. Students must know that their teacher considers their work important and that their homework counts in the teacher's total evaluation of their performance. In the case of the sample lesson, the students' books could be displayed in the classroom after they are checked by the teacher.

Using the Clinical Model
You have now looked at the clinical model in terms of its general characteristics, its individual steps, and its instructional purposes, as well as in terms of an exemplary lesson developed using the clinical model. *Criteria* for each step of the model were provided that will help the new teacher create meaningful, exciting lessons for his or her students. As pointed out earlier, when used correctly, the model is very effective in bringing about student learning.

The clinical model provides a guideline for daily planning; that is, the teacher creates daily learning experiences for his or her students using the model to formulate the lesson. How successful these lessons will be depends on the skill and creativity of the teacher in designing and delivering instruction based on the model. The goal of the preceding section has been to reveal to the new teacher how to use the model to its maximum effectiveness, which can be done by paying close attention to the criteria described for each step of the model. The authors invite you to plan a social studies, science, or math lesson using the model and see the results firsthand.

The Generic Model

In contrast to the clinical model, the generic model of lesson planning does not call for a set sequence of activities. Rather, it leaves up to your discretion the type and sequence of activities to use. For example, to cover a particular topic in math, you may decide that the lesson should start with a Think-Pair-Share activity (see under Cooperative Learning Structures in Chapter 2) for the opening seven minutes of the lesson as a way of gaining immediate student involvement and determining their backgrounds. Using the clinical model, you would not start a lesson with such an independent group activity. Thus, the generic model provides the flexibility for you to employ what you think makes the most sense strategically in terms of activities for a particular lesson. Because there is no set order to follow, there is a greater demand placed on your creative abilities to design the type and sequence of activities that will work.

To give you an understanding of how to use the generic model for lesson planning, discussion will focus on (1) a description of the format and how it should be used and (2) an actual classroom example as a working model to guide your efforts.

Format Design
One of the most useful aspects of the generic model of lesson plan format is its compactness. It is a user-friendly reference and prompt as you attempt to carry out your lesson. As you look at Figure 10–23, notice how all the key ingredients that go into a lesson have a place on this planning blank. The five essential parts of this lesson plan format are the heading, the objective(s), the important notes, and the reflective comments. They are briefly described here, as well as their value and important criteria to address.

FIGURE 10–23   Generic Lesson Plan

Content Area _____   Grade Level _____   Date _____   Teacher _____

Unit _____   Topic _____   **Focus Today** _____

Objective(s): _____

_____

	Time Allot.	Activities		Resources Needed
Focusing:				
Concluding:				

Important Board/Overhead Notes	**Classwork**	**Homework**

Reflective Comments

The Heading

Description: This is the first two lines of the format where you list the *Content Area, Grade Level, Date, Your Name, Unit, Topic,* and *Focus Today*.

Value: This information helps you stay organized. Over time, you accumulate hundreds of lesson plans with their related materials. Few things are more disconcerting than to have lesson plans floating all over the place as the school year goes by. By maintaining this heading style, it becomes much easier to set up and periodically update a lesson plan filing system. One simple way to file your lesson plans is to place them in a three-ring binder by unit and topic. For each content area, you can keep a separate binder and insert related materials and revised lesson plans as needed.

The Objective(s)

Description: This is where you write a concise statement or statements of what the students will accomplish as a result of the lesson activities.

Value: The objective(s) is the "accomplishment factor" of your lessons that tell you what the students will learn that day. To use an analogy, it is hard to get somewhere if you do not know where you are going. The objective(s) is the *where* of classroom instruction. It is crucial to think through and write down objectives that tell what the students will be able to do after the lesson that they could not do before it. This part of the lesson plan is so important that it is worthwhile here to examine several criteria that need to be addressed so that you conceive of and state your lesson objectives in the most effective way possible.

> *Criterion 1:*   Always state objectives in terms of what the students will do, not what you will do.

Example: Students will be able to state five occupations found in their community.

Important Explanatory Note: The objective relates to student learning. If you were to state as the objective, "To teach about five occupations found in our community," simply teaching your lesson would mean the objective had been met. Obviously this would be worthless from the standpoint of student learning. Unfortunately, you will often see objectives stated incorrectly in this way.

> *Criterion 2:*   Always state objectives so they are observable and measurable.

Example: Students will be able to accurately place the names of the 13 original colonies on a blank map.

Important Explanatory Note: Meeting this criterion can always be accomplished by using an *action verb* (such as *state, compare, define, describe, plac*e, or *explain*) in constructing your objectives statements. Do not use passive verbs such as *appreciate, understand, learn*, and so on. The reason for this is that you and the students can observe whether or not and to what extent concrete actions have been accomplished. How do you measure something that is not observable? You can try to make assumptions, but over time, you can really go way off track if that is your general *modus operandi* regarding instructional objectives. In fact, the way to know whether students have *appreciated, understood*, or *learned* is through demonstrated behavior. In other words, once you have determined the extent to which students have accomplished your observable/measurable objectives, then you *and they* will know if they have appreciated, understood, or learned something.

> *Criterion 3:*   Always state objectives so that they serve as clear guides for the creation of your lesson activities.

Example: Students will be able to compare the characters Big Froggy and Happy Rabbit in the story "The Friendly Animals."

Important Explanatory Note: With the objective stated as it is in the preceding example, one is ready to think of the specific *ways* the students can *compare* these two characters. For example, the students can be asked to write a paragraph, make a list of similarities and differences, or draw a picture in their attempts to compare these two characters. Thus, by properly conceiving of the objective, the ability to shift right into designing a solid activity or set of activities for the accomplishment of that objective is greatly facilitated. Imagine if the objective had been, "To learn about the story's two main characters." Not only do you not know what the students are to accomplish from this objective but you are also still very far from figuring out what they should do to "learn about" the story's two main characters. An essential fact about formulating your instructional objectives is that if you address Criteria 1 and 2, you will find that Criterion 3 is automatically addressed also.

The Activities

Description: This is the *heart* of the lesson plan. Here, you describe the sequence of activities that will occur as the means for accomplishing your objective(s). In short, the activities describe what the students are to do. It is wise to think of your first activity as a *focusing* experience and your last activity as a *concluding* experience to the lesson. You can also note the time allotted to each activity and the resource materials needed for each activity.

Value: If the objective is the *where* as in "Where are we going with the classroom learning venture?" then the activities are the *how*, as in "How do we get to that destination?" The classroom where either the *where* or the *how* (or both) is not clear is bound to be an ineffective learning environment. The activities can arguably be considered the most critically important of the teacher's creations. Your activities paint the picture of what you expect to see happening in the classroom during instruction. As such, the activities are yours and the students' road maps to learning. A crucial point must be made here. *You* have complete control over how this road map is drawn. You may have many state, district, and school guidelines and curriculum requirements to follow, but no one tells you what the specific lesson activities should be. The classroom teacher has full creative license *and responsibility* here. This points out how valuable it is to develop skill in designing instructional activities. For this reason, several criteria are presented and discussed here to guide your efforts at designing instructional activities. You should note that the first two criteria should *always* be met, whereas the last three should be met according to the nature and level of learning involved.

Criterion 1:   The activity should maximize student interest and attention.

Discussion: As you saw in examining the nature of the learning process, learning cannot even begin to take place in students who are paying little or no attention to what is supposed to be learned. It follows that students' attention is directly related to their levels of interest. To reiterate briefly, here are several ways to make activities interesting to the students:

- Make the activity relevant to the students.
- Address various learning modalities.
- Be enthusiastic and interesting in your presentation and attitude.
- Pace the activities well so things do not get boring or bogged down.
- Allow the students to be *actively working* most of the time.

- Provide for hands-on experiences whenever possible.
- Include interesting and engaging resource materials in presenting the activities.
- Allow for positive student interaction whenever possible.

Criterion 2:   The activity should involve most of the students most of the time.

Discussion: It is a clearly established fact that people learn very little from what they hear, as compared from what they do. The operative word here is *do*. As you sit down to design your lesson activities, always ask yourself: Will this activity have the students actively engaged in and responsible for doing something? Most of the time, you should be able to answer yes. By planning your activities in this way, you not only maximize student involvement but you also build the students' sense of responsibility by their being accountable for doing the specific work at hand.

Criterion 3:   The activity should build students' backgrounds on the material to be covered.

Discussion: This criterion applies to those activities focused on the Preparation phase of PAR (also discussed in Chapter 1 as the Perception phase of the learning process). It is natural that to build student background, you must first determine what their current background is concerning the material being presented. Understanding concepts and finding meaning in material is possible for students only when they have a working vocabulary (i.e., essential information) in that material. As stated in Chapter 1, activities focused on this level of learning call heavily on your powers of creativity. You must make what is inherently dull—that is, factual information necessary to build background—come alive to gain interest. Effective teachers know how to do this and thus set the stage for the next higher level of learning (i.e., conception). Look at the following example of an activity that a fourth-grade teacher used to build student background about the science topic of Whales.

Example of Effective Background Building Activity

Large outline sketches of seven different types of whales have been posted along the walls of the classroom. Students have been assigned to groups of four each. Each group is to do research on one of the seven types of whales using their handouts "Sharks of the World." The aim, initially, is to come up with four facts about its type of whale. Then, each group is to go up to the poster of its whale and write those facts inside the outline shape of the whale so others can easily read them. Finally, students are to take a guided (by the teacher) tour along the perimeter of the classroom, to read about the facts that have been researched by other groups about the types of whales being studied. In guiding the tour, the teacher fills in other interesting information about whales and also entertains the students' questions.

Important Note about This Activity.   Why does this activity work so well in building background? Because it engages student interest and provides for their *full*, hands-on involvement from beginning to end. Compare this successful approach to one where the teacher merely lectures about the seven types of whales, or where the class covers this material through round-robin reading from their science textbooks.

Criterion 4:   The activity should build student comprehension of the material to be learned.

Discussion: This criterion applies to those activities focused on the Assisting Understanding phase of PAR (also discussed in Chapter 1 as the Conception phase of the learning process). Once student background has been built, the foundation is there for helping students develop understanding of the material. The activity, or more likely the activities, you will design should accomplish this need to provide students with opportunities to connect the background facts together in ways that have meaning to them. Following is an example of an effective comprehension activity based on the whale activity just reviewed.

Example of Effective Comprehension Building Activity
The groups of four students each who just completed their initial research on the seven types of whales are now asked to prepare a five-minute presentation. The presentations are to focus on why and how each group's particular type of whale looks, eats, and lives where it does. Students are to refer to their textbooks, their handout on whales, and selected issues of *Discovery* and *National Geographic* magazines that have been placed in the classroom library.

Important Note about This Activity.   Again, notice how this activity meets the first two criteria concerning engaging interest and maximizing involvement. You can be sure the students will walk away understanding this material much more by preparing for and then giving their presentations than if you had simply chosen to explain the information to them.

Criterion 5:   The activity should foster student creativity.

Discussion: This criterion applies to those activities focused on the Reflection phase of PAR (also discussed in Chapter 1 as the Ideation phase of the learning process). Learning is best assimilated and retained when students have opportunities to take what they have come to understand and apply it in original and creative ways. These acts of application leave a lasting and vivid impression of the material in the students' minds. It is at this point that you can really say learning has occurred. The following example takes the whale activity to its logical conclusion in terms of the level (i.e., ideation) of the learning process involved.

Example of Effective Fostering Creativity Activity
The students are asked to open their large illustrated journals. They are then to choose a theme from the Theme Menu on the board to write about one of the seven types of whales being studied. They also have the option of creating their own theme to write on. Among the themes to choose from are: A Day in the Life of the _____ Whale; Why the _____ Whale Is My Favorite; and The Adventures of Mr./Ms. _____ Whale. The large illustrated journal is set up to have very wide margins all around each page so the students can feel free to illustrate their written text.

Important Note about This Activity.   Here is an opportunity for the students' imaginations to come into play. Imagination is based on a solid background and understanding of the material being studied. The students are going to remember their experiences learning about whales in this class for some time to come.

The Important Notes

Description: This is a space on your lesson plan blank for indicating the important board notes you will need to put up, as well as telegraphic indications of the class work and homework to be completed. With this section of your lesson plan blank filled in, you have all the essential information needed to begin to make it a living reality in the classroom.

Value: When you get into the classroom and are in the midst of the energetic, quickly moving environment that is an elementary classroom, any reference and prompt that will jog your memory and allow you to keep your lesson flowing is a blessing indeed.

The Reflective Comments

Description: On this section at the bottom of your lesson plan blank, you can comment on any aspect of the plan and the experience implementing it in the classroom.

Value: Nothing teaches like experience. With this in mind, any notes you make to yourself about how the lesson went are bound to be helpful the next time that particular lesson has to be presented. Perhaps you will note that the time allotment should be adjusted, or maybe you will make a recommendation to yourself on how to modify one of the activities so it will be more workable the next time. If you do not reflect on the lesson soon after it has been presented, your opportunity to gain from and improve on the experience will be lost. Therefore, the importance of the Reflective Comments section of your lesson plan blank cannot be minimized. In Figure 10–24, a working example of the generic lesson plan is presented to visually summarize the preceding discussion and to guide your efforts at lesson planning.

FIGURE 10–24 Exemplary Model of Generic Lesson Plan

Heading

| Content Area | Science | Grade Level | 1 | Date | 10/6 | Teacher | Ms. Good |

| Unit | The senses | Topic | Sight | **Focus Today** | Colors of the Rainbow |

Objective

Objective(s):
- Students will make the colors orange, green, & violet using primary colors yellow, red, & blue.
- Students will explore and predict other color mixtures and possibilities.

	Time Allot.	Activities	Resources Needed
Focusing:	4"	#1 Quick Review: "You are the scientist, so let's discuss what we already know about the sense of sight." (Refer to each student as "Dr. _____.")	What We Know Pocket Chart & Large Info. Cards
	6"	#2 Presenting Colors: Put large color wheel on overhead to display 3 primary colors (yellow, red, blue); demonstrate directions for mixing two colors at a time on a wax-paper covered color wheel to get orange, green, and violet.	Overhead transparency of color wheel, a straw, 3 plastic cups, water, & food coloring
Activities	15"	#3 Exploring Colors: Students explore mixing colors at their desks, using materials as was just demonstrated.	32 color wheels, 32 straws, wax paper, 96 cups, water and food coloring
Concluding:	25"	#4 Original Experimentation: "Let's take a vote, scientists. Would you like to experiment more?" Students do original mixture experiments on their color wheels using crayons; students share results of their experiments with colors.	Sets of crayons

Notes

Important Board/Overhead Notes

Color Wheel

(color wheel diagram: Violet, Red, Blue, Orange, Green, Yellow)

Mixed	I Predict	I Got

Today as a Scientist, You:
- Explored
- Observed
- Compared
- Communicated

Classwork
- Review "sight"
- Exploring Colors (at desks)
- Experiment with Colors: Crayons
- Rug Time to share results

Homework

Share what you discovered with your parents when you get home.

Reflections

Reflective Comments

1. Big success, overall
2. Students had a little trouble carrying out mixing directions at first
3. *Next time:* Walk class through their first color mix

References for Section III

Armento, B., Klor de Alva, J. J., Nash, G. B., Salter, C. L., Wilson, L. E., & Wixson, K. K. (1994). *A message of ancient days*. Boston: Houghton Mifflin.

Dunston, P. J. (1992). A critique of graphic organizer research. *Reading Research and Instruction, 31* (2), 57–65.

Hom, K. J. (1990). *The effects of an integrated social studies curriculum on inner-city middle school students' attitudes toward and achievement in social studies*. Unpublished doctoral dissertation. United States International University, San Diego, CA.

Hunter, M. (1982). *Mastery teaching: Increasing instructional effectiveness in elementary, secondary schools, colleges and universities*. El Segundo, CA: TIP Publications.

Rafoth, M., Leal, L., & DeFabo, L. (1993). *Strategies for learning and remembering: Study skills across the curriculum*. National Education Association of the United States.

Richardson, J. S., & Morgan, R. T. (1990). *Reading to learn in the content areas*. Belmont, CA: Wadsworth.

Section *IV*

Classroom Management

"I had great ideas for planning and presenting my lessons and was full of enthusiasm for trying to make a difference in my students' lives, but it all seemed wasted because I didn't have a way to maintain an orderly classroom." You would be surprised how many new teachers make a statement similar to this. From another perspective, you will often hear principals say how important it is that their teachers concentrate first on establishing a clear and *consistent* classroom management system and then on instructional goals. The rationale is that you will never get a chance to carry out effective instruction if the students are not functioning in a positive manner that demonstrates respect for you, each other, and learning.

What can a new teacher do to create an orderly classroom environment? Chapter 11 will answer this question by presenting you with a strategy for setting up your personal *classroom management plan.* Just as thoughtful and systematic planning is the basis for successful instruction, this also holds true in the realm of classroom management. Your personality and insistence that students behave will not be nearly enough to control your class. There *must* be some system in place that is *consistently* followed for this to occur. To do this takes much thought, advice, and planning.

The aim of this section is to examine the elements found in any good classroom system as a generic approach and understanding that is adaptable to a variety of classroom situations and needs. In addition, five models that have been developed for managing classroom behavior will be looked at to provide a variety of ideas and possibilities as you strive to design the system that works best for you and your students. To achieve this goal, the following chapters will be presented:

- Seven Essential Aspects of an Effective Classroom Management Plan
- Sample Classroom Management Systems
- Diversity and Classroom Management

Seven Essential Aspects of an Effective Classroom Management Plan

If you observe a teacher whose classroom environment is characterized by students actively involved in learning, a sense of mutual respect, and positive behavior, it may be difficult to recognize the different aspects of classroom management that teacher had to consider, plan for, and then implement as an integrated whole to create this environment. In short, an effective teacher makes this integrated whole happen so smoothly and seamlessly that one can fully appreciate what it took to accomplish this only after trying to do it oneself.

Most people involved with elementary teaching will testify to the fact that *consistency* is the key to effective classroom management. It seems obvious, but you can be consistent only if there is something with which to be consistent. This entails a thoughtfully articulated plan that touches all the critical areas that go into management of an elementary classroom. The goal of this chapter, therefore, is to provide you with a window into the seven major aspects of a successful classroom management system so that no matter where you may wind up teaching, you have in mind and in hand well-conceived ideas and plans for carrying out each of these essential aspects. The seven essential aspects covered will be discussed in the following order: (1) classroom rules, (2) classroom rewards, (3) classroom consequences, (4) routines and procedures, (5) room arrangement, (6) communication, and (7) attitude.

Classroom Rules

Your set of classroom rules communicates the expectations and limitations on behavior in the classroom. These rules, therefore, must be very well chosen. The following discussion will focus on how to create and establish your classroom rules as a guiding framework for positive classroom behavior.

How to Create Your Classroom Rules

The best way to go about creating your set of classroom rules is to keep in mind and address the following three criteria as you complete the task:

Criterion 1:   The rules must focus on behaviors that are observable.

It seems appropriate to have a rule such as "Be respectful to each other." However, this rule is vague (what exactly is *respectful?*), and, therefore, difficult to enforce. As a result, you will find yourself debating and negotiating with students over alleged disrespectful behavior, thus interrupting the flow of instruction and creating an adversarial relationship between you and the students. It would be far more useful to state rules that describe the specific observable "respectful" behaviors to be followed, such as "Raise your hand and wait to be called on to speak" or "Keep hands, feet, and objects to yourself." If and when these expected behaviors are not being met, both you and the students know it is so.

Even with rules that spell out behavior expectations as clearly as this, there will be a wide range of gradations in how much, if at all, the rules have been violated. This is natural because so many situations arise all day long, day after day, in the dynamic atmosphere that is the elementary classroom. Imagine, then, just how impossible it would be to maintain even a semblance of consistency where the rules and concomitant expected behaviors are unclear or vague. You would have *no* chance. By basing your rules on observable behaviors, you gain a tremendous advantage in that you can freely and frequently *praise* students who are carrying out these behaviors. Few things work as well in creating an environment students want to be in as periodic acknowledgment of their good-faith efforts.

Criterion 2:   The rules must be relevant to your students and particular situation.

No set of rules is perfectly appropriate or applicable in every classroom situation. There are some classrooms where it is absolutely essential to have a rule (e.g., "No swearing or teasing"), yet in other classrooms the need for this rule does not even come to mind. In addition, the grade level you teach can be a factor in choosing your rules. For example, in the primary grades, where the students can be likened to "little bundles of energy," the rule "No running in the classroom" might be useful. Again, this also depends on who your students are and what their previous training has been. There is also the question of your school's overall discipline plan and the extent to which your classroom rules need to align with this plan. For example, a school that is attempting to instill a sense of accomplishment and encouragement in its students might ask all teachers to include "Complete all work to the best of your ability" among the set of rules they develop.

Criterion 3:   Keep the number of rules developed limited.

Manageable and *consistent* are the bywords when trying to attain a classroom characterized by positive student behavior. This is possible when your rules are not only relevant and stated in terms of observable behaviors but also reasonably few in number. Too many rules lead to confusion and complications. You cannot micromanage student behavior by having many rules covering numerous situations and needs. If you do this, the students will feel oppressed and tend to rebel. As you will see in the examples of actual sets of classroom rules presented in Figure 11–1, less is more. This means you should have rules that are comprehensive in nature so that they are applicable throughout the day in all activities in which the students are involved.

Teachers who find the need to have a rule covering most every activity and circumstance in the classroom usually do so out of insecurity and because they fail to make the distinction between classroom rules and classroom routines and procedures. Rules pertain to the general behaviors that are expected all the time. Routines and procedures

FIGURE 11–1   Sets of Model Classroom Rules (Various Approaches)

• Always Do Your Best • Listen and Follow Directions • During Independent Work, Stay On Task • Cooperate with Others • Move Quietly in the Classroom	• Use Kind Words • Use Kind Actions • Let Others Learn • Care for Materials • Cooperate with Adults and Children
• Follow Directions • Keep Your Hands, Feet, Mouth, and Objects to Yourself • Raise Your Hand and Wait to be Called On • Stay in Your Seat Unless Given Permission to Get Up • One Person Talks at a Time	• We Will Stay in Our Seats • We Will Respect the Rights and Property of Others • We Will Raise Our Hands • We Will Work Quietly • We Will Listen
• Be Courteous, Cooperative, and Respectful • Respect the Rights, Safety, and Property of Everyone • Be on Time, Prepared to Work, and Stay on Task • Behave in a Way that Does Not Disrupt Teaching • Have No Unauthorized Food, Drink, or Gum	• **Give Encouragement** • **Respect Others** • **On** Task • **Use Quiet Voices** • **Participate**

pertain to the specific details of how a great number of things are to be done in the classroom (e.g., sharpen pencils, go to bathroom, entering and leaving)—in short, how all the business of the classroom is to be conducted. Specific directions are spelled out for how each routine and procedure is to be carried out. Your classroom rules, on the other hand, involve the behaviors that are to pervade all routines and procedures and every aspect of instruction as well.

As you try to determine which rules are going to be the best for you, it is helpful to avail yourself of ideas from a variety of sources. Fellow teachers, especially those teaching at your grade level, will have some useful advice on what rules work for them and why. You can also come across interesting ideas in professional education journals, teacher magazines, and books on classroom management. Be careful, though, not to overwhelm or confuse yourself with too many ideas about classroom rules. If you follow the three preceding criteria, you will have the proper perspective for judging and adapting any ideas that may come your way.

How to Establish Your Classroom Rules

The next task you face after creating a viable set of classroom rules is how to establish these rules so they effectively guide behavior. There are too many instances where a set of classroom rules posted in the room remains nothing more than a wall decoration. These rules are not being enforced by the teacher and thus not followed by the students. Posting your rules does not mean they have been established. To establish your set of classroom rules, the following recommendations should be considered:

1. *Teach Your Classroom Management Plan:*   You certainly know every detail of your classroom management plan, but how the students are informed of this plan is of utmost importance. This is why successful teachers *always* create a definite plan for teaching their new class of students the management system that they have developed. Teaching your classroom management plan can be accomplished through a formal lesson(s). For example, on the first day of school, you can present a formal lesson on the topic of Our Classroom Community. This lesson plan could look very much like the one depicted in Figure 11–2. Notice in this lesson how allowance is made for student discussion and input as the classroom rules are being presented. You want the students not only to know the rules but also to understand and accept that the rules are for their benefit.

2. *Enforce Your Rules:*   Translate your words into deeds! Remember one essential fact: You can be 100 percent sure that you have the undivided attention of your students at the very beginning of the first day of school. All eyes and ears are on you. The students are extremely curious to know what their new teacher is like, what he or she will allow and not allow, and what his or her expectations are for them. Their antennae are up and never as tuned into you as during the first part of the first day of the school year. Knowing the certainty of this, it makes all the sense in the world for you to use this "first-day" phenomenon to your advantage. If the students are bent on figuring you out as soon as they can, take the initiative to make sure they get the precise message you want them to get.

FIGURE 11–2   Teaching Your Classroom Rule

Content Area __Classroom Management__   Grade Level __3__   Date __Sept. 7__   Teacher __Mr. Good__

Unit __Classroom Behavior__   Topic __Our Classroom Community__   **Focus Today** __Classroom Rules__

Objective(s): __Students will list behaviors important to a positive classroom community.__

__Students will be able to state the five classroom rules.__

Time Allot.	Activities		Resources Needed
5"	#1 Quick Think:	"I want each of you to list the behaviors you think are important for making this classroom a great place in which to learn."	Classroom Behavior Log Sheet
12"	#2 Discussion and Categorizing:	Facilitate a discussion by categorizing the ideas students have about important behaviors under the five classroom rules.	Overhead, chalkboard, and Classroom Rules transparencies
25"	#3 Group Posters:	Divide the students into five groups with each group assigned to make a classroom Rule # _____ Poster.	Chart paper, colored markers, rulers
10"	#4 Gallery Walk:	Hang posters under a sign called "Our Classroom Rules" and have the students walk by to see what their classmates created. (Play quiet music during the walk.)	Scotch tape, tape player, and cassette tape

Important Board/Overhead Notes	**Our Classroom Community**	**Classwork**	**Homework**
Rule #1 Rule #2 Rule #3 Rule #4 Rule #5	Rule #1 [ ] [ ] **Behaviors We Look For:** • • • •	• List behaviors • Discuss and categorize • Create rules posters • Gallery walk	Discuss the classroom rules with your parents and get signature on student manual.
Categorizing Behaviors	**Classroom Rules Poster**		

Reflective Comments

(Comments and ideas placed here once lesson has been given.)

Presenting a formal lesson(s) on Our Classroom Community clearly sends this message, but the way business is conducted on that first day sends a louder message. For example, throughout that first day, including the time which your lesson on Our Classroom Community is being presented, hold the students accountable for their behavior. If someone talks out without raising his or her hand, you must communicate that this is not how things will be done in this classroom. The message is not just for that one student who called out. All students will take notice. They will be saying to themselves, "Oh, this teacher means business." You deal with inappropriate behavior similarly every time it occurs, so all students, indeed, do know you mean business. You need not create a series of confrontations; rather, in a calm and firm manner, you consistently hold fast to your expectations for having a classroom that is a community of learners. To settle for anything less is to do a disservice to your students and yourself.

3. *Reinforce Good Behavior:*   Right from the very first day, it is a wise practice to reinforce positive behavior by periodically recognizing and praising students who choose to follow the rules throughout the day. Interestingly, if you were to observe a typical elementary classroom, you would find that most of the students are behaving well most of the time. Yet, most of the comments made concerning behavior are negative. This means that teachers are accentuating the negative and not taking the wonderful opportunity that exists to focus on the positive. Students want attention—some more than others. If misbehaving is the way to get your attention, they will misbehave. From the first day, on the other hand, if they see that they can get not only your attention but praise as well by following the classroom rules, they will tend to choose that route instead.

4. *Model Appropriate Behaviors:*   In addition to pointing out and correcting or praising inappropriate or good behavior, respectively, it is very helpful to *model* the behaviors your classroom rules require. For example, right from the beginning, it is critical that the students know how they are to enter and move about the room. This relates directly to your rule "No running in the classroom." On the first day, you have the great opportunity to model how one should enter and go from place to place in the classroom. Such modeling is one more instance where you can take the initiative concerning how things will function in the classroom. When or where you do not take the initiative concerning classroom behavior, the students will. If you do not take the time to model entering and moving about the classroom, just watch the method they choose. It will not be pretty. Thus, it is important that you determine the ways you plan to model those behaviors most vital to running an orderly classroom so that on the first day they can be modeled and practiced.

Classroom Rewards

A natural and necessary complement to your classroom rules are the rewards and consequences that result from following or not following those rules. The role of rewards and consequences is straightforward. Your system of rewards places the emphasis on positive behavior and seeks to reinforce those behaviors by recognizing and rewarding them. This is why some teachers prefer to use the terminology *positive recognition* for this aspect of their classroom management system. The opposite also applies: Your system of consequences brings students' attention to the limits on tolerable behavior and seeks to keep inappropriate behavior to a minimum. One word sums up the approach that must be used in setting up and applying your system of rewards and consequences: *consistency*. This word should never leave your consciousness as you make decisions about how rewards and consequences will be delivered in your classroom. The following discussion will look at ways to set up a system of rewards and to set up a system of consequences.

Setting Up Your System of Classroom Rewards

Some people preparing to enter the field of elementary teaching proclaim, "I will never bribe my students to behave." This view is understandable to a degree, but it misses the mark in terms of the reality of the classroom situation. First of all, a bribe is given to someone involved in criminal, or at least dishonest, behavior. What does rewarding a child for doing his or her class work well have to do with criminal behavior? This proclamation of bribery simply does not make sense. From another vantage point, some will say, "Students should be thankful for their education and for the benefits it brings. This is reward enough." Again, to a degree, this notion is understandable, but it too is shortsighted as far as what is needed and effective to promote learning in the classroom. Many, if not most, students expect and need some form of extrinsic motivation. It would be wonderful if every student came to school intrinsically motivated to learn for learning's sake. In fact, as teachers, this a fine ideal to have as a goal. You must understand, however, where the students really are in terms of what will motivate them. Then all effort possible should be made to move the current reality toward your ideals.

Figure 11–3 graphically represents the scope of a classroom rewards system. As you review Figure 11–3, notice how the four quadrants indicate that consideration has to be given to individual rewards on both a short- and long-term basis and to class rewards the same way. Within each quadrant, rewards are essentially of three orientations: academic, recognition, and fun. Regardless of which quadrant you are focusing on, however, three questions need to be addressed in setting up your classroom rewards system:

- What behaviors should be rewarded?
- What types of rewards should be given?
- How should rewards be given?

The following discussion looks at ways of setting up your classroom rewards system according to the reward types outlined by the quadrants in Figure 11–3. To do this, the three preceding questions will be addressed for each reward type. In addition, to graphically summarize the ideas presented and, at the same time, provide a practical planning guide, a *Rewards Matrix* will conclude the discussion of each of the four reward types. Within each matrix, the rewards suggested will be categorized according to academic, recognition, and fun.

Short-Term Individual Rewards

In attempting to determine how to set your short-term individual rewards, consider that a short-term reward is one that is given immediately or, at the latest, by the end of the school day. With this in mind, consider three questions.

Question 1:   What short-term individual behaviors should be rewarded?

Anything you can do to reinforce your classroom rules will make your job easier. Therefore, a logical place to start is to reward behaviors derived from your classroom rules. For instance, if one of your rules is "Follow directions the first time they are given," it will not be hard to periodically acknowledge and reward one or a few students complying with this rule. Remember, most of the students can be found behaving appropriately most of the time. There will be no dearth of opportunities to reward stu-

FIGURE 11–3   Types of Classroom Rewards

Timing	Focus		
	Individual Rewards	*Reward Orientation*	*Class Rewards*
Short Term		◄— **Academic** —► ◄— **Recognition** —► ◄—— **Fun** ——►	
Long Term		◄— **Academic** —► ◄— **Recognition** —► ◄—— **Fun** ——►	

dents who are following your rules. Every time you recognize and reward these behaviors, you are reinforcing them.

You have every right, though, to tell the students that not every good behavior by every student will or can be rewarded all day long. Rather, they can be made aware that, without warning, from time to time, you will "catch them being good." They should also come to realize that, over time, your recognition of them will even out among all the students. Rewards lose their meaning and value if they can be attained too easily and often. If, however, you make the rewards too difficult to attain and give them too infrequently, they will have little impact on student behavior. Arriving at a thoughtful balance between these two extremes is what is needed to make your rewards system work. Other behaviors that can be deserving of reward on a short-term individual basis can be helping a fellow student, paying attention, doing individual work quietly, and keeping one's desk and surrounding area neat. You can extend this list by considering which behaviors would be wisest to reinforce because they are pivotal to the smooth functioning of your classroom.

Question 2:   What types of short-term individual rewards should be given?

The rewards you give have one main purpose: to motivate students to apply themselves in positive ways in the classroom. It is safe to assume that rewards will have limited effect if the students do not particularly like them. It is important, then, first to find out the types of rewards that will interest and motivate your students. One way this can be accomplished is through a "getting to know each other" activity. This can be conducted in the following ways:

- *Paired Interviews:*   Have buddy pairs of students interview each other and then use the information they obtain to introduce their buddy to the class. You can give the students a list of questions to ask during the interview. Among these questions can be: What are the things you like to do most? What rewards do you like the most in school? and What are your favorite school activities?
- *Introducing _____ Cards:*   Have each student fill out a preprinted 4" × 6" index card on which they share various information about themselves, including questions like those stated in the Paired Interviews.
- *Around the Circle:*   Have students form a large circle and then briefly introduce themselves to the you and their new classmates. Again, make sure some of the information they share provides some insights into the types of rewards that are likely to motivate them.

In addition to the information obtained directly from the students, you can get many good ideas from other teachers, parents, and your own imagination. Whatever rewards you decide on initially will be modified over time based on the actual experience of what works best for you and your students. But, as with every other aspect of teaching, you need to create a starting point from which to make effective modifications.

Figure 11–4 presents a matrix that lists various types of rewards that can be given to individual students on a short-term basis, along with the behaviors for which those rewards may be given.

Question 3:   How should short-term individual rewards be given?

Two elements are involved in giving rewards: the timing and the method. For short-term individual rewards, the timing is straightforward in that you either provide the reward immediately or some time before the end of that school day. As far as the method for giving short-term individual rewards, there are several possibilities. For example, you could choose to paste a gold star under a student's name on your classroom community pocket wall chart. Or you could add points under a student's name on the Super Citizens clipboard you sometimes carry around the classroom. Whichever ways you choose to deliver the rewards, it helps tremendously if students tangibly experience the rewards. They very much appreciate seeing, feeling, hearing, or doing something that demonstrates a reward has been received.

FIGURE 11–4   Rewards Matrix (Short-Term, Individual)

Rewards		Following Rules	Working on Task	Paying Attention	Desk Area Clean and Neat	Lining Up Smoothly	Helping Someone	Participating	Maturity and Good Judgment	Using Quiet Voices
R	"Wow" Cards									
R	Praise									
R	Stars/ Stickers									
R	Points									
R	Extra Privileges in Class									
R	Positive Letter Home									
R	Positive Phone Call Home									
R	Lunch with Teacher									
A	Read for Pleasure									
A	Computer Time for Assignments									
A	Learning Center Pass									
A	Library Pass									
A	Work on Other Classwork									
F	Food									
F	Toys/Pencils/ Objects									
F	Games									
F	Play a Walkman (Quietly)									
F	Computer Time for Games									

Key: **R** = Recognition Rewards   **A** = Academic Rewards   **F** = Fun Rewards

Short-Term Class Rewards

By definition, short-term class rewards are those given immediately or, at the latest, by the end of the day to either the entire class or to specific groups of students within the class. The most common way of setting up specific group rewards is according to the way students are seated at separate tables or clusters of desks. In this regard, you have the opportunity to catch a group (or groups) of students being good. Often, recognizing and rewarding a group of students within the class sets up positive peer pressure for other clusters of students to emulate their classmates. In this sense, class rewards involve a team dynamic that can prove to be a powerful and positive force in the classroom. Sometimes, individual students need the support, encouragement, and example of fellow students to accomplish what they could not by themselves. By being part of a team effort, students also learn the value and beauty of cooperation as a necessary counterpart to individual achievement.

Question 1:   What short-term class behaviors should be rewarded?

There is a definite similarity between the individual behaviors and class behaviors that should be rewarded. In fact, in many cases, they are exactly the same. For example, if the class, in general, is on task during their seatwork, you may wish to reinforce this behavior by announcing that the class has earned so many points toward a particular reward. You may do the same if the class is maintaining a neat and clean classroom or is being attentive. All three of these behaviors (i.e., on task, neatness, attentiveness) are clearly rewardable individual behaviors, as well. There are, however, behaviors that involve a group effort and dynamic. For example, lining up to enter or leave the classroom is a group activity. Any number of cooperative learning activities also center around group behavior and thus can be the object of class rewards.

Question 2:   What types of short-term class rewards should be given?

One basic principle to bear in mind when determining what types of class rewards to give is that they should be something the class or group can enjoy collectively. For example, for lining up to go to and return from recess in an orderly fashion on a particular day, the class could receive an extra five minutes of music time on the rug that afternoon. In short, for behaving well as a class, all students enjoy the reward of that behavior together. This not only reinforces good behavior but it also allows the students to experience the joys and benefits of working together for the common good. It is hard to think of a better lesson for them to learn!

Question 3:   How should short-term class rewards be given?

Short-term class rewards should be delivered very much along the lines of short-term individual rewards. That is, rewards should be given immediately or by the end of the school day as far as timing is concerned, and in ways that students can see, hear, feel, or do as far as the method of delivery is concerned. The obvious difference is that class rewards involve a group dynamic. When giving such rewards, you are addressing the entire class or a group within the class. In Figure 11–5, a rewards matrix is presented that outlines short-term class rewards.

Long-Term Individual Rewards

Long term refers to any reward earned and given after a period of more than one day. The key word in the previous sentence is *earned*. By their very nature, long-term rewards are like delayed gratification. It is important to understand that a certain level of maturity is needed by a student to be motivated to behave in a particular manner when the reward for that behavior is not coming right away. In addressing the following three questions, this notion of delayed gratification and maturity will be a recurrent theme.

FIGURE 11–5   Rewards Matrix (Short-Term, Class)

	Rewards	Behaviors							
		Following Rules	Working on Task	Paying Attention	Room Clean and Neat	Lining Up Smoothly	Good Sportsmanship at Recess	Positive Collaborative Spirit	Using Quiet Voices
R	Praise								
R	Class/Group Star								
R	Class/Group Points								
R	Membership in Classroom Club								
A	Extra Music Time								
A	Choice of Learning Center								
A	Take Class Book Home to Read								
F	Extra Recess Time								
F	Early Dismissal								
F	Party Points								
F	H.W. Free Pass								

Key: **R** = Recognition Rewards   **A** = Academic Rewards   **F** = Fun Rewards

Question 1:   What long-term behaviors should be rewarded?

A simple way to determine what behaviors should be rewarded on a long-term individual basis is that these behaviors are essentially the same as those rewarded on a short-term basis. The only difference is that you are holding out to the students the possibility of being additionally rewarded if they maintain such behavior over a certain extended period of time. For example, if individual students can periodically earn a gold star under their names for staying on task during instructional activities, they can also be given the long-term reward of a Model Citizen Certificate signed by the principal for accumulating five gold stars in one week. By conceiving your long-term rewards as based on the same behaviors rewarded on a short-term basis, you reinforce behaviors very important to your classroom operation and also effectively deal with the issue of immediate versus delayed gratification.

Question 2:   What types of long-term individual rewards should be given?

Although long-term rewards are often given for the same behaviors as rewarded on a short-term basis, the rewards given are *not* the same. As is evident in the preceding example of the Model Citizen Reward, long-term rewards need to be more substantial than short-term rewards. That is, they need to be something to look forward to and worth waiting for. As you can see in Figure 11–6, the rewards listed on this rewards matrix are of a more substantial nature than the short-term rewards suggested earlier.

Question 3:   How should long-term individual rewards be given?

With rewards that have been earned for a prolonged period of exemplary behavior, not only should the rewards themselves be more substantial but the recognition of the accomplishment itself should also last longer. For example, if a student stays on task for an entire week and thus earns your Model Citizen Certificate, this certificate should be put on display for a period of time. Thus, long-term individual rewards should be more substantial and receive a longer and wider recognition than short-term individual rewards.

Long-Term Class Rewards

As with long-term individual rewards, the same basic principle applies in determining long-term class rewards. That is, your long-term class rewards should be given for the same behaviors for which short-term class rewards are given. The only difference is that the long-term rewards should be more substantial, because the class as a whole has demonstrated exemplary behavior over an extended period of time.

Question 1:   What long-term class behaviors should be rewarded?

The behaviors rewarded on a long-term class basis should almost always be the same as those rewarded on a short-term class basis. This is because (1) these are behaviors you have determined are essential for a positive classroom learning environment and (2) it is crucial that these behaviors be reinforced whenever possible.

FIGURE 11–6   Rewards Matrix (Long-Term, Individual)

	Rewards	Behaviors					
		Following Rules	Working on Task	Paying Attention	Desk Area Clean and Neat	Lining Up Smoothly	Helping Someone
R	Good Citizen Certificate						
R	Positive Call Home by Principal						
R	Photo on "Super Student" Bulletin Board						
R	Lunch with Principal						
R	Recognition at Good Behavior Assembly						
R	Name in Classroom Newsletter						
A	Learning Center Captain						
A	Peer Tutor						
A	Your Choice Box						
F	H.W. Free Pass						
F	Raffle Tickets						
F	Frozen Yogurt Store Visit						
F	Grab Bag Credits						
F	Pass to Popcorn Party						

Key: **R** = Recognition Rewards   **A** = Academic Rewards   **F** = Fun Rewards

Question 2:   What long-term class rewards should be given?

Exactly the same principle holds here as it does for long- versus short-term individual rewards. The long-term class rewards should be harder to earn (i.e., for extended periods of exemplary behavior) and thus be more substantial in nature. A number of suggested long-term class rewards are listed in the rewards matrix in Figure 11–7.

Question 3:   How should long-term class rewards be given?

FIGURE 11–7   Rewards Matrix (Long-Term, Class)

Rewards		Behaviors					
		Following Rules	Working on Task	Paying Attention	Room Clean and Neat	Lining Up Smoothly	Good Sportsmanship at Recess
R	Model Class Award						
R	Class Photo on School-wide Display						
R	Write-up in School Newsletter						
A	Special Field Trip						
A	Computer Center Time						
A	Homework Assignment Cancellation						
A	Erase Any Grade of Your Choice						
F	Class Video and Popcorn						
F	Class/Group Outing						
F	Extra P.E. Period						
F	Free Time for "In-Class Games"						
F	Class Treasure Hunt						

Key: **R** = Recognition Rewards   **A** = Academic Rewards   **F** = Fun Rewards

As you look at Figure 11–7, you can see that the long-term class rewards emphasize a group recognition, participation, and celebration of the accomplishment attained. The feeling throughout the class should be one of team or collective achievement of a laudable goal. In fact, students realize they win on two accounts by attaining long-term class rewards as a result of prolonged exemplary behavior. First, there is the attainment of the reward itself. Second, and quite importantly, they have helped make their own classroom a productive learning environment for themselves.

Your classroom reward system should not be too complex or be designed in such a way that it is a great burden and distraction. To avoid this, yet still obtain all the benefits of a reward system, it should be carefully thought through and planned along the lines just discussed. In this way, students will soon realize you are in control and have taken clear steps to emphasize and maintain a positive classroom environment.

Classroom Consequences

Your classroom rewards aim at encouraging and reinforcing desired and necessary behavior. Similarly, your classroom consequences aim at discouraging and stopping inappropriate and detrimental behavior. Both rewards and consequences are necessary to run an effective elementary instructional program. You cannot overemphasize either one; experience will show that a fine balance between the two is what works.

Before getting into how your classroom consequences can be set up, it will be useful to examine the concept of consequences. It is important to understand the distinction between classroom punishments and classroom consequences. If you look at the concept of *consequences*, you find there is an all-important element there that is not found in the concept of *punishment*. That key element is *responsibility*. Students can be made well aware that if they choose to behave in a certain way, then they must bear the consequences of those actions. In other words, if properly designed and implemented, your classroom consequences not only set the limits on behavior in the classroom but they also teach the students they must take responsibility for their actions. The following discussion looks at how you can effectively set up your classroom consequences plan.

Setting Up Your Classroom Consequences Plan

"By carefully planning effective consequences, and by determining in advance what you will do when students misbehave, you will have a course of action to follow and will be able to avoid knee-jerk responses that are not in the best interests of you or your students" (Canter & Canter, 1992, p. 80). The importance of this statement by Lee and Marlene Canter, which is the cornerstone of their nationally renowned *Assertive Discipline* approach, cannot be overestimated. Consequences for inappropriate behavior are necessary in any endeavor where groups of individuals are functioning according to a set of rules or laws. This is true in any sport, in any occupation, and in numerous other aspects of life in civilized society.

Selecting Your Classroom Consequences

You need to choose effective consequences if they are going to discourage and help correct inappropriate classroom behavior. In addition, they must be consequences that can be given consistently. The obvious question, then, is: What are effective consequences? Several sets of consequences are provided in Figure 11–8. However, these are simply examples of consequences that have been found to work for different teachers in their respective classroom situations. In addition to reviewing these examples as a starting point for selecting your own consequences, it will be a wise move to see if the ones you choose meet the following criteria:

Criterion 1:   You should be able to provide your consequences readily.

As you proceed with the task of choosing your classroom consequences, you must ask yourself: Will I be able to readily and consistently deliver these consequences? You are not meeting this criterion if delivering your consequences interferes with the flow of instruction and also becomes so burdensome on your time and energy that it becomes

FIGURE 11–8   Sets of Classroom Consequences

First time talked to (Warning): turn card to green	Breaking rule once: write name in behavior log
Second time talked to: turn card to yellow and time out	Breaking rule twice: write letter explaining rule broken and apologize
Third time talked to: turn card to red and phone student's home	Breaking rule three times: go to office and call parents to tell which rule(s) broken
(Cards start on blue each day)	Breaking rule four times: go to principal's office
First time: warning and instructed on expected behavior	First violation of rule: print name/date on behavior board
Second time: time-out area for 5 minutes	Second violation of rule: place checkmark next to name, phone call to parents, and 30-minute detention
Third time: time-out area for 10 minutes	
Fourth time: note home to be signed and returned	Third violation of rule: conference with student, teacher, parent, and vice principal
Fifth time: send to principal's office	
Severe Clause: send to principal's office	
First offense: note home	Reprimand 1: fill out warning note (to be signed by parent)
Second offense: phone call home	Reprimand 2: call to parent and 15-minute detention
Third offense: after-school detention and essay on how to avoid breaking particular rule(s)	Reprimand 3: parent, teacher, student, and principal conference

more of a consequence to you than to the misbehaving students. Such impractical consequences rapidly become inconsistently delivered consequences. Rather than delivering them when needed, you deliver them when you can. This is a fatal flaw because it signals that consistency and fairness have gone out the window. Look at the following two examples. The first one is an impractical consequence and the second one is such that it can be readily delivered.

> *Example 1 (Impractical Consequence):*   Stay 30 minutes after class.

Any elementary teacher knows that trying to deliver this consequence will create a major headache. Your time at school before and after the children leave is invaluable for getting various things done. The ability to have flexibility at these times to do errands around the school is critical. Being tied down to your room for 30 minutes after school whenever a student receives this consequence will play havoc with your plans and needs. You will then begin to deliver this consequence inconsistently, thereby negating its effectiveness.

> *Example 2 (Readily Deliverable Consequence):*   Sit and work by yourself for 10 minutes.

Elementary students do not like to be separated from their peers. If you designate a specific area of the room to temporarily place students who choose to ignore certain classroom rules, you will find that you can deliver this consequence immediately and with minimal distraction from what is going on instructionally at the time. Students will come to know very quickly that you will never fail in delivering this consequence when it is called for. This relentless consistency is what has the power to modify student behavior.

> *Criterion 2:*   Your consequences should work for everyone.

Remember this fact: Most of the students are well behaved most of the time. Your classroom consequences, then, should be chosen with this in mind. This means that the consequences do not have to be harsh to be effective. "For 70% of your students a simple warning is all you'll ever have to give" (Canter & Canter, 1992, p. 83). Another way to look at it is that a relatively small percentage of your students will be problematic. It makes little sense to tailor your classroom consequences to only those few students.

> *Criterion 3:*   Your consequences should follow a hierarchy.

Your set of classroom consequences should progress from relatively light to relatively severe for initial to repeated occurrences of misbehavior by any given student within a particular day. For example, if John gets out of his seat without permission, you can say, "That is a warning, John. The rule is to ask permission to get out of your seat." If John behaves inappropriately again during the same day, he then is asked to work by himself for 10 minutes in the designated area of the room. This represents the next level of consequence in the hierarchy. If John breaks yet another rule that day, the consequence would again increase in weight, and so on, if he continued misbehaving, until the most severe consequence would have been reached. The hierarchical design of your consequences sends a clear message that the price gets steeper if students choose to persistently misbehave. Interestingly, you will find that once students *know* that you will relentlessly follow through on this system of consequences, there will be few instances where you will have to deliver any but the first few levels of consequence.

Delivering Your Classroom Consequences

Times when consequences need to be delivered are potential flash points for bad feelings and conflict. This inherent negative potentiality must be minimized if your classroom consequences are going to successfully teach students responsibility for their actions and also not be a distraction from daily instruction. The following three criteria should be used to guide the way you deliver your classroom consequences:

Criterion 1:   Provide a calm response.

Conflicts arise out of reaction. If you remain calm as you deliver consequences to a misbehaving student, it will go a long way toward minimizing a reaction pattern being set in motion. It lets the student know you are not personally angry at or dislike him or her. Further, it shows all students clearly that you are in control of the situation and cannot be brought down to a level of confrontation and frustrated yelling. This last point is of paramount importance. It is no secret that your loss of control in dealing with misbehavior serves as an open invitation for the students to "push your buttons" as often as they can. This becomes their way of taking control of the classroom from you. If this happens, your job and life will become very difficult. Interestingly, if you deliver your consequences in an even quieter voice than you normally use, with a feeling of firmness and resolve behind it, it will tend to have a particularly chilling effect on misbehavior.

Criterion 2:   Provide an immediate response.

If you want to extinguish inappropriate behavior in your classroom, you have to send the irrevocable message that it will be most reliably dealt with immediately when it occurs. This is the only way to be fair. Otherwise, there is no end to how much the students will test you and take liberties.

Criterion 3:   Provide a consistent response.

The one way you want to be completely predictable to your students is in regard to delivering classroom consequences for inappropriate behavior. You want to be so consistent as to when and how you deal with misbehavior that your students will know with certainty that if they do something inappropriate, they will be choosing to receive the consequence of that action. Consistent response demonstrates to the students that you will deal fairly with difficulties whenever they arise. Consistent response also demonstrates your dedication to maintaining a classroom environment where all students' rights to learn are most strongly protected.

Being prepared is the best way to meet these three criteria. If your consequences are planned in a clear, simple, and realistic way, you then have the basis from which to deliver them with a calm, immediate, and consistent response.

Following through on Your Classroom Consequences

The worst thing you can do in the area of classroom management is to threaten consequences and then not give them. If you fall into this pattern, the students will determine very quickly that you are unable or unwilling to deliver the consequences you promise. Once they reach this conclusion, your ability to maintain an orderly classroom will be almost impossible. A key point is that initial impressions and patterns are very difficult to live down. If, after several weeks of school, you bear down and try to follow through on all the consequences you promise, it will be a tremendous struggle to convince the students you are for real. It can be done, but it so much wiser and easier to establish follow-through on delivering your consequences right from the first day. If you pay close attention to the criteria presented earlier, you will be in an excellent position to follow through consistently on consequences that need to be given.

To assure that you have maximum ability to follow through on consequences, it will be useful for you to address the following points:

1. *Have Necessary Materials Ready:*   In light of the myriad of things an elementary teacher needs to tend to on a given day, any preparation you can think of doing to facilitate delivery of your classroom consequences makes it that much more likely you will consistently follow through on them. For example, if one of your consequences involves sending a note home, you should have many copies of a general letter all ready to go. All that you should need to add to these letters is the student's name, date, and a brief description of the inappropriate behavior that occurred. There is no harm at all in the students being well aware how easily it is for you to follow through on this or any other consequence that may need to be given. In this regard, it helps to have a small file box on your desk containing index cards listing each student's parents' names, address, and phone number. Thus, not only can you quickly address letters home but you can also make phone calls as needed.

2. *Keep Your Records Up to Date:*   Being able to follow through on consequences consistently is possible when you know who needs what follow-through. This sounds so obvious, but you would be surprised how often attempts at classroom management have gone down in flames because the teacher either got overwhelmed trying to keep up with this information or simply overlooked its importance. To accomplish this you, need a system of record keeping that readily allows you to answer the following four questions:

- Who behaved inappropriately?
- What was the inappropriate behavior?

- When did the inappropriate behavior occur?
- What consequence is to be given?

If you remain up to date on this information concerning your classroom consequences, and the students know you have this information at your fingertips, it will be one more very strong signal that you mean business—that you care to maintain an orderly classroom. How can such record keeping be accomplished? A simple clipboard and a good supply of forms like the one presented in Figure 11–9 will do the job in good fashion.

As a student behaves inappropriately the first time in a given day, you can bring his or her attention to the classroom rule that needs to be followed and then record this by placing a *w* for *warning* under that rule next to this student's name. In addition, by placing the *w* (in this instance) under the A.M. or P.M., you have a record of when the misbehavior occurred. This way, over a period of time, you can notice patterns of behavior that may provide you with some clues to helping certain students make positive changes. You may even notice class patterns of behavior that suggest some adjustments in your daily routine and instructional program will be beneficial. If the student chooses to break the same or another classroom rule later, you can inform him or her of this and then place a *1* under that rule (A.M. or P.M.) next to the student's name, indicating that the first level of consequence is to be given. By this method of using a daily consequence log sheet, you can immediately and easily record all the information you need to answer the previous four questions. Under Comments, you can note any particularly important points about what occurred that day.

At the end of the day, the daily consequence log sheet can be reviewed for actions you need to take. You can then very easily place each log sheet in a three-ring binder, perhaps labeled Behavior Binder, to maintain an ongoing record. If more substantial documentation is ever necessary, you can always append memos, notes, referrals, and so on to the relevant sheet. In a reverse of the process, this log sheet also shows you all those students who have no or few inappropriate behaviors and thus deserve to be rewarded according to the system you have in place. Your Behav-

FIGURE 11–9 Daily Classroom Consequences Log Sheet

Name and Date	Rule #1: _____ A.M. P.M.	Rule #2: _____ A.M. P.M.	Rule #3: _____ A.M. P.M.	Rule #4: _____ A.M. P.M.	Rule #5: _____ A.M. P.M.	Comments

Key: W = Warning   1 = First Consequence   4 = Fourth Consequence   A.M. = Morning
                     2 = Second Consequence   5 = Fifth (Severe) Consequence   P.M. = Afternoon
                     3 = Third Consequence

ior Binder thus becomes a centrally located and accurate documentation of classroom behavior to share with students, parents, fellow teachers, and administrators as needed and useful.

Routines and Procedures

Your classroom rules set the parameters for appropriate behavior. Your routines and procedures spell out how the nitty-gritty business and functioning of the classroom is to take place. If there is one area of classroom management that is overlooked by new elementary school teachers, it is the establishment of necessary routines and procedures. There is a guiding principle pertaining to routines and procedures that you can be sure will operate in your or anyone's classroom: If there is no agreed-upon way set for carrying out a particular function in the classroom (e.g., sharpening pencils, keeping the room neat and clean), the students will do it the way they wish.

When you consider that there are dozens of routines and procedures necessary to run a typical elementary classroom, students doing things as they wish will create chaos. Remember, during the first days of school, students are extremely observant of what you do and what your expectations are. They also notice very well what you seem to have no expectations for. During this crucial period, each time they see you trying to figure out, on the spot, how a routine or procedure is to be done, they take that as one more signal that you are not in complete control of the situation.

The aim of this section is to show you a practical method for designing a comprehensive plan to establish the routines and procedures you need to have a smoothly functioning classroom. To accomplish this aim, a process consisting of the following four steps will be discussed:

1. Determine the categories for which routines and procedures are needed.
2. List the types of routines and procedures that come under each of the determined categories.
3. Prioritize the various lists of routines and procedures according to how soon they need to be established.
4. Spell out the details of how each routine and procedure is to be carried out.

Step 1:   Determine categories of classroom routines and procedures.

Because there are dozens of routines and procedures to think of in running a typical elementary school classroom, it is hard to know where to begin. Unless you use a systematic approach, not only will you waste time but you will also probably miss thinking of some of the routines and procedures that need to be established. In this first step, then, the task is to create a superstructure for your comprehensive classroom routines and procedures plan. *Superstructure* means the broad categories of classroom functioning for which routines and procedures are needed. In Figure 11–10, eight such categories are suggested. It will be seen in the following discussion how all routines and procedures can fit into one or another of these eight categories. The key is that with

FIGURE 11–10   Eight Categories of Classroom Routines and Procedures

Routines and procedures need to be created and established under each of these categories

1. ROOM USE

2. INSTRUCTIONAL ACTIVITIES

3. TRANSITIONAL ACTIVITIES

4. CLASSROOM MAINTENANCE

5. SPECIAL ACTIVITIES

6. PARENT INVOLVEMENT

7. EMERGENCIES

8. GENERAL PROCEDURES

these categories as a guide, it is much easier to think of the various routines and procedures under them.

Step 2:   List the types of routines and procedures needed.

The task of enumerating the various routines and procedures is facilitated by having categories like those in Figure 11–10 to organize and focus your thinking. At this point, you are ready to list all the routines and procedures that you can think of under each category. In the next two steps, these lists will be modified according to what the realistic priorities are in your classroom. Using the eight categories to accomplish the task in this step not only focuses your thinking but it also makes it easier to explain what you are looking for when asking fellow teachers for their ideas about routines and procedures.

Step 3:   Prioritize your lists of routines and procedures.

In this third step, you get into an important decision-making mode. You are faced with the onerous burden of having somehow to put into operation nearly 100 routines and procedures to effectively run your classroom. Thus, you need a workable way to approach this difficult task. The best way to proceed with determining priorities in the area of classroom routines and procedures is to set time line parameters for yourself that address the following five questions:

• Which routines and procedures must be established by the end of Day 1?

- Which routines and procedures need to be established by the end of Day 1, if possible?
- Which routines and procedures need to be established by the end of Week 1?
- Which routines and procedures need to be established soon after Week 1?
- Which routines and procedures need to be established on a long-range basis?

A simple method to carry out this task would be to code each of the routines and procedures you have listed as follows:

1*   = must be established on Day 1

1   = needs to be established by end of Day 1, if possible

W   = needs to be established by end of Week 1

W+ = needs to be established soon after Week 1

L   = needs to be established on a long-range basis

A thorough set of classroom routines and procedures that have been prioritized according to this coding system for running one particular elementary teacher's classroom is presented as part of the Basic Personalized Model (see the appendix at the end of Chapter 12). In this case, the teacher did not signify routines and procedures that must be established on Day 1.

Step 4:   Spell out how each routine and procedure should be carried out.

If you have successfully carried out steps 1 to 3, you can be confident you are not missing anything important. You also have a very good idea of which routines and procedures you need to spend time spelling out first (i.e., those coded *1*, 1,* and *W*). This latter point is critical because there so many things you need to consider and do at the start of the school year. Any clarity you can gain in how the basic operation of your classroom is going to proceed (i.e., routines and procedures) can indeed be a life saver.

It is recommended that each new teacher design each routine and procedure according to his or her own particular situation, teaching style, and best thinking. The key is that students know whether or not you are on top of how business is to be conducted in your classroom. If you take the time to complete these four steps, your students will see that there are definite ways to do things and that you care enough to set up a well-organized learning environment.

Room Arrangement

Another important aspect of the classroom management system is the physical arrangement of the classroom. *Room arrangement,* for purposes of this text, refers to the use of the total room, floor and wall space included. A thoughtfully arranged classroom contributes to the uninterrupted flow of instruction and student learning activities and, in general, to the smooth functioning of all aspects of classroom life. In contrast, a poorly arranged room can lead to confusion and congestion during periods of student movement and to visibility problems during direct instruction.

This portion of the chapter looks at room arrangement in terms of the parts of the room that need to be arranged by the teacher and some principles that guide how to best arrange those parts. Also provided are diagrams of well-arranged rooms at different grade levels.

Parts of the Classroom to Arrange

Following is a list of parts or areas that should be considered when arranging a classroom.

- Student seating
- Teacher's desk/teaching assistant's desk
- Learning centers
- Special centers/areas
- Rug areas (lower grades)
- Classroom library
- Mail slots/student cubbies
- Academic resources
- Storage areas
- Time-out area
- Wall displays

While arranging each of these parts, it is important to consider several principles that apply to all types of room arrangements.

Guiding Principles to Room Arrangement

Each of the following principles will be discussed next and then the list of room parts/areas in terms of the guiding principles will be examined:

- Ease of movement
- Safety
- Visibility
- Neatness and calmness
- Ready availability of material and resources

Ease of Movement

Students and the teacher must be able to move around the room with ease and without encountering tight spaces or obstacles. The teacher needs to be able to walk easily to all student desks in order to monitor seatwork and behavior. The same practice applies to learning centers or other special areas in the classroom. Students need to be able to get up from their desks without bumping another desk and they need to be able move freely to all areas of the room.

Safety

For fire emergencies, students need to be able to quickly form lines and file out of the room; therefore, there must be adequate space for lines to form and no desks or obstacles near doorways. Generally, all doorways should be kept free and clear, and open floor space should be kept free of objects that people could trip over.

Visibility

Visibility refers both to the student's ability to see the teacher, chalkboards, demonstration areas, and so on, and the teacher's ability to see *each* student in the classroom. It is often said that a teacher must have eyes in the back of his or her head, because it is so important that the teacher be aware of and respond to various student behaviors. In other words, the teacher must constantly reward appropriate behavior and curtail inappropriate or disruptive behavior. The effectiveness of any management system is dependent on the teacher's ability to *see* what students are doing and respond accordingly.

Neatness and Calmness

A neat, clean classroom provides the proper atmosphere in which to attend to what is going on, to study, and to learn. When things are neat and tidy, a sense of orderliness and calmness prevails, which makes it easier for everyone to think and concentrate. When arranging a classroom, it is important to set things up in a way that facilitates the teacher's and students' ability to keep the room neat and clean.

Ready Availability of Materials and Resources

Materials and resources that are used frequently should be kept in easily accessible places. Also, certain centers might be strategically placed near storage areas, such as an art center being located near a cabinet full of art supplies.

Arranging the Parts According to the Principles

Student Seating

One of the most important aspects of room arrangement is student seating. The first decision the teacher must make regarding student seating is whether the students will be seated in individual units or in small groups. In most classrooms, either individual desks are provided for students or small tables that seat two students are provided. Tables are found more frequently at the lower grade levels.

Group seating arrangements are created by putting desks or tables together in small groups, usually to accommodate four to six or seven students. In individual seating arrangements, desks are usually put in rows or in a horseshoe shape. See Figure 11–11 for an illustration of group and individual arrangements. Once the teacher has made a decision regarding group or individual seating, other factors that then affect the particular arrangement include the type of desks or tables available, the size and shape of the room, the nature of the students in the class, and the creativity of the teacher.

When planning the seating arrangements of the students, the teacher should keep several of the guiding principles in mind, including visibility, ease of movement,

FIGURE 11–11   Student Seating Arrangements

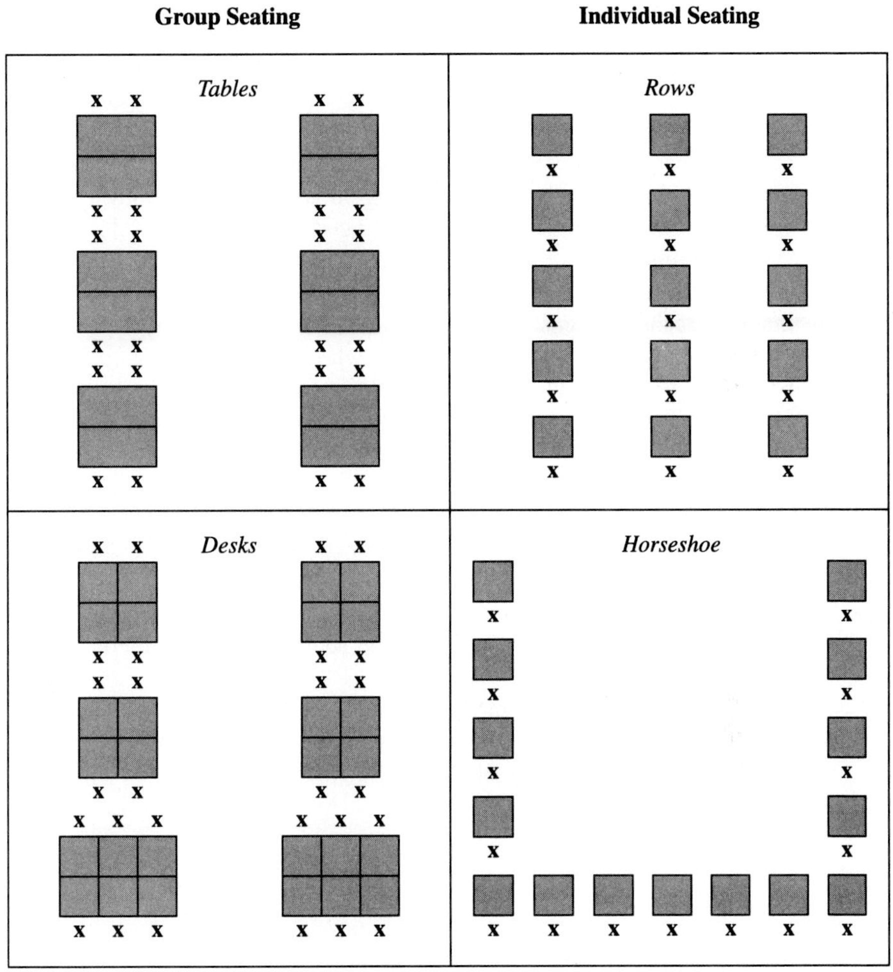

Group Seating   Individual Seating

safety, and appropriate spacing. Again, the teacher should make sure that he or she can see *all* the students in the classroom (and that they can all see the teacher and chalkboards), that he or she can move easily among all of the students' desks, that the desks are a safe distance from doorways, and that desks and groups of desks are sufficiently separated from each other.

Teacher's Desk/Teaching Assistant's Desk

Visibility is probably the most important consideration when deciding where to put the teacher's desk. While seated at his or her desk, the teacher should be able to see *all* the students in the room. Also, the teacher's desk should be in an area spacious enough to allow for individual conferences with students. The teacher's individual preference comes into play regarding what areas in the room are most appealing.

Many teachers have teaching assistants (TAs) for a part of the day and, if possible, a desk should be provided for them. The TA's desk should be in an area where his or her activities (grading papers, tutoring students, etc.) will not interfere with the teacher's activities.

Learning Centers

Learning centers are generally located around the periphery of the classroom, sufficiently away from the students' seating so activities going on in the learning centers will not distract students who are working at their desks.

Learning centers can include computer stations, electronic learning games, puzzles, experiments, art projects, observation activities, or just about any learning activity that the teacher designs. These centers can be used very effectively to provide meaningful learning experiences for students who finish regular assignments early and need something to do. Students can work at their own pace and they can also work collaboratively with one or two other students. Appropriate spacing, ease of movement, and visibility are important principles to keep in mind when arranging the learning centers.

Special Centers/Areas

Special centers or areas can be temporary or permanent. In the temporary category are such things as experiment stations set up in conjunction with a science unit or displays of student work in conjunction with any unit of study. An example of the latter is a model of a whole Western town from the 1800s constructed by the students for a social studies unit on Settling the West.

Examples of permanent special areas include listening centers, art centers, and areas set up for plants or class pets. These kinds of areas need to be set up so they do not interfere with the flow of the regular classroom activities and in such a way that they can be easily maintained.

Rug Areas

Rug areas are especially important in the lower grades, although many are seen in the upper grades, as well. Upper-grade students make use of floor space for cooperative group discussions, process writing in pairs, and working on various kinds of projects, such as creating posters that require large flat spaces to work on. Rug areas provide an area for the class to gather together for stories and instruction on a closer and more intimate basis than when everyone is at his or her desk. Also, teachers often meet small groups for instruction at the rug area. The rug area should be arranged in such a way that the students can see chalkboards, wall charts, and other instructional equipment.

Classroom Library

Most teachers provide a selection of fiction and nonfiction books for students to read in the classroom. Books checked out from the school library or neighborhood library can also be kept in the classroom library. Since books are expensive, most first-year teachers must rely on books borrowed from other libraries until they gradually build up a supply. Student-made books can be included in the classroom library, as well.

Although a classroom library is usually small, by necessity (expense of books), it is a very important part of the classroom. Books provide an avenue for students to expand their horizons and go beyond the confines of their local environment. Teachers model the importance and value of books by maintaining a classroom library and by providing silent reading periods for students daily. The classroom library should be arranged in an accessible place and in such a way that it is inviting and attractive.

Mail Slots and/or Student Cubbies

For the upper-elementary grades, it is convenient to have a mail slot for each student where the teacher can put anything that needs to be taken home (administrative communications with parents, homework, short notes to students, permission slips for trips, etc). Students can check their mail slots as they get ready to go home for the day. There are portable structures made for this purpose that do not take up much space and usually fit on top of a cabinet.

For the younger grades, cubbies (larger square spaces, usually built into a closed space) are more appropriate, as younger children usually carry and/or keep more things in school (such as a change of clothes, painting shirt, etc.). If cubbies are not available, the teacher needs to arrange some place for students to keep the things they bring to school (lunch boxes, toys, show-and-tell objects, etc.). Students need to be taught to always put these things in the space provided for them in a tidy manner; otherwise, they will tend to throw their things on the floor near their desks or in a corner, which creates a very messy-looking room.

Academic Resources

Academic resources include things such as dictionaries, encyclopedias, atlases, thesauruses, standard grammars, and so on. These resources should be grouped in an academic resource section on bookshelves in an area that has easy access for students who need to look things up or take a book back to their desks.

Storage Areas

Storage areas are needed for certain classroom equipment such as playground equipment (balls, jump ropes, hula hoops, parachutes, etc.) and indoor game equipment (bean-bag throw games, holiday decorations, etc.). Usually, some space in the closet is reserved for equipment. It must be accessible, as some equipment (e.g., balls) goes out and comes back each day. It is important that students learn to return classroom equipment to its designated place.

Time-Out Area

A time-out area is a place set off by itself where a teacher can send a student who needs to be removed from the ongoing classroom activity, usually because of disruptive behavior. The time-out area can simply be a desk or a table that is set up with forms and writing materials so the student can describe his or her behavior and state what he or she should have done to avoid the misconduct. The time-out area should always be entirely visible to the teacher and it should be set a good distance away from the regular student seating so that it is definite that the student is being sent away from the group.

Wall Displays

The attractive and purposeful use of wall space has become an increasingly important part of room preparation. Teachers are expected to put up colorful wall displays in conjunction with major units of study, design thematic environments in the classroom, as well as decorate for various holidays. In some classrooms, every inch of wall space is used as a part of various teacher-made displays. Student work is usually displayed on one or two bulletin boards reserved specifically for that purpose.

Although it is important to made good use of the wall space by displaying instructional aids for students, it is not necessary, and perhaps not even beneficial to students, to cover every square inch of wall space with colorful displays. This can cause a kind of overload to the senses, and the students will not be able to appreciate any one display if there are too many. A better approach would be to have one or two thematic displays up at one time, related to units of study. In this case, less is more, as one or two displays will stand out and be noticed by the students. If there are too many displays going on at once, they all get lost in the crowd.

A bulletin board or two should always have displays of student work. Everyone likes recognition, and students are no exception. They enjoy seeing their work displayed and are interested in reading each other's work. Other instructional aids that can be displayed on classroom walls to provide useful information to students are calendars, maps, number lines, alphabets, and grammar rules. All wall displays should be neat and attractive so that they invite student perusal.

Examples of Well-Arranged Classrooms

Figures 11–12 through 11–15 show several diagrams of well-arranged classrooms. As can be seen from the diagrams, various kinds of arrangements are equally appropriate, as long as they are in compliance with the principles of room arrangement.

Communicating the Plan

Once you have developed your personal management plan, there are several important parties to whom you must communicate your plan. These include (1) the school-site principal, (2) the parents of your students, and (3) the students themselves. The following section will look at how and what you need to communicate to each of these parties.

Communicating the Plan to Your Principal

The first person with whom you should communicate regarding your management plan is your principal. Your communication with the principal should include the following:

1. Share your classroom management plan with the principal and get his or her approval of it.
2. Invite the principal to come to your classroom.
3. Discuss what will be done when a student from your classroom is sent to the principal's office.

FIGURE 11–12   Sample Room Arrangement

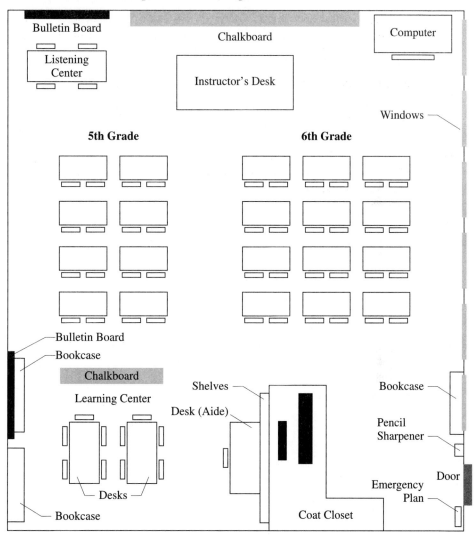

FIGURE 11–13   Sample Room Arrangement

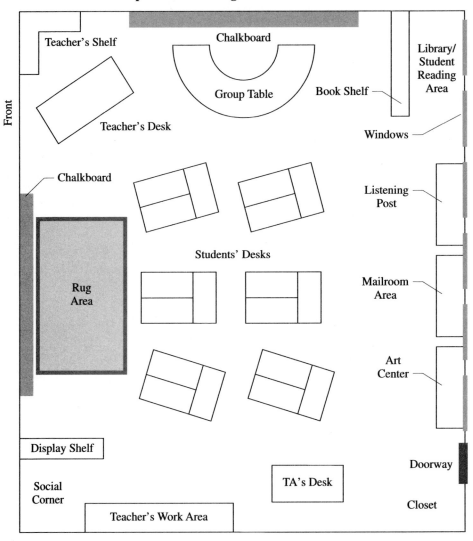

FIGURE 11–14   Sample Room Arrangement

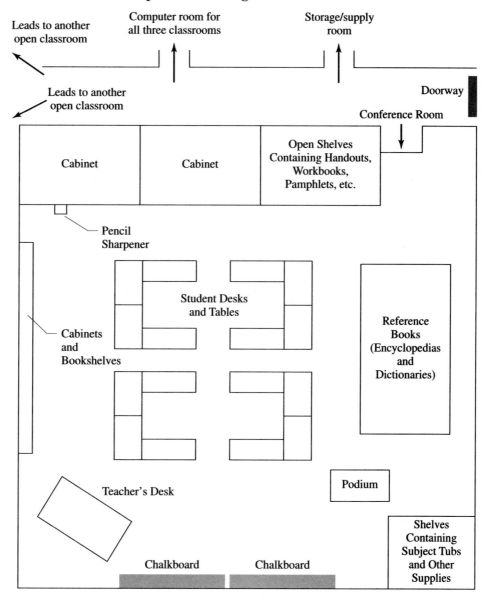

FIGURE 11–15   Sample Secondary Room Arrangement

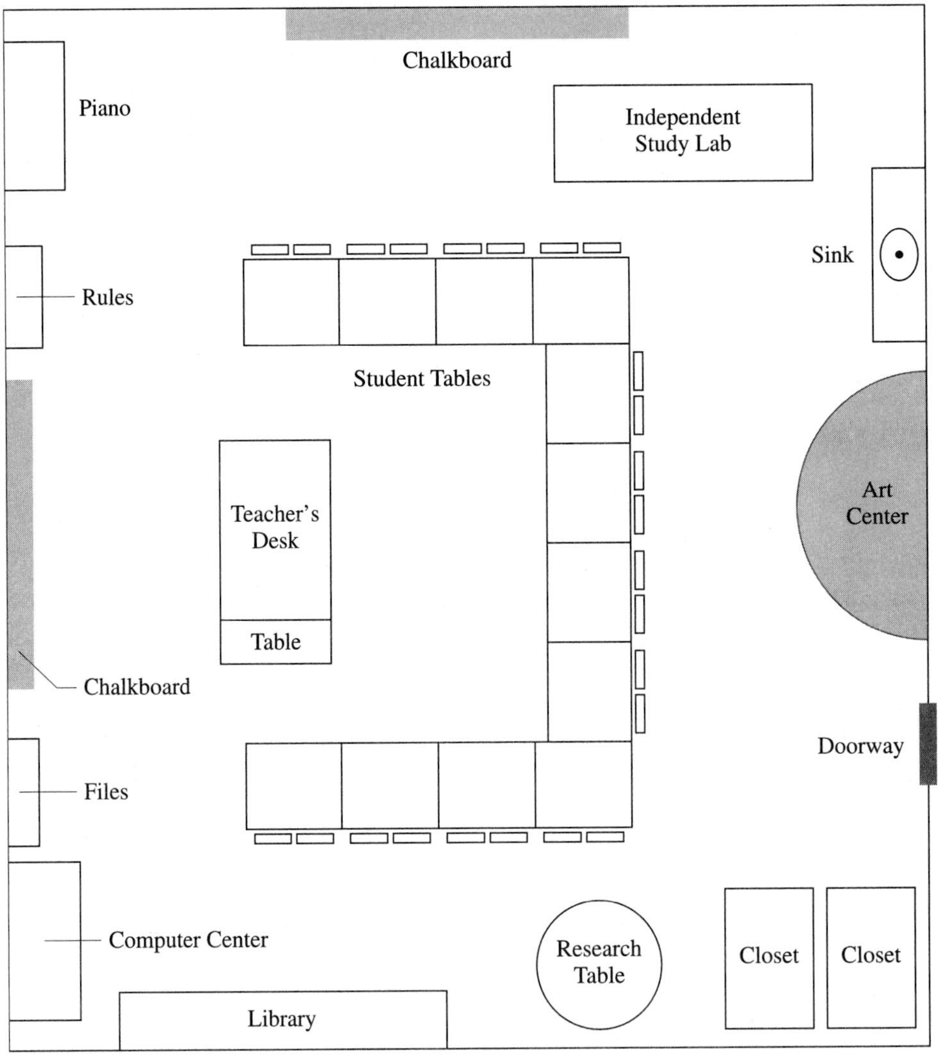

4. Determine alternative consequences in case the principal is out of the office.
5. Inform the principal of any ongoing behavior problems.

The following is a detailed discussion of these suggestions:

1. *Share Your Classroom Management Plan with the Principal and Obtain Approval:*
It is important that you not only show your plan to your principal but also that you request his or her approval and full support of the rules, consequences, and procedures

you have created and plan to implement in your class. With your principal's approval of your plan, you will have the assurance that he or she will support the way in which you run your classroom. If, for example, a dissatisfied parent complains to the principal that your rules are too strict (or too *anything*), your principal can respond that he or she is fully aware of your management system and completely supports it.

If, on the other hand, your principal has not seen your plan because you have not submitted it requesting his or her approval, then the principal can only respond to a dissatisfied parent that he or she "will look into it." The principal must then come to you to ascertain how you run your classroom, and if he or she is not comfortable with some of your rules, it will be hard for him or her to support you in the face of parent criticism. This will reflect poorly on you, so certainly it is a situation you want to avoid.

If you submit your management plan to the principal *before* you implement it, and he or she feels that you should modify or change it somewhat, then you can do so before introducing the plan to the parents or students. It is also possible that there are some schoolwide policies or rules that the principal will want included in the plan. Whatever the particular situation at your school, communicate your management plan to your principal and work with him or her to obtain wholehearted approval and support. You will thereby ensure the appropriateness of your plan and can proceed with confidence to communicate it to parents and the students.

2. *Invite the Principal to Come to the Classroom:*   Once you have implemented your plan in the classroom, your students are familiar with it, and things are running smoothly, it is an excellent idea to invite your principal into the classroom to see your plan in practice. There is nothing as effective as firsthand experience in creating a positive impression in the principal's mind about the merit of your plan and about you as a teacher. It will strengthen your principal's confidence in you and, again, give him or her all the more assurance with which to support you in any kind of situation that may come up. For example, it can happen that a student, being angry that you enforced your consequences due to his or her behavior, will misrepresent what happened to the parent. A hasty parent may come to the school, upset and angry, accusing you of mistreating his or her child. A principal who has been to your room and experienced the positive atmosphere created by your consistent use of your plan can respond to the parent with confidence on your behalf.

Having the support of your principal is a key ingredient to maintaining your credibility with your students and their parents. Students need to know that they cannot undermine your authority by misrepresenting your conduct to their parents or anyone else. By having the principal come into your classroom and experience firsthand how you manage the students, you will ensure his or her support.

3. *Discuss What Will Happen When You Send a Student to the Principal's Office:*   It is helpful for you to have a clear idea of the procedures followed by the administration when a student is sent to the office for discipline problems. Procedures will vary at different schools, but they frequently include a phone call to the parents, a serious talk with the principal, some form of detention, and perhaps the creation of a behavior contract for the student.

4. *Determine Alternative Consequences in Case the Principal Is Out of the Office:*   Principals are very busy people and are, at times, unavailable for one reason or another.

In this case, you will want to have an alternative arrangement for a disruptive student, such as sending him or her to another classroom to do independent work or have some time out in which to consider his or her behavior. There are times in which getting one disruptive student out of the class makes all the difference between being able to proceed with the instruction at hand or having to continually interrupt the instruction to deal with the problem student. Always remember that no one student has a right to interfere with the learning of the rest of the students, and sometimes this means removal of the offending student until he or she can be dealt with at a later time. Having alternative consequences already in place gives you this freedom.

5. *Inform the Principal of Any Ongoing Behavior Problems:* If you have a student who is a continual behavior problem, it is important that you inform your principal of the fact. Sometimes, students have severe problems that are beyond the scope of your expertise as a teacher, and that require the intervention of trained professionals. In these cases, you will want the help of your principal or the administration to determine a process for working with the student. For example, you may be asked to document, in writing, each time the student engages in inappropriate behavior, so that a case can be made for procuring the help of a psychologist or whoever is needed. Having this written record of the student's behavior will also help whatever professional is called in to understand the student and his or her problems. Never neglect your obligation to communicate to the principal or administration severe problems that may occur in your classroom. This is for your own protection and it will also help you solve the problem.

Communicating the Plan to Parents

An important group with whom you must communicate your management plan is the parents of your students. There are several ways in which you can communicate with parents, both to explain your management plan and to keep lines of communication open for progress reports. Consider the following means of communication:

1. Letters
2. Telephone calls
3. Conferences
4. Notes, progress reports, and bulletins

Letters

The most important letter you will be sending to the parents will be the initial letter at the beginning of the school year that explains your management plan. In this letter, you should request parents to indicate that they have read the plan and are in agreement with it. This is usually done by having a portion of the letter that they can tear off, sign, and return to you. Since this letter may be your first communication with the parents, it should contain several types of statements, including:

1. A statement welcoming their child into your classroom
2. A statement of some of your goals for the year
3. A statement inviting the parents to be "partners" with you in their child's education

4. A statement describing your classroom rules and consequences

Figure 11–16 is an example of an initial letter to the parents that includes these types of statements.

FIGURE 11–16   Sample Parent Letter

Dear Parent,

I want to thank you for the opportunity to have <u>Susie</u> in my class this year. I think it is important that you have an idea of what I intend to accomplish as <u>her</u> teacher, and what I need from you in order for <u>her</u> to learn and grow in my class. My goals are to:

- Stimulate <u>Susie's</u> curiosity and encourage <u>her</u> to think critically
- Help <u>her</u> to broaden her base of knowledge so that <u>she</u> can compete, excel, and make choices in <u>her</u> life
- Create an environment in which integrity, honesty, and clear communication are present for <u>her</u> and for the entire class
- Help <u>her</u> to have compassion for other people, other cultures, and nature, and encourage respect for differences
- Help <u>her</u> develop a sense of responsibility for <u>her</u> life and education
- Promote self-confidence and awareness
- Have the school year be fun and filled with many exciting and rewarding experiences.

Please notice that I have used the word *help* a great deal. I cannot accomplish these things on my own. I need your cooperation and teamwork. Together, we can have this year really make a difference, not just in <u>her</u> life, but in yours and in mine as well.

One area that is critical to my being able to get the job done is behavior. I, as a teacher, have the right and responsibility to establish rules and directions that clearly define the limits of acceptable and unacceptable student behavior. <u>Susie</u> has the right to a learning environment free from distractions and disruptions. <u>She</u> also has the right to a teacher who will provide <u>her</u> with consistent positive encouragement to motivate <u>her</u> to behave. I intend to provide that. This may include notes and phone calls home when <u>Susie</u> is doing great work and contributing to class.

We have developed some simple RULES that each student will be required to follow. They are:

1. Follow directions.
2. Keep hands, feet, and objects to yourself.
3. Listen and don't interrupt when someone else has permission to talk.
4. No running, yelling, or gum chewing in class.
5. Be respectful of others.

Occasionally, a student chooses to break the rules. The first infraction initiates a warning. The second instance will require the student to stay 5 minutes after class. The next instance will cause the student to stay after class 10 minutes. The fourth time a rule is broken in a day, the parent will be called. Should the student be having a really bad day, and a fifth infraction occurs, that student will have the opportunity to spend some time with the principal to discuss the merits of appropriate behavior in the classroom. Of course, students will not be allowed to abuse their teacher or other students, either physically or verbally, nor will they be allowed to do anything which endangers themselves or others. In the event this occurs, the student will be sent directly to the principal's office—no warnings or time outs.

(continued)

FIGURE 11–16   *(Continued)*

I certainly don't anticipate having to contact you to discuss a behavior problem with <u>Susie,</u> but should that be necessary, I will look forward to your partnership in resolving the particular issue in a way that benefits everyone.

Please discuss this plan with <u>Susie</u> so that you all understand and agree to it. Sign in the space indicated below and return one copy to me by Friday. Your comments will be greatly appreciated! I need your feedback.

I am always available to you for questions or concerns you may have. Please feel free to contact me. Again, I thank you for the privilege it is to have <u>Susie</u> in my class, and I look forward to meeting you.

Sincerely,

Donald Mizock

We have read the above plan and agree to abide by the provisions set forth.

Date _____   _____   _____
                          Parent Signature   Student Signature

COMMENTS: _____

_____

_____

_____

_____

_____

_____

Source: Reprinted by permission of Donald Mizock.

Some teachers also like to send interest surveys for both the parents and students at the same time that they send the initial letter. This shows parents that you are taking a real interest in their child and in how you can best relate to that child. Figures 11.17 and 11.18 are examples of such surveys. As you can see from the content of the parent survey, the teacher is provided with information about the willingness of parents to help out in the classroom and about the skills or resources they may have to offer.

FIGURE 11–17   Sample Parent Information Form

Dear Parents,

In order to better serve the needs of my students and their families, I am requesting the following informal information from you. Please fill this out and return it to me along with your child's information sheet by next Friday. I look forward to meeting you in person.

Parent(s) current job/occupation(s):_____

_____

Activities/hobbies: _____

_____

Things the family likes to do together: _____

_____

Activities your child likes to do:_____

_____

Is there any time that you might be able to help in the classroom? (Both parents/guardians if possible): _____

_____

Is there any other type of help or expertise which you might be able to offer to the classroom instead of or in addition to your time? (Speaking, computers, etc.):_____

_____

Is there anything else you can tell me about your child or about the family that might assist me in addressing his/her educational, emotional, or other special needs or abilities?_____

_____

_____

_____

Other comments? _____

_____

_____

Source: Reprinted by permission of Donald Mizock.

FIGURE 11–18   Parent Information Form

Name:_____

Occupation: _____

Home Phone: _____   Work Phone: _____

Name:_____

Occupation: _____

Home Phone: _____   Work Phone: _____

When would be the best time to schedule a meeting?

_____

_____

Are you available to work in the classroom?	Yes	No
Are you available to chaperone field trips?	Yes	No
Would you like to be a guest speaker?	Yes	No

Please let me know it you would like to volunteer with any type of home projects or if you have particular interests, talents, or hobbies that you would like to share with our students.

_____

_____

Source: Reprinted by permission of Donald Mizock.

Telephone Calls

It is an excellent practice to give parents a telephone call within the first few weeks of school to introduce yourself and to reiterate your desire to have their cooperation and participation during the school year. Routine phone calls should also be made throughout the year to report positive behavior as well as inappropriate behavior. All too frequently, parents receive phone calls from the school only when their child is in trouble. Therefore, when they hear from the school, they are expecting the worst and may be anxious, if not somewhat on the defensive. Reporting positive behavior to parents (even in the severe behavior problems, you can find something positive to report) helps parents see that you are not just picking on their child or just concentrating on the negative. This will make them more receptive and cooperative in dealing with any behavior problems their child might be having in your class.

Conferences

Most schools schedule parent conferences several times throughout the school year, which affords the teacher an opportunity to discuss the academic as well as the behavioral progress of students with individual parents. Additional conferences can be scheduled if needed. Back-to-school night, which is generally scheduled early in the school year, gives the teacher an opportunity to describe the management plan to parents as a group and to explain what type of cooperation is needed from them.

Notes, Progress Reports, and Bulletins

Positive behavior notes, progress reports, and class bulletins describing classroom events should be sent to parents on a regular basis to keep them informed not only about their child's behavior but also about the kinds of activities going on in the classroom. Parents appreciate being informed about their child's classroom, especially those who work full time and may not be able to visit the class even occasionally. Also, it means a lot to both the student and the parent when the student brings home a positive behavior note. This recognizes the child's efforts to behave in a positive way and will encourage him or her to continue to do so.

This concludes the discussion on communicating your management plan to the parents of your students. The following considers the most effective way to communicate the plan to the students themselves.

Communicating the Plan to the Students

In order to communicate your management plan to the students, it is actually necessary to "teach" it as you would any academic subject. This entails planning lessons and setting aside regular intervals of time in which to deliver your instruction on the plan. There are three important things to communicate to your students about the teaching of your plan:

1. The mechanics of the plan (actual rules and procedures, consequences, etc.)
2. Your determination and expectation that all students can and will follow the rules and procedures
3. Periodic repetition and reminders

Mechanics of the Plan

It is helpful to have a set procedure for teaching the actual mechanics of your plan, as students learn more easily and retain information longer when systematic steps are used in the instruction. The following steps are suggested for teaching the rules, consequences, rewards, and procedures of your management plan:

1. Explain each rule (procedure, etc.) and discuss its importance.
2. State your expectations of the students' ability to follow the rule.
3. Have students write at their desks why they should follow the rule. (This step can vary and can include having the students design a creative poster for the rule, etc.)

4. Have students demonstrate how the rule or procedure is to be followed. (For example, if the procedure being discussed is how materials will be distributed, have several students do a dry run of materials distribution.)

5. Review rules (procedures) and their importance periodically. Students need to be reminded, especially about why the rules are important. Save the students' written comments from step 3 and read them back to the students periodically.

Expectation Regarding Rules and Procedures

A key ingredient to the success of your management plan is your own will and determination that it will be followed by all the students. In order to be this determined, you must care deeply about the welfare and learning of your students. Your concern for the students as well as your determination to have the kind of classroom environment in which everyone is safe, secure, and able to learn must be communicated to them.

How do you communicate your concern for your students? First of all, of course, you have to have it. Second, there are different ways in which you can communicate it to the students. One way is to tell them directly that you intend to see that everyone follows the rules (procedures) because you are very concerned about each child in the class and that you want each person in the class to feel safe, secure, and free to learn. Another way to communicate your concern and determination is by enforcing your rules, consequences, and rewards consistently. Keep up on your record keeping so you can follow through on consequences. Provide rewards for those who consistently follow the rules. Do not ignore the students who quietly follow rules and who do not draw attention to themselves. Their behavior needs to be publicly recognized and rewarded so that everyone can see that you value their behavior.

Think about your students. Try to identify their talents and encourage them to develop them. Determine their interests and use the information to help motivate them socially and academically. Find time occasionally to speak to each student individually and ask about his or her interests and how things are going for him or her in the classroom.

Repetition and Reminders

It is important to review rules and procedures from time to time and to reiterate their purposes and importance. You can do this in many different ways. One way is to read back to students the original written assignment of stating why they think they should follow each rule. Another way would be to do a web with the class in which you put the rule in the middle of the chalkboard, circle it, and make spokes coming out from the original circle. The students then write their suggestions on the spokes as to why the rule is important. Yet another way would be to put students into cooperative groups and have them design a graphic to explain the importance of the rule. The main point is to review rules and procedures periodically so that their purposes and value remain in the minds of the students.

Final Word on Communicating Your Management Plan

Be patient and do not accept anything but full compliance with your management plan. Stick to your determined efforts, even if the plan does not seem to be working. It *will* work! Sometimes, students cannot quite believe that you will not relent and slack off, and they may test you for some period of time. However, once they realize that you mean business and that you will enforce consequences consistently, no matter what, they will respect you and follow the management plan.

Attitude

Through discussion of the first six aspects of a comprehensive classroom management plan, you have seen that there is much work to do and many decisions to make in preparation for having a positive classroom right from the beginning of the school year. This seventh aspect, *attitude*, is the unifying thread that ties all the other aspects together and solidifies them. In this sense, attitude is like the master aspect, in that it governs what you will do and how you will do it in the area of classroom management. While all the other six aspects can be planned very carefully, your attitude is directly related to your personality and character. You can think of how you want to come across, but much is already there inside of you as the person you are.

The most important attitude to have is one of *care*. This sounds obvious only because it is so important. But what does care mean in regard to classroom management? It means that deep inside you, there must be an unwavering conviction and will that you care too much about each child's right to a safe and orderly learning environment to let anyone or anything interfere with or detract from it. To the extent you have this attitude, your students will respond. This attitude is also what will motivate you to make all necessary preparations and decisions (i.e., steps 1 to 6), and be alert to all potential problems in your effort to create a positive learning environment.

Students know when their teacher means business and when he or she cares about their behavior and well-being. There are some children who will be problematic no matter who is teaching and with what attitude. The overwhelming majority of students, however, can be most definitely influenced in a positive direction by your consistency, fairness, and care in how you run your classroom and deal with them.

Sample Classroom Management Systems

Three model classroom management systems will be presented in this chapter. You will see that each system has a different approach to one or more of the main aspects of classroom management.

Basic Personalized Model

The sample classroom management plan (see the appendix at the end of this chapter) is one teacher's personalized approach to the seven aspects of classroom management. This system is designed to fit both the teacher's personality and the classroom and school environment where he or she is teaching.

Sample Student Manual (Detailed)

The model presented in Figure 12–1 represents an effective approach to establishing a classroom management plan with a student manual as a central, organizing element. For the purposes of this book, only the contents/title and first page are shown here as an idea of what you can do. The contents of your student manual can be designed to fit your style and areas of emphasis. This manual is discussed, understood, and agreed to from the first day of school. Because of its clearly written and comprehensive nature, the manual serves as an excellent communication link with the home concerning how this particular classroom is expected to function. Further, because what is spelled out in this manual is followed with care and consistency, it is a useful and ready reference for both students and teacher in dealing with the various situations that arise from day to day.

FIGURE 12–1   Sample Student Manual (Detailed)

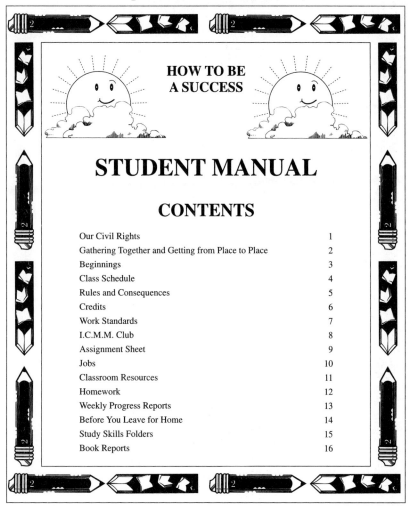

HOW TO BE
A SUCCESS

STUDENT MANUAL

CONTENTS

(continued)

Sample Student Manual (to Be Filled In)

This manual, as shown by the sample pages in Figure 12–2, is similar in some ways to Figure 12–1. The one major difference is that key information is missing when it is first handed out to the students. In this way, as the manual is reviewed on the first day, students are fully involved by filling in the missing information as each aspect of the manual is discussed. There is also a degree of flexibility built in to this approach in that some of the missing information can be determined by mutual agreement right then and there as it is presented and discussed.

FIGURE 12–1   *(continued)*

OUR CIVIL RIGHTS

I HAVE A RIGHT TO BE HAPPY AND TO BE
TREATED WITH COMPASSION IN THIS ROOM:
THIS MEANS THAT NO ONE
WILL LAUGH AT ME OR
HURT MY FEELINGS.

I HAVE A RIGHT TO BE MYSELF IN THIS ROOM:
THIS MEANS THAT NO ONE WILL
TREAT ME UNFAIRLY BECAUSE I AM
BLACK OR WHITE,
FAT OR THIN,
TALL OR SHORT,
BOY OR GIRL.

I HAVE A RIGHT TO BE SAFE IN THIS ROOM:
THIS MEANS THAT NO ONE WILL
HIT ME,
KICK ME,
PUSH ME,
PINCH ME,
OR HURT ME.

I HAVE A RIGHT TO HEAR AND TO BE HEARD IN THIS ROOM:
THIS MEANS THAT NO ONE WILL
YELL, SCREAM, SHOUT,
OR MAKE LOUD NOISES.

I HAVE A RIGHT TO LEARN ABOUT MYSELF IN THIS ROOM:
THIS MEANS THAT I WILL BE
FREE TO EXPRESS MY FEELINGS AND OPINIONS
WITHOUT BEING INTERRUPTED OR PUNISHED.

Five Classroom Management Models

The following discussion will familiarize you with selected models that have been developed for managing classroom behavior by noted individuals from the fields of psychology and psychiatry. The intent here is to provide you with a cross-section of ideas for setting up your own management system. The variety of perspectives presented can be useful in giving you a range of possible courses of action for dealing with the many different situations you will face. In some situations, you will feel more inclined to use a certain aspect of one model; in other situations, you will probably use a different model. It is likely that you will find yourself adapting ideas from these models in ways that best suit your personal style and the nature of the class you are teaching. For each model, the major premise supporting the theory is stated and then followed by suggested courses of action for the classroom.

Dreikurs Model

Rudolf Dreikurs (1968) approached the problem of misbehavior from the perspective of being a psychiatrist.

Major Premise

For the most part, misbehavior in the classroom is due to students' desire for recognition. In their attempts to get such recognition, they turn to four "mistaken goals" in the areas of (1) attention getting, (2) power seeking, (3) revenge seeking, and (4) displaying inadequacy.

FIGURE 12–2   Sample Student Manual (To Be Filled In)

(continued)

FIGURE 12–2 *(Continued)*

Special People!

Fourth-grade teachers are _____ , _____ ,

_____ , _____ , and _____ .

Our principal is _____ .

Our secretaries are _____ and _____ .

Our health aide is _____ .

Our librarian is _____ .

Our custodians are _____ and _____ .

Our reading specialist is _____ .

2

A Portrait of Your Day

Time	Subject

School begins at
_____

Recess
_____

Lunch
_____

Dismissal
_____

Library
_____

Special Programs
_____
_____

Procedures:
1. _____ to the yard from the inner circle.
2. Use the _____ on your way out to play.
3. Play _____ and follow school rules.
4. Get a _____ before the bell rings.
5. Line up _____ when the bell rings.

3

Source: Reprinted by permission of Elizabeth B Comer.

Courses of Action Suggested

In general, the teacher should be careful not to reinforce the four mistaken goals. Specifically, it is important to help students understand the benefits of positive behavior and action by creating a classroom environment in which students find the following:

- Taking responsibility leads to freedom.
- Guidance is available to all.
- A sense of belonging is fostered.
- Inappropriate behavior always brings unpleasant consequences.

Ginnott Model

Haim Ginnott (1971) looked at classroom management as a psychologist.

Major Premise

Discipline is a series of little victories that result when the teacher sends sane messages that address the situation and not the student's character.

Courses of Action Suggested

First and foremost, the teacher is a role model whose own level of self-discipline is a key factor in classroom discipline. The teacher also serves as a guide in moving students away from inappropriate behavior to behavior that is positive and lasting. It is recommended that teachers:

- Model the behavior they hope to see in their students.
- Use praise carefully by praising specific acts and not the personality (e.g., "These math problems are done neatly and correctly"; not "You are a good girl for completing your math problems correctly").
- Aim for classroom discipline that produces student self-discipline, responsibility, and concern for others.

Glasser Model

William Glasser (1965) examined the dynamics of classroom behavior from a psychiatrist's perspective.

Major Premise

Reduction of misbehavior in the classroom can be accomplished by providing an environment and curriculum that meets the students' basic needs for belonging, power, fun, and freedom.

Courses of Action Suggested

Teachers should help students make good behavioral choices as a path leading to personal success. Two main things should be done to achieve motivated and well-behaved students:

- Create an atmosphere and activities that satisfy the students so they choose appropriate behavior as a means of satisfaction.
- Provide ample opportunities for team or cooperative learning, as these better meet students' needs and thus increase work output and reduce behavior problems.

Jones Model

Fred Jones (1987) looked at classroom discipline from a psychologist's viewpoint.

Major Premise
Most misbehavior in the classroom is not hostile defiance; rather, it is "massive time wasting" in which students are talking, goofing off, or moving around the room without permission.

Courses of Action Suggested:
The teacher should help the students support their own self-control as a way of decreasing such behavior in the following ways:

- Use body language to set and enforce behavior limits (e.g., posture, eye contact, facial expression, simple gestures, and proximity).
- Set up incentive systems that prompt the students to be on task, complete their work, and act positively (e.g., some class time to talk quietly for completing the work assigned, increased time on preferred activities such as art, physical education, music, or a film).
- Provide efficient help by arranging classroom seating so that students are within easy reach (e.g., shallow concentric semicircles), using graphics (e.g., models or charts) to show examples or directions, and cutting to the bare minimum the time used to give individual help (i.e., so more students can be helped).

Kounin Model

Jacob Kounin (1977) studied classroom management from a psychologist's perspective.

Major Premise
Good classroom behavior depends on effective lesson management. There is a decided *ripple effect* on the whole class when one student's misbehavior is handled with clarity (i.e., specifying the unacceptable behavior and giving reasons for stopping it) and firmness (i.e., projecting an "I mean it" attitude). Also, the ripple effect can occur when praise or encouragement is given, because the class understands which behaviors are desired and rewarded.

Courses of Action Suggested
There are four essential things the teacher should do to foster good classroom discipline:

- Have a sense of "with-itness" where he or she knows what is going on in all parts of the room at all times.
- Plan and make smooth transitions from one activity to the next to maintain the momentum that is essential to group functioning and work.
- Foster alertness and accountability by avoiding a predictable pattern or calling on students for responses.
- Instill a feeling of progress and use a variety of instructional materials and strategies that maintain interest and involvement (i.e., avoid boredom).

Appendix: Sample Classroom Management Plan*

The primary intent of this plan is to provide an initial structure for behavior and classroom management that can be refined and modified over time. Some of what is included here may prove unworkable, and I am fully prepared to scrap that which is ineffective or inappropriate.

Having a general framework and some ideas, organized somewhat into a plan as outlined herein, does provide a feeling of preparedness and reassurance, and, at the very least, some tools with which to deal with behavior and management issues as they arise.

Rules

1. Follow directions.
2. Keep hands, feet, and objects to yourself.
3. Listen and don't interrupt when someone else has permission to talk.
4. No running, yelling, or gum chewing in class.
5. Be respectful of others.

Positive Recognition

At the very minimum, I plan to provide as much positive communication with parents as I possibly can. This will include notes home and phone calls. I am committed that each child in my class wins. I am prepared to issue awards and stickers for outstanding work and have class parties and treats, as is appropriate for the grade level I teach.

Possibly my greatest ongoing challenge will be to discover the individual strengths of each child, and to promote those in a very positive way. I want every student to know that he or she is talented in some area, and capable of contributing to others.

Consequences

The most appropriate consequence structure for elementary grades seems to be:

1. Warning
2. Five minutes after class

---

* Reprinted by permission of Donald Mizock.

3. Ten minutes after class
4. Teleconference with parent—student makes the call if possible, teacher makes the call if necessary
5. Student sent to principal

Severe Clause.   Any physical or verbal abuse or disrespect of teacher or other students, or any behavior or activity that endangers the student or others, will necessitate immediate dismissal to principal—no warnings or time outs.

I also like the idea of a behavior journal. The student has the opportunity to be clear about making choices to break rules, and to effectively clean up his or her messes. This is an important step toward being responsible for one's own actions.

Record Keeping

Initially, I will maintain my record of rewards and consequences on a daily clipboard. Each student will know that the slate gets wiped clean every day.

Communication

I plan to send a letter to parents the first week of school outlining my goals and objectives for the classroom, as well as behavior guidelines. I intend to create a partnership with parents, keeping them informed and encouraging them to communicate their concerns and their ideas with me. One of my goals is to get parents more involved in the education of their children. I may experiment with designing homework assignments that require the participation of a parent or guardian.

I also think that having some background information about students and their families would be very useful. A parent survey or information form would likely be the most efficient way to gather this information; however, I would look forward to speaking informally with each of the parents individually.

An open line of communication with the school principal is also important in being able to get the job done. My own personal goals and philosophies for education need to be integrated within the framework of the philosophical constructs of the school itself. I would encourage and do everything I could to help foster communication and a sense of partnership among the teachers and between faculty and administration. I have discovered that there is, indeed, strength in numbers, and that if any of us is to succeed in truly making a difference in the lives of young people, we need to work together an a team, with common goals and complimentary methods.

Classroom Management Routines and Procedures

The following outline of management routines and procedures for the various areas listed is intended to be completed and modified with further classroom experience. (The priority key is as follows: 1 = by the end of the first day, W = by the end of the first week, W+ = soon after the end of the first week, L = long range.)

Priority	Room Use
1	**Teacher's Desk/Area** • Off limits without teacher's permission
1	**Student's Desk/ Storage Area** • Off limits to other students unless given permission • Students will straighten desk area before leaving each day
1	**Drinking Fountain** • One person at a time at the drinking fountain • Each person waits his or her turn
1	**Pencil Sharpener** • One person at a time—each person waits his or her turn • Pencils should be sharpened before class begins each day
1	**Trash** • All trash goes in the basket
1	**Equipment and Supplies Area** • Off limits without teacher's permission
1	**Chalkboard**
W	**Library/Resource Materials** • All resource material removed from the room must be signed out • Everything must be returned to its original location
W	**Audiovisual Equipment** Off limits without teacher's permission

Priority	Instructional Activities
1	**Notebook/Journal** • Students will read and write only in their own journal—student journals are private
1	**Participation** • Students are encouraged to ask questions and participate—one person at a time/ raises hand to be recognized • The rest of the class pays close attention to the question asked
1	**Homework (Assigned/Collected/Graded)**
1	**Obtaining Help** • Asking for help is a very smart thing to do—raise your hand or quietly get the teacher's attention
1	**Individual Seatwork** • Work quietly by yourself • Work on the given assignment only • Clear desk of all unnecessary items
W	**Group Work** • Work quietly • Everyone participates • Stay in assigned groups
W	**Out-of-Seat Work**
W	**Whole-Class Instruction**
W	**Tests/Quizzes** • Do your own work—do not look at your neighbor's paper • Work quietly • Answer each question the best you can

Priority	Transitional Activities
1	**Entering & Leaving the Room** • Don't run—line up quietly at the door • Be careful not to bump or shove your neighbor • Be sure that things are put away where they belong
1	**Collecting & Distributing Materials**
1	**Starting & Ending the Day**
1	**Lunch/Recess**
1	**Changing Activities**
1	**Rearranging Seating**

Priority	Classroom Maintenance
W	**Chalkboard Cleaning** • Cleaned each afternoon by class helper • Washed each Friday afternoon by class helper
W	**Putting Away Materials & Supplies** • "A place for everything and everything in its place" • Don't waste materials and supplies • Let teacher know when supplies are running low
W	**Trash Disposal** • Trash basket emptied and wiped out each afternoon by student helper
W	**Room Cleaning**
W	**Room Appearance & Beautification**
W	**Equipment Maintenance**
W	**Plant/Animal Care**

Priority	Special Activities
L	**Field Trips**
L	**Guest Speakers**
L	**Class Party**
W	**Minimum Day**
L	**School Assembly**
L	**Special Presentation**

Priority	Parent Involvement
W	**Communication with (Written/By phone/In person)**
W+	**Volunteers**
W+	**Conference**
W+	**Newsletter**
W+	**Monitor/Observer**
W+	**Homework Assistance**

Priority	Emergencies
W+	**Illness & Injury**
W+	**Fighting**
W+	**Bad Weather**
W+	**Security Awareness**
W+	**Drills/Events**
W+	**Postemergency Information**

Priority	General Procedures
1	**Bathroom Use**
W	**Interruptions**
W+	**Library, Resource Room, Office**
W+	**Counselor, Nurse**
1	**Cafeteria**
W	**Playground/Nutrition**
W	**Classroom Monitors**
1	**Response to Bells**
1	**Referrals/Time Out**

Communication

Dear Parent,

I want to thank you for the opportunity to have **Susie** in my class this year. I think it is important that you have an idea of what I intend to accomplish as **her** teacher, and what I need from you in order for **her** to learn and grow in my class. My goals are to:

- Stimulate **Susie's** curiosity and encourage **her** to think critically
- Help **her** to broaden **her** base of knowledge so that **she** can compete, excel, and make choices in **her** life
- Create an environment in which integrity, honesty, and clear communication are present for **her** and for the entire class
- Help **her** to have compassion for other people, other cultures, and nature, and encourage respect for differences
- Help **her** develop a sense of responsibility for **her** life and education
- Promote self-confidence and awareness
- Have the school year be fun and filled with many exciting and rewarding experiences

Please notice that I have used the word *help* a great deal. I cannot accomplish these things on my own. I need your cooperation and teamwork. Together, we can have this year really make a difference, not just in **Susie**'s life, but in yours and in mine, as well.

One area that is critical to my being able to get the job done is behavior. I, as a teacher, have the right and responsibility to establish rules and directions that clearly define the limits of acceptable and unacceptable student behavior. **Susie** has the right to a learning environment free from distractions and disruptions. **She** also has the right to a teacher who will provide **her** with consistent positive encouragement to motivate **her** to behave. I intend to provide that. This may include notes and phone calls home when **Susie** is doing great work and contributing to the class.

We have developed some simple RULES that each student will be required to follow. They are:

1. Follow directions.
2. Keep hands, feet, and objects to yourself.
3. Listen and don't interrupt when someone else has permission to talk.
4. No running, yelling, or gum chewing in class.
5. Be respectful of others.

Occasionally, a student chooses to break the rules. The first infraction initiates a warning. The second instance will require the student to stay 5 minutes after class. The next instance will cause the student to stay after class 10 minutes. The fourth time a rule is broken in a day, the parent will be called. Should the student be having a really bad day, and a fifth infraction occurs, that student will have the opportunity to spend some time with the principal to discuss the merits of appropriate behavior in the classroom. Of course, students will not be allowed to abuse their teacher or other students, either physically or verbally, nor will they be allowed to do anything that endangers themselves or others. In the event this occurs, the student will be sent directly to the principal's office—no warnings or time outs.

I certainly don't anticipate having to contact you to discuss a behavior problem with **Susie**, but should that be necessary, I will look forward to your partnership in resolving the particular issue in a way that benefits everyone.

Please discuss this plan with **Susie** so that you both understand and agree to it. Sign in the space indicated below and return one copy to me by Friday. Your comments will be greatly appreciated! I need your feedback.

I am always available to you for questions or concerns you may have. Please feel free to contact me. Again, I thank you for the privilege of having **Susie** in my class, and I look forward to meeting you.

Sincerely,

Donald Mizock

....

We have read the above plan and agree to abide by the provisions set forth.

| Date | Parent Signature | Student Signature |

COMMENTS: _____

_____

_____

_____

_____

_____

_____

Parent Information Sheet

Dear Parents,

In order to better serve the needs of my students and their families, I am requesting the following informal information from you. Please fill this out and return to me along with your child's information sheet by next Friday. I look forward to meeting you in person.

Parent(s) current job/occupation(s): _____

_____

Activities/hobbies: _____

_____

Things the family likes to do together: _____

_____

Activities your child likes to do: _____

_____

Is there any time that you might be available to help in the classroom (both parents / guardians if possible)? _____

_____

Is there any other type of help or expertise that you might be able to offer to the classroom instead of or in addition to your time (speaking, computers, etc.)? _____

_____

_____

Is there anything else you can tell me about your child or about the family that might assist me in addressing his or her educational, emotional, or other special needs or abilities? _____

_____

_____

_____

Other comments? _____

_____

_____

Student Information Sheet

My favorite activities/hobbies: _____

_____

_____

What I like most about school: _____

_____

_____

What I like least about school:_____

_____

_____

What I hope to accomplish this year in school: _____

_____

_____

What I hope to accomplish this year outside of school: _____

_____

_____

I am really good at: _____

_____

_____

My favorite subjects are: _____

_____

_____

What I would like you to know about me is: _____

_____

_____

_____

STUDENT NAME: _____

Behavior Journal

Student's name: _____ Date:_____

The rule I broke: _____

_____

_____

I chose to break this rule because: _____

_____

_____

_____

_____

This is what I could have done instead: _____

_____

I also want to say: _____

_____

_____

_____

Student Signature: _____ Date:_____

Diversity and Classroom Management

This chapter addresses managing classrooms characterized by diversity. The term *diversity* is used in a broad sense, to include not only children of various ethnic and racial backgrounds but also children with emotional, mental, and physical disabilities. The overall issue of diversity and classroom management are handled in this one chapter because many behavior problems arise out of issues related to diversity—especially out of the failure of traditional classrooms to meet the needs (academic, social, and emotional) of diverse learners.

For the teacher, there are two aspects of this issue that must be actively embraced. The first is on a personal level and involves self-examination and commitment. The second involves acquiring knowledge and using strategies that assist teachers in achieving learning and behavior goals with diverse learners. Discussion, then, is divided into the following two main parts: (1) the teacher's personal challenge with regard to diversity and (2) strategies and approaches for teaching diverse learners. Teachers can and should positively affect the humanity of society by creating inclusive, multicultural classrooms where children learn to respect, appreciate, and enjoy differences as well as discover the underlying similarities among themselves.

The Teacher's Personal Challenge with Regard to Diversity

Today's classrooms are characterized by many different kinds of diversity—color, ethnic backgrounds, socioeconomic status, ability levels, languages, and family stability and situations, to name a few. To be effective teachers in these classrooms—that is, to help students achieve success in academic activities, in social interaction, and in realizing personal self-esteem—requires knowledge of special strategies and techniques. It also requires much more than this. It requires that (1) teachers look at themselves as well as at their students, (2) teachers become learners willing to learn from and with their students, (3) teachers become problem solvers, and (4) teachers commit to creating inclusive, multicultural communities of learners in the classrooms. Let us look at each of the above briefly.

Teachers Look at Themselves

As a teacher, you must look within and honestly examine your own attitudes, biases, and stereotypes regarding the diverse populations of students within your class. Reflect on how your attitudes and cultural limitations could be interfering with your ability to teach students who are very different from yourself. Your past experiences, which, in many cases, are homogeneous in nature, may blind you to the humanity of individuals who differ from you in significant ways.

> *Whatever our ethnic or cultural backgrounds, we teachers bring our own views, values, and dreams to the classroom. At the same time, we tote our own cultural baggage—assumptions, interpretations, misconceptions, stereotypes, and prejudices.... In* White Teacher, *Vivian Paley (Paley, 1979) advises us that our goal "is to find a way of communicating to each child the idea that his or her special quality is understood, is valued, and can be talked about. It is not easy, because we are influenced by the fears and prejudices, apprehensions and expectations which have become a carefully hidden part of every one of us." (Tamura, 1996)**

Tamura (1996) also has suggested that teachers ask themselves the following three questions:

> *1. What do I represent? What symbols and values epitomize who I am? What personal experiences have shaped how I view myself and others around me? Simply put, we need to understand our own attitudes, anxieties, biases and expectations before we can presume to understand, and attempt to meet, the needs of others.*
>
> *2. How do I view differences? Am I open to different ideas? Do I consciously examine both sides of an issue? Can I imagine what it might be like not to understand what others say and do—or not to feel welcome? A "Multicultural Person of the 21st Century," notes Carlos Cortes, must learn "to judge on the basis of prejudice" (1994, p. 8). In our teaching and learning roles this might mean accepting refried beans as part of a balanced breakfast or considering how westward expansion affected pioneers and American Indians.*
>
> *3. Do I recognize both differences and similarities? How am I different from others? How am I the same? How do these differences and similarities affect my view of myself? My relationships with others? (pp. 23–25)**

---

* *Source:* Tamura, L. "No Longer Strangers." *Educational Leadership* 53, 6: 23–25. Reprinted by permission of the Association for Supervision and Curriculum Development. Copyright © 1966 by ASCD. All rights reserved.

A reflective approach toward teaching is a necessity so that you continually examine the intended and unintended consequences of your instruction and interactions with students. Once you have looked at your own beliefs and attitudes honestly, then you are in a position to learn about and appreciate other cultures and to help your students understand and take pride in their own cultural heritages.

Teachers Become Learners

It is important to learn about the cultural backgrounds of the students in your class and the contributions of those cultures to U.S. society. All teachers need to develop cross-cultural competencies. Demographic trends show that while the number of ethnic minority students is rapidly growing in U.S. classrooms, the teaching force for those classrooms is becoming increasingly more white.

> *Students of color are the majority in 23 of the 25 largest school districts in the United States. By the year 2000, students of color are projected to reach as high as 40% of the student population in U.S. public schools. The teaching profession, however, has become increasingly White and middle class. The implications of this disparity become obvious when we account for the powerful influence that biography (culture, family, prior schooling experiences, social class) has on the daily life in classrooms. (Powell, Zehm, & Garcia, 1996)*

This means that white middle-class teachers will be teaching in ethnically and culturally diverse classrooms. These teachers need to discover cultural values that have special meaning to an ethnic group and how those values may affect attitudes and behaviors in the classroom. If teachers do not make this effort, cultural misunderstandings can occur to the detriment of teachers and students alike. For example, white teachers generally expect a child to look directly at them when they are addressing that child. However, this is considered disrespectful in many Native American tribes; children are taught to bow their heads as a sign of respect when being addressed by elders. A white teacher may demand, "Look at me when I'm speaking to you," without understanding that the child *is* trying to be respectful according to his or her understanding. These kinds of misunderstandings can cause undue frustration to the teacher and feelings of confusion, guilt, and alienation for the student. This is an example of why it is so important for you, as the teacher, to inform yourself about the cultural characteristics of your students. Learning about cultures takes time and commitment and is really a life-long process.

All teachers must also be informed about the disabilities that may be represented in classrooms. Learn to listen to and learn from your students as they express their needs and concerns. And, if you want your students to be continual learners, you must also be continually learning.

> *A relevant curriculum must contain more than short stories, essays, and grammatically correct sentences. I realized long ago that revitalizing the curricu-*

lum had to begin with me, and so I began to gather an extensive repertoire of materials and experiences with different voices. Now my library spans the seven continents, my address book overflows with foreign addresses, and my wardrobe contains an array of ethnic clothes. As I encounter writers from all over the world, filling gaps in my own education, I know I am continuing my own growth. (Wass Van Ausdall, 1994)

Teachers Become Problem Solvers

All teachers must be problem solvers. As a teacher, you will need to tackle the behavior, instructional, and social problems that arise in diverse classrooms in creative and proactive ways. There will not always be tried and true ways of solving for the kinds of problems that may present themselves in diverse and inclusive classrooms. Most likely, you will have to team up with parents, administrators, and other teachers to find and try new solutions to new problems.

Teachers Commit to Creating Inclusive Classrooms

Finally, you must commit to the process of making your classroom an inclusive community of diverse learners. Teachers are the leaders in their classrooms. They set the tone, model social behaviors, and endorse political agendas just by being who they are. Because teachers influence so many lives, they have a special responsibility to examine their own inner "hidden" biases and prejudices so that they can overcome these to create the kinds of classrooms where all children feel welcome, valued, and appreciated.

Strategies and Approaches for Diverse Learners

Although it is somewhat artificial to look at diverse learners in distinct categories or groups since differences exist within groups also, it is nevertheless helpful to enable a discussion of specific strategies that are relevant to specific problems and situations. It should be understood, however, that many of the specific strategies discussed are not only helpful to diverse students but to all students to learn more easily and better. Discussion will focus on strategies for working with the following groups:

1. Ethnic and racial minorities
2. Children with severe behavior problems
3. Children with Attention Deficit Hyperactivity Disorder
4. Children with mental disabilities

Ethnic and Racial Minorities

Successful teaching in ethnically diverse classrooms involves becoming a culturally sensitive person and creating a multicultural classroom. Both of these endeavors require time and study. There are many excellent books and periodical articles devoted to this topic, and it is wise to become a student of this literature as part of a teacher's efforts to restructure the classroom to meet the needs of ethnically diverse students. Offered here are a few suggestions that might constitute a starting place in building a multicultural classroom. These suggestions include the following: (1) sharing personal culture, (2) class meetings, and (3) using literature as an entry into understanding cultures.

Sharing Personal Culture

An effective way to have students share their cultures is to have them interview each other in pairs. By structuring questions that enable students to identify similarities and differences, the teacher will enable them to gain a greater understanding and appreciation of each other.

Another strategy involves having students create and share Me Bags. In this activity, children are given large brown bags and are instructed to collect things at home that are of value to them—things that they like or that have special meaning for them. The students then bring these bags to school and share the contents with the class.

Having children share special cultural abilities is yet another way of enabling them to gain a sense of self. For example, a student in your class is a recent immigrant from another country. Because of language and cultural differences, this child's shyness is presenting a roadblock to learning basic communication skills. You will find that you can help this child overcome the shyness and more fully participate in classroom life by ascertaining any particular skill or interest he or she has that might be shared with classmates. Perhaps the student has considerable ability in playing soccer and can teach others his or her skills during play time, or perhaps the skill will be in dance or music or artwork. Whatever the case may be, by tapping into such a student's area of strength and involving him or her in sharing, teaching, and demonstrating the skill with others, a giant stride will have been made in terms of practicing communication skills and in social adjustment.

Class Meetings

Conducting class meeting is an excellent way of teaching students to practice fairness and respect for all students. This strategy provides a wonderful opportunity to have students not only understand but also experience the meaning of the word *community*. If designed and run correctly and in the right spirit, students can gain invaluable insights into shared decision making, conflict resolution, and mutual respect. There are several considerations to be aware of as you conceive of your own plans for classroom meetings.

First, make sure there are clear ground rules to establish how the meetings will be conducted. Examples of ground rules are (1) Wait your turn to speak; (2) Listen attentively and respectfully to what others have to say; (3) All ideas are important to us; (4) We aim for understanding and consensus to solve problems. Remember one key to success of these meetings is that every child feels free and has a right to express his or her opinions and concerns. Second, provide a nonthreatening way for any student to point out a classroom-related problem. You may simply wish to place a nicely decorated box labeled "Classroom Matters" at a convenient place in the room so students can drop notes in, thus setting the agenda for upcoming classroom meetings. Third, think carefully about how you will facilitate the meeting so that the students truly feel it is their meeting. In this regard, be sure you provide opportunity for as many students as possible to express themselves, clarify ideas or questions when necessary, and, most of all, keep the focus on positive discussion leading to workable solutions. These meetings can be a living experience of cooperation and a unique opportunity for the students to develop a sympathetic awareness of the needs and concerns of their classmates.

Using Literature to Understand Culture

Still another strategy to promote diversity in the classroom is the use of literature from and/or about various cultures to help students understand their own cultures and the cultures of others. There are many literature books available that describe the struggles of minority students in their neighborhoods and schools or that provide multicultural perspectives on familiar themes. Often, these stories provide the basis for classroom discussions and/or journal entries in which students share their personal struggles and concerns. Two very good sources for multicultural book titles are (1) *Teaching Tolerance*, a magazine published by the Southern Poverty Law Center in Montgomery, Alabama, that is mailed twice a year at no charge to educators, and (2) *Multicultural Education*, the magazine of the National Association for Multicultural Education.

All the strategies discussed here help create a sense of self-worth in the individual child as well as create an appreciation for other's ideas and individualities. Helping children develop respect for themselves and others prevents many behavioral problems before they begin.

Children with Severe Behavior Problems

A very thorough approach to developing a personalized classroom management plan has been discussed in Chapter 12. Most students will respond positively to the consistent use of a sound management plan. However, with the increase in students with disability labels entering the general education classes, "teachers find themselves working with youngsters who are sometimes disruptive, who disregard rules, who appear not to respect the personal space and belongings of others, or who neither pay attention nor follow directions" (Ayres & Hedeen, 1996). These students can cause interruptions of precious instructional time and wear on the nerves of teachers and students alike. Most distressingly, such children do not respond to regular management procedures; therefore, teachers need to create special strategies and procedures for working with them. Ayres and Hedeen (1996) have suggested that teachers follow four principles to help create the special approaches they will need to obtain the cooperation of these special students:

1. Use a team approach in working with students who have severe behavior problems. School psychologists, special educators, administrators, and other students can all share insights to help plan strategies that will guide these youngsters to more appropriate behaviors.
2. Have the team develop shared positive goals for the student(s) involved. In other words, instead of focusing on how to stop negative behaviors, structure goals in terms of positive behaviors the team agrees the student can develop.

3. Remember, when a child acts out consistently, he or she is trying to communicate something. If you can discover what a child is trying to say through misbehavior, you are in a better position to help the child choose more acceptable ways of getting his or her needs met.

4. Have the team develop proactive, preventive plans that will preempt misbehavior by channeling the child to alternative behavior routes.

Usually, teachers engage with students on behavior issues only after the student has committed an offense. Ayres and Hedeen (1996) have suggested that educators identify positive skills that these children can learn to use as alternatives to negative behaviors. Many examples are given of possible solutions to problems that are common with this population of students who exhibit severe behavior problems. A few are paraphrased here to give you an idea of some creative solutions to tough problems.

1. *Transitions:* Some students have difficulty stopping an activity in order to move on with the rest of the class to something else. Here are a few possible solutions to resistance to change:
   a. Some 10 minutes before a class transition, Rachael's teacher sets a timer on Rachael's desk for 5 minutes. She is instructed to put everything away and get ready to move on when the timer goes off.
   b. Larry has been given an item to be used in the next class activity; it is his responsibility to carry it to the new location of the activity. This gives Larry a role that he enjoys and it makes him willing to move on.

2. *Create a Sense of Control:* All individuals enjoy having control over their own lives; children are no different. They want to make their own choices, but there is a problem when their choices cause harm or disruption to the classroom activities. Ayres and Hedeen (1996) have suggested that instead of asserting complete authority over these youngsters, it is more effective to find areas in which to offer them choices within an overall structure. Here are a few examples:
   a. Laticia's teacher gives her many choices throughout the day regarding what kind of writing utensil she wants to use, where she wants to work, what color paper she prefers, and so on.
   b. William has many ideas about what he wants to do. In order to assure that his resulting actions are acceptable to the class, the teacher has William write down his plan and run it by his teacher (who might suggest modifications) before he acts on it.

3. *Follow Classroom Rules:* Some children seem unwilling and/or unable to follow the regular classroom rules without special assistance. Here are some suggestions about what that assistance might be:
   a. Tony uses swear words in class. He cannot seem to control himself, and, in fact, is encouraged by the response of other students who giggle when he does so. The teacher holds a class meeting to solicit ideas from the rest of the students. They decide not to laugh when Tony swears and to compliment him when he uses proper language.

b. Carrie's problem is that she continually shouts out in class without raising her hand. She seems unable to stop this behavior even when verbally reminded. The teacher moves Carrie's desk to the front of the room and tapes a card on her desk that outlines the procedure for communicating with the teacher in class (get an idea, raise your hand, wait to be called on, speak in a soft voice). The teacher has Carrie practice the sequence twice a day. If Carrie forgets to raise her hand, her teacher merely has to point to the card on the desk to remind Carrie to do so.

These strategies are devised to give teachers a way of reaching children with severe behavior problems. Teachers of these children must be problem solvers and use the help of colleagues to create innovative solutions. You will have to create solutions to the unique problems that will arise in your classroom, as well. The four principles will help you to find or create the solutions you need.

Children with Attention Deficit Hyperactivity Disorder

Students with Attention Deficit Hyperactivity Disorder (ADHD) exhibit such traits as extreme restlessness, inability to pay attention, excessive talking, apparent aimless movement such as wandering around the classroom, fidgetiness, and disorganization. Often, these children find it extremely difficult to sit still for any length of time and they seem to be truly unable to control their restless behaviors. Typical treatments for these children have been the use of drug therapy (usually Ritalin) and behavior modification strategies that employ reward systems such as receiving tokens for appropriate behaviors. However, Thomas Armstrong (1996) has suggested that there are more natural, holistic approaches for working with ADHD children. He has pointed out that ADHD students function more normally in classrooms that use hands-on, self-paced activities and that utilize project-based approaches that allow students to construct meaning based on what they already know about a subject. The following list of interventions is recommended by Armstrong to help children who have been labeled ADHD at school and at home. It is necessary, of course, that parents and school personnel work together to create a regime of interventions for these children.

Strategies and Interventions for Children Labeled ADHD

1. Cognitive. *Use focusing and attention training techniques (for example, meditation and visualization), self-talk skills, biofeedback training, organizational strategies, attributional skills (including the ability to attribute success to personal effort), and higher-order problem solving.*
2. Ecological. *Limit television and video games, provide appropriate spaces for learning, use music and art to calm or stimulate, find a child's best times of alertness, provide a balanced breakfast, and remove allergens from the diet.*
3. Physical. *Emphasize a strong physical educational program, martial arts training, physical touch and appropriate movement, outdoor activities, noncompetitive sports and games, and physical relaxation techniques.*

4. Emotional. *Use self-esteem building strategies, provide positive role models and positive images of the future, employ values clarification, offer individual psychotherapy, and identify talents, strengths, and abilities.*

5. Behavioral. *Use personal contracting, immediate feedback, natural and logical consequences, and consistent rules, routines, and transitions; involve the child in a selection of strategies.*

6. Social. *Stress effective communication skills, social skills, class meetings, family therapy, peer and cross-age tutoring, and cooperative learning.*

7. Educational. *Use computers, hands-on learning, high-stimulation learning resources, expressive arts, creativity development, and multiple intelligences, whole language, and attention-grabbing activities.*[*]

Children with Mental Disabilities

Today, more and more students with mental disabilities are being mainstreamed into regular classes for lengthy periods of time—not just for nonacademic activities but during hard-core academic subjects, as well. Many of these children have Down syndrome, autism, or learning disabilities. Some are not capable of attaining most of the academic skills taught while they are in the regular classroom; others are capable of learning the regular curriculum with various kinds of aids and supports. All of these children, however, despite the severity of their disabilities, seem to benefit from being included in the regular classes and are more likely to reach their individualized education plan goals than when they remain totally segregated in special education classes. An interesting result of mainstreaming children with severe or mild mental disabilities into the classroom is that the students without disabilities seem to benefit from the integration, as well. "When students with severe disabilities are included in the regular classroom, all students develop social, communication, and problem-solving skills, as well as the ability to get along with others in a diverse community" (Farlow, 1996).

Children who have disabilities benefit from having positive role models of their own age in regular classes and also by forming friendships that extend beyond the classroom onto the playground or to the local neighborhood. Once the children in regular classes get to know their peers who are disabled as individuals, they will begin to greet them and associate with them outside of the classroom, as well. This acceptance means a great deal to the students who have disabilities and it will boost their self-esteem (and, as a natural result, their appropriate behaviors) immensely.

Some of the following suggestions and strategies are offered for the regular classroom teacher whose classroom is "inclusive" of students with mental disabilities:

1. As with the other special disabilities that have been discussed (severe behavior problems and ADHD), the regular classroom teacher becomes a part of a team of individuals who work together to create the kinds of interventions and supports each child with disabilities will need to have in the classroom.

---

[*] Reprinted by permission from Thomas Armstrong, Ph.D., author of *The Myth of the A.D.D. Child: 50 Ways to Improve Your Child's Behavior and Attention Span without Drugs, Labels, or Coercion.*

2. All students, with or without disabilities, should be prepared for the mainstreaming. Teachers should discuss the nature and severity of the disability honestly with the "regular" students so they can gain a better understanding of the student who will be integrated into the classroom. Often, students have misconceptions about various disabilities, and these can be dispelled during these preparation sessions. (In one preparation session, some students expressed concern with the possibility of "catching" severe mental retardation from certain students. These students not only learned that they would not catch anything but also that children with mental disabilities were fun to be with, and they became strong advocates for the mentally disabled on the playground and on field trips.) The students with disabilities should also understand the purpose of the mainstreaming and become familiar with some of the materials they will be using in the regular class. It can be arranged that students with mental disabilities get to know some of the students in the regular class through tutoring in the special class, so that when the integration occurs, friendships have already been formed. In the beginning, a buddy can be assigned to the student to help show him or her the ropes.

3. Specific strategies should be planned out by the support team (comprised of the regular teacher, special education teacher, parents, administrator, school psychologist, etc.) that enable the child with disabilities to have the fullest participation possible in regular class activities. This will vary in accordance with the severity of the disability. The following suggestions and strategies offer possible avenues for inclusion of students who have disabilities:

a. Use pictorial representations of ideas and concepts on worksheets and tests.

b. Read information to the student for assignments and tests and allow him or her to respond orally.

c. Use neighborhood volunteers or classmates to read information to the student ahead of class so he or she comes to class well prepared.

d. Use audiotaped directions to help the student complete worksheets or tests, or to simply practice following directions.

e. Provide cooperative group activities in which the student can make specific types of contributions. For example, he or she may be asked to be the one who brings materials or keeps track of on-task behavior, contributes drawings, or has a part in a dramatization.

f. Provide various types of supports for the student to aid him or her in academic work (e.g., tape a number line onto his or her desk or provide manipulatives such as counters to aid in math problems). Provide graphic organizers, diagrams, or pictures to remind the student of concepts or sequences. Also allow him or her to draw pictures to respond to academic questions.

g. Provide hands-on activities such as science experiments and social studies projects (e.g., building a miniature replica early American Western town) in which the student can make a useful contribution (such as paint the buildings).

h. Give the child meaningful jobs within the classroom such as checking off completed assignments or being a team leader in a sports event.

i. Solicit the help of the other students to think of ways to provide academic as well as social support in daily classroom routines. Once the other students come to know the student who has a disability as a person, they often think of more creative, ingenious, and meaningful ways to help that child than the teachers do.

This chapter has described possible strategies for dealing with some of the more complex management problems that may arise in diverse and inclusive classrooms. Many of these strategies are proactive, meant to prevent the need for students to act out to get their needs met. In all cases of complex management problems that may arise in your classroom, you are called on to be a creative, innovative, problem solver. The chapter has provided a means for you to create your own personalized management plan—one with which you are comfortable. Most of your students will respond positively to a sound, organized plan enforced consistently. However, one can never be blind or without common sense when enforcing rules and consequences. Sometimes, extraordinary circumstances arise that will require you to be extraordinary in your solutions to problems. You can get help in inventing these solutions. Many times, you will be a member of a team that will have to invent these creative strategies to achieve appropriate behavior or inclusion of a child into the regular classroom. Other kinds of problems may come up, too, such as having a child with AIDS in the class or a child coming from an abusive family situation. These problems require extra time and some brilliant thinking on your part. While these challenges require your dedicated effort in finding solutions, there is a great reward and satisfaction in knowing that you have made positive changes in the lives of many young people. And *that* is what teaching is really about.

References for Section IV

Alter, Gloria. (1995). Diverse learners in the classroom. *Social Studies and the Young Learner, 7* (4), 2.

Armstrong, Thomas. (1996). A holistic approach to attention deficit disorder. *Educational Leadership, 53* (5).

Ayres, Barbara J., & Hedeen, Deborah L. (1996). Been there, done that, didn't work. *Educational Leadership, 53* (5), 48.

Canter, L., & Canter, M. (1992). *Assertive discipline*. Santa Monica, CA: Lee Canter & Associates.

Carger, C. L., & Ayers, W. (1995). Diverse learners in a multicultural world. *Social Studies and the Young Learner, 7* (4), 6.

Cortes, C. (1994, May). A curricular basic for our multiethnic future. *ACCESS, 123*.

Dreikurs, R. (1968). *Psychology in the classroom* (2nd ed.). New York: Harper and Row.

Farlow, Leslie. (1996). A quartet of success stories: How to make inclusion work. *Educational Leadership, 53*, 51–55.

Ginnott, H. (1971). *Teacher and child*. New York: Macmillan.

Glasser, W. (1965). *Reality therapy: A new approach to psychology*. New York: Harper and Row.

Jones, F. (1987). *Positive classroom discipline*. New York: McGraw-Hill.

Kounin, J. (1977). *Discipline and group management in classrooms*. New York: Holt, Rinehart and Winston.

Paley, V. G. (1979). *White teacher*. Cambridge, MA: Harvard University Press.

Powell, R., Zehm, S., & Garcia, J. (1996). *Field experiences: Strategies for exploring diversity in schools*. Englewood Cliffs, NJ: Prentice-Hall.

Tamura, Linda. (1996). No longer strangers. *Educational Leadership, 53*, (5), 23–25.

Wass Van Ausdall, Barbara. (1994, May). Books offer entry into understanding cultures. *Educational Leadership, 51* (8), 32–35.

S e c t i o n *V*

Evaluation

Why do elementary school teachers carry out evaluation? The answer is straightforward: to understand and help students and to become better teachers. The key to understanding the meaning and role of evaluation is found within the word itself: *evalu(e)*ation. In essence, elementary teachers conduct evaluation to determine the *value* of their efforts on their students' well-being in all the areas examined in the five sections of this book. This can be illustrated best by posing the following five questions, which are at the heart of classroom evaluation:

- How well do I understand and carry out my roles and responsibilities as an elementary teacher?
- How well do I understand and use various teaching methods to deliver instruction?
- How well do I plan on a long- and short-term basis?
- How well do I manage my classroom to create a positive learning environment?
- How well do I use various modes of evaluation to measure student ability, progress, and achievement?

As you can see from these questions, evaluation tells you at least as much about your efforts as a teacher as it does about the students. Indeed, the relationship between instruction and evaluation is so close that fair and effective evaluation can be said to be possible *only* when the teacher's efforts in the classroom are based on thoughtful and organized plans. Why is this so? Because it is possible to reflect on the value of a particular instructional intervention only when there is a course of action (i.e., a plan) followed. Once you have designed a plan and then carried it out, even if it wound up being modified in its actual delivery, then you can say to yourself: How well did that course of action promote student learning and growth? Without working from carefully developed plans, answering such a reflective question, whether it be concerned with the short or the long term, is impossible. Put simply, you cannot correct, fix, or modify something if there is *no* something. All you can really do is muddle along aimlessly. This crucial fact is obvious but, unfortunately, it is often overlooked.

The aim of this section is to provide ways you can reflect on the students' and your own efforts as a means of both determining and increasing their growth and your effectiveness. To evaluate accurately and thoroughly, you need to accomplish three essential tasks:

1. Determine what to look at (i.e., Chapter 14, Areas to Evaluate)
2. Determine how to look at those areas (i.e., Chapter 15, Ways to Evaluate)
3. Determine what the resulting evaluation information means (i.e., Chapter 16, Maintaining and Using Evaluation Information)

Chapter *14*

Areas to Evaluate

Before you can evaluate your students, and thus your instructional program and efforts, you first need to know what it is that needs to be examined. It is crucial to obtain a comprehensive profile of how each student and the class as a whole is functioning, but it has to be done in a way that is manageable—especially for a new teacher! To do this, you have to be focused in your approach. In other words, you have to have a clear picture of what aspects of student functioning you are going to look at in relation to the content covered and in the context of daily life in the classroom. Only when you know what you are going to look at can you determine both how to look and how to utilize the resulting information. If your conception of the areas to evaluate is incomplete, unbalanced, or just plain inappropriate, your entire effort at classroom evaluation will be useless to you and unfair to the students. This chapter focuses on the following three areas, which will provide you with the comprehensive and balanced view needed for successful evaluation. As you saw in the discussion of learning in Chapter 1, the three areas listed here constitute the three aspects of human consciousness (i.e., knowing, feeling, and willing).

- Cognitive functioning (content-area knowledge)
- Affective functioning (social and emotional development)
- Conative functioning (self-discipline and will)

Further, you will discover that it is necessary to conduct three phases of evaluation of students' functioning in these areas, as follows:

- Diagnostic phase (baseline data on initial *ability* level)
- Formative phase (ongoing monitoring of *progress* being made from baseline level)
- Summative phase (benchmark determination of *achievement* up to a fixed point)

A matrix will be presented for the areas of cognitive, affective, and conative functioning, respectively, as a focused guide containing key questions of what needs to be looked at over the three phases of evaluation. After reviewing these three matrices, it should become quite clear that determining students' abilities, progress, and achievement in cognitive, affective, and conative functioning requires a multidimensional approach to evaluation that goes well beyond simple on-demand testing.

Cognitive Functioning

Cognition is the "knowing" (or mental) aspect of human consciousness. In the most practical and useful sense to an elementary teacher, evaluation of cognitive functioning looks at students' familiarity with *facts*, understanding of *concepts*, and ability to *apply* concepts in the various content areas. This parallels the three phases of the learning process, as pointed out in Figure 14–1.

In the same way that you design instruction to take your students through the three levels of the learning process, so, then, do you need to determine to what extent they are able to accomplish learning at each level for the content involved. There is a great strategic advantage to knowing exactly that you want to determine students' abilities, progress, and achievement through the three levels of the learning process, because then you can begin to make intelligent decisions and plans for how best to look at these things. For example, if you know you want to determine to what extent students' backgrounds have been built, you can then figure out the different and most effective ways to determine whether students have become familiar with and remember essential facts about a topic in a particular content area. Similar will be the case for determining conceptual understanding and the ability to apply those concepts. The matrix in Figure 14–2 graphically depicts the general scope evaluation needs to take to obtain a complete picture of students' cognitive functioning, and thus be most effective.

In each box of the cognitive functioning matrix, a question is posed that represents the focus of what should be looked at for that particular level of cognition and phase of evaluation. It is important to note that the questions under the Diagnostic Phase serve as a way of not only obtaining baseline data but also of determining readiness at that level. Think of how much a child would be set up for failure if he or she is placed in activities requiring application of concepts (i.e., ideation level) before having an under-

FIGURE 14–1   Parallel between Evaluating Cognitive Function and the Learning Process

Evaluating Cognitive Functioning	Phase of the Learning Process
Familiarity with facts	*Perception Phase:* Taking in essential facts to build background
Understanding concepts	*Conception Phase:* Putting facts together to derive meaning
Applying concepts	*Ideation Phase:* Generalizing facts and concepts to form creative and original ideas

FIGURE 14–2 Cognitive Functioning Matrix

Cognitive Functioning	Diagnostic Phase	Formative Phase	Summative Phase
Perception Level (familiarity with facts)	What is the student's readiness for developing a background in particular content?	To what extent is the student developing a background in the content?	How well has the student's content background been built? (leading to diagnostic phase at conception level)
Conceptual Level (understanding of concepts)	What is the student's readiness for understanding particular content area concepts?	To what extent is the student developing an understanding of concepts in the content?	How well does the student understand content concepts? (leading to diagnostic phase of ideation level)
Ideation Level (application of concepts)	What is the student's readiness for creatively applying particular content area concepts?	To what extent is the student developing the ability to creatively apply content concepts?	How well can the student creatively apply content concepts? (leading to readiness for wider and higher perceptions)

standing of the concepts involved (i.e., conception level). This sad situation occurs all too frequently. Therefore, you must be vigilant in your efforts to evaluate cognitive functioning as outlined in Figure 14–2. If you do this skillfully, then you will notice that time and again you are setting up your students for success. And we all know that nothing breeds success like success.

It remains now to address the need to evaluate cognitive functioning in the curriculum covered for each content area. To do this, a profile of cognitive functioning is presented in Figure 14–3. This profile is a simple bar graph that provides a general picture of how well your class has been involved in the learning process (i.e., cognitive functioning) as you proceed through the various units and topics of the different content areas. It can also be used in the same way for keeping track of individual students as part of more detailed record keeping. To form this profile, the lists of content area units and topics can be taken directly from your overall content area curriculum plans. As you proceed through the various units and topics of each content area, you can use information from your evaluation to graphically represent how far along in the learning process the class and/or individual students are. The resulting profiles tell you a great deal about your students' cognitive functioning in the content areas, as well as where you can productively make some adjustments in your instructional program.

Affective Functioning

Affection is the "feeling" aspect of human consciousness. It has a powerful influence on almost every activity and situation in which students are involved. It is obvious how important it is to evaluate students' cognitive abilities as far as content knowledge is

FIGURE 14–3   Profile of Cognitive Functioning

Content Curriculum	Familiarity with Facts (Perception)	Understanding Concepts (Conception)	Applying Concepts (Ideation)

Unit #1

Topic 1
Topic 2
Topic 3
Topic 4

Unit #2

Topic 1
Topic 2
Topic 3
Topic 4
Topic 5

Unit #3

Topic 1
Topic 2
Topic 3

Unit #4

Topic 1
Topic 2
Topic 3
Topic 4

concerned, but equal attention needs to be given to looking at how they function in the affective domain.

> *Students in kindergarten through twelfth grade "dwell" in the affective domain, i.e., feelings, emotions, and strong attitudes are very much a part of almost every waking hour. Conversely, teachers "dwell" mainly in the cognitive domain, where student achievement is perceived to be the single most important* raison d'etre *of schooling. It is our contention that because of this perceptual mismatch, teachers and students don't "meet" intellectually in the classroom. Put another way, their needs are so different—teachers driven to impart knowledge, students to discover the range of emotions inherent in each new day—that real communication sometimes does not occur in classrooms where the focus of instruction is content. (Richardson & Morgan, 1990, pp. 37–38)*

This quote points out that students' cognitive functioning cannot be evaluated in a vacuum. In a given student, what may appear as an inability to mentally process information and concepts may, in reality, be an emotional problem. There is a classic example of a boy whose academic achievement was so poor that he was targeted for special education, until he miraculously started scoring at the top of his class. This prompted the teacher to investigate the child's home situation, from which she learned that the boy's father had just recently overcome alcoholism. The timing of this coincided exactly with the boy's academic turnaround. Within a short time, the boy was placed in a gifted and talented education class. By not evaluating affective functioning, this teacher mistakenly concluded that this student was a slow learner—the opposite of what was the case. What do teachers need to look at in terms of students' affective functioning? The matrix presented in Figure 14–4 provides a practical and focused guide for making such evaluations.

The questions in each box of Figure 14–4 are meant to serve as a starting point to focus your efforts at determining what will be most useful to evaluate in the area of affective functioning. However, unlike with the area of cognitive functioning, your efforts to evaluate students' affective functioning will be accomplished mainly through observation. There are no tests or quizzes you can give the students to determine accurately how they are feeling. Ongoing activities such as journal writing, sharing time (of ideas, perceptions, problems), and creation of expressive picture collages can provide insights about students' feelings. The surest way to look at your students' affective

FIGURE 14–4   Affective Functioning Matrix

Affective Functioning	Diagnostic Phase	Formative Phase	Summative Phase
Motivation/ Interest	What is the student's apparent interest in school and different kinds of work?	How and to what degree is the student's interest in school and work changing as different situations and interventions are experienced?	How far has the student gotten toward being fully interested and engaged in school work and learning?
Social Interaction	What is the student's apparent ability and interest in working, playing, and interacting with others?	How and to what degree is the student's social interaction changing as various activities and situations are experienced?	How far has the student gotten in being able to interact positively with others?
Self-Concept	What is the student's level of self-esteem and how does the student view himself or herself?	How and to what degree is the student's self-esteem and self-concept chganging as time progresses?	How far has the student gotten in attaining positive self-esteem and a healthy, realistic self-concept?
Attitude	What is the student's attitude toward school, learning, and others?	How and to what degree is the student's attitude changing toward school, learning, and others?	How far has the student gotten in having a positive, respectful attitude toward school, learning, and others?

functioning is to see how they approach the following: various kinds of work; interactions with their classmates, you, and others; situations that arise; and school in general. In this regard, evaluating affective functioning is more subjective than looking at cognitive functioning.

Conative Functioning

Conation is the "willing" aspect of human consciousness. In evaluating your students' conative functioning, you are seeking to understand their varying abilities to take action; put more simply, you are asking: How able are my students to do different things? Evaluation in this area, as with the affective area, is carried out largely by observing the students as they are functioning in the classroom and school environment. The conative functioning matrix presented in Figure 14–5 provides three essential areas for you to focus on in making these observations.

Evaluating students' conative functioning is of utmost importance. You may well have students who are considered "bright" (i.e., high cognitive functioning) and motivated (i.e., high affective functioning) yet perform poorly in school. It is difficult to understand and solve such problem cases. Although it is not possible to separate a student's cognitive, affective, and conative functioning, it is useful to recognize that one of the three aspects may be the seat of the problem at a given point in a particular student's development. By considering that a student's difficulties may lie principally in the area of conative functioning, several courses of action to spur his or her progress will present themselves. For example, take the bright and motivated student just

FIGURE 14–5   Conative Functioning Matrix

Conative Functioning	Diagnostic Phase	Formative Phase	Summative Phase
Self-Discipline	What is the student's apparent level of self-discipline in terms of behavior and approach to work?	How and to what extent is the student's self-discipline in behavior and work changing as different situations and interventions are experienced?	How far has the student gotten toward being self-discipline in behavior and work habits?
Concentration/ Attention	What is the student's ability to pay attention and concentrate when needed?	How and to what extent is the student's ability to pay attention and concentrate changing as time progresses?	How far has the student gotten toward being able to pay attention and concentrate for longer periods of time?
Perseverance	What is the student's ability to persevere in completing a task and accomplishing a goal?	How and to what extent is the student's ability to persevere in various tasks changing over time?	How far has the student gotten toward being able to persevere in completing tasks and achieving goals?

described. Upon closer scrutiny and using the Conative Functioning Matrix as a guide, you may discover that this child lacks the self-discipline to follow through consistently with class work and homework assignments. At this point, you can begin to work with the student and those at home to create a structured routine for approaching work at school and home that, little by little, will build the self-discipline that has been lacking.

In evaluating cognitive, affective, and conative functioning, consider this word of caution: Skill and discernment take time, thought, and practice. Sometimes, it may appear that a student's main problem is in one area when, in reality, it masks a problem in another area. For example, a child who is unable to concentrate on the work at hand (i.e., apparent low conative functioning) may actually suffer from a poor self-concept (i.e., low affective functioning). This child may simply give up his or her efforts at a task at the first hint of difficulty because in his or her life no one ever instilled a feeling of self-confidence. In this case, conative and cognitive functioning will outwardly seem to be low (i.e., concentration and little academic progress); however, the main problem area to work on is that of affective functioning. A degree of clarity can be achieved by creating a composite profile, such as the one shown in Figure 14–6, for each student.

Maintaining this profile allows you to note your perceptions and reflections on each student's functioning in the three areas in relative terms and in a single place. In a sense, this profile gives you a picture of each student's intelligence quotient (IQ), emotional quotient (EQ), and action quotient (AQ), respectively. The work required is complex and demands a dedicated effort in order to understand and help the children entrusted to your care.

These three areas of human consciousness are a most relevant and practical focus for your efforts at evaluation. The next chapter will examine how you can actually go about carrying out evaluation of these three areas in the course of daily life in the classroom.

FIGURE 14–6   Composite Student Profile

Name:	Date:

Areas of Functioning	Evaluation Continuum Low ————————————— High
Cognitive Familiarity with Facts Understanding Concepts Applying Concepts	
Affective Motivation/Interest Social Interaction Self-Concept Attitude	
Conative Self-Discipline Contration/Attention Perseverance	

C h a p t e r *15*

Ways to Evaluate

Now that you have a clear picture of what needs to be evaluated, the focus turns to figuring out the most effective ways to accomplish this work. The aim of this chapter is to describe how you can evaluate your students' abilities (diagnostic phase), progress (formative phase), and achievement (summative phase) in the areas of cognitive, affective, and conative functioning. To do this, the following three modes of evaluation will be examined:

- Performance Tasks
- Portfolio Assessment
- Observations of Class Work

Performance Tasks

One of the best ways to evaluate students is to place them in situations where they are required to perform a particular task concerning content being covered. Performance tasks, by their nature, tell you primarily about your students' cognitive functioning, and they tend to emphasize the summative phase of evaluation. The performance tasks to be discussed here are shown in Figure 15–1 in relation to the three phases of evaluation.

In looking at Figure 15–1, you will notice that, with the exception of homework and quizzes, the performance tasks are mainly concerned with what the students have achieved at a particular time. From a grand viewpoint, it is possible to make the argument that all evaluation is formative, in that the growth of children and the teachers' efforts to learn about and help them are ongoing. To an extent, this is true, in that you should use every opportunity and information available to better understand your students and adjust your classroom program to foster their growth. Nonetheless, the general structure of the educational system necessitates that standards be set, judgments made, and grades given at designated points during each school year. In this regard, tests are taken, projects are presented, and reports are written mainly as culminating

FIGURE 15–1   Performance Tasks

Performance Tasks	Diagnostic Phase	Formative Phase	Summative Phase
Test	Secondary Use		Primary Use
Quizzes	Primary Use	Primary Use	
Homework		Primary Use	
Projects			Primary Use
Reports			Primary Use

events to discrete periods of learning in the content areas. Performance on these tasks goes a long way toward determining students' academic grades. Your goal is to run a caring, interesting, and nurturing classroom where performance on tests, projects, and reports becomes the reflection and expression of your efforts to diagnose ability, monitor learning, and tailor instruction so that student learning is maximized.

Tests

Tests are the best known and most used way for evaluating student achievement. Remember, testing can tell you only about your students' cognitive functioning—and only to a certain degree, depending on what level or levels of cognitive functioning you are testing. A test full of factual recall questions will tell you little or nothing about what your students think those facts mean. Although tests are mental tasks (i.e., in the cognitive realm), students' resulting performance is definitely influenced by how they are functioning in the affective and conative areas. This is why it is so important that you effectively use observations of class work as a primary means of determining how students' affective and conative functioning is impacting their academic progress and accomplishments.

A tremendous difference exists between the tests you make up and ones that come ready-made from textbook publishers or other sources. You are an individual who has specific ways that you cover content material with your students. Your students themselves are individuals who have been placed together in your classroom and who create a unique group dynamic. It is, therefore, impossible to find any ready-made test that can fit or address your classroom situation perfectly. Even when ready-made tests purport to be criterion referenced (i.e., tests reflecting your instructional objectives and activities), they are not. This is because only you can design such tests—you alone know precisely what you covered and how you covered it! Unfortunately, as a new teacher who has literally hundreds of things to keep in mind and do, it is not easy to find the time to create your own tests. However, at least you have a fighting chance of being able to design your own tests if you have a clear and workable method for how to do it. The following discussion will provide you with such a method. This discussion will look at (1) the difference between objective tests and essay tests, (2) setting up a simple instructional/learning index for rating your instructional emphasis, and (3) creating criterion-referenced tests by using a table of specifications.

Objective versus Essay Tests

The basic difference between objective tests and essay tests is that the former focus on *closed* questions where there are definite, predetermined correct answers, and the latter focus on *open* questions where there are many possible correct responses. Figure 15–2 lists the characteristics of objective and essay tests to help you determine when it is best to use one or a combination of both.

As you can see, both types of tests have their place in the economy of classroom evaluation. Objective tests will determine familiarity with facts (i.e., perception level of the learning process) and essay tests will determine understanding and application of concepts (i.e., conception and ideation levels, respectively, of the learning process). Often, the wisest course is to design tests that have both objective questions and some form of essay questions (i.e., requiring short or long responses or both) as one way of evaluating students at the conclusion of a particular topic or unit.

Instructional/Learning Index

The basis for creating a fair and useful test to evaluate your students' levels of accomplishment is found right in your daily lesson plans. By examining the lesson plans you used to cover specific material that you are planning to test students on, and by reflecting on how those lessons proceeded, you can make sure the resulting test is rooted in what the students actually experienced in the classroom. For example, if you are setting out to create a test on punctuation after covering this topic during a portion of Lan-

FIGURE 15–2   Objective versus Essay Tests

Objective	• Aims at objectivity in scoring; two or more persons should reach similar scores when grading the same tests • Requires a relatively large number of items to obtain desired results • Samples relatively large segments of course content • Scoring is mechanical and relatively fast • Includes multiple choice, true/false, matching, and completion • Is effective for measuring recall and recognition of factual information • Encourages memorization of information rather than higher levels of thinking
Essay	• Scoring is subjective; responses allow for originality, creativity, and varying writing styles • Requires only a few well-designed questions to obtain the evaluation information desired • Samples a specific segment of course material due to depth of response called for • Encourages understanding of concepts, organization of ideas and information, and development of writing skills • Stresses creativity and imagination and thus effectively measures higher level of thinking and understanding

guage Arts Time over a two-week span, you might create an instructional/learning index that looks something like the one presented in Figure 15–3.

In looking at Figure 15–3, it should be noted that your analysis of the lessons given on the topic to be tested should derive the following four key pieces of information:

1. *Content Covered:* Breakdown of the subtopics/concepts covered
2. *Time Emphasis:* Number of lessons spent covering each subtopic/concept
3. *Learning Emphasis:* Degree to which each level of the learning process was emphasized
4. *Learning Attained:* Degree to which students were able to function at each learning level

Table of Specifications

Once you have filled out the Instructional/Learning Index, you can readily set up a Table of Specifications as the final preparation to creating your test. Figure 15–4 shows a table of specifications for creating a test on punctuation that is based on the information on the Instructional/Learning Index in Figure 15–3. This Table of Specifications shows that a simple method of percentages is used to determine the amount

FIGURE 15–3   Instructional/Learning Index

Language Arts Content Covered	Usage Unit	Punctuation Topic		12/1–12/12 Dates	10 Days
Content Covered	**No. of Lessons**	**Learning Emphasis**		**Learning Attained**	
Periods	5	P ✓ C ✓ I ✓		P ✓ C ✓ I	
Commas	3	P ✓ C ✓ I		P ✓ C ✓ I	
Question Marks	3	P ✓ C ✓ I ✓		P ✓ C ✓ I ✓	
Exclamation Marks	2	P ✓ C I		P ✓ C I	
Apostrophes	1	P ✓ C I		P C I	

Note: P = perception (factual) level, C = conception (understanding) level, I = ideation (application) level

FIGURE 15–4   Table of Specifications

Language Arts	Usage	Punctuation	12/15
Content Covered	Unit	Topic	Test Date

Content to Test	**Learning Level Percentage**			
	Factual Recall	Understanding Concepts	Applying Concepts	Percentage of Test
Periods	20	9	6	35
Commas	13	4	3	20
Question Marks	12	5	3	20
Exclamation Marks	8	5	2	15
Apostrophes	7	2	1	10
Percentage of test	= 60	= 25	= 15	= 100%

of the test to be given to the various portions of the content covered, as well as the level of learning (i.e., cognitive functioning) at which to test that content. Both determinations are made from what was learned in reflecting on the lessons presented and setting up the Instructional/Learning Index. Now all that is left is creating the test questions. Remember, by doing what was necessary to set up both the Instructional/Learning Index and Table of Specifications, you will have thoroughly and thoughtfully reviewed the content to test.

For this example on punctuation, the teacher decided that (1) factual-level questions would focus on stating rules of usage and finding different punctuation marks in a sentence, (2) understanding-level questions would focus on correcting errors in a sentence, and (3) application-level questions would focus on using different punctuation marks in originally created sentences. Given the percentage breakdowns that have already been carefully made, the various test questions can now be made accordingly. What will result is a test that is eminently fair because it is rooted in what actually transpired in your classroom. The students' test scores, then, will accurately tell you a lot about subsequent adjustments you might need to make in your instructional program.

Quizzes

The quiz is a form of test characterized by three main features: (1) the items focus on an aspect of a single content area topic, (2) there are few items to answer, and (3) only a short time period is allotted for answering the items. The quiz can be employed equally well to determine students' readiness for learning a particular topic (diagnostic evaluation) and to determine how much they are learning about a particular topic being studied (formative evaluation). Quizzes can be given by surprise—that is, the *pop quiz*—to keep students on their toes. Often, however, quizzes are announced in advance as a sort of mini-tests.

Because quizzes focus on evaluating student learning of an aspect of a single content area topic, they tend to be less threatening to students. Giving a series of quizzes leading up to a culminating unit test allows the children to consolidate and reinforce their understanding of material in discrete, manageable amounts. In this regard, the use of quizzes can be an effective way of discouraging cramming for the single all-important test and eliminating the anxiety that goes with it.

Projects

Of all the work students are involved in, projects have the widest scope for learning and growth. This is because projects can be used as individual or group efforts. They can take several forms, as follows:

- *Presentations:* Projects in which an individual student or group of students prepares and delivers an oral report about some facet of a content area topic being studied
- *Demonstrations:* Projects in which an individual student or a group of students prepares and delivers a hands-on demonstration of some concept or creative application in a particular content area
- *Role-Plays:* Projects where a group of students act out a particular scene or situation to bring alive some aspect of a particular content area topic

In evaluating students' work in projects, it is easy to see how all three areas of cognitive, affective, and conative functioning are going to come into play in a major way. This is especially true for group projects, where interdependence and interaction are vital.

Homework

Homework is an excellent part of the students' work to include in your overall evaluation strategy. After all, it is done nearly every day of the school year, it is based on a continuation of classroom learning experiences, and it requires the student to complete a prescribed task independently. Given these three characteristics, it is no wonder that a great deal can be learned by evaluating students' homework. However, for homework to be a strategic and useful part of your classroom evaluation plans, there are certain guiding criteria that need to be followed:

Criterion 1:   Give clear and precise directions.

If you want your students to do their homework so that what they hand in reflects their true level of ability and understanding, the work task assigned must be clear and precise—*to them!* If the directions are not clear, chances are students will feel at a loss when they attempt to complete the work—if they make an attempt at all. Many times, students have difficulty completing work in the classroom, with you and with other sources of assistance readily available. Imagine how much more difficult it is for them as they try to complete work by themselves away from everyone. Obviously, this points up the tremendous benefit of having parents who take the time to help their children with their homework. Sadly, you cannot count on this benefit being available to all children. The directions for doing homework should not be something you think of on the spot and rattle off in a few seconds. To do so could well render the resulting work useless as evaluative information.

Criterion 2:   Give homework that is a direct extension of what has been accomplished in class.

For reasons similar to those just discussed, homework should be a logical outgrowth of what the students worked on in class that day. Clear and precise directions for completing a task for which the students are not amply prepared will be of no value. If your students are asked to do work that was not covered or only marginally covered in class, only a few especially bright, field-independent learners will succeed. For most, it will be a road to failure. These children will develop a fear of and dislike for any homework, which will have significant negative implications for the rest of their school years.

Criterion 3:   Give homework that is at appropriate levels for learning.

This criterion is very similar to the previous one, but it is worth mentioning separately because of its importance. First, you do not want to ask students to attempt higher-level (i.e., conception or ideation) work if they are not ready for it. If they do not have a background on a particular topic, what is to be gained from reviewing their homework in which concepts needed to be understood or applied creatively? There will be little surprise when you find that half the class did not do the work, and the other half did it poorly. The only thing you will have learned is that you need to do a better job of building their background in that particular content area topic. That is valuable information, but, in the meantime, the students will have had an experience that erodes their confidence and their interest in doing homework.

Criterion 4:   Set up a workable system for reviewing and correcting homework.

You simply will not be able to review thoroughly and correct every piece of homework. It is a physical impossibility. You also do not want to go to the other extreme of not looking at any homework and just wind up placing a check on it if the page appears somewhat completed. To figure out exactly what you can do in a way that is both practical and informative about your students' progress takes time and experience. In addition to your own experience and thinking, the advice of your fellow teachers will be of great help here. Your attempts in this area will point up the value of giving homework assignments that are not too long. First, overly long assignments will discourage students. Second, such assignments are really unnecessary, as you only need to have students do a focused and reasonable amount of work to derive the practice and reinforcement they need. Third, you will have given yourself so much work to look at that there will be a strong tendency to resort to the "check-it-off" mode of correction.

Criterion 5:   Provide immediate feedback on corrected homework.

This criterion is predicated on Criterion 4 being met. The goal of evaluation is to determine the value of the students' and your efforts so that continuous improvement can be made. This noble goal should not be abandoned when it comes to homework. Therefore, as part of your workable routine for reviewing and correcting homework, there should be provisions for going over the work with the students either collectively, individually, or some combination of both ways. Some teachers establish a routine of reviewing homework as part of the daily schedule. Others rely more on writing comments on the homework that they then hand back. Yet others have their students maintain homework notebooks that become the subject of a mini-conference between the teacher and individual students.

If you follow these five criteria, you will have the basis for making homework not only an integral part of your grading system but also a factor in your judgments about how your students are doing and what their instructional needs are.

Reports

Students' reports as part of your evaluation plan hold a unique place. In one sense, projects can be looked at as reports that are presented; the pure book report or research report that is to be handed in, however, involves much greater skill in terms of writing and organization. Reports also require greater attention as to how students express themselves. In the written report, all ideas, insights, conclusions, feelings, and understandings have to be conveyed in a clear, organized fashion—all through the written word. In making an oral presentation, the use of language can be less precise, as there is more flexibility for conveying the message in an oral and live medium, especially if visuals and manipulatives are included.

Perhaps the most valuable information you can gain about your students from their work in completing reports is in the area of study skills. All of their study skills (as described in Chapter 2) will be required. The students will need to do some research, organize notes, draft outlines, structure their thoughts, and persevere in a disciplined way until the final product is completed. There are two phases to the writing of a report that can provide you with insights into how your students function: (1) observation and conferencing as the report is being planned and written and (2) reading the completed report.

Portfolio Assessment

Portfolio assessment is fast becoming the most preferred choice of alternative assessment methods at all levels of education. It has been called "the most significant trend in education today" (Teacher Created Materials, Inc., Workshop, 1994, San Diego). Teacher education programs are requiring candidates to prepare portfolios to exit credential programs and to use portfolios to represent themselves to prospective employers. Many university professors prepare portfolios as part of yearly retention/ promotion procedures. Elementary teachers are now discovering the many advantages of using portfolios to evaluate student growth and to inform instruction.

To guide the discussion of this significant assessment process, four questions relevant to the use of portfolios in the elementary school classroom will be considered:

1. What are portfolios?
2. What are the advantages of portfolio assessment over traditional assessment methods?
3. What are the components/characteristics of portfolio assessment?
4. How can portfolios be used by a new teacher?

What Are Portfolios?

Portfolios are collections of students' work obtained over a period of time for the purpose of measuring student progress. They can be used for any content area of the curriculum and they can contain many different kinds of samples of student work such as written work (letters, reports, plays, essays, poems, math papers) audio tapes, video tapes, projects, artwork, and so on.

> *A portfolio is a purposeful collection of student work that exhibits the students' efforts, purposes, and achievements in one or more areas over time. The collection must include student participation in selecting contents, deciding criteria for selecting (content) and judging merit, and clear evidence of student reflection, along with reflections and judgments by the teacher. (Teacher Created Materials, Inc., Workshop, 1994, San Diego)*

What Are the Advantages of Portfolio Assessment over Traditional Assessment Methods?

Today's classrooms are characterized by the variety of meaningful learning tasks and activities that students engage in, both on an individual basis and collaboratively. Students are involved in social and scientific inquiry in which they confront real problems of the school or community. Through prescribed methods, the students search for solutions to those problems—they do experiments, present oral reports, write letters to political representatives to express concerns, argue for or against controversial issues, read and express opinions; in other words, they engage in authentic learning activities. Reading and writing skills are more frequently taught in the context of these kinds of meaningful learning experiences rather than in isolation as discrete skills (as they were in the past).

Standardized tests do not adequately measure the abilities and skills of students as they engage in processes that lead to final products as a part of a complete learning experience. Specifically, standardized tests tend to measure discrete skills. For example, through a series of multiple-choice questions, a student may show knowledge of grammar and syntax, but this is no measure of his or her ability to actually write an essay or a story. Although the nature of learning tasks has evolved and changed radically over the past few decades, evaluation procedures and the means of reporting how students are doing have remained unchanged.

Portfolio assessment is a means of evaluation that is more in accordance with what students are doing in today's classrooms. Some of the advantages of portfolio assessment are as follows:

1. Students participate more directly in the evaluation of their work and progress; thus, they feel more in control of their own learning. After an initial evaluation, the teacher and student sit together to discuss where the student is, compared to the standard, and where the student should go from that point. The teacher helps the student set his or her own learning goals. The students learn to evaluate their work according to standard criteria and then to set their own goals, taking more and more responsibility for their own learning. Students also learn to observe *how* they learn and they think and they begin to engage in metacognition. Traditional evaluation procedures (e.g., tests) do not involve students in a process of understanding and determining their own cognitive growth.

2. Portfolio assessment relates directly to what is going on in the classroom. For assessment to be fair and accurate, it must reflect the nature and learning characteristics of the students and the kinds of skills and abilities and content that the students are learning. Standardized tests do not usually match the school curriculum and thus do not measure what students have been doing in their daily learning activities. Portfolios, on the other hand, are made up of work that is produced in the day-to-day classroom activities. Thus, it is a fair and accurate measure of the learning that the student has been engaged in through his or her classroom activities.

3. Portfolio assessment informs instruction. The teacher and student work together and set learning goals for the student. The teacher then gives the student individual instruction and small-group instruction in accordance with those learning goals. Thus, the instruction is informed by the evaluation procedure that indicated the areas in which the student did not meet standard criteria. This, then, helps the teacher to teach directly to the needs of the students. This kind of assessment is of great benefit to the students' learning.

> *I realized early in my career that students experienced optimal learning when I allowed my assessment methodology to shape my teaching. In doing this, assessment provided information that was directly useful in forming decisions about teaching and learning for my students. For assessment to provide this type of information it has to be a process in nature that takes advantage of both subjective and objective evaluation. This is best achieved when the students are examined in a variety of contexts as well as by determining not only what a child has learned but how a child is learning. (Wooton in DeFina, 1992)*

4. Portfolio assessment provides a picture of how a student is progressing over time, whereas standardized testing provides a snapshot of a single performance at one particular moment.

5. In portfolio assessment, students do not compete against other students and are not measured against the performance of others. Each student measures his or her growth against where he or she stood at the initial evaluation. Thus, students compete only with themselves.

6. Portfolio assessment provides the ideal circumstances in which the teacher can individualize instruction for each student, so that instruction is geared to meet the individual needs and levels of the students. Because of the conference, individual instruction, and small-group instruction, the needs of individual students are met.

7. The portfolio assessment process pulls parents more directly into their child's learning by inviting their input into the discussion of the student's progress. It also invites them to contribute to the portfolio in the form of written comments. This participation enables parents truly to become partners with the teacher and the student to further the student's learning.

Figure 15–5 provides a comparison of portfolio assessment to standardized testing in a summarized form. Portfolio assessment is a process that offers many advantages over traditional evaluation procedures. The following discussion will focus on the components of portfolio assessment and how a new teacher would go about initiating this type of evaluation.

What Are the Components/Characteristics of Portfolio Assessment?

Component parts and procedures of portfolio assessment can vary quite a bit, depending on how the teacher decides to set it up. There are, however, some basic parts and procedures that should be included in any type of portfolio assessment. In order to provide an example of a workable portfolio, it is helpful to examine the components and procedures in terms of a content or subject area. In this case, the authors have chosen to describe a writing portfolio. Portfolio assessment is not a linear process; rather, it is a cyclical process and various procedures may occur several times during the cycle or at different stages in the cycle. The following linear listing of component parts and procedures must be viewed with this in mind.

Introduce the Portfolio Concept to Students/Parents

To introduce the portfolio to students, explain the purpose of portfolios and how students will be using them in an age-appropriate manner. Discuss with the students what kinds of work they may choose to put into their portfolios. In the case of a writing portfolio, this could include letters, stories, essays, poems, journal writing, interviews, position statements, research papers, autobiographies, reflections, and so on. All students do not have to select the same things; there is room for individuality here. However, each student must make a commitment as to what will be in his or her portfolio.

FIGURE 15–5   Comparison of Portfolio Assessment to Standardized Testing

Portfolio Assessment	*Standardized Testing*
• Occurs in the child's natural environment	• Is an unnatural event
• Provides an opportunity for student to demonstrate his/her strengths as well as weaknesses	• Provides a summary of child's failures on certain tasks
• Gives hands-on information to the teacher on the spot	• Provides little diagnostic information
• Allows the child, parent, teacher, staff to evaluate the child's strengths and weaknesses	• Provides ranking information
• Is ongoing, providing multiple opportunities for observation and assessment	• Is a one-time "snapshot" of a student's abilities on a particular task
• Assesses realistic and meaningful daily literacy tasks	• Assesses artificial tasks, which may not be meaningful to the child
• Invites the child to be reflective (metacognitive) about his/her work and knowledge	• Asks child to provide a singular desired response
• Invites the parent to be reflective of child's work and knowledge	• Provides parent with essentially meaningless and often frightening numerical data
• Encourages teacher-student conferencing	• Forces teacher-andministration conferences
• Informs instruction and curriculm; places child at center of the educational process	• Reinforces idea that the curriculum is the center of the educational process

Source: From *Portfolio Assessment: Getting Started* by Allan A. De Fina. Copyright © 1992 by Allan A. De Fina. Reproduced by permission of Scholastic Inc.

The teacher can even have contracts available to ensure that it is clear what types of work samples each student will be placing in the portfolio.

The teacher must decide in what kind of container students will store their collected works (e.g., a hardbound binder, an accordion file, a box) and where these will be kept in the classroom. Students need easy access to their portfolios, so they should be housed in a convenient place where there is enough space for a table or two so students can sit to work on their portfolios. Scheduling and behavior expectations for portfolio use should be explained to students. As a final part of the introduction, students could decorate and label their individual portfolios.

To introduce the portfolio concept to parents, the teacher should send home a letter, again explaining the purpose and advantages of portfolio assessment *and* describing parent participation and input into the process.

Select Criteria and Use Checklists

The first step in deciding on criteria is to decide on specific purposes of the portfolio use in the classroom. For example, in the case of the writing portfolio, the purposes could include the following:

1. To enable students to improve in their overall ability to write, including improving their use of writing conventions, ability to write for different purposes, ability to organize their thoughts, and ability to write in an interesting or engaging style
2. To provide students with the means and ability to evaluate their own work
3. To enable the teacher and each student to make collaborative decisions regarding learning goals for the student
4. To provide a means for parent participation in the child's growth and progress
5. To give students ownership of their own work and responsibility for their own learning

Once these purposes have been decided, the teacher must then decide on the criteria that will be used to evaluate student work. This decision will probably be affected by outside factors, as well as the teacher's own thoughts and ideas. For example, the district or school may already have criteria or checklists developed for portfolio evaluation that fit in with the existing grading and report card system. If this is not the case, the teacher can turn to district objectives for content area and grade level, and he or she can also review textbooks and other resources for the appropriate content area and grade level.

The criteria or checklists that are to be used to evaluate student work are extremely important; they are the key to student self-evaluation and goal setting. They also provide the teacher with specific knowledge of the strengths and weaknesses of each student in the content area. This information enables the teacher to design meaningful instruction and to report on student progress and assign grades if necessary.

It is important that the teacher take the time to teach the use of the criteria or checklists to the students, to ensure that they are able to evaluate their own work. This may not happen all at once, but must be taught through direct lessons and demonstration and during the student/teacher conferences. Figure 15–6 is an example of a checklist for essay writing.

The use of evaluative criteria and checklists is what makes portfolio assessment more than just a collection of student papers. It actually provides the vehicle for real student progress and authentic student participation in and responsibility for his or her own learning.

Student/Teacher Conferences

The initial student/teacher conference is held after the student has produced enough work from which he or she can choose samples to be included in the portfolio. (Beforehand, you should establish how often students will make entries in their portfolios over a specific period of time, such as a grading quarter.) In the conference, the teacher helps the student go through the established criteria or checklist to evaluate the strengths and weaknesses of his or her work. Together, the student and teacher decide on several specific goals the student will work to achieve related to their joint evaluation. Both the

FIGURE 15–6   Checklist for Essay Writing

Student _____

Essay Title _____

  1. The essay focuses on a particular subject.

     Range Score: 0 > 10 points.   Points: _____

  2. The essay has appropriate beginning, middle, and ending sections.

     Range Score: 0 > 10 points.   Points: _____

  3. The sequence of events is logical.

     Range Score: 0 > 10 points.   Points: _____

  4. The essay maintains its voice (first person or third person).

     Range Score: 0 > 10 points.   Points: _____

  5. Verb tense and agreement are appropriately used.

     Range Score: 0 > 10 points.   Points: _____

  6. The essay is written using complete sentences.

     Range Score: 0 > 10 points.   Points: _____

  7. The essay contains appropriate descriptive language.

     Range Score: 0 > 10 points.   Points: _____

  8. The essay is correctly punctuated.

     Range Score: 0 > 10 points.   Points: _____

  9. The essay uses rules of capitalization.

     Range Score: 0 > 10 points.   Points: _____

19. The essay has been proofread for spelling errors.

     Range Score: 0 > 10 points.   Points: _____

     Total points for the essay:

Source: From *Portfolio Assessment: Getting Started* by Allan A. De Fina. Copyright © 1992 by Allan A. De Fina. Reproduced by permission of Scholastic Inc.

student and the teacher should make notes on these decisions and include them in the portfolio, perhaps in a special section for goals. Any other relevant ideas, thoughts, or reflections by the student or teacher should be entered and dated. These can include comments about how the student is feeling about his or her skills and abilities, or observations and/or suggestions about the student's work habits, organization skills, and so on. These comments and goals statements will be discussed in the next conference.

    It is only through periodic conferences that growth and progress can be evaluated by the teacher and student together. Periodic conferences are very important to students because it is through this vehicle that the teacher helps students analyze progress and growth. The students should gradually be able to take an increasingly larger role in the conferences so that eventually they are presenting their materials to the teacher and the teacher's role becomes that of offering some guidance and reflective comments. Students need recognition and appreciation of the efforts they have made toward their goals, and teachers can provide this in the periodic conferences.

The teacher must decide how often and when he or she will confer with students. For example, in order to have a conference once a month with each student in a class of 30 students, the teacher will have to confer with 7 to 8 students a week. It would be wise for the teacher to devise a written schedule to be sure each child is met with in a specified period of time. The schedule should be posted so that the students know exactly when their conferences are coming up.

Individual and Small-Group Instruction
Based on the results of the portfolio evaluation conducted in the student/teacher conference, the teacher provides individual instruction and small-group instruction specifically to provide teaching to the goals determined in the conference. For example, if a student has set proper use of paragraphing for a goal, the teacher would provide individual instruction to the student in that skill and small-group instruction to several students at once who all may have chosen to work on that skill. In conjunction with this instruction, students again produce work from which they must select samples to go into their portfolios. It is important that the students themselves select the samples of their work to be included in the portfolios and that they make their selections using the criteria and/or checklists the teacher has introduced. This gives them practice in evaluating their own work, which is an important step in their assuming responsibility for their own learning. This time around, they will have more of an idea of how to evaluate their own work and select their best work.

Parent Participation
Several times a year, parents should also attend the conferences. Their comments and suggestions should then be included in the "comments" page of the portfolio. Parents often have insights about their children or can provide information that is helpful in the formulation of new goals. Once the students, teacher, and parents have observed and evaluated the progress made by the student, new goals can be set, and the assessment cycle begins again.

How Can Portfolios Be Used by a New Teacher?

Portfolio assessment involves a whole way of thinking about assessment and its relation to instruction; in other words, it is based on a philosophy of learning and evaluation that is grounded in authentic measures of student growth and involves the student in the evaluation process. In order for the new teacher to understand the philosophy of the portfolio assessment process, and to use this understanding to build such a process into the classroom teaching and learning structure, the following guidelines are suggested:

Guideline 1:   Inform yourself about portfolio assessment.

Read, read, read! Read all you can about the portfolio assessment process. *Portfolio Assessment: Getting Started* by Allan De Fina (Scholastic, 1992) and *Practical Portfolios* by Susan B. Mundell and Karen DeLario (Teacher Ideas Press, 1994) are particularly helpful for the new teacher or any teacher who has not had any experience with this assessment process but would like to begin using it in the classroom.

Another way to become informed is by attending workshops, seminars, and inservices on portfolio assessment. Many school districts have their own inservice training programs on portfolio assessment to promote its use in the district. Also, various commercial organizations offer seminars on portfolio assessment. For example, Teacher Created Materials gives seminars each year in various cities across the country.

Finally, talk with other teachers who are doing portfolio assessment. The greatest resource for teachers is other teachers. Seek out those teachers who do portfolio assessment in their classrooms; they will have many insights and suggestions based on their own experiences.

The portfolio assessment process is not a sequence of steps that can be followed like a recipe. Rather, it is a whole way of viewing assessment and its relation to instruction. As one teacher put it, "to 'do portfolios' means to look at instruction and time differently" (Grosvenor in Dalheim, 1993). According to Allan De Fina, "If portfolio assessment is going to live up to its promise, then it is not enough for teachers simply to mindlessly follow a set of instructions. They must understand the philosophical thinking behind portfolio use" (De Fina, 1992). It is for this reason that the authors strongly urge anyone interested in using portfolio assessment to study, read, and investigate before implementing the procedure in the classroom.

Guideline 2:   Begin simply; choose one content area in which to use portfolio assessment.

Do not be overly ambitious in the beginning; portfolio assessment is a complex process with many components and different possible procedures. Begin slowly by choosing one content area in which to use it. Remember, this first time everything will be new, and new procedures take extra time to think through and set up properly.

Guideline 3:   Make thorough preparations before implementation.

Preparation involves making decisions, organizing materials and schedules, and communicating with all potential participants in the process.

Making Decisions.   Many decisions must be made before the process begins. These include:

- In which content area will portfolio assessment be done?
- How will the purposes and procedures of portfolio assessment be communicated to students and parents?
- How and where will the portfolios be housed?
- How often will students have access to their portfolios?

- Who will have access to the portfolios besides the owners?
- How often will students make entries into their portfolios?
- When and how often will there be conferences?
- What criteria and/or checklists will be used to evaluate student work?
- How and to what extent will parents be involved?
- How will the portfolio assessment be translated into grades for report cards, if necessary?

Organizing Materials.   Materials that need to be procured include:

- Each student must have a container in which to house his or her works, such as a three-ring binder, accordion file, or hanging file box.
- Various kinds of forms will be used to accommodate various kinds of entries into the portfolios such as visitor comment pages, self-reflection pages, evaluation/goals pages, attitude surveys, and so on. (Some examples of these kinds of form pages are included in the next few pages.)
- Evaluation criteria and checklists for the specific learning tasks and skills that will be evaluated must be compiled. (Some examples of evaluation criteria and checklists for a writing portfolio are provided in the next few pages.)

Communicating with All Potential Participants.   The teacher must communicate with the following:

- The students must understand *why* they will be doing portfolios and *how portfolios will benefit* the students.
- The parents must understand the purposes and advantages of portfolio assessment and the extent and nature of parent involvement.
- Other possible contributors to an individual's portfolio could be the school principal, assistant principal, other teachers, other students, and resource personnel.

   Guideline 4:   Refine the process.

It is important that the teacher reflect on components and procedures he or she uses in the portfolio process as it is happening. A record of notes and comments should be kept in an organized fashion so that the teacher can refer to these with the purpose of honing and refining the process, for the current year and the following year. For example, if the teacher notes that a particular format for conferences did not work as anticipated, this could be noted with comments regarding how it might have worked better. Such information should be incorporated into the next round of conferences.

Examples of Evaluative Criteria, Checklists, and Forms
Figures 15–7 through 15–14 are examples of ways to solicit information, keep records, and provide evaluative criteria for students and the teacher. These examples have been gathered from various sources and are intended to show how surveys, forms, and checklists could be set up for a writing portfolio. It is likely that you will want to use modifications to meet the needs of particular situations.   *(text continues on page 345)*

FIGURE 15–7 **Evaluative Criteria for a Writing Portfolio, Upper Grades**

Inventory of Writing Skills
Upper Grades

Name _____ Date _____

The Writing Process	Date/Grade:								
Uses the process in a meaningful way									
Integrates writing in his/her life									
Pre-writing Strategies									
Uses lists									
Uses brainstorming									
Uses rehearsal skills (drawing, talking, role-playing, etc.)									
Uses clustering									
Uses organization strategies (outlining, mapping, etc.)									
Takes notes									
Writing									
Accesses prior knowledge									
Writes to communicate									
Is appropriate to audience, purpose									
Revising									
Initiates revision									
Adds or deletes information									
Considers word choices									
Revises for quality and clarity									
Editing									
Is concerned about correctness									
Uses a variety of resources									
Publishing									
Uses a variety of techniques									
Spelling									
Uses resources to assist in spelling									
Identifies own spelling errors									
Conventions									
Punctuation									
Uses end punctuation									
Uses commas									
Uses quotation marks									
Capitalization									
Uses proper capitalization									
Grammar									
Knows subject/verb agreement									
Knows verb tense agreement									
Composition									
Includes beginning/middle/end in stories									
Uses complete sentences									
Paragraphs unified/coherent/developed									
Uses elements of story (plot, setting, characters, etc.)									
Uses transition words									
Uses figures of speech									
Writes in many genres									

Source: Taken from *Portfolios and Other Alternative Assessments.* Published by Teacher Created Materials, Inc., © 1993. Reproduced by permission.

FIGURE 15–8   Evaluative Criteria for a Writing Portfolio, Lower Grades

Inventory of Writing Skills
Primary Grades

Name _____   Date _____

The Writing Process Date/Grade:								
Symbolic Representation								
Uses oral language								
Uses pictures								
Uses dictation								
Spelling								
Uses scribble writing								
Uses random letters								
Uses initial consonant spelling								
Uses initial/final consonant spelling								
Uses initial, interior, and final consonant spelling								
Uses vowel (may be wrong vowel)								
Uses conventional spelling of high frequency words								
Uses conventional spelling in parts of the story								
Uses resources to assist in spelling								
Identifies spelling errors								
Conventions								
Prints scribble or letters horizontally across the page								
Leaves space between words								
Punctuation								
Uses "and" as punctuation placeholder								
Uses periods at end of thoughts								
Uses question marks for expression								
Uses exclamation marks for expression								
Uses commas for expression								
Uses quotation marks								
Capitalization								
Puts capitals at beginning of sentences								
Uses capitals for proper nouns								
Grammar								
Knows subject/verb agreement								
Composition								
Writes 1-5 sentence stories								
Writes 6-10 sentence stories								
Writes 11-20 sentence stories								
Story has beginning/middle/end								
Uses dialogue								
Writes in several genres								

Source: Taken from *Portfolios and Other Alternative Assessments.* Published by Teacher Created Materials, Inc., © 1993. Reproduced by permission.

FIGURE 15–9   Checklist for Lower-Grade Writing Portfolio

**Student-Teacher Conferencing Checklist
(Writing Guidelines for Young Children)**

Student's Name _____ Date _____ Grade _____

When writing in my journal, I can do the following:

_____   I wrote about something I am interested in.

_____   I wrote a story about real people, places, and things.

_____   I wrote a make-believe story.

_____   I started at the top of the page.

_____   I wrote from left to right.

_____   I drew pictures to go along with my story.

_____   I used both capital letters and small letters.

_____   I left spaces between all of the words.

_____   I put a period or an exclamation mark at the end of every sentence.

_____   I put a question mark at the end of each question.

_____   I started each sentence with a capital letter.

_____   I made the people in my story talk.

_____   I put quotation marks around the words of the people in my story.

_____   I tried to use some new words in my story.

Other things I did when I wrote my story are

_____

_____

_____

_____

_____

Source: From *Portfolio Assessment: Getting Started* by Allan A. De Fina. Copyright © 1992 by Allan A. De Fina. Reproduced by permission of Scholastic Inc.

FIGURE 15–10   Portfolio Conference Record: Evaluation and Setting Goals

Conference Record for _____ *(Student Name)*			
Subject of Conference: _____			

Date	Observations	Areas of Positive Growth	Needs/Goal Setting

Source: Taken from *Portfolios and Other Alternative Assessments.* Published by Teacher Created Materials, Inc., © 1993. Reproduced by permission.

FIGURE 15–11   Portfolio Conference Record: Evaluation and Setting Goals

Name of Student _____

Teacher's Name _____

Date of this report _____

Strengths	Teacher's Comments:	Student's Comments:
Should Work On	**Teacher's Comments:**	**Student's Comments:**

Source: Excerpt from *Portfolios and Performance Assessment: Helping Students Evaluate Their Progress as Readers and Writers* by Roger Farr and Bruce Tone, copyright © 1994 by Harcourt Brace & Company, reprinted by permission of the publisher.

FIGURE 15–12   Writing Attitude Survey Form

Name _____ Date _____

1. Name some different types of writing a person may do. _____

_____

_____

2. Why should you learn to write? _____

_____

_____

3. Do you consider yourself to be a writer? _____ Explain your answer. _____

_____

_____

4. Do you like to write? _____ Why or why not? _____

_____

_____

5. What are some strategies you use to help you write? _____

_____

_____

6. Where do you get your ideas for writing? _____

_____

_____

7. How does reading help you to become a better writter? _____

_____

_____

8. What makes a piece of writing "good"? _____

_____

_____

Source: From *Practical Portfolios* by Susan B. Mundell and Karen DeLario. © 1994. Teacher Ideas Press, P.O. Box 6633, Englewood, CO 80155-6633. Reprinted by permission.

FIGURE 15–13   Student Self-Reflection Form for Writing

Name _____ Date _____

1. How have your opinions about writing changed since your first survey?

   a. _____

   _____

   b. _____

   _____

2. Do you think these changes are positive changes? Why or why not?

   _____

   _____

   _____

3. Tell something new you have learned in writing.

   _____

   _____

   _____

   _____

4. Complete the following statements: From my Creative Writing Checklist, I can tell I have improved on

   _____

   _____

   _____

5. Now I would like to concentrate on improving

   _____

   _____

   _____

   _____

Source: From *Practical Portfolios* by Susan B. Mundell and Karen DeLario. © 1994. Teacher Ideas Press, P.O. Box 6633, Englewood, CO 80155-6633. Reprinted by permission.

FIGURE 15–14   Visitor Comment Page

It is very important that all visitors, including the student, record their visits to the portfolio. This allows a running record of how often and for what purpose the portfolio is used. The work involved in creating and maintaining this portfolio will be well justified by frequent visits from many people, including teachers, students, parents, and administrators.

Date	Name	Purpose	Visitor Comments

Source: From *Practical Portfolios* by Susan B. Mundell and Karen DeLario. © 1994. Teacher Ideas Press, P.O. Box 6633, Englewood, CO 80155-6633. Reprinted by permission.

Observation of Class Work

An informal way to gain valuable information about students is by merely observing them as they are engaged in class work. For purposes of this discussion, *class work* is defined as any cognitive, affective, or conative action done by the students as they function in the classroom. The information a teacher gains through observation is often more revealing and significant in terms of learning about students' skills, talents, abilities, needs, and interests than are the more formal assessments such as tests, written assignments, and even portfolios. The information gained from observation can reveal hidden talents and abilities of children as well as help the teacher find unique ways to motivate individual students.

The discussion of observation of class work will consider the following three questions:

1. What kinds of things should be observed?

2. How can observations be noted and organized?

3. How can the information gained through observations be used to increase student growth?

What Kinds of Things Should Be Observed?

Observing just about everything can be of value. However, this task can be made more manageable by categorizing what is observed into three different types of behaviors: (1) cognitive behavior, (2) affective behavior, and (3) conative behavior.

Cognitive Behavior

Cognitive behavior refers to how children acquire knowledge (i.e., how they learn and remember facts, how they understand concepts, and how they apply what they know). In more general terms, it refers to how the mind works.

The human mind develops in an uneven fashion. As a child grows, he or she does not acquire mental capacities in a rigid sequence from basic to more complex abilities. It is possible for a child to function at what is considered a higher level of thinking before he or she masters all aspects of the related lower level of thinking. For example, a child may be able to construct an intricate story line for a creative writing assignment before mastering all the mechanics of writing. There was a time when this pattern was not generally recognized; teachers would only allow those students who showed mastery of language conventions to do creative writing. Yet, the child who is allowed to go ahead and write his or her story may find the mechanics of writing easier to learn in relation to his or her own work. Sometimes, the only way to discover this uneven functioning and use it to help a child grow cognitively is through the informal observations of the teacher.

Consider the case of Alex. Alex had a learning disability. He could not remember certain types of information; for example, he could not remember sound/symbol relationships in reading instruction. He could not, therefore, remember that the letter *G* is pronounced "ga" in a word such as *goat*. Alex also could not remember whole words, no matter how many times he was told what they were. Therefore, Alex could not read. He spent year after year in special education classes receiving repeated instruction in what he could not do, which was to sound out words or remember them by sight recognition.

One day, one of Alex's teachers noticed that although Alex could not remember facts, he did seem to be able to remember concepts. She specifically noticed that when she gave him the definition of a noun and then read him a sentence, he was then able to tell her which words in the sentence were nouns. The fact that Alex could learn and remember concepts meant that he could learn content-area knowledge. Yet, because he could not read, no one had thought to give him instruction in science, social studies, math, and language arts. By providing someone to read for Alex (classroom aides, other students, and the teacher when possible), he was able to learn all kinds of concepts. He could be examined in this knowledge by using modified testing procedures. By providing Alex with the support he needed (someone reading to him), it not only made various kinds of knowledge accessible to him, but it improved his self-image greatly. For the first time, Alex was successful in school.

Although Alex's case is extreme, the principle is the same for all children—and that is, children may possess cognitive abilities that cannot be measured by standardized tests or may not be detected through formal instruction. Sometimes, it takes a special key to open the door to these abilities, and that key may be something the teacher happens to notice in even a casual exchange with the child. Even though the authors provide a structure to the process of observing children in class work, the essential point is that the teacher must always be alert and watchful, because sometimes the tiniest observations lead to big breakthroughs.

Characteristics of cognitive functioning cover a wide range of intellectual behaviors such as remembering, describing, interpreting, applying, making inferences, predicting, memorizing, analyzing, synthesizing, and evaluating, to mention a few. Whenever the teacher notices a characteristic of a child's intellectual functioning that seems significant, it should be noted on the anecdotal records. For example, supposing the teacher notices that Jack has trouble identifying main ideas in the context of written material. Jack has just read a paragraph in his social studies text and he is unable to identify the main idea of the paragraph because he cannot distinguish it from supporting detail. All the information seems of equal value to him and he does not see the hierarchical relationship of the material. Since the teacher notices this in the middle of a lesson, he or she merely makes a quick notation in an anecdotal record book such as "Jack could not distinguish main idea from supporting detail in social studies text" and then dates the entry. At a later time, the teacher may review the anecdotal information with a view as to how the information can be used to identify where Jack is having difficulty and how he can be helped. In this particular case, the use of graphic organizers might help Jack understand the relationships of ideas in a text.

Another example is the case of Kerry. Her teacher noticed that she seemed to be able to grasp ideas and understand written material better when she read aloud. Having noticed this characteristic of Kerry's cognitive functioning several times in various circumstances and written it down, the teacher eventually made arrangements so that Kerry could read aloud softly during silent work periods or work with another student so she could voice concepts and ideas aloud. These arrangements did, in fact, improve Kerry's overall performance in academic tasks.

These are examples of observations of various kinds of cognitive functioning. It is impossible to enumerate all the areas and/or situations in which you might observe these behaviors in your own students. However, Figure 15–15 enumerates a few critical behaviors that are useful to observe.

Affective Behavior

The affective domain of learning is characterized by emotions, feelings, and attitudes that directly influence a child's ability to learn. For example, if a child has a negative attitude toward math (due to prior failure and humiliation), it will be difficult for that child to attend to a math lesson or to work on a math assignment.

Children who are under stress or who are in an anxious emotional state (for whatever reason) find it very difficult to attend to and achieve at academic tasks at school. For example, Linda was a first-grader who could not count or read numbers past the number 6. She was a very alert little girl who interacted with other children well and

FIGURE 15–15   Cognitive Behaviors to Observe

1. How does the student approach a mental task or an academic assignment (in terms of organization)?
2. How does the student respond to questions (haphazardly or in a logical manner)?
3. What kind of questions does the student pose?
4. Can the student repeat information heard or read in his or her own words?
5. How does the student apply information?
6. Does the student seem to rely on any kind of special support to enhance his or her own understanding (such as repeating information out loud)?
7. Does the student notice and attend to detail?
8. How does the student respond to instructions?
9. How does the student express his or her ideas?

who adored her teacher. Linda's teacher suspected that the child's learning difficulties were caused by some kind of emotional stress Linda was experiencing rather than by an inherent learning disability, because she had noted on many occasions that Linda seemed to crave her attention and affection. Looking over her anecdotal records, she saw that many of her comments about Linda were regarding the frequency and persistence with which Linda sought out her attention and approval. Upon further investigation, the teacher found out that Linda's parents were separated and that Linda had witnessed many violent scenes between them. Because Linda's home life continued to be unstable, the teacher tried to give her as much emotional support as possible by praising and encouraging her frequently.

As in the cognitive domain, it is impossible to enumerate all of the affective behaviors that teachers should note in their anecdotal records. However, several are listed in Figure 15–16.

Conative Behavior

Conative behavior involves a child's will or determination, which affects his or her perseverance, mental discipline, and concentration. Children vary significantly in their ability to concentrate and persevere on learning tasks. Some children just give up, even if only mildly frustrated, whereas others will continue to make effort despite many failures and great frustration.

The conative domain of functioning is important because when a person studies to learn new information or concepts, or when a person applies knowledge to new situations or struggles to solve a problem, there is a point when it all boils down to sustained

FIGURE 15–16   Affective Behaviors to Observe

1. How does the child interact with other children?
2. How does the child interact with adults?
3. What is the child's attitude toward academic subjects (confident, positive, fearful, negative)?
4. How does the child seem to feel about himself or herself?
5. Does the child have any special interests?

periods of mental work and concentration. Study and learning cannot be fun all the time, and it is often by the use of a person's will that he or she perseverses to put in the time and mental effort to accomplish a mental task. The same is with children who are required to memorize and learn many things in school. Once the will has seen the individual through a difficult mental task, there is a reward of immense satisfaction when understanding is finally achieved or a problem is finally solved. But one has to struggle through the tedious mental effort to experience this satisfaction. This is the role of will—it supports the cognitive by enabling the individual school child to persevere.

Will can be developed in children by helping them establish routines, gradually increasing their time on task, discussing the importance of perseverance and mental discipline, demonstrating its value, and encouraging efforts made by students in that direction. Therefore, when a teacher notices that many of his or her comments about an individual child seem to have to do with perseverance and mental effort or self-discipline, the teacher can begin to think about possible interventions that are geared to developing the child's will. Figure 15–17 notes behaviors the teacher may observe in the conative area of functioning.

How Can Observations Be Noted and Organized?

It cannot be predicted when or in what kind of classroom activity the teacher may observe student behavior that is significant and worthy of note. The teacher may be delivering instruction, directing a small-group activity, tutoring an individual, or otherwise be quite involved in classroom activities when he or she observes student behaviors that are of value. There must be an organized system of making notations that can be executed quickly and in some kind of organized way. The authors suggest that the teacher obtain a hard-cover three-ring binder and organize it as follows:

1. Make two major divisions in the binder—one for initial entries to be made immediately following the observation for any child in the class, and one for entries to be copied into later for each individual child in the class.
2. The first section will contain notation sheets for each of the three categories of behaviors described earlier: cognitive behaviors, affective behaviors, and conative behaviors. (Figures 15–18 through 15–20 are examples of how these whole-class notation sheets could be designed.) It should be mentioned here that the three types of student functioning—cognitive, affective, and conative—are interrelated, and

FIGURE 15–17   Conative Behaviors to Observe

1. Can the child work on a mental task (age appropriate) for a sustained period of time?
2. Can the child see a task through from beginning to end?
3. Can the child pay attention to various external stimuli (such as teacher lecturing) determining sustained focus on the stimuli?
4. Does the child make an effort to push himself or herself to reach a goal?
5. Does the child show determination in the face of difficulties?

FIGURE 15–18   Whole-Class Anecdotal Notation Sheet: Cognitive Behavior

Date	Student	Cognitive Behavior
10/18	Jerry W.	Jerry seemed to understand his math better when he worked with Donald
10/18	Carol S.	Carol asked very insightful questions in social studies
10/20	Larry T.	Larry wrote a very persuasive letter to our representative

FIGURE 15–19   Whole-Class Anecdotal Notation Sheet: Affective Behavior

Date	Student	Affective Behavior
2/13	Linda	Linda repeatedly brought her work to me to ask if it was "a good job"
2/13	Howie	Howie refused to even start a math assignment and started to cry when I encouraged him to do at least a few of the problems

FIGURE 15–20   Whole-Class Anecdotal Notation Sheet: Conative Behavior

Date	Student	Conative Behavior
3/1	Mary S.	Today, Mary announced that she was going to read "the whole silent reading period" with no interruptions — she accomplished her goal
3/1	Michael	Michael pushed himself to get through all 16 of today's math problems
3/2	Howie	Howie was able to force himself to do three problems — I think this is a matter of will — I know he can do this level work

there is not always such a clear division of the type of behavior being observed. For example, a student's behavior may seem to be influenced by strong negative feelings as well as a lack of will. In this case, record the behavior in the area that seems to be the stronger factor at work for the particular instance.

3. Keep an entry sheet for each individual student in the second half of the binder. Entries made during class time can be transferred to the individual student's record sheet during nonclass time when you have some quiet time not only to transfer the entries but also to reflect on accumulated comments on individual children. (Figure 15–21 is an example of an individual anecdotal record sheet.)

How Can the Information Gained through Observations Be Used to Increase Student Growth?

In order to make the fullest use of anecdotal records of classroom observations, the following guidelines are suggested:

FIGURE 15–21   Individual Student Anecdotal Record Sheet

RECORD SHEET OF JOHN N.

Date	Observed Behavior
3/10	John continually pops out of seat, very apologetic when reprimanded.
3/11	Although John has earnestly promised to stay in his seat, he continually gets up and walks around; he seems unable to control this behavior.
3/12	John continues to get up frequently; seems to need to move.

1. Record all three types of student behaviors (cognitive, affective, and conative).
2. Set aside time to review notations and transfer comments to individual student record sheets.
3. Reflect on an individual's recorded behaviors, think of possible solutions to problems, and try out various interventions.

Record All Three Types of Student Behaviors
Most teachers focus on the cognitive behaviors of their students, often to the exclusion of the affective and the conative domains. All three types of behaviors are important and contribute to the overall functioning of the individual. Cognitive growth is directly influenced by the nature and development of the affective and conative aspects of consciousness. These can enhance or impede cognitive development.

> *It seems important to note in this connection that the development of the intellectual faculties is conditioned upon the corresponding development of the sensibility and the will. The activity of the mind in knowing depends, among*

other things, on the acuteness and energy of the senses, the intensity of the emotions and desires, and the energy and constancy of the will. (White, 1886)

In order to further the intellectual growth of your students, you must understand each child as a whole, made up of three areas of consciousness (cognitive, affective, conative). Furthermore, you must understand how intellectual processes are being influenced by the emotions and the will (or lack of it). By observing children during class work and noting their emotional states, perseverance, and determination, you will gain insights into causes of difficulties children may be having in the cognitive realm. Other ways of evaluating students—such as tests, performance areas, and portfolios— provide measures almost exclusively of cognitive behaviors. It is through the direct observations of a student's functioning in all types of classroom activities that you will gain the insights into how the cognitive might be influenced by affective and conative factors. That is why observation of class work and anecdotal record keeping are so important. They provide a unique view of the child.

Set Aside Time to Review and Transfer Comments
Schedule a specific weekly time for yourself to attend to your anecdotal records. This way, you will keep up with what is happening with various students and you will be ready to use your observations to help students.

Reflect, Think, and Try
Reflect on each student's individual record sheet, noting repeated behaviors or behavior patterns. Think of possible solutions to problems that you note. Sometimes, by reviewing accumulated comments, you will see a pattern not previously noticed. Try various kinds of interventions. Think of yourself as a scientist, in that you are trying to solve problems you have detected in your observations. Try different things. If one thing does not work, try another. You may also be able to involve the student in coming up with solutions to his or her own difficulties. Once you have thought of a possible intervention, note it in your records, try it in class, and then note and record the results. Figure 15–22 shows an individual student record sheet in which the teacher has thought of an intervention, tried it, and recorded the results.

Observing children as they function in class, making anecdotal records, and reviewing those records provides the teacher with a valuable picture of the "whole" child and gives the teacher insights into how he or she can help students function effectively in the classroom. Observation of class work is an invaluable method of evaluating children and using the evaluation to further student progress and growth.

Using Observation Information to Further Student Growth
Through the observations you make, performance tasks you give, and portfolios of work that you set up, there will be no dearth of evaluation data for you to process. This chapter has discussed how you can use this information to better understand and help your students as well as increase the effectiveness of your own efforts. What remains is to know how to set up a grading system that intelligently and systematically utilizes the information generated and to set up your grade book accordingly (Chapter 16).

FIGURE 15–22   Individual Student Record Sheet with Intervention Strategy

RECORD SHEET OF JOHN N.

Date	Observed Behavior
3/15	*John out of seat every 10 minutes — wants to please but can't seem to control himself.*
3/17	*John still out of seat often even though he was interested in assignment.*
3/18	*Possible intervention strategy — set up a second desk for John across the room — tell him when he feels the irresistible urge to move, he can go to his "second" desk.*
3/19	*Strategy worked well — John went between his two desks and completed his work.*

Like it or not, grades are everyone's bottom line when it comes to the educational enterprise. Parents are keenly aware of the implications that high or low grades have on their children's future opportunities. Except for the very youngest ones, students are also aware of this fact. The goal of this chapter was to present evaluation as more than a limited look at cognitive functioning. Rather, it has been shown that the entire being of the student must be regarded if real evaluation is to be carried out. There is no need to give in to the prevailing bottom-line mentality in designing and carrying out your classroom evaluation plan. There is also no reason to allow this mentality to permeate your classroom grading system. Of course, academic grades still have to be given and the school's report cards need to be filled out. By using the information you obtain by evaluating cognitive, affective, and conative functioning, you are in a solid position to complete both of those required tasks.

Chapter 16

Maintaining and Using Evaluation Information

Numerous ideas were presented in Chapter 15 about understanding and helping your students through various means of evaluation. This chapter looks at your need to set up a grading system and a grade book so that evaluation information can be productively utilized.

Setting Up Your Classroom Grading System

You should take several steps prior to setting up your classroom grading system, as follows:

- Ask about your school's policy on grading, including the type of report card used.
- Speak with fellow teachers, especially those teaching at your grade level, for advice.
- Consider the nature and design of your instructional program and what will be emphasized.
- Consider the areas and ways you plan to evaluate student ability, progress, and achievement.

By carrying out these steps, you will have given yourself the background you need to begin to delineate the areas of student work and functioning that will be graded. Figure 16–1 lists areas for grading according to the three areas of human consciousness—cognitive, affective, and conative—all in relation to typical areas to be graded on a report card.

Notice that the various ways of evaluating cognitive functioning (presented in Chapter 16) form a solid basis for giving academic grades. Similarly, your evaluation of affective and conative functioning provides the basis for giving work-habit grades. Add

FIGURE 16–1   Areas for Grading

Academic Grades	***Cognitive Functioning***
	• Tests and Quizzes • Classwork • Homework • Projects • Reports • Portfolios
Work-Habit Grades	***Affective Functioning***
	• Effort in Work • Working with Others
	Conative Functioning
	• Completion of Work Assigned • Staying on Task • Listening
Citizenship Grades	***Citizenship***
	• Respects Others • Follows School and Class Rules • Demonstrates Self-Control

to this the area of citizenship grades, which can easily be derived from the records you have kept as part of your classroom management plan, and you have a complete, fair, and informative picture of your students' lives in your classroom. This is a picture that can be readily transferred to almost any report card. Only one critical step remains before your classroom grading system is complete: assigning a relative weight to the various ways of evaluating cognitive functioning for assigning academic grades. For example, in thinking through this important decision, you may realize that over the course of a typical grading period, the students will be given approximately 12 hours of language arts homework. During that same six-week span, they will also be asked to write one book report, which will require approximately 5 hours of work. It could well seem reasonable to you, then, that homework should be a somewhat larger part of the language arts grade than the book report. This is just one example of the line of thinking you might take. Following are several factors to consider in making this decision about weighing different evaluation tasks for the purpose of assigning report card grades:

- Consider class time and student time spent on different kinds of work.
- Consider the learning level involved in completing certain kinds of work (i.e., the difficulty of mental effort required, as, say, in a creative science project demonstration).
- Consider the group dynamic involved in completing projects (i.e., the combination of mental effort and social skills required).

- Consider the importance of work directly related to various goals and objectives as spelled out in your instructional plans and as stated by your school and district.
- Consider the scope of different evaluation tasks (i.e., a unit test, a small spelling test, or an encyclopedia research activity in class).

Once the decision has been made, it becomes a central part of your classroom program and, as such, it needs to be communicated clearly to your students and their parents at the very beginning of the school year.

Setting Up Your Grade Book

Knowing what things you need to look at, how you will go about looking at them, and the relative weight they are to be given places you in an excellent position to set up your grade book. This task should not be taken for granted. If you fail to start the school year with a clear, organized approach to keeping track of grades, you can very quickly lose control of all the evaluation information that will be generated every day. As a result, your stress level will increase, your ongoing picture of student progress will be hazy, and objectivity and fairness in grading will be diminished.

Considering the number of evaluation tasks students will be graded on in each of the content areas, the most organized and manageable way to record grades is to maintain a separate ongoing evaluation/grading folder for each content area where all evaluative grades are placed on a regular basis. Your single, official grade book can then be used to record the cumulative grades from each content area as well as regular information concerning citizenship, general work habits, and attendance. To try to keep all your grading information in one terribly congested master grade book will be a nightmare. You will spend untold hours trying to make heads or tails of the information at report card time. If you must use one master grade book, then a workable variation on the concept of separate content grading folders can be achieved by dividing the grade book into *ongoing* and *cumulative* sections. Further divide the *ongoing* section into content areas. Regardless of which of the two methods you choose, a typical page for both the ongoing and cumulative grades will look very much like the ones shown in Figure 16–2 (ongoing evaluation information) and Figure 16–3 (cumulative evaluation information).

With accurate and complete records maintained in the ways described here, you accomplish two critical tasks: (1) creation of a formative and summative evaluation profile of each student and for the class, in general, and (2) a thorough record to use for conferences with individual students, parents, fellow teachers, and school administrators.

One important final word on evaluation is necessary: It should be recognized that evaluation *is* instruction. The different ways you evaluate students are actually instructional experiences for them. These experiences can inhibit and demoralize them, or they can open up new possibilities of continuing improvement and growth. If you carry out an evaluation system where you consider the whole child by looking at the areas of cognitive, affective, and conative functioning, then students will feel supported, encouraged, and increasingly confident as they complete the different evaluation tasks.

FIGURE 16–2 Ongoing Evaluation Information

SECOND QUARTER

PERIOD _____ SEMESTER, 19 _____

SUBJECT Social Studies

INDICATE CALENDAR DATE

GRADE

The Blank Columns at the Right May Be Used to Indicate Assignments

Identification No. and/or Name ▶

Text Book No.

	1st WEEK					2nd WEEK					3rd WEEK					4th WEEK					5th WEEK				
	M	T	W	T	F	M	T	W	T	F	M	T	W	T	F	M	T	W	T	F	M	T	W	T	F
	HW #1		HW #2		Quiz	HW #3	HW #4	HW #5			HW #6		Grp. Proj.			HW #7		Grp. Proj.				Portfolio		TEST	

1
2
3
4
5
6
7
8
9
10
11
12
13
14
15
16
17
18

FIGURE 16–3 Cumulative Evaluation Information

SECOND QUARTER

PERIOD _____ SEMESTER, 19 _____

SUBJECT	*Social Studies*																		
INDICATE CALENDAR DATE																			
GRADE																			

		ACADEMIC							WORK HABITS							CITIZENSHIP		
Identification No. and/or Name ►	*Tests*	*Quizzes*	*HW Cls. Wrk.*	*Reports*	*Grp. Proj.*	*Ind. Proj.*	*Portfolio*	*Effort*	*w/ Others*	*On Task*				*Respect*	*Rules*	*Self-Control*
1																	
2																	
3																	
4																	
5																	
6																	
7																	
8																	
9																	
10																	
11																	
12																	
13																	
14																	
15																	
16																	
17																	
18																	

References for Section V

Dalheim, M. (Ed.). (1993). *Student portfolios.* Washington, DC: National Education Association.

De Fina, A. A. (1992). *Portfolio assessment: Getting started.* New York: Scholastic Professional Books.

Farr, R., & Tone, B. (1994). *Portfolio and performance assessment.* Fort Worth, TX: Harcourt Brace.

Jasmine, J. (1993). *Portfolios and other alternative assessments.* Huntington Beach, CA: Teacher Created Materials, Inc.

Mundell, S. B., & DeLario, K. (1994). *Practical portfolios.* Englewood, CO: Teacher Ideas Press.

Richardson, J. S., & Morgan, R. F. (1990). *Reading to learn in the content areas.* Belmont, CA: Wadsworth.

White, E. E. (1886). *The elements of pedagogy.* New York: American Book Company.

Resource Bank of Instructional Activities

As experienced teachers and supervisors of teachers, the authors have found that one thing teachers are always in need of are effective activities to achieve their instructional purposes. In other words, while planning, most teachers determine fairly rapidly and easily *what* they want their students to learn, but have more difficulty deciding *how* the students will achieve the particular learning the teachers have in mind. The *how* is usually done through instructional activities. The activities presented here have been adapted from the Richardson and Morgan text, *Reading to Learn in the Content Areas*, by teachers and student teachers in the San Diego County area for use in classroom instruction. Although they are presented in the framework of the PAR, they can be used in other types of planning models as well, both in block-type approaches and in daily lesson planning. Once the teacher is clear on his or her instructional objective, it also becomes clear which of the activities will be useful in achieving that objective.

As stated earlier, each phase of the PAR has an instructional purpose; the *P* (preparation) phase is meant to determine and build background, the *A* (assistance) phase is meant to give students a purpose to read and to assist their comprehension of written material, and the *R* (reflection) phase is meant to cause students to reflect on what they have read. Therefore, if a teacher is interested in finding an activity to prepare his or her students for new reading material—for example, whether or not he or she is using the PAR model— the activities presented in the *P* phase will be useful to that teacher.

Although the activities in this section are presented as being either *P*, *A*, or *R* activities, most of them, with slight modification, can be used at *any* phase of the PAR. It is up to the teacher to modify the activities to suit his or her instructional purposes.

Because of the universality of the instructional purposes of the PAR (in most instructional sequences, it is desirable to prepare the students for the learning, to assist their comprehension, and to have them reflect), the practitioner will find this a very useful section—a resource bank from which to draw for instructional activities. It is the authors' hope that teachers and student teachers will use this section as a resource and that they will refer to the many activities and examples presented here as they are actually planning instructional sequences for their classrooms.

In the discussion of these activities, focus will be on the following:

1. A description of the activity
2. Instructions on how to construct the activity
3. An example of the activity constructed by elementary school teachers

To begin, here are some activities that can be used in the *P* (preparation) phase of the PAR.

Instructional Activities for Preparation

The preparation phase of the PAR has two instructional purposes: to *determine* background and to *build* background. Discussion will first focus on activities that can be used to determine the students' backgrounds for various topics of instruction.

Activities for Determining Background

The Maze
Description.   The Maze is an activity in which certain words are deleted from a passage of the text material to be read by the students. In place of the deleted words are three words (the deleted or correct word among them) from which students must select what they think is the correct word. In selecting which words to replace by three choices, the teacher may follow a repeating pattern, such as every fifth word, or choose key meaning words for replacement. Figure A–1 shows a maze that was developed for a third-grade class regarding California deserts.

Instructions for Creating a Maze.   Follow this sequence of steps to create a maze:

1. Select a representative passage from the material students will be reading.
2. Delete words at regular intervals, either by using a pattern (every fifth or tenth word) or by choosing key meaning words.
3. In place of the deleted word, offer the students three choices: (a) the correct word (which is the deleted word), (b) a grammatically correct but semantically incorrect word, (c) a word that is neither grammatically nor semantically correct in the sentence.
4. Administer the Maze to students before starting a unit of study. Check responses to determine how much knowledge students have regarding the topic of study.
5. In the instructions to the students for the Maze, be sure to inform them that the only purpose of the Maze is to see what they already know about the topic. It is not a test, they are not expected to know all the answers, and they will not be graded on it.

FIGURE A–1   Example of a Maze

Below is a passage for you to read. Sometimes, there will be three words where there should be only one. Your job is to circle the word that best fits in the sentence. This exercise will help me know better how to help you read this material. This is not a test! Do your best.

The dry desert climate presents problems for living things. Climate is the _____ (usual weather, animals, rain level). How do plants and animals live in such a dry climate?

The cactus has a special way for staying alive in the _____ (ocean, desert, oven). Its _____ (long roots, branches, veins) spread out around it and are not very deep in the soil. When rain comes, the cactus uses the roots to draw _____ (blood, water, oil) up into its trunk. The cactus saves the water for use during _____ (the holidays, rainy weather, dry weather). Animals have their own ways of staying alive in the desert. Many desert animals get much of their water from their _____ (food, mom, skin). Animals must also find a way to _____ (avoid, deal, swim) with hot desert temperatures. The earth is _____ (cooler, hotter, dirtier) under the soil. Desert life is not easy for plants or animals. However, with their special ways of staying alive, the desert is full of life.

Answers: usual weather, desert, long roots, water, dry weather, food, deal, cooler

Source: Reprinted by permission from Sandra Flores.

Some teachers like to inject a little humor into this exercise by making one of the choices very ridiculous or outlandish so that students learn to relax and enjoy it; this way, it becomes a motivating factor rather than one that creates anxiety or stress. In fact, for all the determining background activities, once students get used to doing them and realize they really are not being judged or evaluated, they will tend to relax, respond honestly, and enjoy the activity.

What-I-Know Sheets

Description.   What-I-Know Sheets ask students to indicate, in their own words, what they already know about a topic, what they know after reading the material, and what they still do not know even after reading about the topic. In this instance, only the first question is relevant to determining background, where the students indicate what they already know about a topic before they have read about it in class.

In a variation of the What-I-Know Sheets, students are asked what they already know and what they would like to know about a topic before they learn about it. They are asked the same two questions at the end of the unit of study. Figure A–2 shows the first type of What-I-Know Sheet.

What-I-Know Sheets are used at each phase of the PAR; that is, the students respond to the first column to indicate what they already know during the *P* phase, the second column to indicate what they know now after the reading during the *A* phase, and, finally, what they still do not know about the topic during the *R* phase of the PAR. By returning to this activity at the various stages of the PAR, students are made aware of what they have learned from their reading as well as what they still might learn from further reading.

FIGURE A–2   What-I-Know Sheet

The teacher has students fill out the first column individually; this *determines* their background. Next, the teacher has students tell what they wrote in the first column as a whole class activity; this *builds* their background. After the students have read their texts, the teacher has them write and share their entries for column two; this *assists* their comprehension. Finally, at the end of the unit, the teacher has students think about what they still might not know about the topic; this causes students to *reflect* on the topic.

Topic: Migrant Workers in Florida during the Depression
Purpose: To have students become aware of the plight of migrant workers in Florida and to cause them to reflect on the human, economical, and political implications of such abusive situations, then and now.
Level: Fifth grade

What I Already Know	What I Know Now	What I Still Don't Know

Source: Reprinted by permission from Jill Seman.

Teachers can profitably use the What-I-Know Sheet activity as a springboard for discussion and reflective thinking. Although the format of this activity is relatively set, variation is possible through the manner in which the teacher uses it—such as varying the way in which students fill out their sheets (various group and individual formats) as well as the manner in which students obtain their information for each column.

Instructions for Creating What-I-Know Sheets.   The following steps are helpful in creating What-I-Know Sheets:

1. Decide how the What-I-Know Sheet will be used at each phase of the PAR and use a format most compatible with your purpose.
2. Write clear instructions to students as to the purpose of the activity and how to fill out the columns. These instructions may be given orally or in writing, depending on the level of the students.

The Self-Inventory

Description. A self-inventory is an activity in which students indicate their familiarity with key concepts and vocabulary from the material to be read by selecting one of three responses in regard to each term: *I know this, I sort of know this,* or *I do not know this.* Teachers vary the format of this activity in many ways—by changing the wording of the degree of knowledge students select from, by using various symbols to represent the degree of knowledge, and by creating completely new formats for the representation of the key terms. Figure A–3 shows a standard format for the self-inventory.

When this activity is administered before the start of a new unit of instruction, it informs the teacher as to what students already know about the topic. Merely by asking students to tell what they know about the terms they indicated they knew in a group discussion, the teacher begins to build students' backgrounds.

Instructions for Creating a Self-Inventory. Self-inventories are more interesting and motivating to students when the teacher uses various kinds of symbols to indicate the level of familiarity with key terms and also when the teacher uses various formats in which to present the terms. Computers are very useful in designing self-inventories that relate to the unit of study vis-á-vis their format and symbol system. Use the following steps to design a self-inventory:

1. Look over the material to be read by the students and select key concepts and vocabulary. Try to select terms that students are likely to know as well as those they may not know; this way, they will not feel totally discouraged when doing the activity.
2. Decide on a symbol system for students to use to indicate the level of familiarity with the key concepts and vocabulary.

FIGURE A–3   Example of a Self-Inventory

Put a "smiley face" next to the words you know.		Put a question mark next to words you do not know very well.		Put a "frowning face" next to the words you do not know.	

1. ecology	6. conservation
2. ecosystem	7. pollution
3. rain forest	8. environment
4. habitat	9. greenhouse effect
5. preservation	10. acid rain

GOOD JOB! YOU FINISHED!

Source: Reprinted by permission from Randy Wesson.

3. Design a format compatible with the unit of study, if possible. (This can be done simply by adding a drawing or visual to the worksheet.)

4. Write clear instructions to students, informing them of the purpose of the activity and reassuring them that it is not a test.

The Recognition Pretest

Description.   In the Recognition Pretest, students are given questions with several possible responses provided. They are merely to indicate which of the possible answers they think are correct, much like a multiple-choice question. Figure A–4 is an example of a recognition pretest developed by a fifth-grade teacher.

FIGURE A–4   Example of a Recognition Pretest

"This is not a test!" I repeat, "This is not a test!" YOU be the TEACHER, and tell me what you know about the four statements below. Circle *y* for *yes* if you think the word phrase completes the statement accurately. Circle *n* for *no* if you don't think it does. EXAMPLE: For the first statement, if you think an ARCHAEOLOGIST is a person who makes keys, then you would mark:

    ⓨ/n   makes keys

1. An ARCHAEOLOGIST (are - key - ah - la - gist) is a person who
   - y/n   makes keys
   - y/n   digs up fossils
   - y/n   spends time looking at planets and stars
   - y/n   studies people who lived a long time ago
   - y/n   is kind of like a detective

2. A TRIBE is
   - y/n   a small bird
   - y/n   a community of people
   - y/n   another word for a newspaper
   - y/n   a group of Native Americans
   - y/n   a band of people who share the same culture

3. The term BERING STRAIT refers to
   - y/n   a geographical location between Alaska and Asia
   - y/n   the direction a ship heads when it goes forward
   - y/n   a narrow passageway
   - y/n   a place where bears are
   - y/n   an area of water

4. By the time Christopher Columbus sailed for America, in 1492 A.D., there were already this many cities in California
   - y/n   0
   - y/n   2
   - y/n   10
   - y/n   50
   - y/n   100

Source: Reprinted by permission from George Theissen.

Instructions for Creating a Recognition Pretest.   To create a recognition pretest, use the following steps:

1. Look over the material to be read by the students and identify key phrases or sentences.
2. Turn the sentences or phrases into questions.
3. Create possible responses to the questions, one of which is the correct answer, one or two that sound plausible, and one that is obviously incorrect.
4. Write clear instructions to the students regarding the purpose of the activity and how to respond to it.

The PreP (Prereading Plan)

Description.   The PreP (Prereading Plan) is a simple and nonthreatening way to elicit information about students' prior knowledge (or lack of it) related to the topic.

The PreP consists of a set of three questions posed by the teacher, each of which asks for a specific type of information that requires a specific type of thinking on the part of the students. The first question, which is intended to elicit initial associations with the topic, asks students merely to note what comes to mind when they hear the name of the topic of study—for example, "What comes to mind when you hear the term *Han Dynasty?*" The teacher writes the students' ideas on the board.

The second question, intended to cause students to reflect on those initial associations, asks them to consider what made them think of the responses they gave to the first question—for instance, "What made you think of (paper, yin/yang, silk, etc.)?" This helps the students become aware of their own thinking, especially in terms of how they associate and store information.

The third question, which helps students reform knowledge, asks them to synthesize the shared information from the first two questions to see if they can discover any new ideas about the topic before they read about it in the text—for example, "Based on our shared ideas and before we study the lesson, have you any new ideas about the Han Dynasty?" At this point, the activity is building the students' backgrounds.

Instructions for Creating the PreP.   The PreP is a very simple activity to prepare because it consists of three specific types of questions that remain consistent; what changes is the topic about which they are asked. The main decision the teacher has to make with regard to the PreP is how to structure the activity. For example, the teacher could take students' first responses and write them on the board. Or the teacher could have students note their responses to the first question on paper and get into pairs to create a combined list. Then they could discuss with each other what made them think of their responses, and they will see how, in some cases, they stimulated each other's thinking processes.

It should be remembered that it is perfectly acceptable for the teacher to modify any of the PAR activities mentioned herein to suit his or her purposes. The authors encourage this practice, which may even lead to the creation of a whole new activity. The important thing that should remain constant is that the activity will fulfill the purpose of the phase of the PAR in which it is used.

The following steps may be used to construct a PreP:

1. Decide how to phrase the topic to be studied.
2. Write the three questions, phrasing them in the specified manner:
   a. What do you think of when you hear _____?
   b. What made you think of that?
   c. Based on our shared responses, can you think of any new information about our topic?
3. Decide how to structure the activity in the classroom.

Figure A–5 is an example of the PreP activity used for a math topic.

Activities for Building Background

Anticipation/Prediction Guides

Description.   Anticipation/prediction guides consist of a series of statements, regarding the material to be read by the students, to which they react *before* reading and *after* reading. The students are instructed to agree or disagree with the statements before they read in their texts and they are told to be prepared to explain why they agreed or disagreed. After they have responded to the written questions, the teacher conducts a class discussion by asking students how they responded to each question and why they

---

FIGURE A–5   PreP (Prereading Plan) MATH

This activity will be used to determine what knowledge students in a fourth-grade class already possess about line graphs. Once the teacher determines the level of knowledge students bring to the study of line graphs, he or she can gage the speed and depth of instruction.

Phase 1: Initial Associations
Teacher: "Tell me what comes to your mind when you hear the words *line graph*?"

As students relate their responses, the teacher writes them on an overhead or chalkboard. This activates students' prior knowledge or related knowledge.

Phase 2: Reflections on Initial Associations
Teacher: "What made you think of 'vertical axis' (or measurement, visual picture, or whatever answers were given)?"

This phase helps students become aware of their own thinking processes, especially regarding patterns of association.

Phase 3: Reformation of Knowledge
Teacher: "Based on our shared responses, are there any new ideas you now have about line graphs?"

This phase helps students to gain new insights about the topic by using their synthesizing thinking skills and to verbalize, as well.

Source: Reprinted by permission from Jill Seman.

responded that way. At this point, a lively discussion may ensue as some students become quite passionate in the defense of their opinions. Hearing each other discuss the statements and using the vocabulary they will encounter in their reading, their backgrounds are built.

This activity also creates a motivation for the children to read the lesson so they can see if their responses were correct. Since they respond to the same statements after reading, the activity further assists their comprehension of the material as it focuses their attention on main points from the reading. Since they have invested previous thinking on the matter and made a commitment to an opinion (agreed or disagreed), it will be easy for the students to pay attention when the points come up in the reading and then make their second responses according to what they read. Figure A–6 is an example of an anticipation/prediction guide.

Instructions for Creating an Anticipation/Prediction Guide.   The following steps are helpful in creating an anticipation/prediction guide:

1. Examine the material to be read by the students and pull out the main points and concepts.
2. Write a statement that is either true or not true about each main point or concept.

FIGURE A–6   Example of an Anticipation-Prediction Guide

Directions: Read these statements to yourself as I read them aloud. If you agree with a statement, be ready to explain why. We will check all statements we agree with in the prereading column. Then we will read to see if we should change our minds after we read the lesson.

Prereading   *Postreading*

_____1.   The Californians wanted California to become   _____
                         a state.

_____2.   All of the California delegates could speak   _____
                         English.

_____3.   Women and Indians were allowed to vote in   _____
                         the state of California in 1849.

_____4.   After California became a state, the borders   _____
                         were made smaller.

_____5.   Women were not allowed to own land in   _____
                         California.

_____6.   Every delegate at the convention agreed that   _____
                         California should not allow slavery.

_____7.   California became the thirty-first state in the   _____
                         United States.

Source: Reprinted by permission from Donna Ramirez.

3. Set up the format of the worksheet so that students have space to respond to the statements *before* and *after* the reading of the text material.

Graphic Organizers

Description.   Graphic organizers are visual representations of knowledge. Under the umbrella of the term *graphic organizer* come many different forms of visuals such as webs, semantic webs, story maps, time lines, structured overviews, Venn diagrams, and pictorial representations of ideas. Graphic organizers have been used extensively in this book to represent ideas and relationships of ideas, concepts, or aspects of concepts. All of these different forms can be fit into one of four categories of graphic organizers: (1) hierarchical, (2) conceptual, (3) sequential, and (4) cyclical.

Hierarchical graphic organizers are those that arrange main concepts, subconcepts, and supporting details in rank order. They often use a box type of pattern. The *conceptual* graphic organizer includes a central idea, category, or class with supporting facts such as characteristics or examples. Webs, Venn diagrams, mappings, and some pictorial graphic organizers are examples of this category. The *sequential* graphic organizer arranges events in chronological order such as a time line, story map, or a model for a linear process. The *cyclical* graphic organizer depicts a series of events within a process in a circular formation. Figure A–7 is a hierarchical graphic organizer that shows all four types of graphic organizers.

When graphic organizers are used prior to reading, they build background. When used simultaneously with reading or directly after reading, they assist comprehension and memory. Used at the end of a unit of instruction, graphic organizers aid in thinking

FIGURE A–7   Four Types of Graphic Organizers

and reflection. Research has shown that the effects of graphic organizers are strongest when students are instructed in their use and they construct their own (Dunston, 1992).

Directions for Creating a Graphic Organizer. Follow these steps to construct a graphic organizer:

1. Examine the material to be read by the students and identify the organizational pattern of the writing (sequential, compare/contrast, simple listing, analytical, cause/effect, etc.).
2. Choose the type of graphic organizer that best suits the identified pattern.
3. Identify the main ideas and the supporting details.
4. Construct the graphic organizer so that it depicts the relationship of the main ideas to the supporting details.

DRTA (Directed Reading Thinking Activity)

Description. The DRTA is an interactive reading activity in which the teacher intermittently questions students as they read a passage, asking them to predict what will come next based on what they have read to that point. The technique can be used with fiction and nonfiction material.

The DRTA has three phases: predicting, reading, and proving. In the first phase, students make a prediction about what will come next (based on a preview of the material and/or what they have read just before). Next, they read what they have made a prediction about; and last, they verify (or prove) their predictions. To assist students in making predictions, the teacher asks a question, has them make a prediction, then has them read a specific amount of text to find and verify the correct response. The eventual goal is that the students will learn to use this method by themselves as they read—in other words, they will learn to generate their own questions before and during reading.

During the predicting phase of DRTA, background building occurs and students are given a purpose to read the text (i.e., to verify their predictions). "Predicting prepares readers for comprehension [because] when readers are asked what they think might happen next and then read to verify their prediction, they are being encouraged to read purposefully" (Richardson & Morgan, 1990).

During the reading and proving phases, comprehension is assisted, so the DRTA fulfills the purposes of *P* and *A* at the same time. Figure A–8 is an example of a DRTA developed for a second-grade social studies unit on winter. The students can respond orally to the questions (which can lead to an interesting class discussion) or in writing. They can also write their predictions down first, then share them with the class.

Instructions for Creating the DRTA. The following steps are helpful in creating the DRTA:

1. Examine the material to be read by the students and identify places where predictions can be made about what is to come.
2. Divide the reading material into short passages based on places identified in step 1.
3. Write a question for each of the passage divisions.

FIGURE A–8   Example of a DRTA

Reading with a Purpose: DRTA

Goal: Teacher introduces the season of winter by using the DRTA method to read *White Snow, Bright Snow* by Alvin Tresselt.

Activity: DRTA (directed reading to develop comprehension)
                Teacher reads only first half of book.

Teacher: Look at the cover of the book. What do you think the story is about?
Students: Children playing in the snow.
Teacher: In which season does it snow?
Students: Winter.
Teacher: Good. Do the children look happy or sad?
Students: Happy.
Teacher: Why do you think so?
Students: Because they're playing and skiing, and they have sled.
Teacher: I think they look happy, too. But what about this man here? What is he doing?
Students: Sliding down a hill?
Teacher: On purpose?
Students: No, by accident.
Teacher: So maybe there are advantages and disadvantages of snow. Right?
Students: Right.
Teacher: How many of you think that snow is fun, but it can also be dangerous?
Students: It's bad when there is a snowstorm.
Teacher: Correct. Now I'm going to read the first part of the story titled *White Snow, Bright Snow* by Alvin Tresselt, and I want you to pay attention to the words he uses to describe snow. What are the words he uses in the title to describe snow? "_____ Snow, _____ Snow?" When I'm done, I'm going to use two of these words to describe snow, and make up a new title.

After reading the first half, divide students into groups and go over the story again with each group. Point out adjectives for *snow* so that they can choose two for a new title. Have them write words on cut-out snowflakes. Students will create a new story in the form of a pop-up book.

Source: Reprinted by permission from Brigette Fontenot.

Analogies

Description.   Analogies are a wonderful way to build students' backgrounds for a topic that is somewhat removed from their realm of experience. The analogy makes the topic more comprehensible by providing a description of a process, event, or phenomenon with which students are familiar and to which they can relate that can be compared to an unfamiliar process, event, or phenomenon about which they will be reading. Analogy is one of the most effective ways of helping students understand and even empathize with historical situations that seem so removed and unrelated to their lives, or with scientific explanations of processes that seem difficult and complicated. Figure A–9 is an analogy written for a social studies unit about the struggle for rights

FIGURE A–9   Example of an Analogy

I am going to give you a couple of situations. As I read them to you, I want you to imagine how you would feel in each one if such a thing happened to you.

Suppose you live on a big ranch in the mountains. You love where you live because there are so many fun things for you to do. You ride your horses through the trails and the meadows, you go fishing in the lakes and streams, and you climb your favorite tree and think about the big treehouse you plan to build in it soon. There are so many things for you to enjoy, and you are so happy there with your family, friends, and pet animals.

But one day something happened that surprised you. Some Martians came to explore your family's ranch. They realized that your land had many valuable things they needed on Mars. Because they needed them so badly, they just took everything from you without asking your permission. Soon, they cut down all the trees, including your favorite one, because they needed the wood. Then they decided they needed some of your animals for food for their friends on Mars. On top of all this, they decided they needed to come take over all your land for their people and wanted you to go live on Mars!!

Is that crazy?!?! You don't want to live on Mars. You don't know anything about Mars. You wouldn't know how to act or behave or what to do. Everything would be so weird to you because all you know how to do is climb trees, play with your pets, fish in the streams, and run through the woods and meadows, but on Mars there aren't trees, rivers animals, or meadows.

What would you do? How would you feel about these Martians coming down and deciding they needed what you had so they were going to take it away from you without even asking?

After reading this situation, I want you to imagine that this happened to you and I want you to write about it in your diary. Begin: "Dear Diary: ," and tell your diary what you are feeling and why you feel this way. Then, in the next paragraph, describe what you think would be the best way to address the problem. Finally, write out a solution to the problem that you think would be appropriate.

Source: Reprinted by permission from Nicole Elias.

in America. It is intended to help students understand how some Americans have been denied basic rights—in some cases, even rights that are needed in order to survive.

Instructions for Creating an Analogy.   Follow these steps for writing an analogy:

1. Identify a process, event, or phenomenon in the material to be read by the students that you think will be difficult for them to understand or relate to.
2. Think of a comparable process, event, or phenomenon with which students can identify that is a part of their experience or understanding, and write the analogy in an interesting manner.
3. Decide how to use the analogy in classroom instruction and write clear instructions for the students.

Preguiding Questions
Description.   A preguiding questions activity is similar to the anticipation/prediction guides in that students respond to the questions both *before* and *after* reading the text

material. This activity works best in situations where students possess some background knowledge about the topic at hand, either because they have been studying things related to it or because they have life experiences that relate to it.

For example, Figure A–10 is a preguiding questions activity developed by a fifth-grade teacher for a science lesson about earthquakes for a Los Angeles classroom. The students had some background knowledge due to their personal experiences with earthquakes.

The teacher put her students in small groups to discuss the questions and write the best answers they could to each question, using their personal knowledge and their prediction skills for those questions about which they were unsure. The students then read the selection together in their small groups and answer the questions again after reading. Finally, each group shares with the class their answers to the questions *before* and *after* reading. This activity is an excellent one for involving students in using all their communication skills—reading, writing, listening, and speaking.

Directions for Creating Preguiding Questions.   Follow these steps for creating preguiding questions:

1. Select three or four points from the material to be read by the students; any more than this will make the activity too long.
2. Write questions for each of the points, phrasing them so they require an explanation, not just a yes/no answer.
3. Form students into small groups so they can pool their collective knowledge and make educated predictions.
4. Use this activity when the students already have some background knowledge for the topic at hand.

Determining Background Activities Extended
The following determining background activities can be easily made into background-building activities by the addition of a class discussion of the students' individual responses:

FIGURE A–10   Preguiding Activity for a Lesson on Earthquakes

Directions: Today you will be doing detective work in your science groups.

1. Have your group leader read each question, one at a time.
2. The group leader will lead a discussion on each question, giving each group member a chance to contribute his or her ideas.
3. Pooling your knowledge, write the best answer you can to each question. Use your prediction skills if you are unsure (i.e., make an *educated* guess).
4. Read your textbook aloud together.
5. Again write answers to the questions. Compare your answers before and after reading.
6. Share your comparison with the class.

Source: Reprinted by permission from Madeleine Serrano.

1. Maze
2. Self-Inventory
3. What-I-Know Sheets
4. PreP
5. Recognition Pretests

This concludes the discussion of the first part of the PAR—that is, the *preparation* phase. Two things should be accomplished in the preparation phase: the background of the students (for the material to be learned) has been determined and/or the backgrounds have been built. Now it is time to move on to the next phase of the PAR—the *assistance* phase.

Instructional Activities for Assistance

The *A* of PAR stands for *assistance*. In this phase of PAR, the goal is to provide students with a purpose to read and then to assist their comprehension of the written material. In each of the two parts of assistance, there are a variety of activities that will further the goals of (1) setting a purpose for reading and (2) assisting reading comprehension. The following pages will first look at activities that are intended to provide students with a *purpose* to read, and then instructional activities that are meant to *assist* students in understanding what they are reading.

Activities for Setting Purpose

Mystery Clue Game
Description.   The Mystery Clue Game is a very enjoyable activity that provides students with a purpose to read their textbooks or whatever reading assignment they have been given. It can be used with both fictional and nonfictional material. This group activity requires students to collaborate to "solve" a mystery by sharing clues provided by the teacher. Figure A–11 is a mystery clue game using a format to facilitate group work.

Directions for Creating a Mystery Clue Game.   Please see pages 178–179 for details on how to create a Mystery Clue Game.

Jot Chart
Description.   Jot charts are a form of graphic organizers that enable students to compare and contrast information. These charts have the phenomena being examined on one side and the characteristics of the different phenomena on the other side. Figure A–12 shows a jot chart created for a sixth-grade lesson on Ancient Greek Culture that compares the roles of the different gods and goddesses, their relationships, their sanctuaries, and religious festivals in which they play a part. The students fill in the chart as they read the text. This gives them a purpose to read and makes the reading more enjoyable, especially when they do the activity in pairs or small groups.

FIGURE A–11   Mystery Clue Game

Mystery Words	*Clues*
1. soil	• contains humus • can erode or blow away • decomposers help it • can slide • plants need it
2. trees	• provide homes • breathe in what we breathe out • when decayed, they turn into humus • need birds and animals • are a natural resource
3. animals	• live in different environments • help spread seeds • are part of the food chain • help keep nature in balance
4. naturalists	• Ansel Adams • John Muir • John James Audubon • Audubon Society • Sierra Club
5. conservation	• our survival depends on it • to save our natural resources • to save wildlife • to be aware of everything we use and cut down or use • to use wisely our natural resources
6. habitat	• each living thing requires its own particular kind • the place where plants and animals live • a place that provides everything needed to live • could be a forest, a desert, or coastal wetlands • includes water, shelter, food, soil, and climate

Source: Reprinted by permission from Cherie Firmery.

Instructions for Creating a Jot Chart.   Follow these steps for constructing a jot chart:

1. Look over the material to be read by the students to see if it contains information that can be compared in several different ways.
2. Decide on the events, people, processes, or phenomena to be compared. Write these as one side of the chart.
3. Decide on the areas in which the comparisons will take place—list these at the top of the chart.
4. Decide how the chart will be used in classroom instruction (i.e., individual activity, group activity, etc.).
5. Write clear instructions for the students.

FIGURE A–12   Example of a Jot Chart

The purpose of this chart is to assist you in developing an understanding of the materials being studied about ancient Greek culture.

This is your Jot Chart. Fill in the chart as you read through the material. Refer to this chart to study and learn major points of this unit.

Jot Chart

God/Goddess	Role	Relation	Sanctuary	Religious Festival
Zeus	god of			
Poseidon	god of			
Hera	goddess of			
Ares	god of			
Dionysus	god of			
Apollo	god of			
Demeter	goddess of			

Source: Reprinted by permission from Margaret Parro.

Preparation Activities Extended

The Maze, PreP, What-I-Know Sheets, and Recognition Pretests can all become purpose-setting activities by adding a purpose-setting statement, such as "Read the text to find out if your choices in the maze were correct." In the case of the What-I-Know Sheets, the students can read with the purpose of filling in the second column. With the recognition pretests, they can read to see if they made the right choices. As stated earlier, most of the PAR activities mentioned here can be modified to work at different phases of the PAR, and some of them, such as the What-I-Know activity, are designed to extend through all three phases of the PAR.

Activities for Assisting Comprehension

Mapping

Description.   Mappings (also called *webs*) are a form of graphic organizer that depict a central idea or concept with its subconcepts or characteristics and the supporting detail. Mappings can be done as an interactive whole-class activity, an individual activity, or a small-group activity. They assist comprehension because they show the relationships of concepts and ideas. If students are creating maps as they read, they are forced to pay attention to these patterns of relationships.

Figure A–13 is a typical mapping. Its central concept is California becoming a state, and there are four subcategories of related issues with supporting detail.

Instructions for Creating a Map.   Follow these steps to create a map:

1. Identify a main concept in the material to be read by the students. Do not try to map a whole chapter; that is too much for one map. Focus on one section of the lesson or chapter.
2. Identify subcategories (may be section headings) and the supporting detail.
3. Write the main concept in the center of the paper (board chart, overhead sheet, whatever you use).
4. Decide how to use the activity in class (i.e., individual, whole-class interactive, or small-group activity).
5. Write clear instructions for the students.

Cubing
Description.   Cubing is a strong activity for engaging students in using thinking skills as a means to comprehension. In this activity, students are asked to read about an issue that has two sides or more and then respond to six levels of questions, each of which requires a specific type of thinking. These levels of thinking are parallel to the generally accepted reading comprehension levels, such as those of Bloom's taxonomy.

FIGURE A–13   Mapping for Developing Comprehension

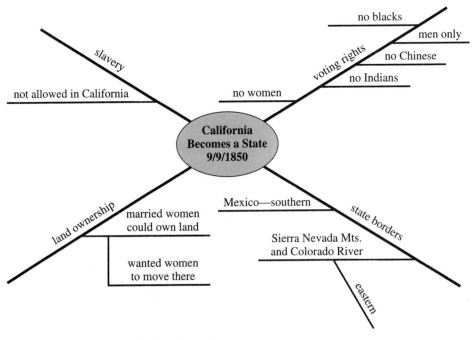

Source: Reprinted by permission from Donna Ramirez.

A motivational factor that can be added to this activity is having the students put their answers on actual cubes (square tissue boxes covered with paper); each level of response goes on one side of the cube. Even upper-grade students enjoy making the cubes and using them during class discussions. This activity provides students with a purpose for reading as well as enhancing their comprehension. Figure A–14 is an example of a cubing activity developed for a fifth-grade class studying reform movements in the United States.

Cubing can be used at all levels and for all subjects, and although it works extremely well when students are reading about a controversial issue, it is actually effective with any kind of subject matter. For example, a cubing exercise developed for a first-grade unit on transportation can have the students respond to the six levels of questions on "boats" and "planes."

We encourage elementary school teachers to try using this valuable exercise because it helps students develop, use, and understand their own thinking processes.

Instructions for Creating a Cubing Activity.   Use the following steps for a cubing activity:

1. Write down the six question levels (i.e., describe it, compare it, associate it, analyze it, apply it, and argue for or against it). For each one, write directions specific to the topic at hand, as in Figure A–14.
2. Ask students to bring in square tissue boxes and cover each side with butcher paper.

FIGURE A–14   Cubing Exercise

Cut out the cube that is outlined on the poster board. You will each have your own cube. Bend it into shape. Write the following six underlined phrases onto the cube, one on each side. Use this cube to perform the activity below.

On a separate paper, write your answers to the directions requested by each phrase on the cube. Write your answers in the sequence they are given below. In parenthesis next to each direction, I have provided a description of what is being requested.

1. Describe it.   (The reform movement.)

2. Compare it.   (Compare the antislavery movement to the women's rights movement. Include differences and similarities between slavery and lack of suffrage.)

3. Associate it.   (What does the reform movement make you think of? How does it make you feel?)

4. Analyze it.   (Was the reform movement effective?)

5. Apply it.   (Identify a problem in society today. Describe how the reform movement techniques could be used to address this issue.)

6. Argue for or against it.   (Are you for or against the reform movement? What are your opinions and the reasons for them?)

Source: Reprinted by permission from Nicole Elias.

3. Have the students write each of the question levels on one of the sides of the cubes.
4. Either in small groups or individually, have the students write in the answers on each side of the cube.
5. Cubes can be used as the basis of a lively class discussion.

QAR (Question-Answer Relationship) Activity

Description.   The QAR activity consists of a series of four questions, each of which is a little different in terms of how the student will look for the answer in relation to the reading material. The answer to the first-level question can be found in the text (i.e., the words are right in the text).

The answer to the second-level question can be found in the text, but it is not directly spelled out; the student must think about what the author is saying. To get the answer to the third question, the student must combine his or her own knowledge with what the author says. Finally, for the fourth question, the student relies only on himself or herself; the answer is in his or her head. Figure A–15 is an example of a QAR prepared for a fifth-grade history lesson about Texas becoming a state.

FIGURE A–15   QAR Activity

Settlement of Texas

1. Q: What did the advertisements say about Texas that lured thousands of Americans there in the 1820s and 1830s?
   A:

   QAR: Right There

2. Q   There were two things that the settlers were required to do if they settled in Texas. What were they?
   A:

   QAR: Think and Search

3. Q: If there were 100,000 Americans in Texas in 1835, then how many Mexicans were there?
   A:

   QAR: You and the Author

4. Q: How would you feel if you were a Mexican in Texas in 1835?
   A:

   QAR: On Your Own

Conflict with Mexico

5. Q: What two things did Mexican officials outlaw in 1830?
   A:

   QAR: Right There

6. Q: What event led the settlers to form their own government?
   A:

   QAR: Think and Search

FIGURE A–15   *(Continued)*

7. Q: How would you describe the relationship between General Santa Anna and the settlers?
   A:

   QAR: You and the Author

8. Q: How do you think Davey Crockett and Jim Bowie felt as they were defending the Alamo?
   A:

   QAR: On Your Own

The Mexican War

9. Q: Mexico reacted angrily to something the United States did in 1845. What was it?
   A:

   QAR Right There

10. Q: The United States did something to provoke the Mexican government. What was it?
    A:

    QAR: Think and Search

11. Q: Why do you think the Americans felt they needed to invade Mexico from two different directions?
    A:

    QAR: You and the Author

12. Q: How did the Treaty of Guadalupe Hidalgo and the Gadsden Purchase affect the United States?
    A:

    QAR: On Your Own

Source: Reprinted by permission from Mark Jessup.

Instructions for Creating a QAR Activity.   The following steps will help you create a QAR activity:

1. Look over material to be read by students and identify a topic that consists of several events or related issues.
2. Write the questions on the four specified levels: (a) can be answered directly from text; (b) answer is in text but student has to think or reason to find answer; (c) student combines what he or she knows with what is in text; and (d) student answers from ideas in own head (text not needed for direct reference).
3. Walk students through this activity several times before allowing them to try it on their own.
4. Provide immediate feedback when students do the activity independently.

Instructional Activities for Reflection

Reflection activities are critical thinking activities. Chapter 6 described in detail how to teach critical thinking activities. Please refer to that chapter when teaching the following activities, as they require the same type of modeling as well as continued practice.

Activities for Reflecting on Learning through Critical Thinking

Cause-Effect Guides

Description.   Cause/effect guides are intended to help students identify causal relationships in written material. Sometimes, it is difficult or impossible to identify the causes of events and phenomena because they are unknown and cannot be traced. However, students typically do not consider they are of phenomena and events when they read about them, even when the causes are apparent or at least traceable. It is a very good practice for students to question events and phenomena they read about in terms of causes. This helps them become more wise and shrewd in their reading and thinking abilities. Figure A–16 is an example of a cause/effect guide developed for a middle-grade lesson on China.

Cause/effect guides can be modified for lower grades by using simpler language and more obvious connections. Figure A–17 shows a cause/effect guide created for a second-grade lesson on bananas.

A modification of the cause/effect guide is the cause/effect story guide. This activity is created by listing events in a story, then choosing the key events and listing them graphically to show how they are related sequentially, revealing a causal pattern.

Instructions for Creating Cause/Effect Guides.   Use the following steps:

1. Look over the material the students are to read and identify major events or phenomena and their causes.
2. List the events on one side of the worksheet.
3. List the causes, out of order, on the opposite side.
4. Write instructions as to how the students should connect the events (phenomena) to their causes.

Fact/Opinion Worksheets

Description.   Fact/opinion worksheets are intended to help students identify opinions as opposed to facts, as a means of detecting bias in written material. With the help of the teacher, elementary students are capable of determining what is merely the author's opinion rather than fact, and what kinds of inferences the author is making. This is an important skill for students to develop, because as adults they will need to be able to determine the accuracy of written material in order to make informed decisions. Figure A–18 is a fact/opinion worksheet created for a fifth-grade history lesson on life in the middle colonies.

FIGURE A–16   Example of a Cause/Effect Guide

Match the following causes with its effect.

_____ **1.** Cheng defeats the Zhou.

_____ **2.** Qin Shihuangdi becomes first emperor of unified China.

_____ **3.** Empire is divided into 36 provinces.

_____ **4.** Qin establishes a bureaucracy.

_____ **5.** Qin standardizes writing, measurement, and money.

_____ **6.** Lisi hated the works of Confucius and other dissenters.

_____ **7.** The Chinese believe in an afterlife.

_____ **8.** Qin wanted to protect his empire.

A. The Great Wall of China is built using forced labor; many lives are lost.

B. The feudal state of Qin became ever larger and his control of China spread.

C. The Empire became more unified as the different regions were able to communicate and trade with each other.

D. This action unified the many warring states since each section was firmly controlled by a governor and a devender.

E. Book burning and other forms of censure were practiced, resulting in loss of books, ideas, and people's lives.

F. His innovative ideas and reforms helped unify China, ended the feudal system, and brought about opportunities for any man to own land.

G. Qin was buried with a clay army of over 6,000 life-sized warriors to guard him after death.

H. This did away with the inheritance of governmental posts from father to son and opened offices to workers who were appointed, trained, paid a salary, and, unless the worker was at the top or bottom of the hierarchy, had a superior to answer to and people below to supervise.

Source: Reprinted by permission from Linda Jones.

Directions for Creating Fact/Opinion Worksheets.   To construct a fact/opinion worksheet, follow these steps:

1. Look over material to be read by students and select factual statements as well as statements of opinion.
2. If there are no opinion statements, make up some related to the topic.
3. List the facts and opinions together on a worksheet and write clear instructions for the students.
4. Decide how this activity will be used in the classroom instruction. This worksheet can be used as a basis for lively discussion on which statements are facts and which

FIGURE A–17   Example of a Cause/Effect Guide

_____ **1.** This is why bananas grow well in Honduras.

_____ **2.** This is why boxes of bananas are put into containers.

_____ **3.** This is where the ship brings bananas into the United States.

_____ **4.** You must eat a banana when it is yellow.

a. keeps the green bananas cool

b. if ripe, bananas can spoil quickly

c. hot sunshine and a lot of rain

d. Gulfport, Mississippi

Source: Reprinted by permission from Jill Seman.

FIGURE A–18   Fact/Opinion Worksheet

Place an O by the sentences that state opinions and a F by the sentences that state facts.

_____ **1.** Quakers wore plain black clothes without any jewelry.

_____ **2.** Clothing of any color except plain black shows special privileges.

_____ **3.** Quakers addressed all people as equals; this showed that they had bad manners.

_____ **4.** Pizza and tacos are the best contributions from the Italian and Mexican cultures.

_____ **5.** Cultural and religious diversity existed in Pennsylvania.

_____ **6.** Women could not vote for Assembly members.

_____ **7.** In the middle colonies, some ethnic groups spoke only their native languages.

_____ **8.** Only women should be allowed to vote for political representatives.

_____ **9.** Smallpox and measles killed many of the Native Americans.

_____ **10.** Ethnic tensions caused all of the problems in the middle colonies.

Source: Reprinted by permission from Bo Varnado.

are opinions. For such a discussion, require students to state *why* they have identified a statement as either fact or opinion.

Semantic Webbing

Description.   This activity is also designed to give students practice in distinguishing fact from opinion, but in this case, the format is a graphic one. Several facts and several opinions are listed on the lines of the web. Students are asked to discuss in small groups which are which, and then they are asked to fill in the blank lines with facts only from the text. Figure A–19 shows an example of a semantic web.

FIGURE A–19   Sematic Web: Struggle for Rights

Instructions: Decide which statements are facts and which are opinions about each of the different examples we studied, and then fill in the remaining spaces with facts we learned from the lesson for each example.

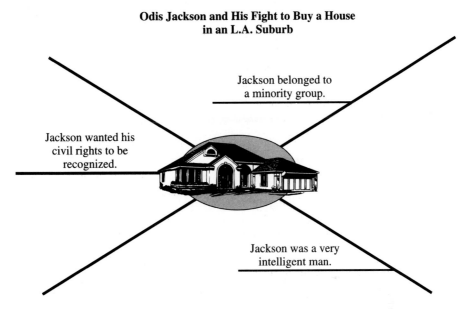

**Odis Jackson and His Fight to Buy a House
in an L.A. Suburb**

Jackson belonged to
a minority group.

Jackson wanted his
civil rights to be
recognized.

Jackson was a very
intelligent man.

Source: Reprinted by permission from Nicole Elias.

After the students have completed their webs, the groups can report their results to the class. By having students explain the reasoning behind their decisions, the teacher is helping them verbalize their thinking processes, which, in turn, helps them understand their own reasoning processes. For students who are not so adept in reasoning, it provides valuable examples of how to think things through.

Instructions for Creating a Semantic Web.   Follow these steps:

1. Look over the material students will be reading and identify a topic, event, process, or phenomenon on which to focus.
2. Identify facts and opinions from the reading about the chosen topic (event, process, phenomenon) and include them on the graphic.
3. Leave some blank lines for students to add more facts.

TRIP Cards

Description.   The TRIP (Think–Reflect In Pairs) Card is a cooperative activity done in pairs. Student pairs are given cards, one side of which has a question about an event, process, phenomenon, or topic, and the other side on which is the correct answer. Students quiz each other with the cards and keep track of correct answers. Each correct answer is worth a certain number of points, which enables students to see how they are doing. With the correct response on the back of each card, they can give each other immediate feedback as to the correctness of their answers. Figure A–20 is a TRIP Card activity created for a fifth-grade history lesson on Texas statehood.

In a variation of this activity, student teams develop their own TRIP Cards, trade cards with other pairs of students, and then see how many responses they can get correctly.

Instructions for Creating TRIP Cards.   The following steps are suggested:

1. Formulate questions pertaining to major ideas, facts, and events as well as important supporting detail.

FIGURE A–20   TRIP Cards

Front of Cards	*Back of Cards*
Americans headed for Texas for these two reasons. (5 points each)	1. Rich farmland 2. Grassy plains for cattle
Settlers were given farm-sized plots if they promised the Mexican government what two things? (5 points each)	1. Become Mexican citizens 2. Join the Catholic Church
Why did the settler population grow much more rapidly than the Mexican government expected? (5 points)	Because many settlers brought slaves with them
Who became dictator of Mexico in 1834? (5 points)	General Antonio Lopez de Santa Anna
What was the name of the main conflict between the settlers and the Mexican army? (5 points)	The Battle of the Alamo
In what year did Texas become a state? (5 points)	1845
What was the name of the agreement in which Mexico gave up all claims to lands in Texas? (5 points)	The Treaty of Guadalupe Hidalgo

Source: Reprinted by permission from Mark Jessup.

2. Obtain cards (such as unlined index cards) and write the questions on one side of the cards and answers on the other side.
3. Decide how to use the cards (e.g., student pairs work together to think of the answers, student pairs quiz each other, students create their own questions and answers, etc.).

Many activities have been given here for the various phases of the PAR Planning Framework. Teachers are invited not only to use these activities and see the results but also to create their own. One of the most demanding and creative aspects of a teacher's job is to find and/or create meaningful activities to accomplish instructional goals and objectives. By presenting these various activities, it is the authors' hope that we have provided some assistance in your continual search for substantial instructional activities.

References

Dunston, P. J. (1992). A critique of graphic organizer research. *Reading Research and Instruction, 31* (2), 57–65.

Richardson, J. S., & Morgan, R. T. (1990). *Reading to learn in the content areas.* Belmont, CA: Wadsworth.

Index